INDESTRUCTIBLE TRUTH

Indestructible Truth

Truth

*The Living Spirituality of
Tibetan Buddhism*

REGINALD A. RAY

SHAMBHALA · BOSTON & LONDON · 2000

SHAMBHALA PUBLICATIONS, INC.
Horticultural Hall
300 Massachusetts Avenue
Boston, Massachusetts 02115
www.shambhala.com

9 8 7 6 5 4 3 2 1

FIRST EDITION
Printed in the United States of America
⊚ This edition is printed on acid-free paper that meets the
American National Standards Institute Z39.48 Standard.

Distributed in the United States by Random House, Inc.,
and in Canada by Random House of Canada Ltd

LIBRARY OF CONGRESS CATALOGING-IN-PUBLICATION DATA

RAY, REGINALD A.
    Indestructible truth: living spirituality of Tibetan Buddhism /
Reginald A. Ray.
        p.   cm.
    Includes bibliographical references and index.
    ISBN 1-57062-166-7
    1. Spiritual life—Buddhism.   2. Buddhism—Doctrines.   I. Title.
BQ7634 R39   2000
294.3'923—dc21   00-030128

To the Ven. Chögyam Trungpa Rinpoche

(1940–1987)

Contents

CONTENTS

Acknowledgments

This book was made possible in part by a sabbatical grant provided by the Naropa University community, to whom I owe a continuing debt of gratitude. Thanks to my friend Peter Goldfarb and the Goldfarb Foundation for underwriting some of the expenses involved in the research of this work. I also want to express my appreciation to the Tibetan teachers who have graciously allowed me to quote from their books, their unpublished teachings, and private conversations, and particularly to Sakyong Mipham Rinpoche, Dzigar Kongtrul Rinpoche, and also Ringu Tulku Rinpoche for assistance provided while he was teaching at Naropa University. Many thanks also to my longtime friend and respected colleague Larry Mermelstein, Director of the Nālandā Translation Committee, who gave the manuscript a close reading and provided indispensable perspectives and numerous helpful suggestions. Thanks to others who read parts of the manuscript or offered useful advice, including John Rockwell, Jules Levinson, Phil Stanley, Scott Wellenbach, and Dan Hessey. I am particularly grateful to my Shambhala editor, Kendra Crossen Burroughs, whose steadiness, detailed eye, and sense of style has helped this book come much closer to what it has wanted to be. Thanks to Emily Bower and Liz Monson, Sakyong Mipham Rinpoche's editors; Vern Mizner, editor for Dzigar Kongtrul Rinpoche; and L. S. Summer, who prepared the index. Thanks to my students at Naropa University and the University of Colorado who read early drafts of this book as part of their course assignments and who helped me see what it was I needed to say and how to say it. I owe a special debt to my wife, Lee, for help at each stage from initial discussions about the book's scope, through the writing and editing, down to the time of final proofreading. As always, much of her insight and wisdom is expressed herein and I continue to regard my work in general as largely a product of our partnership. I also owe a debt, not yet entirely clear, to my daughters, Tara and Catherine, who, as second-generation dharma practitioners, are testing the validity of Tibetan Buddhism with their lives.

Finally, I wish to express my gratitude to the late Chögyam Trungpa Rinpoche, to whom this book is dedicated. Brought up in traditional Tibet, he did not hesitate to enter into the chaos of the modern world. Uncompromising in his sense of the true dharma, he nevertheless was always willing to meet his Western students far more than halfway. In life, he expressed a moving and remarkable trust in the ability of modern people to hear and receive the authentic Tibetan tradition. In death, his legacy continues to call all of us out from the pettiness of the modern materialistic view, to a life lived in the largest possible terms and dedicated to the welfare of others.

INDESTRUCTIBLE TRUTH

Introduction

TRUTH MAKES LITTLE SENSE AND HAS NO REAL IMPACT if it is merely a collection of abstract ideas. Truth that is living experience, on the other hand, is challenging, threatening, and transforming. The first kind of truth consists of information collected and added, from a safe distance, to our mental inventory. The second kind involves risking our familiar and coherent interpretation of the world—it is an act of surrender, of complete and embodied cognition that is seeing, feeling, intuiting, and comprehending all at once. Living truth leads us ever more deeply into the unknown territory of what our life is.

In the case of Tibetan Buddhism, it is possible to know a great deal about the subject, yet remain aloof and removed, unaffected by what one knows. It is the pitfall of both the professional scholar and the amateur anthropologist who know everything about their subject but remain strangely indifferent in the face of what they know. All of one's knowledge, then, amounts to mere items in the museum of "cultural artifacts" that, though occasionally interesting, are finally of no fundamental use or importance to anyone.

Tibetan Buddhism is a way of experiencing the world. In many ways, it is quite different from the dominant trends not only in Western, but now in the "modern, technological culture" that is rapidly encircling the globe. There are many parts of the traditional, conservative, medieval culture of Tibet that we will never be able to appreciate or understand. But there are other parts, particularly of its Buddhist heritage, that can help us see with new eyes the limitations and possibilities of our own contemporary situation.

It is not so surprising that Tibetan Buddhism should have much to say to modern people. If the lifespan of the human race is compared to that of a hundred-year-old person, the psychological style of modern culture is only a day in length. Even the time since the cataclysmic transformations wrought by the rise of agriculture five thousand to ten thousand years ago represent only a few months. For the rest of the 99 + percent of our human history, we have shared a common way, very much more embedded and embodied than what we now experience. It should not be surprising that in the brief period of modernity, we have not fundamentally changed any more than a person a hundred years old, in the last day of his life, can expect suddenly to become someone different. Beneath the surface of our modern speed, ambition, and self-importance is a person not very much different from our forebears in temperament, capacities, and—yes—spirituality.

Buddhism is a particularly interesting tradition because it has one foot in the past and one in the present. On the one hand, it arose at a time when India was undergoing transformation from a more primitive to a "high" civilization. Buddhism has the same literacy, scholasticism, professional elites, institutionalization, hierarchies, political involvements, and monetary concerns as do the other "high religions" that evolved after the invention of agriculture and that we now largely identify as our own ways of being religious. At the same time, the Buddha claimed, "I follow the ancient path," and by this he meant to show a "way back" to a more fundamental experience of human life than the one evolving in his day. Tibetan Buddhism, perhaps more than any other form of Buddhism, has retained the raw and rugged experience of this "primordiality" as the basis of its spirituality. In this sense, it is concerned not with truth that is fixed and dead, but with truth that is alive and constantly emerging. And it is only this kind of truth that is "indestructible" because it is not a reified version of the past, but a reflection of what is ultimately so in the immediacy of the present.

For many years, I have taught a course at Naropa University and the University of Colorado called "Tibetan Buddhism" for students with little or no background in either Buddhism or matters Tibetan. In my teaching I have always felt it important, particularly at the introductory level, to open up a dialogue between my students and the living spirituality of Tibetan Buddhism. In order to do this, I have sought an introductory text that would [1] provide an outline to the subject in relatively short compass; [2] not be overly technical or burdened with the myriad details of Tibetan Buddhist history; [3] address the spirituality or "practice" of the tradition, rather than focusing primarily on philosophy, dogmatics, or political history; [4] give due attention to the "Practice Lineage" traditions of the Nyingma and the Kagyü, so often underplayed in the story; and [5] strike some balance between a Western scholar writing about Tibetan Buddhism and Tibetans speaking about their tradition in their own voices.

There are, indeed, several excellent introductions to Tibetan Buddhism on the market, yet none quite fits the bill. I have thus written two books, this one and another shortly to be published, for my students and also for others wishing a circumscribed, nontechnical introduction to Tibetan Buddhism.

This book provides a survey of Tibetan Buddhism in its more exoteric aspects. It opens with a discussion of the Tibetan sacred cosmos, with its living elements, forces, and beings and the critical role of ritual as a means for communicating with the unseen world. There follows "Tibet's Story," which explores the Indian sources of Tibetan Buddhism, including the monks, layfolk, hermits, and mad saints, representing conventional and unconventional approaches to spirituality, with whom the Tibetans studied. Included here also are the stories and histories of those Tibetan masters and schools—the Nyingma, Sakya, Kagyü, and Kadam/Geluk—that shaped Tibetan tradition down to modern times. A section on "core teachings" details the inspiration and practices of the shared spirituality of all Tibetans, including the so-called "Hinayana" and "Mahayana," that provided a many-faceted path to wholesomeness, mental stability, compassion for others, and self-perfection. The book concludes with a survey of the major philosophical orientations that underlie the spiritual life in Tibetan Buddhism and provide its rationale, including Buddhist psychology (Abhidharma), the teachings on emptiness (Madhyamaka), and the doctrine of buddhanature. The forthcoming companion volume, *Secret of the Vajra World:*

The Tantric Buddhism of Tibet, introduces the reader to the most important tantric or Vajrayana ideas and practices as they existed in Tibet.

In comparison with other introductions, *Indestructible Truth* and *Secret of the Vajra World* are distinctive in several respects.

1. Most introductions on the market today tend to focus on Tibetan Buddhist history or philosophy. In these books, I emphasize the spirituality of Tibetan Buddhism. By this, I mean Tibetan Buddhism as a way of life, practice, and transformation.

2. In keeping with long-standing academic practice in the West, most existing introductions tend to place relatively more emphasis on the Geluk traditions as being definitive of Tibetan Buddhism as a whole. Such works have placed at the center of the picture the Geluk monastic forms of Tibetan Buddhism, as they existed in Central Tibet, and as they emphasized study, scholarship, and debate. This is an imbalance, for it leaves aside the many non-Geluk lineages, traditions, and practices that were found alongside the Geluk form in Central Tibet and also that existed—indeed predominated—in other parts of the country. My books attempt to redress that imbalance.

3. For the relatively well-informed reader, let alone for someone new to the topic, Tibetan Buddhism can seem bewilderingly complex. It emerges from five centuries of interaction with Indian tradition and includes some fourteen centuries of history in Tibet of schools, institutions, lineages, religious figures, and texts that can be overwhelming in their detail and diversity. In these books, I have felt it important to be highly selective and to discuss only those elements of Tibetan Buddhism that are needed to tell the basic story.

For this reason, I have attempted to keep technical details to a minimum. For example, each of the Tibetan schools and lineages has its own rich history. I have not tried to lead the reader through this temporal labyrinth but have rather provided an outline of each school's development and filled this out with stories and other material to suggest the general character of each. In a similar way, I have presented Tibetan philosophy in its major orientations and attempted to show the implications of each for the spiritual life. Readers interested in the many schools and subschools, along with their various theoretical positions and refutations of other schools, have many excellent works they may turn to. In a similar way, I have presented the core Buddhist discipline of meditation in general terms along with concrete examples, and have kept to a minimum discussion of the relatively theoretical and abstract descriptions of levels and stages, with their subheadings and complex correlations that one finds in much Tibetan "path" literature. Finally, although indigenous shamanic practice and the developed Bön religion are referred to in this book, I have not devoted separate sections to them. They are certainly important in the overall picture of Tibetan religious and cultural life, but devoting chapters to them would have led me too far afield from the central topic.

4. I have wanted to include in my presentation the voices of living Tibetan teachers to indicate something of the idiom of the traditional teachings and to allow a contrast with my own way of presenting the same subjects. Hence I have told the story of Tibetan Buddhism by relying to a significant extent on the words of Tibetan teachers themselves.

It is my aspiration that this approach will render Tibetan Buddhism accessible to those who do not have any previous background and also provide new information and perspectives to those who do. In particular, I hope that my emphasis on the spirituality of the tradition will help readers, at whatever level, to gain new appreciation of why Tibetans, both those in Tibet and those in exile, feel so deeply about their heritage and why Westerners might choose to explore this tradition. And, beyond this, I hope the reader will find for him- or herself at least an intimation of the primordiality that Tibetan Buddhism is finally about.

At least for me personally, then, the ultimate importance of Tibetan Buddhism for the contemporary world lies in something that is more than Tibet or even Buddhism itself—it lies in the potential of this tradition, perhaps in a unique way, to incite us to recover what we modern people are at our root and fundament. And, in this tumultuous and harrowing day and age, unless we can recover our human basis, we may not have much hope of continuing forward. Still, such a momentous project cannot be approached in the abstract, and it certainly cannot be accomplished by just thinking about it. We need to meet a human presence, see a human face, and hear a human voice in order to learn. And in order to learn, we must be willing to open ourselves and risk change. The Tibetans, through their measureless suffering and their incredible generosity, present themselves to us as resources, as friends for such an endeavor.

Tibet
PEOPLE AND PLACE

TIBETAN BUDDHISM WAS, UNTIL RECENTLY, THE MAJOR form of religious belief and practice throughout the regions where Tibetan civilization prevailed. Beginning sometime prior to the seventh century CE, Buddhism began to make its appearance in Tibet, and it developed from that time to become the major religious orientation of the Tibetan people. In its prime, Tibetan Buddhism was one of the world's most vital, diverse, and spiritually profound traditions. After some fourteen centuries of free and well-favored development, Buddhism and indeed Tibetan civilization as a whole suffered calamitous attack under the 1949 Chinese invasion and subsequent political appropriation and repression of Tibet. At the same time, as is often said, Tibet's loss was the world's gain, for since the Chinese occupation hundreds of thousands of Tibetans fled into exile. Among these were many gifted teachers who have, since the 1960s, been presenting their traditions to the rest of the world. There are now hundreds of groups of non-Tibetans practicing Tibetan Buddhism, on virtually every continent, in every major city, and in many out-of-the-way places; and the tradition is studied in many colleges and universities, both Western and Asian.

Tibetan civilization flourished throughout an extensive portion of Asia, including both the region we think of as Tibet proper, "political Tibet," and also other areas extending into other political entities. These include principally portions of Assam in the east, Bhutan, Sikkim, and parts of Nepal to the south and southwest; and Ladakh to the west. Although heavily damaged in Chinese-occupied Tibet, Tibetan Buddhism continues to be practiced in these other Tibetan cultural locales.

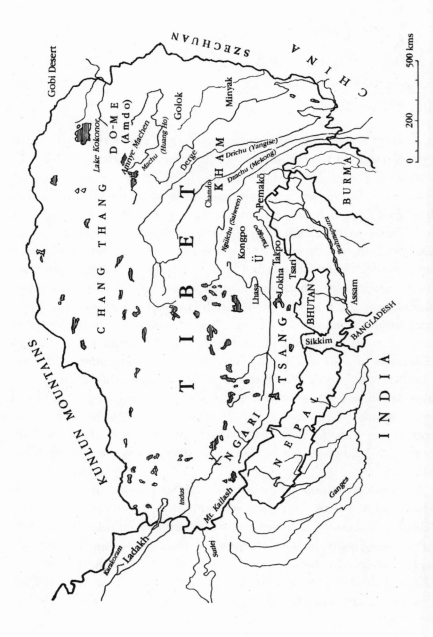

Tibet proper is bordered on three sides by stupendous mountain ranges, from twenty thousand to nearly thirty thousand feet in height—in the south the Himalayas, to the west by the Karakoram range, and to the north by the Kunlun range (see map). These mountains are completely impassable for most of the year and even in the best of seasons presented the traveler with dangerous and sometimes insurmountable obstacles. Although open to the east, the seemingly endless deserts, plains, and lower mountains meant that anyone wishing to travel from Central Tibet to Beijing, for example, could plan on an eight-month journey. While these physical barriers did not completely isolate Tibet from the rest of the world, they certainly impeded outside influence. Tibet's relative isolation was reinforced by cultural and geopolitical factors. Up until the Chinese invasion of 1949, Tibet had functioned as a kind of buffer between British India to the south, Russia to the north, and China to the east. These great powers preferred a steady state in which outside meddlers did not enter Tibet and thus kept it cordoned off. Within Tibet itself, the highly conservative religious culture was not welcoming to outsiders. The combined result of geographical, political, and cultural factors meant that up to the middle of the twentieth century, Tibetan civilization was able to develop its own unique character and to suffer the encroachments of modernity in a much more gradual and incidental way than most other traditional cultures.

In order to understand the character and diversity of Tibetan Buddhism, it is important to know something about Tibetan geography, as it has impacted Tibetan politics, society, and culture.[1] The territory of Tibet proper may be divided into three roughly equal sections. The northern third of the country is a vast, uninhabited desert, cut by mountain spurs and ranges. For most of the year it is bitterly cold and swept by fierce winds. Although in the past no one lived there, it was periodically visited by hunters and by traders seeking salt, soda, and borax. The middle third of Tibet, although still high and cold, is made up of rolling hills and grasslands, interspersed with lofty mountain ranges and great lakes. Here Tibetan nomads, incredibly hardy and tough, tended their flocks of yak, sheep, and goats, living in felt tents year round, and moving with the seasons to find the best pasture lands. The southern third

9

of the country is composed of a series of river valleys that, although still high, are (because of their more southerly latitude) relatively moist, temperate, and fertile when compared with the rest of Tibet. It was in this southern third of Tibet that most of its some three million people lived, in hamlets, small villages, and a few larger towns, supporting themselves mainly by farming.

The inhabited regions of Tibet were quite diverse in social and political configuration, and this diversity was reflected in the arena of religion as well. Central Tibet, made up of the districts of Ü and Tsang along with several other provinces, was a particularly rich farming region, and the location of the greatest population density and the largest towns. Society here was defined by large estates owned by wealthy nobility, and also by landed peasants and landless fieldworkers. Owing in part to its concentration of people and its relative wealth, Central Tibet was politically the most centralized of the Tibetan regions and also socially the most hierarchical and stratified. This region and particularly Tibet's largest town, Lhasa, was the seat of the Dalai Lama and the site of his famed residence, the vast Potala, with its thousands of corridors, rooms, and temples. Central Tibet and Lhasa were also the stronghold of the Geluk school and included the largest monasteries in the country. It was here that, since the seventeenth century, the Tibetan central government was located, headed by the Dalai Lama and staffed by monks of the ruling Geluk sect and nobility loyal to them. The Sakya school was also strong in Central Tibet with its central seat in Sakya.

East Tibet, known as Kham, includes the valleys of several great rivers (the Salween, Mekong, and Yangtze) and the pastureland between them. Although more spread out, Kham had a population roughly equal to that of Central Tibet. Owing to its proximity to China, a number of important trading routes lay in Kham, along with several major towns including Derge and Chamdo. Kham was politically more decentralized than Lhasa, and its different regions were governed sometimes by hereditary princes and sometimes by lamas from their monastic seats. The Nyingma and Kagyü schools were particularly strong here, with a few medium-sized monasteries in the valleys and numerous retreat centers in the surrounding hills and mountains.

Amdo, in northeastern Tibet, was inhabited mostly by Tibetan no-mads with their flocks and also by Mongolian herdsmen who were like-wise followers of Tibetan Buddhism. It is here that the sacred lake of Kokonor is found and also that Tsongkhapa, the founder of the Geluk sect, was born. Owing to its ever-moving nomadic population, Amdo is less politically centralized than either Central Tibet or Kham, and the various nomad groupings were mostly self-governing. Owing to Geluk conversions in the area, the Geluk sect was particularly strong, having a number of large monasteries. The Nyingmapas were strong here as well and also had a number of large monastic establishments.

The other Tibetan cultural regions existing today outside of the areas of Chinese occupation show similar social, cultural, and political diver-sity. Tibetan areas of India and Nepal are mostly agricultural in nature, with the various schools all represented. Bhutan and Sikkim have popu-lations composed of Tibetans, partly Tibetanized hill peoples, and im-migrants from Nepal. These are also primarily farming areas and have been dominated by the non-Geluk orders. In the more mountainous areas, until the Chinese occupation closed the routes to Tibet proper, trade provided a major form of livelihood.

Thus it was that although Central Tibet was nominally the seat of the ruling Geluk sect, in fact the various regions of Tibet were quite autonomous both politically and culturally. Several factors contributed to this relative independence. For one thing, the large distances and relatively poor communication between Central Tibet and the various other regions meant that each area was able to develop its own charac-ter. In addition, the various Tibetan regions were culturally diverse, each with its own particular history, its own way of speaking, and its own dress, food, artistic traditions, and so on. Furthermore, different Tibetan regions predominated in one or another types of social setup: some were relatively populous, centralized agricultural states; others were still agricultural, but more sparsely populated and spread out; still others were essentially nomadic; and others were urban, containing merchants, the nobility, government officials, artists, with the social di-versity implied by such a mix. The relative independence of the differ-ent areas was also encouraged by the fact that the style of Buddhism followed in the different regions differed, as did local shamanic ritual practices. Finally, Tibetans as a people tend to be fiercely independent and are not particularly amenable to outside control of their affairs. A Golok (or Golog), from northeastern Tibet, gives expression to this sense of independence—even from the Geluk rule from Central Tibet—in this speech quoted by John Rock:

> You cannot compare us Golog with other people. You obey the laws of strangers, the laws of the Dalai Lama, of China, of any of your petty chiefs. You are afraid of everyone. And the result is that you are afraid of everything. And not only you, but your fathers and grandfathers were the same. We Golog, on the other hand, have from time immemorial obeyed none but our own laws, none but our own convictions. A Golog is born with the knowledge of his freedom. . . . Our tribe is the most respected and mighty in Tibet.[2]

In spite of all this diversity, certain patterns bound Tibetan civilization together more or less as a unified whole. Primary was, of course, the Tibetan language, spoken throughout these various areas, in various dialects. Second only to language, Tibetan culture was unified and defined by Tibetan Buddhism itself, providing a history, a worldview, and a manner of living more or less characterizing all Tibetans, including those who were not nominally Buddhist, principally the followers of Bön. Institutionally, the culture was bound together by the importance of monasteries, whether large or small, to every Tibetan whatever their region or manner of livelihood. Even—perhaps particularly—among the nomads, the monasteries played a central role, not only for religious purposes but for the medical services its lamas could provide, mediation in times of dispute, protection in conflict, storage of grain, and so on.

A correct understanding of Tibetan Buddhism, both in its homeland and in exile, is not possible without an appreciation of the diversity of Tibetan culture as well as its unity. It may be argued that the dharma throughout Tibet has, as is often said by Tibetans, to have "one single taste." At the same time, it is clear that there is no one style or tradition of Tibetan Buddhism that can stand as a standard for the rest. The more scholastically and politically oriented Geluk school is no more definitive of Tibetan Buddhism than the more meditative lineages of the Nyingma and the Kagyü. Those who lived in the huge monasteries of Central Tibet could take no particular pride of place over meditators residing in small hermitage communities or the solitary hermits living walled up in a cave, in retreat until death. The strength and vitality of Tibetan Buddhism lay, perhaps, in its ability to include and accommodate so many different manifestations of human spiritual aspiration and practice.

In an age in which world culture is becoming more and more standardized, this is certainly a point worth considering. Buddhists in Tibet might disagree over which view was the more profound or which approach the most effective, but few would dispute that the very fact of religious diversity in Buddhist Tibet came directly from the hand of the Buddha himself, as one of his greatest gifts to his followers. With this view in mind, then, let us consider the rich and varied landscape of Tibetan Buddhism, both as it existed in its homeland and as it is now beginning to flower in the modern period in the rest of the world.

PART ONE

The Sacred Environment

1

The Cosmos and Its Inhabitants

TRADITIONAL TIBETANS LIVED IN A WORLD THAT IS, IN many respects, quite different from the one assumed in modern Western culture. It is not so much that the classical Tibetan worldview contradicts the findings of modern science, but rather that it emphasizes different things and has a different overall shape and configuration. Most important, in the classical Buddhist view, the world is defined not only by what we can perceive with our physical senses and think about rationally. It is equally made up of what cannot be seen, but is available through intuition, dreams, visions, divination, and the like. The senses and rational mind provide access to this immediate physical world, but it is only through the other ways of knowing that can one gain access to the much larger context in which this physical realm is set. Can modern people have experience of this traditional Tibetan cosmology? Tibetans will tell you that their experience of the universe is accessible to anyone who cares to know it. If you know where to look and how to look, they say, you will see for yourself what we are talking about.

THE SCOPE OF THE COSMOS

The Tibetan cosmos is a vast one, beginningless and endless in terms of time, and limitless in extent. Our immediate world—in a model derived from ancient Indian cosmology—is conceived of as a flat disk. At its center is Mount Meru, the "world mountain," surrounded by oceans (figure 1.1). In these are situated the four continents, Aparagodaniya in the west, Uttarakuru in the north, Purvavideha in the east, and our human "island," Jambudvipa in the south. Each of these is flanked by two subcontinents, making eight subcontinents in all. Extending above and below, with Mount Meru as the central axis, are six realms, six distinct types of existence in which sentient beings live. (See the "wheel of life" illustration, figure 14.2, page 389.) Below Mount Meru and extending downward are the hungry ghost realm (*preta-loka*) and, below that, the multileveled hell realm (*naraka-loka*), places of intense suffering. Occupying our human space, level with the base of Mount Meru, is the animal realm. These three—the realms of the hells, hungry ghosts, and animals—make up what is called the three "unfortunate" or "lower" realms. The human realm is the lowest of the three "fortunate" or "higher" realms. On the upper slopes of Mount Meru and extending upward are the jealous god realm and the realm of the gods, also divided into several levels.

This configuration represents our "local universe." However, our own Mount Meru, with the four continents and the six realms, is but one of trillions, indeed an infinite number of such worlds that exist. The existence of worlds, each inhabited by sentient beings, thus extends on and on throughout space, with no end. The life span of the worlds is called a great *kalpa* and is divided into four. In the kalpa of creation, the worlds come into being; in the kalpa of duration, they have their life and support sentient beings; in the kalpa of dissolution, they are destroyed in a final conflagration; and in the final kalpa, there is nothing but empty space. Then the entire process of manifestation begins again. The process of creation, duration, and destruction goes on and on, repeating itself ad infinitum throughout endless time.

This context of space and time, with the innumerable worlds, provides the arena for *samsara,* "cyclic existence." Samsara refers to the condition of beings who have not yet attained liberation, whose existence is still governed by belief in a "self" or "ego." Those still within samsara are thus blindly driven, through the root defilements of passion, aggression, and delusion, to defend and aggrandize the "selves" that they think they possess. This action produces results or karma that be-

FIGURE 1.1 *Mount Meru, the world mountain at the center of the universe.*

come part of who they are. It is in accordance with their karma that they are born in one of the six realms in one of the innumerable worlds. Here they live out their lives, exhausting some previously generated karma but also creating further karma toward the future. When samsaric beings die, they are subsequently reborn in the same or another realm, again in accordance with their karma. Normally this process, and the cycles of pain and pleasure that it entails, goes on without end. The various samsaric worlds are known as "impure realms," that is, places where the condition of samsara prevails among the inhabitants.

The situation is not hopeless, however, for an alternative is provided. In addition to the six realms of samsara, there are other realms of being that stand outside of samsara. These are the pure realms, characterized by enlightenment, the abode of the "realized ones," those who have attained liberation from samsara and who dwell in various pure lands. These beings are the celestial buddhas with their various manifestations; the *yidams* (personal deities), male and female, also called wisdom dakinis and herukas; the great *bodhisattvas* such as Avalokiteshvara (figure 1.2) and Tara (figure 1.3), who will come to the aid of beings; the dharma protectors (*dharmapalas*) who watch over and guard the dharma itself and those on the path; the enlightened men and women who have passed beyond this world; and others. These various enlightened ones represent a state of realization that is available to suffering sentient beings. In fact, according to the type of Buddhism followed in Tibet—Mahayana Buddhism—the state that they embody is the ultimate and final destiny of all humans and other sentient beings. All are on the path that will one day lead to the attainment of the complete and perfect enlightenment of a fully realized buddha.

The "home" of these enlightened beings is, as mentioned, one of the pure lands. These are places where samsara does not prevail and where the inhabitants are pure beings, such as enlightened buddhas or high-level, celestial bodhisattvas. In the pure lands, everyone has an abundance of compassion and understanding. All live with a peerless motivation, the dharma is heard continuously, and life is simple and free from obstacles. In sometimes elaborate and colorful accounts, all the problems that exist in an impure realm are said to be absent, every scent is sweet,

FIGURE 1.2 *Avalokiteshvara, the celestial Bodhisattva of Compassion.*

FIGURE 1.3 *Tara, the feminine counterpart of the Bodhisattva of Compassion.*

every sound melodious, every sight pleasing. Although the pure lands are said to be innumerable and to exist throughout space and time, nevertheless, certain of them are most important. Best known is the realm of Sukhavati, situated in the west, the dwelling place of Amitabha (or Amitayus) Buddha, Avalokiteshvara, and Tara. Shakyamuni Buddha himself is said to have come from this pure land. Also important are Abhirati, the home of Akshobhya Buddha to the east, and Vaiduryanirbhasa, also in the east, home of the Medicine Buddha, Bhaishajya-guru. These pure lands are considered rather remote, although one may aspire to be born in one of them after death.

There are other places understood as being on a higher spiritual level than the samsaric realm, but they are more proximate to our earthly existence and more accessible. One such place well known to Tibetans is the Potala, a sacred mountain identified with several sites in South and Southeast Asia and the earthly home of Avalokiteshvara. In Tibet, the Dalai Lama's immense "winter residence" was called the Potala in recognition of his identity as a human incarnation of Avalokiteshvara. Padmasambhava—also known in Tibet as Guru Rinpoche—is similarly said to dwell in the palace of Lotus Light on the glorious Copper-Colored Mountain on the subcontinent of Chamara.

One of the most interesting of such pure places is the so-called mythi-cal kingdom of Shambhala, a realm in which all of the inhabitants live in an enlightened society and preserve the most sacred traditions of the world. James George, Canadian high commissioner to India and Nepal, provides the following description of Shambhala:

> What, then, is Shambhala? It is a complex idea, a myth, an im-age, but it is also a place, a center that exists on earth. It has been called the navel of our world, the link with the world of the sacred. It is traditionally located in the part of Central Asia where Tibetan Buddhism flourished. . . . The Tibetan tradition speaks of Shambhala as a mystical kingdom or sanctuary shel-tered behind high mountains. There the most esoteric traditions are preserved while spiritual values are eroded or disappear in the world outside. According to Tibetan texts, the hidden way to this sanctuary is so long and arduous, so guarded by natural and supernatural obstacles, that it is ultimately accessible only to those rare searchers who, purified in mind and heart, are single-minded in their aim. Anyone who has visited Buddhist monas-teries of Central Asia will have heard of such searchers—holy men who, after a lifetime of discipline and meditation, disap-pear into the mountain wastes never to return.[1]

FIGURE 1.4 *The Kingdom of Shambhala, a pure realm of enlightenment.*

Although the "home" of the buddhas and high-level bodhisattvas is outside of samsara, they appear in our world to help us enter the path of liberation and follow it to its conclusion. The human Buddha Shakyamuni thus appeared twenty-five hundred years ago, bringing the dharma to this world for the first time and founding a lineage of the study and practice of the teachings. Likewise, the celestial buddhas,

FIGURE 1.5 *King of Shambhala.*

bodhisattvas, protectors, dakinis, and departed teachers appear in our world in various ways, bringing blessings, protection, and guidance on the path.

The Tibetan cosmology, then, is not meant to present a disembodied, abstract "scientific" picture. It rather shows us the *realms of potential experience* that make up this cosmos. It describes the various realms of being—only one of which is human—that are possible and exist within the totality of being. Some of these modes of being are defined by the suffering of samsara, while others represent liberation from samsara. Traditional Tibetan cosmology, then, contrasts with modern conceptions of the universe that are essentially rationalistic, gained by ignoring all experiential data except ones that conform to limited physical criteria such as matter, extension, and motion, and that can be proven to any observer through logical demonstration. The Tibetan picture has been gained through different means and includes different "data."

There are now many Tibetan teachers who understand very well the kind of universe that is described by modern science, including the geography of this world and its structure and constitution, and the expanding universe that has become available to us through astrophysics. Their response to our ideas is, "Yes, but all of this is just Jambudvipa, the human world. There are other continents [spheres or "islands" of possible experience] and other realms, and these are outside of and beyond this human realm. You cannot see them by using scientific instruments."

However, even Jambudvipa has more dimensions and subtleties than modern people usually ascribe to their world. The dominant modern Western cosmology, defined by scientific materialism, regards this world in terms of the operation of so many "physical laws" of physics, chemistry, biology, botany, and so on. Within this perspective, a complete explanation of the universe can be provided through reference to "scientific" principles, yielding a natural world that is dead, without any enlivening spiritual presence and essentially without meaning.

In the traditional Tibetan view, however, the animate and inanimate phenomena of this world are charged with being, life, and spiritual vitality. These are conceived in terms of various spirits, ancestors, demigods, demons, and so on. One of the ways Tibetans recognize a spirit is through the energy that collects in a perceptual moment. A crescendo of energetic "heat" given off by something indicates a spirit. It is something like when we might say that a rock, a tree, or a cloud formation is "striking" or "dramatic" or "compelling." A rock outcropping that has a strange and arresting shape, that perhaps seems strong and menacing, will indicate the existence of some kind of nonhuman presence. Likewise, a hollow in a grove of trees where a spring flows and the flora are unusually lush and abundant, that has a particularly inviting and nurturing atmosphere, will likewise present itself as the home of a spirit. The unusual behavior of a natural phenomenon or an animal will suggest the same as will the rain that ends a drought or the sudden irruption of an illness.

It is not only things that are unanticipated or surprising that indicate the presence of a nonhuman being. Every river and mountain has its spirit embodiment or inhabitants. Each human habitation has a spiritual presence as part of its own being. As this variety suggests, spirits themselves also appear with various levels of development and motivation. Some are malevolent; some are neutral; and others are generally beneficent.

The traditional cosmological perspectives create a uniquely powerful environment for the practice of Tibetan Buddhism. The boundless temporal and spatial vistas reveal the fragility, brevity, and ultimate futility of human life, taken on its own terms. The view of the phenomena of this world as spiritually charged allows intimacy, relationship, and mutuality with the relative world. The understanding of samsara as the endless repetition of life followed by death followed by life, all governed by karma, suggests that lasting happiness in the ordinary sense is not attainable. The introduction of buddhahood as standing outside of samsara provides an alternative to this daunting and frightening prospect. The fact that buddhahood is not only available but is the ultimate and final destiny of all instills fundamental optimism and a sense of the value of life. And the limitless time frame in which this can be achieved enables people to relax and to take their spiritual journey at its own pace. In this way, Tibetan Buddhism has achieved the seemingly contradictory goals of revealing the radical inadequacy of samsara, leaving its adherents little option but to look to a spiritual path, while at the same time rousing them to a sense of confidence, joy, and well-being at their human condition and its literally infinite possibilities.

THE "PROOF" OF EXPERIENCE

This conception of the cosmos and its inhabitants is not just an abstract, theoretical map with no connection to experience. Quite to the contrary, Tibetans find it continually confirmed and proved by the happenings and events of their lives. Let us consider the example of the *dharmapalas,* the deities who protect the dharma and its practitioners from harm. Chagdud Tulku recounts a trip he made to Tibet in 1987, nearly four decades after the Chinese occupation. During this visit, he was able to visit the Chagdud monastery, or *gompa,* in East Tibet, seat of the line of Chagdud incarnations of which he is the current rebirth. The important texts, statuary, and other sacred objects of the gompa had been removed by the local people and carefully hidden away to escape Chinese depredations. Upon arrival at the monastery, Chagdud Rinpoche was able to see that, unlike other monasteries in East Tibet, Chagdud gompa itself had escaped destruction or even serious harm by the Chinese. The lamas and local villagers ascribed this to the activity of the main protector of the monastery and told the following story. As mentioned, valuables that could be removed from the monastery were hidden away.

> A Tibetan from another region, however, did attempt to destroy the large, clay statues that remained in the monastery, particularly an old, very sacred Guru Rinpoche statue in the dharma protector shrine room. He came and found the heavy wooden doors locked, so he climbed up to the small windows under the roof and was about to enter when he saw a large tiger—a vision, but completely real to him—leap in front of the statue. He fled, and afterward became very ill, vomiting blood.
>
> Still not convinced of the power of the dharma protectors, he returned and, using authority invested in him by the Chinese, ordered the doors opened. Inside he saw a shiny black rock, slightly larger than a man's head. "What is this?" he demanded. "It is the life force stone of the dharma protectors," someone replied.

"Don't tell me stupid lies," the would-be-saboteur said harshly. "What dharma protectors? What life force? This is a rock—only a rock—that I will take outside now and throw away."

He reached down and seized it, but it did not move. He ordered another man to help him, then another and another. When four men could not lift the stone, he stepped back and started to mutter incoherently. At that moment, at a distant spot on the riverbank, his son fell into the water and drowned. This man lost his sanity and never regained it. The Chinese and their henchmen scoffed at the idea that these events were related, but no one had much personal enthusiasm for destroying Chagdud Gonpa after that.[2]

Experiences such as this that point to the presence and activity of normally unseen forces are shared by everyone and contribute to the cultural consensus about what is real and what is not.

A similar kind of evidence of the unseen is provided by divination, which is also part of the daily lives of ordinary Tibetans. Through divination one is able to supplicate an embodiment of enlightenment with which one feels a particular connection—perhaps a certain buddha, bodhisattva, or protector—and ask for information and direction concerning a specific problem or dilemma. Underlying the practice of divination is the assumption that the universe is an interconnected, organic whole in which every part is causally connected with every other part. According to the Buddhist teachings on karma, the large patterns of past, present, and future are "written," so to speak, in the totality. Divination seeks to "read" this karmic pattern so that events that are in the process of unfolding can be detected and deciphered. Deities, who are unconstrained by the limitations of human existence, know this totality and can be consulted for information about it. The validity of the process and the reality of the beings whom one is supplicating are indicated by the effectiveness of the results.

An incident from the life of Chögyam Trungpa Rinpoche illustrates how divination works. When he was escaping from Tibet, along with a party of a hundred and seventy people, it was necessary to pass through an area thick with Chinese soldiers. At this point, the party came to an impasse and faced three equally dismal alternatives. First, they might try to cross a turbulent river, with some likelihood that the Chinese were on the other side waiting. Second, they could continue as they were, proceeding alongside the river, risking almost certain encounter with the Chinese who were occupying the area; or third, they could join forces with a larger group of Tibetan refugees and try to fight their way through. The close proximity of the Chinese was evident, and Trungpa Rinpoche felt that they might appear at any moment. It gradually became clear that options two and three were not viable, and the party was left with no alternative but to cross the river. Still, there was fear and hesitation. Rinpoche at this point performed a divination to try to determine whether there were, in fact, Chinese on the other side of the river and whether, in crossing, they would be walking into certain capture. It indicated that no Chinese were present. The party crossed the river and continued toward safe haven in India. In commenting on the practice of divination, Rinpoche makes the following observation:

> Divination is generally used when you are somewhat trapped by the situation. You really have no alternative but you are too cowardly to commit yourself to your actual intuition of the straightforwardness. So you turn to the pretense of divination. And what happens in divination is that, even though you may be highly biased in your view of the situation, you pretend not to be. You step out of the situation altogether and then you open your mind and allow yourself to make a decision in accordance with the divination practice. Or, more precisely, once you are there in no man's land, the answer is there already. Then you come back to your own territory and make a decision.[3]

The practice of divination can sometimes provide even more dramatic indication of the reality of the unseen dimensions of existence and their inhabitants. Particularly striking in this regard are the oracle priests of Tibetan Buddhism. These priests, often ordained monks living in the great monasteries, call upon one of the protector deities to take possession of them. In his famous book, *Seven Years in Tibet,* Heinrich Harrer provides a vivid account of one of the most famous monastic oracles in Tibet, the Nechung oracle. As Harrer witnessed the possession:

> He looked as if the life were fading out of him. Now he was perfectly motionless, his face a staring mask. Then suddenly, as if he had been struck by lightning, his body curved upward like a bow. The onlookers gasped. The god was in possession. The medium began to tremble; his whole body shook and beads of sweat stood out on his forehead. Servants went to him and placed a huge, fantastic head-dress on his head. This was so heavy that it took two men to carry it. The slender body of the monk sank deeper into the cushions of the throne under the weight of his monstrous mitre. . . . The trembling became more violent. The medium's heavily laden head wavered from side to side, and his eyes stared from their sockets. His face was swollen and covered with patches of hectic red. Hissing sounds pierced through his closed teeth. Suddenly he sprang up. Servants rushed to help him, but he slipped by them and to the moaning of the oboes began to rotate in a strange exotic dance. Save for the music, his groans and teeth-gnashings were the only sounds heard in the temple. Now he started beating on his gleaming breastplate with a great thumb-ring, making a clatter which drowned the full rolling of the drums.[4]

Eventually the oracle became calmer, and a cabinet minister began to put various questions to the deity who had possessed the oracle. Answers were provided, often in a cryptic expression that required deciphering. From these, the appropriate direction for certain state and monastic dilemmas was drawn.

Another kind of confirmation of the unseen realms of Tibetan cosmology is provided by the *deloks* (or *delogs*), "those who die and return," people who go through the experience of death, journey to the usually invisible realms of samsara and nirvana, and then return to life to report their experiences. Chagdud Tulku, whose mother was one of these visionaries, provides the following account:

31

As a child in Tibet, I sometimes found my mother, Delog Dawa Drolma, surrounded by an audience listening with utmost attention as she told of her journeys to other realms. Her face was radiant as she spoke of the deities in the pure realms; tears flowed as she described the miseries of hell beings and pretas, or tormented spirits. She told of encountering deceased relatives of certain people, and she relayed from the dead to the living concerns about unfinished business (perhaps buried coins or jewels that could not be located) or pleas for prayers and ceremonies. She also brought back spiritual advice from high lamas who had passed from this world, to which lamas on this side of death responded with deep respect.[5]

Chagdud Tulku comments that his mother, in making this journey to the other worlds lay "for five full days . . . cold, breathless, and devoid of any vital signs, while her consciousness moved freely into other realms, often escorted by the wisdom goddess, White Tara."[6] Her direct experience of other realms gave authority to her words, which were trusted without hesitation. This was so not only because great lamas treated them with such high regard,

> but also because she knew the whereabouts of buried coins and actions of the deceased before their deaths—things that she could not possibly have known without having been told directly by those she encountered as a delog. Later in her life one of the most generous contributors to her projects was a Tibetan businessman who had been an adamant non-practitioner of religion until my mother conveyed to him information about buried money from his deceased sister.[7]

Knowledge of other realms is sometimes obtained while one is in one's body in a relatively normal state. Consider the following account by James George, whose comments on Shambhala were quoted above. One day George and his wife were visiting with the young Chögyam Trungpa Rinpoche. George describes the meeting as follows:

Ironically, I feel that I came the closest to encountering Shambhala while sitting in the study of Canada House in New Delhi one evening in 1968. We had as our guest the well-known Tibetan teacher Chögyam Trungpa Rinpoche . . . and we asked him what he thought of the tradition of Shambhala. To our astonishment, he replied very quietly that, although he had never been there, he believed in its existence and could see it in his mirror when he went into a certain state. He could reach this state by the traditional process of *prasena,* or "conjuration," through performing a special ritual invocation (*sadhana*).

That evening in our study he produced a small metal mirror of the Chinese type. After looking into it intently for some time, he began to describe what he saw. Within a vast circle of high snow-capped mountains lay a green valley and a beautiful city, in the center of which rose a terraced hill with a small palace or temple on top of it. Around this hill was a square, walled enclosure, and around this again were other enclosures containing temples, gardens and sacred monuments. The most singular thing about the inhabitants of the city was that they were of all faiths, races, and nations, and appeared to come from the four corners of the earth.

Four years later, in Bhutan, I saw for myself the scene that Trungpa had described. It was in a painting that resembled in almost every detail the city that he had seen in his mirror. I saw it at the home of one of the senior officials and nobles of Paro, Mr. Paljor Dorji. Mr. Dorji confirmed that his painting, which was several centuries old, was of Shambhala.[8]

Another sort of specialist who can provide unusual testimony about the existence and nature of the unseen world is the hermit, meditating in retreat. As in other Buddhist cultures,[9] in Tibet those who have spent much or all of their lives in solitude, meditating day and night, tell stories of meeting various beings from the unseen realms. Sometimes divinities would visit the meditator's cave, hoping for instruction in the dharma, which was not available in their realm. And often as not, the yogin would comply by spending much of the night teaching the gods and goddesses the path to liberation. The great yogin Milarepa, for example, frequently encountered various spirits, demons, and deities who found their way to his cave. If the beings were ill-intentioned, he would convert, banish, or dispel them; if they were well-intentioned, he would teach them.

Finally, the unseen world is known to Tibetans through the accounts of masters who are considered fully realized. Tulku Urgyen Rinpoche gives the following account:

> In the past, masters like Kyungpo Naljor, Tilopa and Naropa visited Uddiyana [in northwestern India] and described the visions they had there of Vajra Yogini's pure realm, which is full of terrifying charnel grounds and frightening eternal fires and so on. More recently a group of normal people went there and returned saying that all they saw were some big boulders and a small pond of water. "We didn't see anything; it's just a normal place," they told a master named Gendun Chopel, who died a few decades ago. In response, he said, "While you don't even see the unchanging nature of mind which is inseparable from yourself, how can you ever have visions of deities through sadhana practice?" In other words, if you are unable to see what you already continuously possess, how can you expect to perceive Vajra Yogini's pure land? . . . We must first be well-established in dharmata; then it is possible to see the divine city of Vajra Yogini.[10]

THE CLASSIFICATION OF BEINGS
OF THE UNSEEN WORLD

The Tibetan universe is thus a complex and multifaceted one with many kinds and levels of inhabitants. It may be helpful to put these into some kind of order for the reader. The following fourfold schema, suggested by Geoffrey Samuel, while not strictly traditional, is useful in providing a general idea of the scope and dimensions of "being" found in Tibetan Buddhism.[11]

Beings Transcending Samsara

1. *The selfless and compassionate beings of Buddhism, such as the various buddhas, bodhisattvas, protectors of the dharma, and departed masters who remain available to practitioners in a nonmaterial form through the means of supplication, ritual, and meditation.* A buddha is an enlightened being who has passed completely beyond samsara. Buddhas may be human, such as the buddha of our world, Shakyamuni. They may also be purely celestial such as Amitabha, the buddha of compassion, who, as mentioned, lives in an enlightened pure land "in the West," known as Sukhavati. A bodhisattva is a being who has vowed to attain the enlightenment of a buddha and who is at some point along the path to that goal. Bodhisattvas may also be human or celestial. As human beings, they may be ordinary persons like ourselves or people of great attainment. Examples of celestial bodhisattvas are two emanations of Amitabha, the male bodhisattva Avalokiteshvara, and the female bodhisattva Tara, who are embodiments of pure compassion and among the most-loved deities in the Tibetan pantheon. Celestial bodhisattvas are closer than buddhas to ordinary human beings and may be supplicated in times of need. It is believed in the cases of both Tara and Avalokiteshvara that they will respond without fail to those who call upon them with faith and devotion. Some of Tibet's most revered incarnate lamas, including His Holiness the Dalai Lama and His Holiness the Gyalwa Karmapa, are considered to be human incarnations of Avalokiteshvara.

One somewhat specialized class of buddhas are the tantric *yidams,* or "personal deities." A yidam is an enlightened being whom one takes as the subject of one's Vajrayana practice. These buddhas are understood to be embodiments of one's own inner realized nature. Two well-known yidams in the Kagyü lineage are the male Chakrasamvara and the female Vajrayogini.

The dharmapalas, or "protectors of the dharma," are also beyond

TABLE 1.1

CLASSIFICATION OF THE BEINGS
IN THE INVISIBLE WORLD

TRANSCENDING SAMSARA	
Category	*Examples*
Buddhas	Human: Shakyamuni Buddha Celestial: Amitabha
Bodhisattvas	Avalokiteshvara Tara
Yidams	Male: Chakrasamvara Female: Vajrayogini
Dharmapalas	Mahakala
Gurus	Padmasambhava (Guru Rinpoche)
Dakinis	Yeshe Tsogyal

WITHIN SAMSARA	
Category	*Examples*
Indian Deities	Brahma, Indra
Deities of this world: neutral deities of the atmosphere mountain deities deities on the earth deities under the earth, in waters deities of human habitations deities of the human person	 tsen gyalpo, nyen sadak nagas (lu) field god, tent god, hearth god right shoulder: god of father's lineage left shoulder: god of mother's lineage
Deities of this world: malevolent	dön mamo rakshasas pishachas maras

samsara and are classified according to two types. First are the "wisdom dharmapalas," who are embodiments of the fierce or protective energies of the buddhas and are therefore considered in their very nature to be enlightened. The various *mahakalas* are examples of this type (figure 1.6). Second are the "worldly protectors," who function as guardians of the dharma but who are not considered to be themselves enlightened. Rather, they were originally worldly deities who were tamed by a master such as Padmasambhava and made a vow henceforth to act as guardians, carrying out the intentions of the buddhas. Thus, although they still have not attained the final goal of liberation, for all intents and purposes in their activity they function as dharma protectors.

Also existing in enlightened realms outside of samsara are various realized *gurus* or teachers who have passed away and dwell in pure lands. For example, Padmasambhava though departed, still lives in his pure realm, the Copper-Colored Mountain, from which he responds to the supplications of his devotees. The dakini Yeshe Tsogyal, similarly considered enlightened and dwelling with Padmasambhava, is the subject of prayers and supplications on the part of those who particularly look to her.

This category of beings who dwell outside of the boundaries and territories of samsara is the most important for Buddhist practice for it is to these buddhas, bodhisattvas, protectors, and departed masters that the various higher rituals and meditations of Vajrayana Buddhism are directed.

Beings within Samsara

2. *Indian deities*. The Indian deities were inherited by the Tibetans when Buddhism was transplanted into Tibet. These deities are generally not of much daily importance to Tibetans either in the context of Buddhist practice or in the arena of worldly life with its difficulties, problems, and demands. However, they can be of significance to the meditator. Along with other deities, the Indian divinities are thought to dwell on one or another of the various levels of the god realm. Here they have some practical importance since meditators, upon entering

FIGURE 1.6 *Mahakala, one of the most important dharmapalas,
or guardians of the teachings.*

various meditative trances, may encounter one or another of them in
the course of their practice.

3. *The gods of this human world, including local deities of mountains,
lakes, and other geographical features as well as those who inhabit structures*

38

such as houses. The *lu* or *nagas,* for example, live under the earth in springs, rivers, lakes, and wells and preside over that part of the under-world. One infringes on the nagas' realm when one changes or obstructs the flow of water, causes pollution, or in some other way defiles their watery domain. Unless the responsible persons have gone about their work according to appropriate rituals and have obtained the nagas' leave, they may fear some illness, such as leprosy which is connected with the nagas. Owing to their connections with water, the nagas also preside over the weather. In the case of drought or too much rain, ritual offerings to the nagas are indicated.

Another example of deities residing in natural phenomena are the *sadak,* earth lords, considered masters of the soil. These beings preside over specific locales and become upset and angry if the earth within their territory is disrupted or defiled in any way. On the earth also are worldly spirits known as the *nyen,* living on the shoulders of mountains. A broken and unrepaired ritual relation with them results in sickness, accident, and death. On mountains reside the *gyalpo* and above the earth, in the air, live the *tsen.*

Examples of spirits associated with man-made phenomena are the field god, the tent god, and the hearth god.[12] The hearth, for example, is the center of the life of the Tibetan family, and it has a strong and definite presence within the family's dwelling. Here the energy, health, and prosperity of the family is concentrated. It is the job of the female head of the household to maintain a good relationship with the hearth deity. She manages this by making offerings to the hearth god and by being in all ways respectful of the hearth. If the hearth is inadvertently defiled through a pot boiling over or through dirt or refuse falling into it, rituals must be performed to purify the misdeed and to reestablish a positive relationship with the spirit of the hearth.[13]

4. *Beings whose intention toward human beings is always malevolent.* This category, encompassing all those considered as *dön,* or harmful spirits, includes various ill-intentioned nonhumans, some of whom may have been malevolent humans in their last life.[14] An example of such invariably inimical beings are the *mamo,* black, ferocious female demon-

esses who delight in instigating chaos, disrupting human affairs, and bringing all kinds of misfortune on human beings. Their appetite for destruction is whetted by confusion and degeneration in human society—when families quarrel and relatives feud, when exploitation, corruption, and poverty go unaddressed, when clan takes up arms against clan. When aroused, the mamos send sickness and plague to humans; they bring disaster to projects; they incite widespread warfare; and they bring down calamity on crops and livestock. Nevertheless, evil intentioned though they are, the mamos' wrath can to some extent be appeased by various kinds of offerings and rituals.

In this malevolent class as well are the *rakshasas* and the *pishachas,* flesh-eating demons who attack unsuspecting prey. Included also are the *maras* or *dü,* who, as emanations of Mara, tried to prevent Buddha Shakyamuni's enlightenment, are thoroughly and viciously anti-dharmic and create obstacles to yogins and other serious dharma practitioners.

This fourfold classification, as Samuel points out, fits the traditional Tibetan situation only in a very rough way. Categories 3 and 4 in particular have no sharp dividing line. In practice, nonhuman beings can be met at any bend of the road and can present any conceivable face. Often, in practice, one is not initially certain even whether it is a spirit that lies behind a phenomenon or event, or, if so, whether the spirit in question is ultimately well- or ill-intentioned. Once a spirit or deity has made its presence known through some kind of untoward event, some calamity, threat, or blessing, then one may go to the appropriate lama or diviner to determine the source of the event in question. One seeks in particular to know what actions may need to be taken to bring about a positive relationship with the energy or being in question. Thus the situation is about as complex as life itself, and as full of unanticipated encounters. One needs to be alert and attentive to recognize and relate properly with the spirits one meets.

With these various samsaric deities and beings, we certainly seem to be describing a strictly Tibetan context and reality. Interesting, then, is the illustration provided by a man, American by birth and residing in the United States, who had been plagued by an illness that could not be definitively diagnosed and resisted treatment. After making the usual rounds of Western doctors and alternative health practitioners, this person—who was not a Buddhist—happened to consult a Tibetan physician. After hearing the man's story, the Tibetan inquired if the man had been working around any wells, ponds, or streams prior to the onset of his sickness. The man thought back and replied that, yes, he had been moving some large stones in a stream that ran through his property. The physician suggested that a local *naga* had been offended and that this was the cause of the malady. He advised his patient to return to the stream and put the stones he had displaced back in their original locations, and I believe an offering to the naga was also prescribed. Skeptical to the core but desperate, the man complied. He later reported that his illness had resolved itself within a short period of time.

Tibetan Buddhism itself has ways of classifying these various nonhuman beings. The most important and influential system is that of the six realms, mentioned above, a schema that the Tibetans inherited when Buddhism came from India to Tibet. This system classifies only those beings within samsara. Those in a state of liberation and therefore outside of samsara, are beyond karma and cannot be located or placed in any sense. While two of the six realms (the human and the animal) represent physical beings, the other four include beings who are not physical as we are: the realms of hell-beings, of pretas or hungry ghosts, of jealous or warring gods, and of gods.

Another important schema, also inherited from India, similarly provides an overall picture of samsara and of the place of visible and invisible beings within in it. This is the schema of the three realms, or *dhatus* (table 1.2), which include the desire realm (*kama-dhatu*), the form realm (*rupa-dhatu*), and the formless realm (*arupa-dhatu*). The desire realm includes all beings who, driven by desire, are preoccupied by the search for pleasure as opposed to pain. Included here are the hell-beings, hungry ghosts, animals, jealous gods, and humans, as well as the lower gods. The form realm, which is composed of four substages, is inhabited by the higher gods, who have appearance but are not material and solid as physical beings in our world are. Their state of being is defined by peace and

TABLE 1.2

THE THREE REALMS (DHATUS)

AND THEIR CORRELATIONS WITH THE EIGHT LEVELS
OF MEDITATIVE ATTAINMENT (DHYANAS)

REALM (DHATU)	TYPE OF HEAVEN /DEITIES	MEDITATIVE ATTAINMENT	COMMENTS
3. Realm of Formlessness: *Arupa-dhatu*	Gods whose basic state of being embodies this attainment	8. Neither perception nor nonperception	These gods have a being that has no "form"; they are defined by various states of mind, more and more ethereal as one moves
	same	7. Nothingness	
	same	6. Infinite consciousness	
	same	5. Infinite space	
2. Realm of Pure Form: *Rupa-dhatu*	Akanishtha heaven* Abodes of pure deities	4. Concentration Equanimity Beyond pleasure and pain	five abhijnas (psychic powers) attained here
	Complete beauty Immeasurable beauty Limited beauty	3. Concentration Equanimity	
	Radiant gods	2. Concentration Rapture Joy	
	Great Brahmas Brahma-priests Retinue of Brahma	1. Discursive thought Detachment Rapture Joy	
1. Realm of Desire: *Kama-dhatu*	Gods of Desire (includes gods and jealous gods): Tushita heaven Heaven of the 33 Four great kings Human beings Hungry ghosts Animals Hell-beings	Ordinary samsaric states of mind of the six realms	

*The heavens listed under the "realm of pure form" represent a selection from the some two dozen mentioned in the sources (Kloetzli, "Buddhist Cosmology," 115).

equilibrium. The formless realm, also composed of four stages, is inhabited by gods who have no particular shape, size, or boundaries. Nevertheless, they still possess some kind of identity or self, although in a very subtle and attenuated form. And they are still subject to the operation of karma. The formless realm is thus composed of gods whose being is identified with either infinite space, infinite consciousness, nothingness, or neither perception nor nonperception. Again, although the upper two of these three dhatus embody states of being obviously ethereal and divine by any standard, they are still considered to lie within samsara. This is so because eventually the karma of these states will exhaust itself and the beings in them will suffer rebirth in other, usually lower realms. The schema of the three realms clearly emphasizes "godly" conditions of being and, as we shall see below, is intended to help meditators locate "divine" states of mind they may experience. By contrast, the schema of the six realms is of much more practical use for most people since it gives greater emphasis to the lower worlds with which we have most contact and into which most of us may expect rebirth.

To what extent can human beings encounter the inhabitants of other realms? Among the nonhuman realms, it is the animal realm of which we are most aware. Hell-beings are so far removed from our realm and so preoccupied with their own suffering that we human beings do not normally encounter them. If we are accomplished meditators, we may encounter deities who live in the god and jealous god realms, but otherwise we will not normally encounter them either. If ordinary human beings are to have any experience of the nonmaterial realms, it is most likely they will see beings from the hungry ghost realm in the form of "ghosts" or other disembodied spirits.

The hungry ghost realm is interesting because, within Tibetan cosmology, it performs a somewhat different function in comparison to the other nonvisible realms. While the god realm, the jealous god realm, and the hell realm are all rather clearly defined and have beings within them that conform to the definition, the hungry ghost realm seems to be a kind of catchall category for beings of a variety of types and temperaments. As mentioned, this realm includes ordinary ghosts as well as demons and malevolent beings of various sorts falling into category 4.

These classifications and their correspondences are very rough and imprecise. For Tibetans, when an unseen being makes itself known, the important point is, as mentioned, not where it should be placed in one of these schemes; of much more interest is whether it is generally beneficent or malevolent and what kind of ritual relationship needs to be established with it. In the context of the vitality and immediacy of Tibetan religious life, here as elsewhere, theoretical considerations tend to take a backseat to more practical considerations.

People are more or less preoccupied with different kinds of spirits and deities depending on their particular concerns and work. For those involved in farming and therefore concerned about the weather and the availability of water, good relations with the nagas are critical. Those looking after a monastery will be particularly attentive to the Buddhist protectors, and Westerners are sometimes surprised at just how much time and energy is given within the typical monastery to maintaining proper relations with the protector deities. Those engaged in retreat practice, will spend a great deal of time in relation with their personal deities (yidams). Nevertheless, it is true to say that everyone is in some way concerned with all the classes of deities, for high lamas are enlisted by laypeople for help with the lower-level spirits, while ordinary laypeople will have special buddhas, bodhisattvas, and dharma protectors whom they supplicate.

The way in which one communicates with these nonhuman beings is through ritual and ritualized activities. The spirits, gods, and deities do not generally respond to ordinary human language. For example, to say, "Leave me alone," does not have the pointedness, power, or effect—or, frankly, the appropriate decorum—that ritual has with its supplications, confessions, offerings, praises, and purifications (see chapter 2).

CONCLUSION

To what extent can the contemporary Western Tibetan Buddhist practitioner dispense with some or all of these unseen, nonhuman beings? Within the Tibetan perspective, this cosmology of the unseen worlds is a critical aspect of the tradition. The manifestation of a spirit or deity is a significant event, for it is an overture on the part of the invisible world toward human beings. Some kind of relationship is being called for. If the deity in question is a Buddhist deity, this is an event of spiritual power and importance that can provide important direction in one's life. If the spirit is a worldly one, positive or negative, information can be obtained about how to conduct one's life, in terms of the unseen world, the interconnected world beyond perception. From the Tibetan point of view, relationships with the unseen world are essential to a full and successful human life. Ignoring one's relationships with the whole world of unseen spirits and spiritual beings is, in fact, as senseless and counterproductive as ignoring the people and conventions of one's own immediate human society. It is simply not possible to live in such a way.

Buddhism is normally thought of as a nontheistic tradition, and this raises the question of how such spirits, gods, and deities are to be understood within the Tibetan Buddhist framework. Certainly in Tibetan life, whether it is a question of the malevolent mamos, the potentially beneficent hearth god, the deities of the god realms, or the dharma protectors or tantric yidams, the nonhuman beings are understood at least on one level as more or less independent, objective entities. They are beings with whom one must be in constant relation, even though they are nonhuman and usually not visible.

At the same time, however, from the point of view of the philosophical and meditative tradition, all such nonhuman beings are ultimately seen as aspects of one's own mind and not separate from it. But what does this actually mean? Frequently, particularly in the West, this standard Buddhist assertion is taken to indicate that such spirits and deities, taken as external beings by ordinary Tibetans, are not really external at all; that in fact they are mistaken projections of psychological states. This, then, becomes a justification for treating them as in fact nonexistent and provides a rationale for jettisoning them from Western adaptations of the tradition. The problem with this approach is that it reflects a misunderstanding of what is meant by the statement that such entities are aspects of mind and inseparable from mind.

The deities are more properly said to be aspects of one's own innate mind or reflexes of one's awareness. For example, the buddhas, although apparently objectively existing beings, are fundamentally nothing other than our own enlightened nature. The protectors are representations of the wrathful and uncompromising energy of our own awareness. And the gurus are objectifications of the teaching and guiding principle as it exists within each of us. In a similar manner, the various samsaric spirits and demons may be seen as embodiments of peripheral states of one's own mind. These apparently externally existent beings, then, are false bifurcations of the primordial nondual awareness that lies at the basis of all experience. So far, so good; but here is the really critical point: *it is not only the beings of the unseen world that have this status, but all of the phenomena of duality.* In the Tibetan view, ourselves, other people, trees, mountains, and clouds, indeed all of the phenomena of the entire so-called internal and external universe, are nothing other than false objectifications and solidifications of nondual awareness.

To say this is not, however, to discount their external and "objective" existence within the relative world of apparent duality. In the examples cited above, the samsaric beings of the six realms as well as the Buddhist deities existing in the state of nirvana make their appearance to us ordinary, unenlightened people as external, objectively existing beings. In fact, on this level, they can appear as significantly more real, vivid, and powerful than the ordinary physical universe that surrounds us. On one level, then, such beings certainly do exist and are important co-inhabitants of our cosmos. Thus to say that they are aspects of mind is not to deny their existence on the relative level. Nor does it obviate our responsibility to deal with them and relate to them on their own level and as they present themselves to us.

What, then, does it mean to say that these unseen beings are all aspects of mind? It means simply that the way we experience and conceive of them has to do with our own psychology and level of awareness. Ultimately—and this is something that we shall explore more in detail below—the apparent duality of subject and object is not given in reality. It is a structure that we, out of fear and ignorance, impose on the world. When we see the phenomenal world truly as it is, we realize a level of being that precedes the subject-object split. This is the true nature of "experience," "awareness," or "nondual mind," understood at this point as interchangeable categories. When Tibetans say that the spirits, gods, and deities are aspects of mind and nothing other than mind, they mean it in this sense, that their fundamental nature—as indeed the nature of all phenomena—is nondual awareness.

2

Living in the Sacred Cosmos

THE COSMOS, THEN, IS A VAST ARENA OF LIFE AND activity, with many levels and kinds of beings. Human beings are just one clan, so to speak, among many others. Even the other clans within samsara—the gods, jealous gods, animals, hungry ghosts, and hell-beings—form part of one large grouping and, beyond the boundaries of the samsaric grouping, there are others. Each sort of being, whether trapped in cyclic existence or free from it, has its own mode of being and its own "place" within the whole. Those who are considered awakened have a mode of being and a "location" that is inconceivable to ordinary human beings. But this very inconceivability is, in a sense, a "place" from our ordinary point of view because it locates them outside of the cycle of transmigration.

None of these beings, whatever level they represent, is unconnected or irrelevant to human life. In fact, we humans are one part of a vast, interconnected web of relationships with all other inhabitants of the cosmos, both those still living within delusion and those who are awakened.

An awareness of these relationships is critical because, to a very large extent, who we are as humans is defined by this network of relations. To be able to know this fact, and to take responsibility for it, gives us a dignified and directed human life. Within Tibetan tradition, the isolated individual—the one who is unaware of the vast cosmos of beings within which we live and who attempts to live as if it did not exist—is lost. He is a *dundro,* an animal-realm being in human form, controlled by ignorance, with its nose to the ground.

Our interconnectedness with the rest of the cosmos rests on deep foundations. Most fundamentally, we share with all other beings the inherent core of buddha-nature—the inner, awakened state that dwells at the heart of all sentient beings as their inmost essence. We might consider all beings as having, like us, membership in the same great family—just as we view our children and our parents equally as family members, even though they are at earlier or later stages of life than we are. In a similar way, we are at a certain stage in our spiritual evolution. The others in the vast sea of being are at other stages in the very same process. Insects, for example, represent an earlier phase in this process, fully awakened buddhas a later one. But fundamentally, we are all made of the same stuff, so to speak.

INTERCONNECTEDNESS OF BEINGS

Our Connection to Beings within Samsara

We are intimately interconnected with all other inhabitants of the six realms because, besides possessing the same buddha-nature as they, we have their lives and their specific destinies written within us. We are related with all beings within samsara, because we humans have been reborn, time out of mind, in every other condition and mode of sentient existence, as hell-beings, hungry ghosts, animals, humans, jealous gods, and gods, not once or on a few occasions, but countless times. Within the animal realm, we have lived as amoebas, insects, all the way up to the most intelligent mammals, over and over. We share the same history of suffering and happiness with every other being within the six realms.

In addition, not one of these countless births is lost to us. According to Tibetan tradition, every experience we have had as a sentient being remains indelibly within us as subliminal memory, imprinted on our inmost consciousness, that part of us which goes on from birth to birth. We may not be conscious of ever having been a bird or a lion, and we may have no memories even of our previous birth; yet the experiences of these and all other lifetimes since beginningless time continue to shape and inform how we experience our human life right now. When we look at a frog or a butterfly, on some level we understand that life form because in other times and places we have *been* a frog and a butterfly. If our intelligence is clear and our heart unobstructed, we have open access to this understanding. Most of us, however, are governed by utilitarian motives, and so we view the frog or the butterfly in self-serving terms. The frog may be something to eat or provoke revulsion; the butterfly may be seen as an object of beauty or as something to complete our butterfly collection. Either way, however, our memory of having been a frog or a butterfly—or a hungry ghost or a god for that matter—is alive and active at a deep level within us.

It is interesting to see how differently adults react to children, depending on how much access they have to their own childhood. The more we remember being children—the more we can still feel the joys and sorrows of that experience—the more understanding of our own children we will have, the more kindness we will show, and the more accurate we will be in our guidance of them. On the other hand, some of us cannot remember ever having been children or, for whatever reason, feel hatred and disgust toward this period of our lives. In such cases, it is far more difficult to understand or genuinely love a child. In just the same way, the more we are aware of our own karmic history, the more understanding we will have of the various kinds of beings within samsara, the more kinship we will feel with them, and the more compassion we will have.

Awareness of connection with other beings within samsara is a matter of the utmost importance for our own happiness and fulfillment. If we are unaware of our relatedness with other people, for example, and habitually view them solely as objects for our own entertainment or aggrandizement, we are violating our deeper sense of connection with them and creating the seeds of future problems for ourselves. Likewise, if we ignore our natural connectedness with animals, viewing them as "fair game" and perhaps killing them for our own pleasure, we are again acting against our inner awareness. In both examples, it is like throwing more and more garbage into the clear well of our inherent nature. In such cases, we are sowing seeds of future confusion and suffering for ourselves.

From the Tibetan point of view, as one moves along the path of spiritual development, one's feeling of kinship with other beings within the cosmos gradually increases. Those of us who are at more preliminary levels of this path will have little or no awareness of linkage with others. As we progress, our sense of relatedness increases. At higher stages of spiritual maturation, one will feel a strong sense of connection to all other beings and an obligation to help them. Fully enlightened buddhas are said to remember every birth they have ever had, as if it were only yesterday. They remember because every experience of every birth is recorded within them, and by virtue of their awakening, the record is completely open.

Our Connection with Enlightened Beings

We are not only in a state of intimate relation with all other beings within samsara. In addition, we are deeply connected with all the various enlightened beings who pervade time and space. This is so because the hearts of the awakened ones are just the same as ours: the buddha-nature. The only difference between us and them is that in our case, the buddha-nature is covered over with veils and hidden, while in them it is fully uncovered and manifest.

It is indicative that when we meet human teachers of high realization, we often have intense reactions. We may feel tremendously strong emotions of love and longing, or perhaps fear and dread. These emotions are a sign of our connection with them. In that teacher we are—in a very real sense—meeting our own future, face to face. We see what we are fated to become, what we *must* become in order to fulfill our own inherent destiny. How could we not in some way be deeply moved by such a meeting?

In revered teachers, a state of realization is embodied in human form. In the celestial buddhas and high-level bodhisattvas, the embodiment is more ethereal and not within the human realm. Nevertheless it is not only possible but essential that, as we go along the path, we also discover and deepen our sense of commonality with these nonmaterial, awakened ones. According to Tibetan tradition, in fact, as we mature, the "sky draws closer to the earth," so to speak, and the celestial buddhas and bodhisattvas seem more and more our ever-present protectors, mentors, and guides.

RITUAL: COMMUNICATING WITH THE UNSEEN WORLD

As human beings, we are fated to act constantly. Even "doing nothing" can be a powerful act, and like any other form of action, it has its karmic consequences. In addition, all our actions are *in relation*—to all those beings with whom we are in connection, and whatever we do has an impact on them. Within Tibetan tradition, to know this and to act in accordance with it is to take responsibility for one's human life.

Of the various beings within samsara, it is only other humans and animals that are normally visible. And even of these, we are only aware of a tiny portion. The beings of the other realms—those of the hells, the hungry ghost realms, the jealous gods, and the gods—are ordinarily invisible. Likewise, we ordinarily cannot see the various spiritual beings that surround us and exist throughout space, realized teachers who have died, high-level bodhisattvas, the various protectors, the fully enlightened buddhas, and so on. And yet, in the Tibetan perspective, to live a genuinely human and fruitful life, we need to discover our relation with all these various beings of samsara and beyond, and to act in ways appropriate to our connection. Within Tibetan tradition, the way to do this is through ritual (*choga*).

The Language of Ritual

Ritual is action that expresses a relationship. It is the vehicle of communication with another and is itself that communication. Ritual may be performed in relation to beings whom we know and see, and also in relation to those in normally invisible realms.

When we pass people on the street, we act in certain ways depending on our relationship with them. If we do not know them and do not wish to know them, we may lower our eyes and avoid their glance. If it is a good friend, we may smile and greet them warmly, perhaps shaking hands. If it is someone we do not like, we may frown and move away. These gestures are all ritualized behaviors that express our relation with the other and also reaffirm that relation. We can also use simple rituals like these to alter our relations. Perhaps there is someone with whom we have had difficulty and we want to change the relationship. As we approach them, instead of doing the expected and averting our gaze, we may look at them and smile. Such a simple ritual has the power to change the course of our own and the other's history. Each of these actions—smiling, frowning, looking at someone, looking away, shaking hands—is part of a ritual vocabulary used in our culture to communicate various kinds of relationships.

In Tibetan Buddhism, ritual is used in relation both to the seen and the unseen world. In Tibet, different vocabularies are used in different instances, depending on which beings one wishes to be in relation with. In each case, one engages in ritual to express one's link and to communicate. In the pages that follow, we will examine ritual in more detail. At this point, I wish to provide some basic orientation to the general topic and its role within Tibetan tradition.

The essence of ritual is communication. Why do we need to communicate with other beings? Because communication is the exchange of energy and experience. As human beings on the spiritual path, we need continually to be in a process of exchange with others, both seen and unseen. Other beings have things to give us, and we have things to give them. Human life is a process of learning and growing, and this is always a mutual enterprise. The only way that this occurs is through the give and take of communication. The pathways of this exchange are our interconnectedness with other beings. Ritual opens these pathways and allows exchange and communication to occur. Moreover, to progress in our journeys, we need to be in a communicative relation not only with those who are further along than we are, but also with those who are in various states of sorrow, below us.

Ritual Relations with Samsaric Beings

The relations that we have with other beings, both visible and invisible, are infinitely varied and complex. With some beings we have a particular connection, a "karmic link" or "karmic debt." Those we are in a position to help are ones with whom our link is especially strong. With beings who are far removed from us, our connection is weaker.

For example, among the six realms, our fellow human beings, animals, and hungry ghosts—the pretas—are close to us. Other human beings, because they have the same condition as us are the closest, and we are continually interacting with them. We also have many opportunities to interact with animals, and because we humans are in a privileged position, we need to act with kindness and take an attitude of protection toward them. Traditional Tibetan Buddhists prefer not to harm even the smallest insect. Saving animals destined for slaughter is particularly meritorious. Hungry ghosts are also close to us because, though normally invisible, they hover around human situations, looking for kindness and nourishment. Sometimes the pretas become visible in the form of ghosts or spirits. They may be beings of considerable power who insist on their needs by creating obstacles for us. We need to provide help to the pretas both for our own benefit and for theirs.

In Tibetan Buddhism the way to address the needs of hungry ghosts is through specific rituals. As described below, we arrange certain kinds of offerings, ritually empower them with our energy in the form of kindness and good intentions, and then make them available to the pretas. By so doing, we can give them something they desperately desire. For as beings living in the human realm, we are in a unique position to feed their spiritual need, to provide nourishment that alone can allay the terrible hunger and thirst that they, as pretas, continually feel. This nourishment not only alleviates their suffering but, through a strengthened sense of relation with us, brings them closer to a human rebirth. Through this kind of ritual, we not only provide assistance to those in great need, but remove the obstructing influences they may be sending our way and generate an overall better karmic situation for ourselves.

Beings in the god realms or in the hell realms are somewhat more removed from us. In Tibetan Buddhism, a ritual relation is nevertheless maintained with them, although it does not have the tangibility of the relations that we have with other humans, animals, and the hungry ghosts. For example, it is considered important that one make a daily ritual reaffirmation of one's wish that all beings, from those in the deepest hells to those in the highest heavens, may travel the road to liberation.

By way of another example, in a practice described below called *tong-len*, "sending and taking," we perform a contemplation in which we picture beings in each of the six realms, beginning with the hell realms. We visualize their pain and try to feel what they are experiencing. Through our remembrance of them, they are not forgotten and the solitude of their suffering is broken. Moreover, our hearts are opened and the compassion of our inmost nature is released, and we are able to send them relief. In a similar way, one by one, we take each of the other realms and vividly picture the suffering of the beings within it and, experiencing it, send relief. Even the gods, though generally blissful, in their own ways suffer, for the effort required to maintain their ignorance of the pain of others represents a subtle but very real dimension of suffering. Therefore we carry out the same contemplation for them.

In a similar way, there is an "initiation into the six realms" that is performed in Tantric Buddhism in which one is able to "practice" each of the realms. Through the practice, one is able mentally and emotionally to enter into each of the six realms, for a period of time, and experience its joys and its sorrows. In Tibet, six-realm retreats were sometimes undertaken with a guru, who would lead a group through days of experience of each of the six realms. The point of this kind of practice is to bring awareness of beings throughout the various samsaric worlds, to know their experience intimately, and to awaken compassion for them. This is felt to be of immediate and direct benefit to them if for no other reason than that their existence is known and their suffering felt by another. In addition, because one's awareness is educated and the flames of compassion are fanned, one makes oneself more available to benefit others one meets in life.

Ritual Relations with the Awakened Ones

The essence of Tibetan Buddhism is communication with the awakened ones—departed masters, bodhisattvas, buddhas, and so on. We call them to mind, open our hearts to them, and receive their blessings. The way we do this is through ritual. One of the most common ritual means for this is the sevenfold offering of Mahayana Buddhism: one visualizes the being or beings in question, then [1] offers salutation, [2] makes real and imagined good offerings, [3] confesses one's shortcomings and harm of others, [4] rejoices at the existence of the awakened being who is the beloved object of devotion, [5] requests them to teach, thus expressing one's openness and longing for instruction, [6] asks them to remain in connection with suffering, samsaric beings and not disappear into nirvana, and [7] dedicates whatever merit or goodness one has accumulated to the welfare of all beings. In this simple, brief rite, one makes a link with the transcendent ones, affirming and actualizing a specific kind of relationship with them.

The reason that we can do this in the first place is that the buddhas, bodhisattvas, and departed masters already represent who we most essentially are and must in fact become. This is why, in Tibetan Buddhism, even the most devotional supplication to the most seemingly external being is not finally theistic. For, in truth, we are longing to meet our deepest selves face-to-face, and we are supplicating our own hidden being. The path to this goal is first, to discover our inmost being in the other, the awakened one, and then, through relationship with him or her, gradually to come to awareness of that transcendent nature within ourselves.

As we shall see below, there are many ritual stages along this path to awakening. What they share, however, is visualization. We create a mental picture of a departed teacher, a high-level bodhisattva, or a buddha. Then we carry out a ritual in which we open ourselves and communicate with this being in various ways, ritually participating in his or her awakening. In this way, we cultivate our own awakened state.

This process of visualization is a powerful one. For example, in our ordinary life, what we do not visualize as existing does not exist for us.

If we do not *see* another person as human, then for us their humanity does not exist. The same is that much more true for beings who live in nonmaterial forms outside of samsara. We may be surrounded by buddhas and bodhisattvas all the time, but until they have a shape and a name, we do not see them or have access to a relationship with them. For us they might as well not exist. But the moment we give them a form in our mind and begin to communicate with them, they exist, and their wisdom, compassion, and power can enter into our own systems.*
It is the many ritual forms of Tibetan Buddhism that enable us to do this.

Ritual and Western Buddhism

Within traditional Tibet, the reality of ritual is simply accepted as a matter of course. It is assumed that just as there are forms by which to relate to other human beings, so there are other forms, called rituals, that are used to communicate with the nonhuman and nonmaterial realms.

The status of ritual among Western followers of Tibetan Buddhism is, however, more in question. Many have felt unable to entertain the ideas of reincarnation or of the six realms. For them, many of the traditional Tibetan rituals dealing with other beings and other realms do not make sense. Sometimes this extends to thinking that even talk of nonmaterial buddhas, bodhisattvas, and protectors is "symbolic" and that there is nothing that really corresponds to these designations. In that case, many of the Tibetan liturgies are seen as directed to no real object, but are rather understood as psychological ploys to bring about certain effects.

*Some people may feel that they do not know how to visualize as described here. The fact is that, as human beings, we are visualizing all the time. When we see a person we know, we visualize him or her as this person we know, calling up all of our past memories and recognition. We can see how this works in instances where we mistakenly think we see someone we know on the street. We have the experience of seeing this actual person, only to discover that it is not that person at all and we were mistaken.

Even if we Westerners do pay lip service to the traditional Tibetan cosmological ideas, often—as Jeremy Hayward has argued—we remain at heart what he calls "scientific materialists" (1999). In other words, while we may accept the idea of other realms and other beings within and outside of samsara, we do not actually believe in them. Instead, we live as if the world were dead and this reality the only one that exists.

This attitude is reflected in many Westerners' difficulties with Tibetan ritual. Among Western practitioners, there is frequently a kind of dead feeling in ritual, and many of us fall back on the idea that rote repetition, without any particular engagement or feeling, is sufficient. We fall back, in other words, on attitudes to ritual learned in our upbringing, where simply to be physically present was all that was required. In order to survive the many meaningless rituals we may have been subjected to, we also learned to disengage ourselves psychologically and to occupy our time with thinking about other things. What is missing here is the understanding that ritual is a way of communicating with beings who, on the relative plane, *really are there* and *really are important to us.* This lively and compelling sense of ritual is, at present, sometimes hard to come by in Western adaptations of Tibetan Buddhism.

THE ANATOMY OF A COMMON TIBETAN RITUAL: THE LHASANG

The *lhasang*—literally "higher purification offering," which may be glossed as "invocation of the higher beings"—is one of the most common rituals in traditional Tibet. While some rituals are performed strictly for temporal ends and others for spiritual ends, the lhasang is interesting because it is performed for both mundane and supermundane purposes. And, while most rituals are directed to a particular being, the lhasang is a broad invocation that calls upon all the various "good spirits" and well-intentioned deities, as well as upon the various buddhas, bodhisattvas, protectors, and departed teachers of the buddhadharma. Because of its broad conception, the lhasang is multipurpose.

On the one hand, it is performed by laypeople: in times of duress or special need, the male head of the household will do a lhasang on behalf of the entire family. On the other hand, lamas will also perform the lhasang on various special occasions, before a journey, on a special holy day, to support the construction of a building, to bless an important object. In the Western practice of Tibetan Buddhism, the lhasang is a popular and often-performed ceremony both because it is applicable to almost any situation and because it is simple and accessible.

The purpose of the lhasang may be described as twofold. First, it is a ritual of purification, cleansing people and places of any obstructions, obstacles, or negative forces. The fire and the purifying smoke are held to embody a powerful energy that dispels the defilements and negativities of those present. Second, the lhasang is an empowerment in that it brings down blessings in the form of wisdom, efficacy, and power. Juniper is typically burned in the lhasang fire, and the fragrant smoke travels up to the heavens, attracting the higher beings of samsara and the enlightened ones; thus the smoke becomes a kind of passageway or lightning rod down which their blessings can descend, filling participants with a sense of well-being, understanding, and happiness. Many different lhasang rituals were used in Tibet, depending on locale, lineage, and specific purpose. The following summarizes the general format typically possessed by lhasang ceremonies.

Prelude

Prior to the actual lhasang ritual, a hearth or fire pit is constructed, usually out of doors. The green boughs of juniper are collected and laid out by the ritual site. Juniper is typically selected—sometimes along with other aromatic woods such as cedar—because its smoke is especially fragrant and pleasing to the gods. The fire is lit and allowed to burn down so that the heat of glowing coals predominates, rather than open flame. The juniper may be doused with water, as wet juniper produces a heavier and more aromatic smoke. When the officiant is prepared to begin the invocation, the boughs are laid on the coals, and, within moments, the white, fragrant smoke begins to billow up to the sky.

Invocation

The ritual now begins with an invocation to all-powerful and helpful forces, both those within samsara and those beyond it. The invocation is a way of calling these beings to attention and inviting their presence at the liturgical performance of the lhasang. The invocation will usually address general categories of beings and also more specifically particular protectors, bodhisattvas, departed teachers, local deities, and so on. On the general level, then, the lhasang might call upon the three jewels (Buddha, dharma, and sangha), the three bases of Buddhist practice (gurus, yidams, and dakinis), and whatever gods and sages there may be. More specifically, one might invoke certain protectors, the three bodhisattvas most important to Tibetan Buddhism (Avalokiteshvara, Manjushri, and Vajrapani), Guru Rinpoche, other lineage figures, and the like.

Offering

Once the invocation has caused the multitude of helpful beings to gather, offerings are made. The offerings consist both of actual physical substances and those that are conceived with the imagination. The actual or material substances that are offered into the fire vary depending on the intentions of the ritual and the elaborateness that is desired. The juniper, of course, is already being offered, and this consists of the basic offering ingredient. Other material substances may include different kinds of grains, other desirable food substances, varieties of alcohol, and other things that may be deemed attractive to the invited unseen guests. At this time, mental offerings are made, consisting of the visualization of all the good and fine things that the world has to offer. Sometimes to Westerners, the imagined offerings seem less consequential and important than those that are physical. In a Buddhist context, however, the act of holding precious things in mind and then offering them can be equally powerful, whether they are material or not.

The Supplication for Assistance

The invocation has gathered the unseen beings, and the offerings have formed a link between those beings and the human practitioners of the ritual. Next follows the request for assistance, which usually includes two parts. In the first, one supplicates for protection against obstacles and other forms of negativity. This negativity itself is both inner and outer. Inner obstacles or obstructions might include illness, emotional disturbances, resistance, and any other inner impediments to well-being and successful dharma practice. Outer obstacles—as articulated in Tibetan tradition—include the enmity of others in the form of curses, lawsuits, warfare, and other forms of attack, as well as disasters such as failing crops, plague, or famine.

While the first kind of request made in the supplication is for purification of oneself and the removal of external obstacles, the second is for empowerment. Now one requests that one be filled with both mundane and transmundane power and well-being. On the mundane level, one asks for health, material prosperity, and happiness. On the transmundane level, one supplicates for the increase of successful dharma practice, insight, compassion, and a closer relation with one's lineage.

In Buddhism, it is of course believed that all things occur based on causes and conditions. However, the beings of the unseen world, each in his or her own way, are powerful participants in the realm of causality. Worldly deities represent critical, vulnerable points in the way things transpire in the world. By invoking them, making offerings, and supplicating them to provide assistance, it is as if one were relating to a worldly monarch who is all-powerful. Though still within the web of causality, he is able in a unique way to bring about effects and respond to one's needs.

When it is great bodhisattvas and enlightened beings that one is supplicating, their power is that much greater. Particularly within a Western context and with our "otherworldly" religious heritage, one might question whether it is appropriate to ask buddhas for help with, for example, sickness. Aren't they only interested in enlightenment? It is the same as asking whether a realized master would care about our physical suffering and have any interest in helping us recover. For Buddhism, physical and emotional obstacles, while they are with us, can be powerful teachers. But they can also prevent us from engaging in the practice of dharma and from helping others. Poverty, political oppression, and other obstacles can similarly be impediments to the ultimate welfare and spiritual progress of oneself and others. In the traditional Tibetan context, it is believed that the buddhas and bodhisattvas, as well as the human teachers and gurus, look with kindness upon human woe and its relief. They will help where it is appropriate and where they can. At the same time, in every human life, there are sorrows and sufferings that remain our companions; these the practitioner is to regard as expressions of the compassion of the awakened ones, who are holding us closely to teach and train us.

Mantras That Bring Down Power

Typically, the supplication is followed by the repetition of various mantras, series of syllables often with no rational meaning. These are often in Sanskrit, considered the original language of Buddhism and thus particularly holy and efficacious. These mantras are mostly drawn from various powerful sources within Tibetan Buddhism. For example, at this section in the lhasang one might find the syllables OM MANI PADME HUM, the universally known and revered mantra of Avalokiteshvara, or OM AH HUM VAJRA GURU PADMA SIDDHI HUM, the most important mantra of Padmasambhava. In Vajrayana Buddhism, the mantras embody in sound the essence of particular buddhas, protectors, or departed gurus. In saying them, one is directly and powerfully connecting with those beings to whom one is making the supplication.

As the mantra section of lhasang is being chanted, participants may circumambulate the fire, circling it in a clockwise fashion, allowing the juniper smoke to wash over them and bring a more tangible sense to their purification. At this time, it is also common for people to pass various objects through the smoke to purify them, such as clothes one might wear on important occasions or implements used in religious work, such as paintbrushes, sculpting tools, and so on. Trungpa Rinpoche comments, however, that it would not be appropriate to include in this process ritual implements such as *mala*s (rosaries) or bells, which are already pure by their very nature.

Coda

The lhasang now concludes, perhaps with a restatement of what is desired, perhaps with a particularly powerful mantra. The following particularly sacred Sanskrit mantra might well form part of this coda:

> OM YE DHARMA HETU-PRABHAVA HETUM TESHAM
> TATHAGATO HYAVADAT
> TESHAM CA YO NIRODHA EVAM VADI MAHASHRAMANAH
> SVAHA

This mantra represents one of the oldest statements of Buddha Shakyamuni's teaching, found in the Pali canon and elsewhere. Roughly translated, it means, "Whatever phenomena (dharmas) arise from a cause, the cause of them the Tathagata has taught, as well as the cessation thereof. Just so has the great ascetic declared." The coda puts the finishing touches on the lhasang liturgy and seals its intentions.

CONCLUSION

Rituals are performed in Tibetan Buddhism for many different purposes, both spiritual and temporal, and the atmosphere surrounding them obviously varies depending on the situation. General rituals, such as the lhasang described here, are occasions for enjoyment and celebration. This is a natural result of the character of ritual as festive and social in the broadest sense. In the lhasang, the usually invisible powers that undergird and transcend our world are invited as guests of honor. The offerings that are made to them represent a kind of feast that reestablishes one's connection with them and invites their participation in the life of the community. Through the ritual, one is led to take a larger view of one's life and one's world. In Tibetan ritual, one experiences a shift in perspective—sometimes subtle, sometimes dramatic. This shift feels like a diminishing of one's sense of isolated individuality and an increase in one's sense of connectedness with other people, with the nonhuman presences of our realm, and with purposes that transcend one's usual self-serving motivations.

In the lhasang, the shift in perspective can often be quite tangible. Perhaps as the smoke rises up to the sky, the wind abruptly picks up; perhaps a bank of clouds suddenly comes over the mountains or a cloudy sky breaks up and a brilliant burst of sunlight appears. Perhaps an eagle is suddenly seen overhead or the air abruptly becomes more sparkling. Whatever the signs, if the ritual has been done with a whole heart, some kind of confirmation from the nonhuman world may be expected. The shift is also atmospheric, giving birth to relaxation, humor, and expansive joy.

Ritual is a way of reconnecting with the larger and deeper purposes of life, ones that are oriented toward the general good conceived in the largest sense. Ironically, through coming to such a larger and more in-clusive sense of connection and purpose, through rediscovering oneself as a member of a much bigger and more inclusive enterprise, one feels that much more oneself and grounded in one's own personhood. Through ritual, one's energy and motivation are roused and mobilized so that one can better fulfill the responsibilities, challenges, and demands that life presents.

PART TWO

Tibet's Story

3

The Indian Wellspring

THE ACCOUNT OF BUDDHISM IN TIBET BEGINS WITH India and is, to a large extent, intimately tied up with the unfolding of Indian Buddhism. Tibetan Buddhists acknowledge this connection and always tell their own story in relation to that of the dharma in India. This chapter addresses the question "How do Tibetan Buddhists view India, and what aspects of Indian Buddhism do they see as particularly important to their own history?" The following summary, then, does not provide an introduction to Indian Buddhism on its own terms but rather an account of those dimensions of Indian Buddhism that are felt by Tibetans as most important to their spiritual identity.

For Tibetans, India is the "middle country," the sacred land in which Buddha Shakyamuni appeared and in which the major Buddhist traditions so central to Tibet were developed. It is important to remember that for Tibetans, the "history" of Indian Buddhism is not strictly located in the past. The great Indian meditators and teachers have passed away in a physical sense, but their spiritual essence, resourcefulness, and creativity are alive and available to people in the present. Thus it is that Indian Buddhism provides both a "historical" reality and a sphere of truth and agency that are as vital now as ever. In this sense, although Buddhism disappeared long ago from its Indian homeland, Tibetans down to today maintain the highest reverence for India and find in it the ongoing wellspring of the dharma's immeasurable blessings. When a Tibetan makes a pilgrimage to Bodhgaya, the Buddha's birthplace, or carries out a meditation retreat in a cave sacred to one of the Indian Buddhist saints, he or she fully expects to feel the enlightened presence of the departed master and perhaps even to experience him in a dream or vision.

BUDDHA SHAKYAMUNI

How do Tibetans understand the life of the Buddha? Tibetan Buddhists belong to the tradition known as the Mahayana, or "greater vehicle," the type of Buddhism that was prevalent until modern times in North and East Asia. The human ideal of the Mahayana is the bodhisattva, the "enlightenment being" who practices wisdom and compassion and strives for enlightenment for the welfare of all beings. According to the Mahayana, every human being, and, indeed every sentient being, is destined one day to become a fully enlightened buddha, just like Buddha Shakyamuni. Those who came before and already attained buddhahood are found, as mentioned, throughout time and space.

The path to fully enlightened buddhahood that each of us must follow is immeasurably long, involving millions of lifetimes of study, meditation, and selfless work for others. At an early stage in the path, one takes the *bodhisattva vow,* the vow to attain full enlightenment for the welfare of others. Subsequently, the bodhisattva progresses through various stages (*margas,* paths) and levels (*bhumis*). In his (or her) final life, just like Shakyamuni, the bodhisattva is born into a world system in which the dharma is unknown. There he attains enlightenment and initiates the tradition of dharma. As an enlightened buddha, he is endowed with superhuman qualities and powers, and ranks above even the highest gods.

The "life" of Buddha Shakyamuni, then, describes the final birth and last life of Gautama (Shakyamuni's given name), the person destined to become the fully enlightened buddha of our world system. Various Tibetan hagiographies reflect both the human and the superhuman aspects of the Buddha's identity. In fact, within the Indian context, these are seen as inseparable: to fully realize one's human nature is to attain the superhuman pinnacle of existence. In the poet Ashvaghosha's account, the elegant *Buddhacharita* ("Actions of the Buddha"), Gautama (whose dates are roughly 563–483 BCE) is the pampered son of an Indian *raja,* or local ruler. Gautama's father is grooming his son to inherit the throne. In the court, the prince experiences a life of pleasure and indulgence, and any form of pain or suffering is kept out of sight. However, the young prince feels that something is missing and one day leaves the palace grounds to see what the world beyond is like. On his excursion, he encounters the aspects of existence that his father had concealed from him: an old man, a diseased man, and a corpse. Gautama is shocked and deeply disturbed by what he has seen. His pleasure-oriented life now seems completely hollow, and he falls into a deep depression. Neither his palace friends and companions nor his immediate family can provide any solace, and the pleasure he once found in life has vanished. When seen under the shadow of death, even his own royal destiny seems meaningless and futile.

Fortuitously, at this moment Gautama meets a holy man who holds up to him the possibility of renouncing the world and following a path of spiritual practice and exploration. Gautama yearns to follow this path and, escaping in the dead of night from a palace world that cannot let him go, he disappears into the forest to follow a life of wandering and meditation. He cuts off his hair, exchanges his princely garments for a tattered robe, and sets off into the trackless jungle in pursuit of enlightenment. He eventually finds and practices with various teachers and spiritual communities. Most notably, he spends six years engaged in extreme forms of asceticism with five companions, who will later become his first disciples. Discovering that none of his mentors or fellow practitioners have found the way to liberation, he sets off on his own to meditate. Finally, on the first full-moon day of May, he attains enlightenment under a tree in Bodhgaya. Subsequently, the Buddha meets up with his five former companions in asceticism and preaches them his dharma, or the truth of his realization. These five become his first disciples and the first members of the sangha, or Buddhist community. Thus were laid the foundations of Buddhist tradition, summarized in the three jewels (*triratna*), the Buddha, who is the example to follow; the dharma, consisting of his teachings; and the sangha, the community of

FIGURE 3.1 *Shakyamuni Buddha practicing extreme asceticism,*
prior to abandoning this approach for the middle way between
self-mortification and self-indulgence.

people following the Buddha's tradition. According to the texts, after
his enlightenment, the Buddha spent some four and a half decades
teaching the dharma, presenting several cycles of doctrine and practice.
Eventually, he dies at the age of eighty at Kushinagara, in the Salla
grove.

According to Tibetan Buddhism, the biographies of the Buddha's life
found in the *Buddhacharita* and other early texts, in which he is shown

teaching only the four noble truths and the salvation of the individual, are incomplete. This is because they do not mention those periods of his life in which he presented the more advanced teachings of the Mahayana (greater vehicle) and Vajrayana ("adamantine vehicle," an allusion to the diamondlike, indestructible quality of true reality, or emptiness). In the Indian texts found in the Tibetan canon, we learn that first Shakyamuni Buddha taught the four noble truths, known as the "first turning of the wheel of dharma." This collection of instructions is known as the Hinayana or "lesser vehicle" to distinguish it from his later teaching. At later points in his life, the Buddha turned the wheel of dharma (*dharmachakra*) a second and a third time, giving teachings on emptiness and buddha-nature, respectively. Beyond these three turnings of the wheel of dharma, he also gave initiations and instructions for the unconventional lineages of the Vajrayana.

Tibetan tradition, following that of India, maintains that not all of these teachings were given by the Buddha in his ordinary physical body. In the Indian Mahayana view, Buddha Shakyamuni possessed not just a mortal human body, but also a "visionary" body and an "ultimate" body. These are known as the three *kayas,* or bodies of the Buddha. First is the *nirmanakaya,* his physical form, visible to ordinary people. Second is the *sambhogakaya,* a spiritual body of shape, color, and light, but not materiality, in which the Buddha is said to have journeyed to celestial realms to teach the dharma to the gods. The sambhogakaya is ordinarily visible only to people who have considerable attainment. And third is the *dharmakaya,* the ultimate reality, which defines the nature of the Buddha's awareness itself. What is it that makes Gautama a buddha? It is the fact that he is the definitive human embodiment of ultimate reality, the dharmakaya. His inseparability from this final nature of "things as they are" gives him the ability to manifest in the visionary form of the sambhogakaya and to travel in that "body" throughout the universe in a flash, to manifest multiple forms, and to exhibit other miracles. Teachings proceeding from any of the three kayas are considered authentic "buddha word" (*buddha-vachana,* words considered to have been delivered by the Buddha himself). It was in the sambhogakaya form, in particular, that the Mahayana and Vajrayana teachings are understood to have been given. In the Vajrayana, for example, the Buddha is understood to have manifested as various tantric deities along with their mandalas, or retinues, and to have delivered the tantric teachings in that form. To the ordinary, worldly way of thinking, it might seem that the teachings given by the Buddha in his physical body are more "real" or legitimate than those given in a nonmaterial, spiritual body imperceptible to the gross senses. But in the Tibetan view, the latter teachings have greater significance, because they stand in a closer relation to the source, the dharmakaya, from which those teaching ultimately derive.

BUDDHA SHAKYAMUNI'S TEACHINGS

According to Tibetan Buddhism, Buddha Shakyamuni during the four and a half decades after his enlightenment presented a vast array of instruction, both conventional and unconventional. Tibetans organize these into two separate categories. First are the conventional teachings, including the Hinayana and the Mahayana. The Buddha gave these teachings in the three turnings of the wheel of dharma, just mentioned. Each turning contains a comprehensive approach to the spiritual path, including both the general way we should regard reality, "view" (*tawa*) or doctrinal explanation, as well as practices (*druppa*) to be carried out to actualize that view. Second are the unconventional instructions contained in the Vajrayana. It is in the Hinayana and Mahayana that the view of Tibetan Buddhism is articulated and brought to its full maturation, while the Vajrayana comprises a particularly potent and extensive set of meditation practices through which the view may be realized. Because the Vajrayana addresses primary practice and does not present a new and distinctive view, it usually is not considered a separate turning of the wheel of dharma.

Hinayana and Mahayana: The Three Turnings of the Wheel of Dharma

THE FIRST TURNING OF THE WHEEL: HINAYANA

Shortly after his enlightenment, the Buddha journeyed to the Deer Park in Benares, where he encountered his five former ascetic companions.

TABLE 3.1

THE THREE YANAS

As Taught by Buddha Shakyamuni

Yana	Vehicle	Occasion of Teaching	Location	Primary Audience	Content of the Teaching	Main Texts
Hina-yana	Lesser Vehicle	First Turning of the Wheel of Dharma	Deer Park in Benares, NE India	Shravakas Pratyeka-buddhas	Four Noble Truths 1. suffering 2. origin of suffering 3. cessation of suffering 4. the path	Tripitaka Vinaya Sutras Abhi-dharma
Maha-yana	Greater Vehicle	Second Turning of the Wheel of Dharma	Vulture Peak Mountain, Rajagriha, NE India	Bodhisattvas	EMPTINESS All phenomena are without self-nature	Maha-yana Sutras Prajna-paramita sutras
		Third Turning of the Wheel of Dharma	Vaishali, NE India	Bodhisattvas	BUDDHA-NATURE All sentient beings possess the buddha-nature within. THE THREE NATURES (*Svabhava*) Reality may be understood as exhibiting the imaginary, the dependent, and the full perfected natures.	Buddha-nature sutras* *Sandhi-nir-mochana Sutra* *Lankava-tara Sutra*
Vajra-yana	Adaman-tine Vehicle	Revelation of the Vajrayana	Dhanya-kataka, Andhra Pradesh, SE India	King Indrabhuti, Bodhisattvas	SKILLFUL MEANS OF VAJRAYANA including visualization and resting in the nature of mind	Tantras

*The Buddha's teachings on the buddha-nature are found in sutras such as the *Tathagatagarbha Sutra*, the *Shrimaladevi Sutra*, and the *Dharanishvara Sutra*. See chap. 16.

To them he presented the basic Buddhist teachings, consisting of the four noble truths:

1. The truth of suffering, that the experience of pain, frustration, and incompletion are part and parcel of the human condition;

2. The truth of the origin of suffering in the thirst for egoistic security and aggrandizement, including the basic teachings on *karma* or moral cause and effect;

3. The truth of the cessation of suffering or the possibility of *nirvana*, liberation; and

4. The truth of the path, consisting of the noble eightfold path, including the "three trainings"of ethical conduct (*shila*), meditation (*samadhi*), and wisdom (*prajna*). As these three aspects of the path have come to be understood in Tibet, *shila* refers to one or another of the major codes of conduct followed by laypeople, monastics, and yogins. Samadhi includes the various meditative practices known as *shamatha* (mental quiescence) and *vipashyana* (insight). Shamatha involves focusing the mind on an object of meditation (for example the breath) and, through that, bringing the mind into a state of one-pointed stability and calm. Vipashyana is the spontaneous insight that arises from within the open and alert state of mind created by shamatha. The third of the three trainings, prajna indicates the understanding of egolessness that develops through the experience of vipashyana.

In Tibetan Buddhism, as in other Mahayana traditions, the teachings of the first turning of the wheel of dharma are collectively known as the Hinayana, or "lesser vehicle." These teachings are described as "lesser" because they outline a path of individual salvation, through which the practitioner can attain liberation from samsara. The Hinayana practitioner is called a *shravaka*, or "hearer," a person who hears the first-turning teachings and applies them in his or her life. Also mentioned are the *pratyekabuddhas*, meditators who dwell in remote places and aim at liberation, but are not members of the shravaka lineages directly deriving from the Buddha.

The Hinayana is so called to distinguish it from the Mahayana, or "greater vehicle" with its ideal of universal salvation. In fulfillment of this ideal, the Mahayana practitioner takes the bodhisattva vow, striving to emulate the example of Shakyamuni Buddha, being reborn countless times to help sentient beings and finally attaining the realization of a fully enlightened buddha. The designation Hinayana, as it is used in the Mahayana, refers to the first step on the Mahayana path, in which one renounces samsara, takes refuge in the three jewels (Buddha, dharma, and sangha), and follows the path to extricate oneself from one's own suffering, attaining liberation. Seen from the point of view of the Mahayana, the Hinayana is an incomplete ideal and, at a certain point on the path, needs to be transcended in favor of the more universal aspiration of the Mahayana.

The term *Hinayana* has sometimes been mistaken as a designation for specific historical schools, such as the Theravada (which now flourishes in Southeast Asia), Sarvastivada (an early school that was important in northwestern India, from which the Tibetans drew their Hinayana teachings), and other early, non-Mahayana lineages. Tibetans themselves have contributed to the confusion on this point partly because, in later times, they had no actual contact with the early schools and followed the Mahayana view by identifying them all as Hinayana. (For a discussion of this issue, see pages 238–40.)

The Buddha's teachings of the first turning of the wheel of dharma are contained in the scriptures, or "three baskets" (*tripitaka*) of the early schools, the Vinaya (rules of monastic restraint, see below), Sutra (basic doctrines and practices), and Abhidharma (advanced teachings, discussed in chapter 14). In Tibet the Hinayana texts are known in their Sarvastivadin version. The Vinaya contains the rules and conventions that govern Tibetan monastic life and still provide the regulations that define the lifestyle of Tibetan monks and nuns. The sutras are read by Tibetans for their many stories, teachings, and meditation instructions. And the Abhidharma is studied in monastic colleges by those who will specialize in Buddhist philosophy.

THE SECOND TURNING OF THE WHEEL: MAHAYANA I

The Buddha taught the view of the Mahayana in the second and third turnings of the wheel of dharma. The second turning, given on Vulture Peak Mountain near Rajagriha, articulates the truth of *shunyata,* or emptiness, the doctrine that the apparently substantial world that we perceive and think about is, in fact, empty of any solid or objectifiable reality (see chapter 15). As the texts say, the world is like a dream, a mirage, an echo, or a reflection in water. The Buddha's teachings of the second turning are found in the *Prajnaparamita Sutras* in various recensions (8,000 lines, 25,000 lines, and so on).

Some Westerners have misinterpreted the second-turning teachings on shunyata as nihilistic. If all things are empty, it is mistakenly thought, then nothing has any value and everything is finally meaningless. Why bother to be a decent human being? Why pursue a spiritual path? As we shall see below, such an interpretation of shunyata could not be more mistaken. The teachings on emptiness reveal that it is our own ego-centered, self-serving versions of reality that are empty of validity, not reality itself. Once this emptiness is realized, the true beauty and value of the world may be seen and the boundless compassion that exists within each person may be released.

THE THIRD TURNING OF THE WHEEL: MAHAYANA II

Tibetans believe that the Buddha turned the wheel of the dharma for a third time at Vaishali and other places. Two teachings lie at the heart of the third turning. First, the Buddha taught that while all apparent reality is *shunya,* or empty, it is not utterly nonexistent, thus combatting any misunderstanding of the second turning as nihilistic. Once we realize that our own version of reality is relatively worthless, we begin to make contact with a world that is resplendent. This is the teaching on luminosity, or *prabhasvara.* Second, the Buddha articulated the teachings of buddha-nature. The Buddha's third-turning teachings are found in the *Sandhinirmochana Sutra,* the *Lankavatara Sutra,* a series of *Tathagata-garbha Sutras,* and other texts.

The third-turning teachings on buddha-nature are of particular importance for Tibetan Buddhism. In the Indian Mahayana tradition, human beings are seen, in their origins and in their essential nature, as fundamentally good. This basic goodness is called buddha-nature (*tathagata-garbha*) and is said to be endowed with wisdom, compassion, and power. These qualities are free of any taint of an "ego," in other words, of any self-serving or self-aggrandizing tendencies. This is to say that, right at this moment, at the core of the personality of each of us, is the state of realization or enlightenment. All people, whether or not they consider themselves "spiritual," can have occasional glimpses of the state of the buddha-nature, the state of non-ego, in moments of natural warmth, openness, or joy.

In ordinary humans, this state of being is generally covered over and hidden by conceptual thinking, driven by fear and paranoia. However, in a buddha, all of the layers of obscuration have been removed. In a buddha, one sees the complete manifestation of what a human being is in essence and can, in fact, fully become. This state is profoundly human and, at the same time, according to Indian tradition, exalted above even the gods (*devatideva*). The essential identity of ordinary human beings and buddhas is what leads some to call Buddhism nontheistic. Nontheism in Buddhism does not imply a denial of the existence of higher beings called gods (*devas*), for the existence of these is affirmed with the qualifiers that they are still within samsara (they dwell in one of the six realms), are subject to karma, and have traces of ignorance. Buddhism is nontheistic in that it affirms that what is ultimately good and true does not reside outside, in an external deity, but exists within, at our core.

It is through meditation that even the most ordinary and unexceptional person can make contact with the awakened state. For those in the early stages of practice, this may involve no more than a brief glimpse. Nevertheless, such an experience can be a powerful and most helpful blessing: it shows that the teachings of enlightenment refer to something quite real and, often, it leaves in its wake a feeling of relaxation, well-being, and confidence in knowing that one's innermost being is so good and so wholesome.

In Tibetan Buddhism, the path is understood as the progressive removal of the obscurations that cover over the buddha-nature. Various levels of realization of the buddha-nature are described in the tradition. Ordinary people may have glimpses of the enlightenment within, while meditators, retreatants, and yogins have more extended experiences. As they progress along the path of meditation, the obscurations become weaker and more porous. Initially, they seek to rest in the buddha-essence (that is, the buddha-nature) for longer and longer periods while sitting in meditation. Later, they try to rest in the inherent nature as they move about in the world. High-level bodhisattvas represent yet another level of proximity to the buddha-nature within, and immeasurably beyond them is a fully enlightened buddha. For a buddha, the awakened state is fully manifest with no obscurations whatsoever. Everything that he is and does is a direct and spontaneous manifestation of the wisdom, compassion, and power of enlightenment.

WHY THE DIFFERENT TEACHINGS OF THE THREE TURNINGS?

Why, in the Tibetan understanding, did the Buddha present these various conventional teachings of the three turnings of the wheel of dharma? The answer has to do with the Buddha's skillful means, or *upaya,* according to which he presented different doctrines and practices to meet the varying needs and levels of sentient beings. According to the respected Nyingma teacher Tulku Urgyen Rinpoche:

> Through his immaculate wisdom, Buddha Shakyamuni always taught after taking into account the abilities of the recipients. In other words, he would not teach at a level above a person's head. He adapted his teachings to what was suitable and appropriate to the listener. Therefore, we can say that those who heard his teachings only assimilated what was comprehensible to someone of their aptitude. Later, when they repeated what Buddha Shakyamuni had taught, their account was according to what they had perceived in their personal experience.[1]

The Vajrayana: Extraordinary Instructions on Practice

The conventional path described by the Hinayana and Mahayana set out perspectives and methods by which one may attain complete enlightenment. At the same time, the journey described by the conventional vehicles is a long one, extending over innumerable lifetimes. In order to provide a more direct route to realization, in addition to presenting the Hinayana and Mahayana, Buddha Shakyamuni also taught the unconventional instructions of the Vajrayana. Tulku Urgyen explains:

> [The Buddha's] teachings were not only limited to the personal experience of the receivers, who according to some historical texts were shravakas, pratyekabuddhas or bodhisattvas. . . . In addition to delivering these general Sutra teachings, the Buddha Shakyamuni [in his *sambhogakaya* form] also taught in various locations throughout the universe. Manifesting in the form of a deity as the central figure of innumerable mandalas, he taught the tantras. In this way, we should understand that Buddha Shakyamuni himself, appearing in other forms, was the crucial figure in the transmission of Vajrayana teachings.[2]

The three turnings of the wheel of dharma outlining the Hinayana and Mahayana are given in various sutras or "discourses" of the Buddha and are therefore known as the tradition of sutras. The Vajrayana—and in the Tibetan context this refers primarily to what is called the unsurpassable tantra (anuttara-yoga tantra)—is set forth in tantras, or revelations of the Buddha, and is therefore known as the tradition of tantras. As mentioned, the Vajrayana does not articulate a new view or doctrinal standpoint but rather presents an array of meditation practices for realizing the view. In that sense, the Vajrayana may be seen as a subdivision of the Mahayana in which one puts the teachings of the greater vehicle into practice through a more meditative and yogic way of life.

The essence of Vajrayana tradition consists in making a direct connection with the buddha-nature within. It is thus called the fruitional vehicle, because it takes the goal of Buddhist practice—the awakened mind within—as the basis of the path. This sets it in contrast with the Hinayana and Mahayana, which are called causal vehicles because their practice develops the causes by which the enlightened state may eventually be contacted. In the Vajrayana there are two primary methods to make the connection with the buddha-nature within. In the first, one visualizes oneself as a particular buddha or bodhisattva according to detailed iconographic instructions presented in the tantras, and carries out various meditational practices in that mode.[3] A second method involves formless practice of *mahamudra* or *dzokchen,* in which one is first "introduced" directly to the buddha-nature by one's guru and then instructed to meditate upon it.[4] This "introduction" involves "pointing out," in which the guru is able to show us where, within our experience, the essential nature of mind can be met. If the Vajrayana is essentially oriented to meditation, one might ask which view among the three turnings of the wheel of dharma it is specifically putting into practice. The view of Vajrayana is drawn specifically from the second and third turnings of the wheel of dharma, with particular emphasis on the third, containing the teachings on buddha-nature. Through visualization or through an introduction to mind's nature, then, one is able to make a direct link with the awakened buddha-nature within.

Conclusion

Tibetans view Hinayana, Mahayana, and Vajrayana as the three yanas, or "vehicles" that constitute the three major stages of the Buddhist path. In the Tibetan perspective, one follows the path to enlightenment by first practicing the Hinayana, then the Mahayana, and finally the Vajrayana. One first enters the Hinayana by taking refuge in the Buddha, dharma, and sangha, and one then pursues an ethical life and practices meditation. Subsequently, one follows the Mahayana, by taking the bodhisattva vow and working for the welfare of others as well as oneself. And then one enters the Vajrayana, fulfilling one's bodhisattva vow through various methods of intensive meditation practice.

THE TRANSMISSION OF BUDDHA SHAKYAMUNI'S TEACHINGS IN INDIA

According to the Buddha's biography, he attained buddhahood by following a path of solitary meditation. Within the Indian context, this was called forest renunciation, "forest" referring to any place that was isolated and far from human habitations, such as a mountaintop, a hidden cave, or a location deep in the jungle. In India and Tibet, this meant renouncing the world with the aim of achieving realization in the present life and following a "forest" way. In the Buddha's time, forest renunciation generally included wearing a simple robe made from rags, begging for one's food, remaining in solitude, wandering from place to place, living in the open or under a tree for shelter, and spending one's time in meditation. The Buddha taught this very same path as the highest form of spiritual life to his earliest disciples. For example, in the first-turning traditions known in Tibet, Mahakashyapa, known as foremost among the forest renunciants, is the Buddha's chief disciple and successor. Buddhist tradition throughout its existence in India and Tibet reveals a continuity of traditions of forest renunciation. Tibetan tradition teaches that it is only through this life of solitary meditation "in the forest" that buddhahood may finally be attained. In Tibet, the greatest saints have almost always been hermits or forest renunciants.

The Buddha also legitimated two other ways of life for his followers, both of which are also important in Tibet. First, he taught a more collective and communal path of renunciation that eventuated in classical Buddhist monasticism. It was institutionalized monasticism that provided the infrastructure for Buddhism in Tibet. The Buddha also taught the way of the lay follower, emphasizing moral behavior and generosity toward the renunciant dharma practitioners; this was the ideal followed by the great majority of Tibetans. In India, each of these three Buddhist ways of life—that of the forest renunciant, the settled monastic, and the layperson—played an essential role in the transmission of the Buddha's teachings through subsequent generations. At a certain point, a fourth way of life developed in India, that of the lay practitioner or householder yogin, a person who, while living the life of a layperson, also practiced meditation and strove for the highest ideal of realization in this life. One finds this ideal flourishing among certain Yogacharin practitioners (see chapter 16) and among the Vajrayana siddhas, or perfected ones (see *Secret of the Vajra World*). It became particularly important in Tibet among the Nyingmapas, or followers of the "Ancient School," and also among some practitioners of the other schools. It was primarily in terms of these four ways of life that Buddhism was transmitted into the Tibetan environment.

The Sutra Teachings of the Three Turnings of the Wheel of Dharma

THE MONASTIC LIFESTYLE

The sutra teachings, as contained in the Hinayana and Mahayana canons, were preserved and transmitted primarily within the Hinayana and Mahayana monastic communities throughout India. Men and women lived in monasteries or nunneries, followed the rules of individual monastic restraint (218–263 for men, 279–380 for women), and had their collective affairs governed by many regulations and conventions of institutional life also found in the Vinaya. Those who followed the Vinaya to perfection were revered as saints by the laity, and the stature of a monastery was to a large extent dependent upon the laity's judgment that monks and nuns kept the Vinaya rules well. Those so inclined, and particularly the men, focused much of their attention upon the copying, preservation, reading, understanding, and debating of the classical texts. Within the Mahayana tradition, the most renowned figures were scholar-monks who lived in one or another of the great Mahayana monasteries of North India.

WELL-KNOWN SCHOLAR-MONKS

In Tibet, six of these scholar-monks, known as the six adornments, are renowned as being particularly worthy of veneration for their philosophical creativity in developing the essentials of Mahayana thought and for providing the foundation for Buddhist philosophy in Tibet. These six include three "progenitors":

1. Nagarjuna (first to second century CE), venerated as a "second Buddha" and initiator of the Mahayana, the founder of Madhyamaka, the most important Mahayana philosophy in Tibet, and

the one whose works on emptiness provide the ground upon which all other Mahayana thinkers build;

2. Asanga (third to fourth century), master of the third turning of the wheel and founder of Yogachara, who gave extensive teachings on the path and practice of the bodhisattva; and

3. Dignaga (fifth to sixth century), the renowned Buddhist logician;

and three preeminent commentators:

4. Aryadeva (fourth century), Nagarjuna's primary disciple, credited along with Nagarjuna with founding the Madhyamaka school, and commentator on Nagarjuna's works;

5. Vasubandhu (fourth to fifth century), Asanga's younger brother, disciple, and commentator; and

6. Dharmakirti (seventh century), a Buddhist logician renowned for his ability to defeat wrong views.[5]

Other great Indian Mahayanist monks whose thought and writings figure prominently in Tibetan Buddhism include the Madhyamaka masters Buddhapalita (fifth to sixth century), Bhavaviveka (sixth century), Chandrakirti (seventh century), and Shantideva (eighth century); the Yogacharin scholars Sthiramati (sixth century) and Dharmapala (sixth century); and Shantarakshita (eighth century) and Kamalashila (eighth century), who articulated a synthesis of Madhyamaka and Yogachara. The works of these great Mahayana authors are studied and well known in Tibet, and Mahayana thinking in Tibet during the past fifteen hundred years invariably takes its lead from them.

The Vajrayana Lineages

THE SIDDHAS

Traditions of forest renunciation maintained, as mentioned, a continuous presence within the Buddhism of India and greater Asia, although they usually existed on the periphery of mainline, institutionalized monasticism. This peripheral position was an accurate and appropriate reflection of the character of the forest traditions, with their emphasis on radical renunciation (not even a roof over one's head), living in solitude (only trees and animals for companions), intensive meditation practice (throughout both day and night), and realization of the awakened state in the present life. In Asia, at various times, lineages of forest renunciation existed among all the major Buddhist orientations, including the early schools, the Mahayana and the Vajrayana. By the seventh century, when Tibet was poised to begin importing Buddhism from India, the "forest" lineages of both early, non-Mahayana and Mahayana seem largely to have disappeared in India. Now the surviving members of the early schools and the conventional Mahayana are strictly monastic traditions. The only type of forest Buddhism we hear about in India in this and the following centuries is the Vajrayana.

According to the great Tibetan scholar Lama Taranatha (sixteenth to seventeenth century) in his *History of Buddhism in India,* Vajrayana Buddhism can already be located in the time of Nagarjuna (first to second century) in the jungles of India, among a small group of isolated and anonymous meditators who had followed this path to realization.[6] These masters, known as siddhas ("perfected ones"), were practitioners of the unconventional traditions of highest or innermost tantras. According to Lama Taranatha, these masters passed their lineages of practice and realization to only one or perhaps a very few disciples. Tulku Thondup Rinpoche says that "the Tantras of the Inner Yanas, the highest teachings of Buddhism, were introduced into India under the strictest secrecy."[7] By the eighth century, the Vajrayana begins to become more visible in India, owing to its growth and increase in popularity. From the eighth to the twelfth century, we hear of the existence of eighty-four mahasiddhas, or "great siddhas," who lived throughout India, following the Vajrayana traditions, and who taught, performed wonders, and transmitted the Vajrayana teachings to chosen disciples. As we shall presently see, the siddhas played a central role in the transmission of Buddhism to Tibet, and subsequently Tibetan siddhas carried on the teachings of their Indian counterparts in the Tibetan environment down to the present.

The siddhas were men and women who, in their pretantric lives, often found themselves in situations of great distress, dislocation, and

FIGURE 3.2 *One of the Indian mahasiddhas, men and women who were masters of Vajrayana and who helped spread its teachings in Tibet.*

suffering. For them, as for Gautama Buddha, ordinary life held no hope of relief and no ultimate promise of satisfaction. Typically, they encountered a guru who accepted them as disciples and admitted them into Vajrayana practice through the *abhisheka,* or initiation liturgy. Subsequently, they spent many years practicing intensively. Sometimes their practice was carried out in cremation grounds or in solitary retreat. At other times it was carried out in the world, but secretly. Tantric gurus were known for their uncompromising and even ruthless approach to the spiritual path. Not infrequently they would place their disciples in difficult or degraded circumstances to teach them the renunciation of comfort, status, and security, and free their minds for the ultimate. Eventually, their tutelage complete, the disciples attained realization and themselves became known as siddhas.

The siddhas often brought their realization back into the world, where they pursued ordinary lives as men and women lay practitioners, representing all levels of society, working as kings, scholars, blacksmiths, sweepers, and so on. In this way, they used "ordinary life" as the vehicle for their teaching and the transmission of their lineages. The eighty-four siddhas sometimes remained anonymous, appearing as unexceptional, unspiritual people within conventional society. At other times they exhibited their realization in shocking and unconventional ways. Sometimes they were called crazy (*nyönpa*), referring to their uncompromising expression of ultimate wisdom and compassion within conventional society, behavior that seemed "crazy" by ordinary standards. Either way, they carried on their teaching, converting the confused or the wicked and leading disciples deeper into the nature of reality.

According to Taranatha—and this is confirmed by modern scholarship—in its early days, the Vajrayana was strictly a nonmonastic tradition. Among the eighty-four siddhas, as seen in their Indian biographies (the *Chaturashiti-siddha-pravritti*), the great majority have no connection whatever with Buddhist monasticism. There are a few that begin their Buddhist careers as monks, but virtually all of them end up separating themselves from monastic life as they begin to practice the Vajrayana. The staid and conventional atmosphere of the monastery evidently could not contain the energy, boldness, and unpredictability of their spiritual search. The siddhas carry out their practice either in the wilds in retreat or in the context of lay life. By the tenth century, more conventional forms of Tantric Buddhism are beginning to be practiced in Indian monasteries, and in the next two centuries Vajrayana texts are being studied within monastic contexts.[8] However, even during this period, the most serious Vajrayana practice continues to be found among retreatants and lay yogins, outside of the conventional settings of institutionalized monasticism.

CONCLUSION

Within Tibetan Buddhism there are two major ways in which any individual can follow the Buddhist path: the way of study and the way of meditation. While these two are usually combined in differing proportions by most Tibetans, nevertheless it is useful to distinguish them. Chökyi Nyima Rinpoche, representing the viewpoint of the Practice Lineage (those Tibetan lineages emphasizing meditation), describes these two ways as follows:

> The style of the scholar is to study numerous details and carefully reflect upon them, refining one's understanding through using the words of the Buddha, the statements of enlightened masters, and one's personal power of reasoning. By doing so one can establish a clear understanding of the real state of things as they are. . . . A strong fascination with critical questioning and analyzing prevents one from following the approach of a simple meditator and from gaining an immediate certainty about the profound nature of emptiness, the basic wakefulness that is the very heart of all the buddhas. Due to these reasons some people find much greater benefit from the analytical approach of a scholar through which doubts and lack of understanding can be gradually cleared away. . . . This is one type of approach and it is excellent.
>
> Another type of person feels less inclined to study all the details of the words of the Buddha and the statements of enlightened masters, or to investigate them with the power of factual reasoning. Rather, they wish to focus directly on the very core of the awakened state—the wakefulness that perceives every possible aspect of knowledge exactly as it is—personally, within their own experience. Such people are not so interested in taking a long, winding, round-about road through detailed

studies and analytical speculations; rather they want immediate and direct realization. For such people there is the approach of pith instructions [on meditation], including Mahamudra and Dzogchen.[9]

Mahamudra and dzokchen are, as we shall see, the essence and epitome of the meditative lineages of Vajrayana Buddhism in Tibet.

Indian Buddhism made its way to Tibet between the seventh and twelfth centuries. Coincidentally enough, during this period, the dharma in India was in a particularly rich, diverse, and mature manifestation. It is difficult to fully appreciate the tremendous array of Buddhist lineages and teachings that were available to the Tibetans at this time. Those traditions referred to as Hinayana, the Mahayana, and the Vajrayana were all being studied and practiced; scholarly study of the various Buddhist philosophies had reached an apogee of depth and sophistication; the world-renowned monastic university of Nalanda was in full flower, with upward of ten thousand residents from all over Asia; other great monasteries, such as Vikramashila, Odantapura, and Somapuri came into existence; conventional monasticism existed side by side with forest lineages and unconventional teachings; lay practitioners or householder yogins were carrying on tantric lineages; and different regions in India provided different lines and interpretations of all of these currents. When we see the diversity in Tibetan Buddhism at a later time, we can be certain that much of this goes directly back to Indian roots and the Indian environment of the seventh to twelfth centuries. By the end of this period, this richness and creativity in India came to an end, for by 1200 the Muslim campaigns had more or less eradicated institutionalized Buddhism from North India, campaigns that resulted in the burning of Buddhist texts, the killing of monks and nuns, and the destruction of India's major Buddhist monasteries.

4

Foundations

THE EARLY SPREADING

BUDDHISM WAS CARRIED TO TIBET IN TWO WAVES OF importation known by Tibetans as the early spreading of the dharma (*nyingma*) in Tibet, which occurred between the seventh and ninth centuries, and the later spreading (*sarma*), which took place between the tenth and thirteenth centuries. Sometimes these two historical periods are referred to as those of the "Old Translation" (*nga-gyur*) and the "New Translation" (*sar-gyur*); here "translation" refers not only to the literal rendering of texts into Tibetan but more broadly to the transmission of the dharma from one culture to another. During each of these two historical phases important traditions were brought to Tibet that have been maintained to the present. The traditions brought during the early spreading are held principally by the Nyingma, known as the Old Translation school or the Ancient School. Those lineages imported during the later spreading survive mainly in the various schools known as those of the later spreading, or New Translation period, foremost among which are the Kadam, which later transformed into the Geluk, and the Sakya and Kagyü. In this chapter, we will examine the historical process of the early spreading, as understood by Tibetans, and in the next the traditions of the Nyingmapas, the primary holders of the early transmission.

The narrative of the early spreading begins with the account of a series of kings who ruled in Central Tibet. Like others in Tibet's story, the importance of these kings lies in the roles that they played and the meanings they exemplified within the larger cultural pattern. As understood in Tibet, the king's particular function is to join heaven and

TABLE 4.1

THE THREE RELIGIOUS KINGS

KING	CENTURY CE	INCARNATION OF	ACCOMPLISHMENTS
Predecessors: Lha tho tho ri	Pre-7th		In his reign, Buddhist scriptures and symbols fell from the sky.
Namri Löntshan of Yarlung	ca. 600		Made king of the region.
Songtsen Gampo	7th 620?–649	Avalokiteshvara Bodhisattva	Unified Central Tibet. Extended influence through military conquests to east, west, and south. Married two Buddhists, Chinese princess and Nepalese princess. Buddhism instituted at royal court. Sent Thönmi Sambhota to India to bring back alphabet.
Trisong Detsen	8th 754–797	Manjushri Bodhisattva	Invitations to monk Shantarakshita and siddha Padmasambhava. Building of Samye monastery. First ordination of Tibetan monks. Support of both monastics and yogins. Translation of Indian Buddhist texts into Tibetan. Extension of Buddhism beyond the royal court.
Ralpachan	9th 815–836	Vajrapani Bodhisattva	Ardent support of Buddhism. Acknowledged the supremacy of the monastic order over the royalty and the king. Translation of Buddhist texts continued.

earth. Heaven refers to the sphere of spiritual truth and reality, including the world of unseen beings as well as the realm of ultimate reality itself. Earth is the realm of practicality. The king, then, is supposed to provide the connecting link, bringing spiritual reality down and making it real in this world. He is to rule over human society in such a way that it reflects and respects "the ways things are" in the largest sense.

Tibetans say that their first kings originated in the mists of prehistory. Originally, these rulers were sacred beings who came from heaven and returned there at the end of their lives. Sometime later, one of these kings was killed by deception, and thereafter kings died as did ordinary humans. There are three Tibetan "religious kings" who are particularly prominent in the early spreading, Songtsen Gampo (seventh century), Trisong Detsen (eighth century), and Ralpachan (ninth century). The importance of these kings lies in the fact that, in fulfillment of their royal function, they oversaw the bringing of the dharma to Tibet and its transplantation into the Tibetan environment. In their era, kings had been understood as ordinary human beings for some time. Nevertheless, the theme of their heavenly origin continued to play a role in Tibetan thought, for these three kings were later understood as the human incarnations of three celestial bodhisattvas. Songtsen Gampo was seen as the human embodiment of Avalokiteshvara, Trisong Detsen as Manjushri's incarnation, and Ralpachan as the physical form of Vajrapani.

Tibetan legend has it that Buddhism first appeared in Tibet under the reign of Lha tho tho ri, a distant ancestor of Songtsen Gampo. In the reign of this early monarch, we are told that Buddhist scriptures and symbols fell from the sky. We also hear of teachers visiting Tibet at this time from India and Central Asia. These legends perhaps reflect that fact that Tibet had, for some centuries prior to Songtsen Gampo, been surrounded by Buddhist cultures, peoples, and influences, including India to the south and China to the northeast. No doubt, it had had contact with Buddhism through the traders who plied their way along the trade routes bordering and cutting through parts of Tibet.

SONGTSEN GAMPO (SEVENTH CENTURY)

It was with the first of the religious kings, Songtsen Gampo (609–649), understood retrospectively as an incarnation of Avalokiteshvara, that Buddhism makes its first definite appearance. Songtsen Gampo was a powerful leader who unified Central Tibet under his aegis and extended his influence from Shangshung in the west to China in the north and the plains of India in the south. It is recorded that, in service of his imperial vision, Songtsen Gampo married two princesses, one from

China and the other from Nepal. Both were Buddhists, and through their influence the king was converted, Buddhism was instituted in the royal court, and the first Buddhist temples in Tibet were constructed.

Songtsen Gampo's kingdom had as yet no writing, and, aware of the importance of writing in the great cultures of the Indian subcontinent and China, he sent one of his ministers, Thonmi Sambhota, to India to search out an alphabet. This emissary returned with a script that was adapted to the Tibetan language. During this period Buddhism was probably restricted to Songtsen Gampo's court, and the records in fact indicate strong opposition from the Tibetan nobility with allegiance to the traditional shamanic religion. At the same time, the royal connection was crucial to the later history of Buddhism in Tibet because, through the king's conversion, Buddhism became associated with the power and prestige of the royal court. In addition, it was through the patronage of later kings and rulers that monasteries were built, texts were translated, and increasing numbers of people became monks and nuns.

TRISONG DETSEN (EIGHTH CENTURY)

The Building of Samye Monastery

Trisong Detsen (742–797; enthroned 754), the second great religious king of the early spreading, is seen as an incarnation of the celestial bodhisattva Manjushri. Trisong Detsen's contributions included the founding of institutionalized Buddhism in Tibet through the building of the great monastery of Samye in the southern part of the country, the first ordination of Tibetans as monks, the support of both monks and nonmonastic yogins, the translation of texts into Tibetan, and the general extension of Buddhism beyond the royal court.

Samye monastery, modeled on the Indian monastery of Odantapura, was built as an enormous three-dimensional mandala[1] with a circular surrounding wall enclosing the sacred precincts, four gates at the four cardinal directions providing entry into the interior, and a central, multi-storied temple housing the main deity. At Samye, for the first time, Tibetans could be trained as monks and institutional Buddhism was able to gain its first major foothold in Tibet. This was critical because monastic Buddhism eventually came to provide the institutional infrastructure of the tradition, enabling Buddhism to survive in Tibet and come to a position of preeminent importance in its religious life.

The story of the building of Samye tells us a good deal about the coming of Buddhism to the Land of Snow. When Trisong Detsen determined to strengthen the influence of the dharma in his land and wanted to build a great monastery, he invited the renowned Indian Mahayana monk Shantarakshita to come to help him. Shantarakshita accepted the invitation and arrived no doubt with the usual retinue of retainers and assistants, collection of texts, and high hopes for reproducing the Indian model on Tibetan soil. However, so the legend goes, when he attempted to preach the dharma, the local deities rose up in revolt. In Dudjom Rinpoche's account, "Lightning struck Marpori [where the Dalai Lama's residence in Lhasa, the Potala, was later built] and the palace at Phangtang was swept away by a flood. The harvest was destroyed and great calamities befell the country."[2] When an attempt was made to build the monastery at Samye, disaster followed. As one text explains, the building activity was continually assailed by the local deities: whatever had been built during the day was destroyed by the angered spirits during the night.[3]

It was clear that Shantarakshita had attempted to force the Indian model on the Tibetan context without first making a relationship with the local deities. As a conventional monk, this master was well versed in the textual tradition of Indian Buddhism and was himself an exemplar of the Vinaya. He was an able exponent of conventional Mahayana and could have reproduced the monastic model in Tibet, had the environment been willing. But, having lived his life in the relative protection and security of the Indian monastery, he had, by his own admission, no skill in handling the wild and intractable energy of the local Tibetan situation.

What was required was someone who knew how to see and acknowledge the local spirits—the energies and forces of the earth and sky, of the waters, rocks, and growing things, wind and storm, animals, the various nonhuman beings of the place, and so on. Such a person was needed to make a genuine connection with them and, through knowing them intimately—knowing their seed syllable, their inmost identity, so to speak—to bring them into the arena of dharma and enlist their loyalty in the dharma's service. All this Shantarakshita understood, and so he suggested to King Trisong Detsen that he invite the Indian siddha Padmasambhava to "tame" the local gods.

The major themes of Padmasambhava's story are typical of those of the Indian siddhas, but he exemplifies the siddha ideal in a particularly vivid and colorful form. In one of his earlier and most important biographies,[4] we read that a certain king, Indrabodhi of Uddiyana in the northwest of India (the Swat Valley in present-day Afghanistan), is childless and his kingdom is suffering accordingly. In answer to the prayers of his priests, the celestial Buddha of compassion, Amitabha, decides that he will take incarnation to provide the king with a son and to bring help to his suffering subjects. He takes miraculous birth as an eight-year-old child in a lotus in the midst of a lake, hence his name, Padmasambhava, "the one born from a lotus." The child is discovered by the king and declares to him that he has entered the world in order to benefit all beings. The theme of birth from a lotus is an ancient one in Indian Buddhism and serves to show that the child in question is not an ordinary one but a "divine child" come to bring particular benefit to the human world.

The king brings Padmasambhava to the palace where, like Gautama Buddha before him, he is brought up and trained as a prince, learning arts and letters as well as the martial arts. Again, as in the case of the Buddha, Padmasambhava's father wants him to marry and assume the throne. A wife is chosen and for five years the prince experiences worldly happiness. Eventually, again like the Buddha, Padmasambhava comes to realize the illusory and unsatisfactory nature of all worldly things and announces his intention to renounce the world and enter the monastic order. He then departs, leaving the royal life behind him for the uncertain road of the renunciant life.

Here Padmasambhava's journey takes a radical departure from the model of the Buddha. In another part of Uddiyana, Padmasambhava is

FIGURE 4.1 *Padmasambhava, or Guru Rinpoche, active in the First Spreading and founder of the Nyingma school of Tibetan Buddhism.*

accused of the deaths of several people. The ministers of the king demand that he be put to death by hanging. The king replies, "This son is not of human origin; and, inasmuch as he may be an incarnate divinity, capital punishment cannot be inflicted upon him. Accordingly, I decree that he should be exiled."[5]

Like others of the Indian siddhas, Padmasambhava's worldly life has come to an end, and he has no further options within the world. He now goes into exile and for many years practices in one cremation ground after another. He uses corpses for his meditation seat, food left to the dead for his nourishment, and their shrouds for his clothes. When famine strikes, he transmutes the flesh of the corpses and subsists upon it, using the skin of the dead for clothing. During this period of practice, Padmasambhava studies with gurus of Hinayana, Mahayana, and Vajrayana. In particular, he receives tantric initiation and instruction from many realized tantric practitioners, the men known as siddhas and the women as dakinis, or "sky-goers." Eventually, through his practice, Padmasambhava brings his realization to fruition (although, since he was lotus-born, it was in some sense there from the beginning) and comes into possession of miraculous powers. He begins to use these in the service of dharma, taming and converting non-Buddhists and malevolent spirits.

Padmasambhava now meets the princess Mandarava, who herself has refused the intentions of her father to make her marry and who is pursuing a spiritual path. Padmasambhava instructs her, and their relationship deepens. Mandarava's father, furious at this development, has his daughter thrown into a pit of thorns and lice and has Padmasambhava burned at the stake. Both miraculously survive their persecution, the king is converted, and the spiritual relationship of Padmasambhava and Mandarava is accepted. Henceforward, the two practice together in various places and attain realizations. Subsequently, Padmasambhava appears in the guise of other siddhas, such as Virupa and Dombi-Heruka, instructing disciples, preaching to the laity, converting non-Buddhists, and subjugating evil spirits. His renown as a realized siddha of immeasurable power spreads far and wide.

As a siddha, Padmasambhava is the kind of person King Trisong

Detsen needs. Unlike the conventional monastic, he is fully realized. Because of his attainment, he is able to enter any of the six realms at will and see and communicate with their inhabitants, including the spirits obstructing the planting of dharma in Tibet and the construction of Samye. Padmasambhava is also free of conventional constraints: in contrast to the monastic, he is not beholden to an institution, confined by traditional forms of religious thought and practice, or answerable to rich and powerful donors. "Buddhism" is a religion for the unenlightened; in this sense, Padmasambhava stands beyond the pale of Buddhism itself, and ironically, that frees him to do the work that Trisong Detsen needs.

Trisong Detsen conveys his invitation to Padmasambhava. The master arrives and sets about his task. He traverses Tibet on foot, performing divinations. Most important, he meets, makes connections to, and overcomes the various local deities, enlisting their help in the project of establishing the dharma. Samye is built through the combined efforts of Shantarakshita and Padmasambhava, drawing on donations from the royal court and the nobility. Now the local deities provide assistance to the project. In particular, Padmasambhava employs the tamed spirits so that the various walls that are raised during the day by men are made higher at night by the deities. In this way, Samye is completed in a mere five years. Subsequently, Shantarakshita ordains seven Tibetans and these became the first fully ordained monastics in Tibet.

King Trisong Detsen receives many teachings from Padmasambhava. As part of his initiation gift, he offers his queen, Yeshe Tsogyal, to the master. Thenceforward this noble lady becomes the principal consort and primary disciple of Padmasambhava, receiving his major teachings including the most sacred Nyingthig ("essential heart") instructions. After taking initiation from Padmasambhava, she practices in retreat and attains realization. With him, she travels throughout Tibet, practicing in many caves and blessing them. She attains the power of total recall, enabling her to remember everything she has ever heard. This enables her to bring together Padmasambhava's many teachings. At his command, she hides these as *terma* ("hidden dharma treasures," discussed below) in various places to be discovered by later generations. Yeshe Tsogyal is also credited with the most important biographies of

Padmasambhava. Tulku Thondup remarks that "for the followers of [Padmasambhava], Yeshe Tsogyal has the peerless grace and kindness of a mother."[6]

The building of Samye illustrates several important themes in the arrival and maturation of Buddhism in Tibet. First, the dharma was only able to make its way there by taking into account the powers, energies, and forces of the nonhuman environment and by maintaining a healthy relationship with them. Second, it flourished through both the conventional, institutional tradition (embodied in Shantarakshita) and the unconventional, noninstitutional lineages (embodied in Padmasambhava). Third, in Tibet, the conventional Mahayana (Shantarakshita) and the unconventional Vajrayana (Padmasambhava) orientations worked in alliance with each other, supporting, supplementing, and complementing one another.

At this time, King Trisong Detsen organized an extensive translation project to render the most important Indian Buddhist scriptures into Tibetan. At Samye, it is said that over a hundred scholars and translators congregated to translate the various Buddhists texts of Hinayana, Mahayana, and Vajrayana.[7] Tibetan youths were selected based on their intelligence and aptitude, and these were instructed in the art of translation. Great scholars, learned in the Tripitaka, were invited. Tantric masters such as Vimalamitra and Shantigarbha were asked to transmit Vajrayana teachings. And twelve monks of the Sarvastivadin order were brought to Tibet. Finally, acknowledging and affirming the importance of the two streams of Indian Buddhism, two classes of renunciants were identified and supported at this time: monastics living in the monastery setting and yogins living in retreat in the caves around Samye. Under Trisong Detsen, Buddhism was rapidly becoming a well-established Tibetan religion.

The Samye Debates

A further important event occurred under King Trisong Detsen: the so-called Samye debates between Indian and Chinese contingents. The Indian side was led by the conventional monk Kamalashila, disciple of Shantarakshita, while the Chinese side was headed by Hua-shang Mahayana. The Indian side argued for the conventional Mahayana teachings of the gradual path to enlightenment: one should follow the bodhisattva path, study the classical texts, adhere to a moral life, and practice the six *paramitas* (virtues perfected by a bodhisattva; see chapter 13). Through that, one should aim to accumulate vast stores of merit and wisdom throughout countless lifetimes in the service of others on the path to full awakening. This approach, the Indian side contended, was the only true goal for the followers of Shakyamuni, as it benefited both oneself and others. As David Snellgrove notes, "such a doctrine argued in favour of the conventional intellectual and moral training which had guaranteed the stability of Buddhist monasticism since the days of its founder."[8]

The Chinese side held that the superior path lay in meditative realization of the buddha-nature here and now. Hua-shang Mahayana, presenting a viewpoint close to Ch'an (Chinese Zen), argued that within each sentient being is present the ultimate nature of the awakened state. Through meditative training, one can remove the obscurations of this inherent enlightenment so that it can be realized in this life. For Hua-shang, intellectual knowledge and conventional morality are not the essential point and can even be counterproductive and harmful if they get in the way of direct realization of the inherent enlightenment within. Through this path, the spontaneous wisdom of realization fulfills the basic intention of intellectual knowledge as well as the selfless compassion of conventional morality.

The Tibetan accounts of this debate are difficult to evaluate. In particular, it is hard to say for certain whether this debate occurred as stated and, if it did, who was the actual victor. Conventional monastic sources following in Kamalashila's tradition, not surprisingly depict the Indians as the victors, with the Chinese retiring in defeat. But other sources, and perhaps those that are older and more reliable, say that the Chinese emerged victorious.[9]

It does seem to be the case that the "political authority" of the day, represented by the royal court, maintained some suspicion in the face of the more yogic and tantric teachings of practitioners like the Indian siddhas and yogins like Hua-shang Mahayana. Certainly, for those in positions of power with interest in maintaining some degree of social control, robed monks living in established monasteries (supported by the king) and preaching a path of moral behavior are bound to appear as a safer bet than unconventional wandering yogins with untold powers and uncertain alliances. On the other hand, rulers in Tibet, as elsewhere, have always also been interested in precisely the kinds of magical powers uniquely attributed to those yogins, tantrics, and shamans known to have pursued a life of meditation and reputed to have attained realization.

The Samye debates were not purely a contest between India and China. In fact, the two sides were emblematic of the two major Mahayana approaches to the dharma, that of conventional Mahayana monasticism and that of the unconventional tantric yogin. It is interesting that both approaches were known in India and both were also known in China. As we have seen, India had its settled, Mahayana monastics and also its wandering tantric practitioners. Likewise, these two styles existed in China, suggesting that the Samye debates were a focal point of a number of different religious and political trends and disagreements.

The important point about the Samye debates is not really who won, but what they show us about the conversation between the conventional monastic and the yogic viewpoints that was beginning to emerge in Tibet at this time. Each represents an understanding of how best to follow Shakyamuni's tradition. And each has its point to make and its strengths. The conventional approach of Kamalashila outlines a path that is compatible with institutional monastic life, that is readily supportable by the established powers-that-be (in the early spreading, the royalty), and that provides a relatively safe, stable, and reliable, if gradual, method of training. The approach of Hua-shang, by contrast, lays stress on meditation and the realization of the awakened state in this lifetime. Working in tandem with one another, these two approaches have produced a Tibetan tradition that has the depth of real attainment as well as the breadth and durability of an institutional religion.

In a very real sense, the Samye debates are still going on in Tibetan

Buddhism today. The Gelukpas and others who represent the strongly institutional monastic approach accuse others, notably those of the Nyingma order, of "continuing the mistaken doctrines of the Chinese party."[10] The Nyingma school, for its part, holds that the Chinese side champions an essential perspective in the practice of the buddhadharma, and one early text even names Hua-shang as a Nyingma patriarch.[11] From the Nyingma perspective, without emphasis on realization in this life, Buddhism will produce good people but not awakened saints. Thus their critique of a life consisting primarily of study and ethical behavior: when a religion is composed only of "good" and learned people without the freedom, wildness, and accuracy of awakened ones, it can become stuck.

RALPACHAN (NINTH CENTURY)

The third religious king, Ralpachan, understood as the incarnation of the celestial bodhisattva Vajrapani, ruled from 815 to 836. In the sources, he is depicted as unsparing and even naively enthusiastic in his support of Buddhism. The translation of Buddhist texts continued, with terminology becoming more standardized. Ralpachan himself became a monk, heaped gifts and privileges upon the monasteries, and required each family to provide one-seventh of the support needed to maintain one monk. Finally, he showed his utter submission to the Buddhist clergy by tying his long hair in braids with ribbons extending from them and then having monks sit on them.

These acts were considered by some of the nobility, particularly those following non-Buddhist shamanic forms of religion, not simply as benign devotion but as a humiliating and inappropriate capitulation on the part of the court to the growing power of the Buddhist church. The anger and resentment of the non-Buddhist nobility erupted in the assassination of Ralpachan in about 836 by an individual named Langdarma. The assassin seized the throne and over the next several years engaged, so we are told, in a relentless persecution of Buddhism.

CONCLUSION

Langdarma was himself murdered about 842. The later sources tell us that for roughly the next hundred and fifty years, until the beginning of the later spreading of the dharma, there was no unified political authority in Tibet, and the land lapsed into civil strife and internecine warfare. The former support for Buddhism from rulers, nobility, and wealthy families evaporated, and institutional Buddhism disappeared. Later historians view this as a grim period of darkness that was simply an interlude until the later spreading.

However, seen from another viewpoint, this was clearly one of the more important and creative periods in the transmission of Buddhism to Tibet. As later history shows, during this time, Buddhist teachings, practices, and lineages, and particularly tantric ones that did not rely on the court or monastery for their existence, continued to be practiced and passed on from teacher to disciple within individual families and small groups of practitioners. Yogins continued to explore the upper reaches of the Buddhist path in retreat. And many creative and mutually trans-formative interactions occurred between practitioners of the dharma and the various non-Buddhist shamanic and contemplative traditions that existed in Tibet at that time. During this period, yogins and ritual masters of Buddhist and non-Buddhist lineages studied with one an-other, local gods and spirits were "tamed" and brought into the arena of Buddhism, and many indigenous ideas and practices became vehicles of the dharma (such as traditions dealing with death and dying).

We know of the tremendous creativity of this period because when the later spreading begins and Buddhism is newly imported from India, it occurs in a context of strong, profound, and mature individual lin-eages continuing in a decentralized form from the earlier period, lin-eages that are later collectively termed Nyingma, the practitioners of the earlier dharma, or the Ancient School.

5
Nyingma
THE ANCIENT SCHOOL

DURING THE LATER SPREADING OF BUDDHISM IN Tibet, lasting from the latter part of the tenth century (978 CE) until the beginning of the thirteenth, Buddhism was newly imported from India, drawing on the Hinayana, Mahayana, and Vajrayana traditions that were then prominent on the subcontinent. During the later spreading and after, the traditions that we now associate with Tibetan Buddhism were established and took their classical shape. These include the Nyingma, or Ancient School, which traces its lineages and teachings back to the early spreading of the dharma; and it also includes three schools that emerged from the fresh importation of the dharma at this time, including the Kadam (later transformed into the Geluk), the Sakya, and the Kagyü. During the later spreading, other lineages and traditions made their way to Tibet, but did not survive as independent schools. Most notably among these were the Chö lineage of Machig Labdronma, the Shije, and the Jonang.

During the early spreading, as we saw, both monastic and nonmonastic lineages were carried to Tibet. The monastic lineage was set in place primarily with the founding of Samye. The countless individual Vajrayana lineages were practiced and maintained within nonmonastic contexts by yogins and lay practitioners. Prior to the time of the later spreading, the practitioners of these traditions simply thought of themselves as Buddhists (*nang-pa,* "insiders," or followers of dharma), not as belonging to a specific and identifiable school. This situation changed at the time of the later spreading, with new lineages being carried to Tibet and promoted as superior to those of the previous period. This superiority was claimed on the basis that the new lineages represented a fresh importation from the motherland of dharma and, in their view, an uncorrupted embodiment of the true teachings.

It was during the time of the later spreading that those practicing the early-spreading traditions began to think of themselves as belonging to a distinct group, those of the Ancient School. This identity may have been forced on them by the proponents of the new schools, or they may have taken it on themselves in response to the critiques that were being mounted against them. It was only from the time of the later spreading, then, that one sees the consolidation of the Nyingma as the overall designation given to the many Buddhist traditions that had survived from the early spreading.

PROGENITORS OF THE NYINGMA LINEAGE

The lines of teaching that define the Nyingma lineage trace themselves back to several masters who lived before and during the eighth century. Foremost among these is Garab Dorje, the human originator of the dzokchen. This master was born to a Buddhist nun. After casting him away to die, she later found him still alive. Believing him to be some sort of divine child, she retrieved him, acknowledged him as her own offspring, and raised him. At the age of seven, Garab Dorje debated with a company of the king's scholars and confounded them. From this time onward, he was recognized as an emanation—an incarnation of a buddha or high-level bodhisattva. Subsequently, Garab Dorje went into retreat for thirty-two years in a place known for its terrifying spirits. At this time he received numerous revelations, including the profound dzokchen teachings. During this period, Garab Dorje received the instruction to write down all the tantras.[1]

Garab Dorje transmitted the dzokchen lineage to Manjushrimitra, another important Nyingma progenitor. Manjushrimitra met Garab Dorje in the Shitavana charnel ground, became his disciple, and studied under him for seventy-five years. After Garab Dorje had passed away,

SOME DATES OF NYINGMA HISTORY

754–797	King Trisong Detsen reigns
	Padmasambhava in Tibet
	Shantarakshita in Tibet
775	Founding of Samye monastery
792–794	Samye debates
1159	Nyingma monastery of Kathok founded
1286–1343	Rigdzin Kumaradza
1308–1343	Longchen Rabjampa
SECOND HALF OF 17th CENTURY	Building of major monasteries of Nyingma* 1659 Dorje Drak monastery 1665 Palyül monastery 1676 Mindröling monastery 1685 Dzokchen monastery
1730–1798	Jigme Lingpa
1735	Shechen monastery built on earlier foundations*
19th CENTURY	Ri-me movement
1848–1912	Ju Mipham Rinpoche

*Dates provided by Tulku Thondup, *Buddhist Civilization in Tibet,* 23.

his body appeared to Manjushrimitra as a celestial vision, and the departed master dropped a small casket that contained his final teaching, a famous epitome of the dzokchen teachings called "the three words that strike to the heart" (*tshik-sum ne-du*).[2] Tradition says that it was Manjushrimitra who divided the dzokchen into its three classical parts, mind section (*sem-de*), space section (*long-de*), and section of secret oral instructions (*me-ngag-de*). Finally, in Dudjom Rinpoche's words,

> He went to the Sosadvipa charnel ground, to the west of Vajrasana [Bodhgaya], where he taught the doctrine to ugly dakinis,

countless animals, and to many practitioners who adhered to the conduct [of the secret mantra]. He remained there, absorbed in contemplation, for one hundred and nine years.[3]

Manjushrimitra's primary lineal disciple was Buddhajnanapada. This person encountered his guru while on his way to Mount Wu-t'ai-shan in China, sacred place of the celestial bodhisattva Manjushri. While en route, near a white house, Buddhajnanapada comes upon Manjushrimitra dressed as a venerable old householder, wearing his robe as a turban and ploughing his fields with the help of a filthy old peasant woman. The traveler does not realize that the old householder and his wife are people of great attainment. When Manjushrimitra offers him a fish from a latrine, Buddhajnanapada refuses to eat it and is ridiculed by the householder as an Indian with too many scruples and reservations. Finally, Buddhajnanapada realizes that the old man holds teachings that he fervently desires, and he receives instruction. From Buddhajnanapada, the line passes on until it reaches masters such as the translator Vairochana, Vimalamitra, and Padmasambhava.[4]

Just as Garab Dorje had received the dzokchen teachings directly from the celestial bodhisattva Vajrapani, so a certain King Ja, who lived in a place in India known as Sahora, received the mahayoga and anuyoga lineages from the buddha Vajrasattva. The king also received them from the Indian master Vimalakirti. Subsequently, the mahayoga lineage was received by Buddhaguhya, who transmitted it to Vimalamitra, who passed it on to Tibetan translators Ma, Nyak, and others. The anuyoga lineage was passed down to one of the twenty-five disciples of Padmasambhava.[5]

The Nyingmapas consider Padmasambhava, known by his devotees as Guru Rinpoche—whose life story is told above—as the actual founder of their lineage. For them, he is the Second Buddha whose many transmissions and instructions are uniquely preserved in their lineages. Padmasambhava is considered the actual originator of the various traditions and lineages of the Nyingma, not only through his activity during the early spreading, but also in his ongoing revelations down through history to the present. In addition to Yeshe Tsogyal, his primary disciple, Padmasambhava had twenty-five chief disciples, men and women who were instrumental in establishing their master's teachings in Tibet. These yogins and yoginis also are thought to have lived not only during the eighth century, but in subsequent times, in the form of reincarnations who act as *tertöns,* "finders of spiritual treasures," rediscovering *terma,* or teachings hidden by Padmasambhava and destined for later ages.

Devotion to Padmasambhava is a strong and ongoing theme of the spiritual life of all Nyingma practitioners. Although not present in his physical human body, he is considered to dwell in a realm, a "pure land," the Copper-Colored Mountain that exists outside of ordinary time. From there, he responds to the genuine supplications of those who are devoted to him and will come, bringing all kinds of spiritual and mundane assistance. An important practice for Nyingmapas is the Guru Yoga of Padmasambhava, in which he is visualized coming from his pure realm, bringing blessings and relief to his devotees. Yogins and yoginis, on the other hand, seek not simply to receive the blessings of Padmasambhava, but to merge their identity with their beloved guru, who is the immaculate embodiment of their own inherent nature.

The following story, told by Trungpa Rinpoche, illustrates this theme of yogic identification.

There was a great Tibetan siddha called the Madman of Tsang. He lived in Tsang, which is in East Tibet, near a mountain called Anye Machen, where my guru Jamgon Kongtrul visited him. This was about five years before I met my guru. He used to tell us the story of his meeting with the Madman of Tsang, who was an ordinary farmer who had achieved the essence of crazy wisdom. He had these various precious things stored in his treasury, bags and bags supposedly full of valuable things. But the bags turned out to contain just driftwood and rocks. My guru told us that he asked the Madman of Tsang, "How should we go about uniting ourselves with Padmasambhava?" The madman told him the following.

"When I was a young student and a very devout Buddhist,

full of faith, I used to want my body to become one with Padmasambhava's body. I did countless recitations, thousands and millions of mantras and invocations. I used to shout myself half to death reciting mantras. I even felt that I was wasting my time by breathing in during these recitations. I called and called and called to Padmasambhava. I could go on calling on him until my voice breaks down, but it wouldn't make any sense. So I decided not to call on him anymore. Then I found that Padmasambhava was calling on *me*. I tried to suppress it, but I couldn't control it. Padmasambhava wanted *me,* and he kept on calling *my* name.[6]

On one level, this story beautifully illustrates the devotion that Guru Rinpoche's followers could feel for him, the desire not just to emulate him but to identify with his enlightened state of being, and Guru Rinpoche's living presence and his availability to devotees. On a more esoteric level, it exemplifies the realization that Padmasambhava is our innermost state of being, when glimpsed without the covering of ego.

LONGCHENPA

Longchen Rabjampa, or Longchenpa (1308–1363), more than any other person, pulled the various strands of Nyingma teaching into a coherent and unified perspective at the time just after the close of the later spreading. He was deeply learned not only in the Nyingma traditions but also in all the other major strands of dharma available in his day in Tibet; at the same time, he was an ardent practitioner who spent much of his life in retreat, putting the teachings into practice.

In Longchenpa's person and writings one can see, for the first time, the school of the Nyingma with its distinct history, teachings, and practices. Longchenpa also embodies much of the main inspiration and spirituality of the Nyingma not only as it existed in his own day, but as it has continued to exist down to the present. In his voluminous writing, Longchenpa shows himself to be a remarkably brilliant and original person, and the many texts he composed remain among the most important treasures of the Nyingmapas.

Longchenpa was born in south-central Tibet in 1308. He was ordained as a novice at the age of twelve and studied the Vinaya in particular. By the time he reached sixteen, he was studying the New Translation traditions of the various "new schools" of Tibetan Buddhism, such as the Sakya, the Kagyü, and the Shije. From the age of nineteen to twenty-six, Longchenpa studied the major texts and philosophical schools of the Mahayana under a variety of learned teachers. He also received empowerments and oral instructions in the most important Nyingma tantras. Subsequently, he deepened his knowledge of the sutras and tantras and was able to study with noted Sakya and Kagyü masters, including the third Karmapa, Rangjung Dorje (1284–1339).

Concurrent with these years of scholarly study, Longchenpa was also engaged in meditative training and spent much of his time in retreat. During these periods of intensive practice, he is said to have experienced many visions of the tantric deities such as Manjushri, Vajravarahi, and Tara and to have gained various spiritual attainments. When he was twenty-seven, at the direction of the divinity Tara, Longchenpa went to meet the master Rigdzin Kumaradza (1286–1343) who was the holder* of the Vima Nyingthik, the essential heart teachings of dzokchen that derive from the eighth-century master Vimalamitra. At this time, Rigdzin Kumaradza was in a retreat camp in the upper valley of Yarto Kyam with about seventy students. When Longchenpa arrived, the master received him with joy and announced that Longchenpa would be the transmission-holder of the Vima Nyingthik. Longchenpa stayed with Kumaradza for two years, studying the three categories of dzokchen of [1] the mind section, [2] the space section, and [3] the section of oral instructions, with emphasis on the outer, inner, secret, and most secret teachings of this third section.

---

*In any given lineage of teachings, a master will identify certain disciples as the primary "holders" or "transmitters" of a particular line or body of teachings. It then becomes their responsibility to ensure that the teaching, in its full integrity, is passed on to the next generation of practitioners.

The conditions under which Longchenpa and Kumaradza's other disciples lived were, in Tulku Thondup's words, characterized by "severe deprivation."

> In order to combat his attachment to material things, it was Rigdzin Kumaradza's practice to keep moving from place to place instead of settling at one location and getting attached to it. In nine months he and his disciples moved their camp nine times, causing great hardship to Longchen Rabjam and everyone else. Just as soon as he got his simple life settled in a temporary shelter, usually a cave, which would protect him from rain and cold, the time would come to move again. He had very little food and only one ragged bag to use as both mattress and blanket to protect himself from the extremely cold winter. It was under these circumstances that Longchen Rabjam obtained the most rare and precious teachings of the tantras and instructions of the three cycles of Dzogpa Chenpo.[7]

Eventually, Kumaradza empowered Longchenpa as the lineage holder of the Nyingthik transmission, the essence and epitome of dzokchen.*

For the next seven years, Longchenpa practiced in solitude, focusing on the dzokchen teachings that he had received. Thereafter, he spent much of his time in retreat and gave a variety of empowerments and teachings to disciples who were gathering around him. His biography describes this as a time of spiritual experiences and visions that led him and his disciples more and more deeply into the dzokchen. Longchenpa had now begun to write, and several of his most famous compositions date from this time. It was during one of his retreats that Vimalamitra, the eighth-century tantric master and siddha, appeared to him in a vi-

---

*The close relation between retreat "ordeals" such as this and spiritual training is well known among traditional Tibetans. Only when a disciple is pushed beyond his or her own limits are definitive breakthroughs in spiritual understanding likely to occur. It will be interesting to see whether, in the modern Western practice of Tibetan Buddhism, experiences like Longchenpa's will be possible. If they are not, one wonders what impact this will have on the depth and vitality of Tibetan Buddhism in the West.

sion and conferred on him the Vima Nyingthik teachings. This meant that Longchenpa had received this lineage directly from the originator of the cycle itself, ensuring the freshness and potency of the transmission. It is this transmission that Longchenpa principally passed on to his disciples and became central to the Nyingma dzokchen teaching and transmission.

Longchenpa was devoted to his master Rigdzin Kumaradza and visited him frequently to clarify his understanding and develop his realization. When arriving before his master, he would often give him whatever little he might have in the way of food and possessions, to unburden himself of the obstacle of possessiveness. Even as a person of great attainment, Longchenpa never ceased to humble himself and to show selfless devotion to the dharma wherever he found it.

On account of his great accomplishments in the areas of scholarship and meditation, Longchenpa became famous and revered. Given this circumstance, it would have been easy for him to raise funds from donors and to build monasteries, thus institutionalizing his teaching and lineage. However, Tulku Thondup comments, "he avoided all such works because he had no interest in establishing any institutions."

> Anything offered with faith he spent strictly for the service of the Dharma and never for other purposes, nor did he ever use it for himself. He never showed reverence to a lay person, however high-ranking in society, saying, "Homage should be paid to the Three Jewels but not to mundane beings. It is not right to reverse the roles of lama and patron." However great the offerings made to him, he never expressed gratitude, saying, "Let the patrons have the chance to accumulate merits instead of repaying it by expressions of gratitude." He was immensely kind to the poor and suffering people, and he enjoyed with great pleasure the simple food offered by poor people, and then would say many prayers of aspirations for them.[8]

Longchenpa spent most of his life in solitude, in mountain caves, engaged in meditation retreats. He took great joy in the silence, the simplicity, and the purity of this way of life. He often commented on the dignified aloneness of the retreatant's existence and on the power of solitary retreat to open the depths of the mind. Longchenpa says:

> Far from towns full of entertainments,
> Being in the forests naturally increases the peaceful absorptions,
> Harmonizes life in Dharma, tames the mind,
> And makes one attain ultimate joy.[9]

Longchenpa was a great scholar, deeply learned in the various traditions, philosophies, and practices of Buddhism. But he was also the greatest of dzokchen masters, and it was this that he especially practiced, transmitted to his disciples, and wrote about. For Longchenpa, as for the later Nyingmapas, dzokchen is the innermost essence of the entire array of the Buddha's teachings. Longchenpa summarizes the dzokchen perspective:

> The present mind, which is unhindered—
> No grasping at "this" [or "that"], free from any
>   modification or dilutions, and
> Unstained by [the duality of] grasped and grasper—
> Is the nature of ultimate truth. Maintain this state.[10]

In Longchenpa, we see the spirituality of the Nyingma school as it is taking shape at the time of the later spreading. For example, we find the Nyingma rootedness in the lineages and traditions of the early spreading. There is in him deep veneration to Padmasambhava, Vimalamitra, and the other early masters, and a devotion to the teachings and practices that derive from them. At the same time, there is an inclusiveness, seen in the fact that Longchenpa had received teachings and transmissions of all the lineages then present in Tibet. Longchenpa also shows us the vigorous spirituality of the Nyingma, with its emphasis on meditation, on practice in retreat, on the benefits of poverty and a rugged life in the wilds, and on sacrificing everything for the dharma.

Longchenpa's refusal to engage in institution building and its inevitable worldly involvement reflects a particularly important feature of the Nyingma tradition. Prior to the seventeenth century, Nyingma practitioners lived as laypeople or as yogins in small hermitages and retreat centers scattered primarily throughout eastern Tibet. Such an institutional arrangement facilitated a focus on meditation and spirituality, and enabled the Nyingmapas to avoid being drawn into much of the infighting and destructive machinations of Tibetan religious politics. However, perhaps partially in response to increasing persecution by the Gelukpas, during the second half of the seventeenth century, the Nyingmapas began to build larger centers, including four of their main centers in Tibet (Kathok, Palyül, Mindröling, and Dzokchen). The other two were the earlier center of Dorje Drak and Shechen monastery, built in 1735. The institutionalization of the Nyingmapas, however, does not seem to have penetrated too deeply, for even today they still represent the quintessential yogins and meditators, and continue to teach their disciples the virtues of renunciation, simplicity, and retreat practice.

KAMA AND TERMA

Because of the nonmonastic context of their Vajrayana traditions, the Nyingmapas originated as a grouping of many distinctive lineages. This has given the school a diverse and decentralized character throughout its history and has resulted in lineage accounts that are often more numerous and complex than those of the new translation schools.

The Nyingmapas have two primary types of lineage, both understood to derive from Padmasambhava and his disciples. The Kama, or humanly transmitted text lineage, represents teachings that were given at the time of the early spreading by Padmasambhava to his human disciples. These, in turn, were passed on from master to disciple, with the result that the continuity of teachings originating during the early spreading was maintained. In keeping with the style of transmission that was prevalent among the Nyingmapas, many of the Kama lineages were handed down from one family generation to the next.

The second type of lineage among the Nyingma is the Terma, or lineages of revealed "spiritual treasures." These represent the rediscovery of "treasures" hidden during the time of the early spreading by Padmasambhava and other masters and later revealed by tertöns who have appeared from the days of the later spreading and down to the present time.

The Kama, known as the "long lineage of textual transmission," includes texts of the Hinayana (Vinaya), Mahayana (Sutra), and Vajrayana (Tantra). These lineages were carried to Tibet during the early spreading by scholars and yogins not only from India but also from China and Central Asia. These texts are contained in collections that are unique to the Nyingma school, and include the teachings of the Buddha (the sutras and tantras) as well as teachings by the great Nyingma forefathers such as Padmasambhava, Vimalamitra, and Vairochana. Nyingmapas also accept and study the texts of the later spreading, contained in the canon of scriptures translated into Tibetan, known as the Kanjur ("buddha word," those texts spoken by the Buddha) and Tenjur (commentaries on the buddha word composed by others).

The Terma includes not only texts but also other objects of spiritual power such as statues or ritual implements that were concealed by Padmasambhava or Yeshe Tsogyal for future generations and rediscovered by tertöns at a later time. Each generation has its specific character and is in need of a dharma teaching appropriate to it, that it can hear, understand, and apply. Tradition tells us that, anticipating this, Padmasambhava gave many teachings that were what people living in various later times would need and hid these for the later "dark ages." Terma are hidden in various places such as the earth, rocks, or water. There are also "sky terma," which means "texts" that are hidden in space, so to speak, and appear abruptly and spontaneously in the minds of later masters.

Those who discover terma are highly attained bodhisattvas who have been reborn specifically in order to discover particular treasures. Since terma are generally written in secret or coded language (the "language of the dakinis"), it is also the function of the tertön to understand and interpret the meaning of the terma for his or her generation. Nyingma tradition enumerates a long list of tertöns, including three preeminent tertöns, eight great ones, twenty-one powerful ones, one hundred and eight intermediate, and one thousand subsidiary tertöns. The most notable of these are understood as emanations of Padmasambhava's twenty-five great disciples. Tulku Urgyen provides a further glimpse of the tertöns:

> Since the time [Padmasambhava] left Tibet, he has sent a cease-less stream of emissaries representing him. . . . Many of these tertons uncovered what Padmasambhava had hidden in such an impressive fashion that even people who harbored great doubt were forced to admit the validity of termas. Sometimes a terton would open up a solid rock before a crowd of 400 or 500 people and reveal what had been concealed inside. By openly perform-ing such feats and permitting people to witness the revelations with their own eyes, they completely dispelled all skepticism. Through the ceaseless activity of Padmasambhava this type of terton has continued to appear right up to the present day. So, the terma teachings come from Padmasambhava himself and are revealed in an undeniably direct way. This is not some mere legend from long ago; even until recent times, these great ter-tons could perform miraculous feats like passing through solid matter and flying through the sky.[11]

In his autobiography, Chagdud Tulku provides the following account of a terma discovery made by his mother, Dawa Drolma, who was known as a tertön. Chagdud Rinpoche's family, who lived in East Tibet, was making a pilgrimage to Lhasa, several months away by caravan.

> For many months the caravan of pilgrims wended its way through the high, craggy mountain passes, the long valleys and the deep forests that separate Eastern from Central Tibet. Sometimes they stopped at monasteries, but usually theirs was a nomadic existence, with all the pleasures and the hardships that involves. One day as the entourage passed through a valley, my mother suddenly pointed and exclaimed, "Over there is a *terma* that must be revealed now!" The caravan immediately changed direction and traveled until it came to the rock face of a moun-tain. At my mother's direction, a man struck the rock with one strong blow of a hatchet and a large slab fell off, exposing a p'hurba, or ritual dagger, embedded in stone.[12]

Instead of taking hold of the *phurba,* Dawa Drolma immediately turned to her sister, who had continually disparaged her accomplishments, and invited her to pull the phurba from the rock in which it was embedded. When the sister attempted to do so, her hand was burned as if by molten iron. "My mother stepped forward and pulled the p'hurba from the stone as easily as a knife from butter. Inside a hole in the center of the phurba was a scroll inscribed in the secret language of the 'sky goers,' the wisdom beings known as dakinis. The script, indecipherable except to one with profound wisdom, was revealed by my mother."[13]

The Terma tradition is known as the "short lineage of revealed treasures" because, in contrast to the Kama, the termas were all revealed subsequent to the early spreading and therefore the time since their reception is relatively shorter. Tulku Thondup comments:

> For example, if a disciple of Padmasambhava takes rebirth as a Terton in the twentieth century, there is no need to have a long lineage of lamas preceding him. He himself has received the blessing and empowerment from Padmasambhava, attained realization, and is thus second to Padmasambhava in the lineage of transmission.[14]

Through the terma tradition, the Nyingma school has been able to stay in close and continual contact with the spirit, energy, and inspiration of Padmasambhava, its founder and spiritual source. Rather than seeing a pattern of continual decline as time progresses, each successive generation has been able to make a new beginning with a fresh revelation from the founder, a revelation that is suited to its particular needs and capacities. This has meant that within the Tibetan tradition down to today, the spirituality of the Nyingma's has remained living, intense, and fitting. In relation to the importance of terma, Tulku Urgyen explains:

> There is a very important point involved here: namely the purity of transmission. As teachings are passed down from one generation to the next, it is possible that some contamination, or damage, of samaya [the integrity of the transmission] may creep

in, diminishing the blessings. To counteract this, Padmasambhava in his immeasurably skillful wisdom and compassion gives us fresh hidden treasures. . . . [In the terma], the distance from the Buddha [with whom Padmasambhava is identified] to the practitioner is very short when a revelation is fresh and direct; there is no damage in the line of transmission. The purity or lack thereof lies not in the teaching itself, but in how distant the line of transmission is. That is why there is a continual renewal of the transmission."[15]

THE THREE LINEAGES

Something of the style of Nyingma spirituality may be observed in the "three lineages" or methods by which the teachings of dharma are transmitted, whether in the Kama or the Terma tradition. These are the Thought Lineage of the Victorious Ones, the Sign Lineage of the Vidyadharas, and the Hearing Lineage of the Individuals. On the one hand, these three methods of transmission show how the Nyingma lineages were first received by human beings. On the other, they reveal the ways in which the teachings have been passed on from master to disciple throughout Nyingma history. Each of these three lineages corresponds to one of the "buddha bodies," or *kayas* (mentioned in chapter 3), in which enlightened ones appear and from which they communicate with the samsaric beings: the dharmakaya, the ultimate body, reality itself beyond specific form or configuration, the wisdom being of all reality; the sambhogakaya, the "body of enjoyment," the kind of resplendent, nonmaterial form taken by the buddhas, bodhisattvas, and departed masters in religious visions; and the nirmanakaya, the "created body," the form enlightened ones take when appearing as human beings, such as Shakyamuni Buddha.

Most of the teachings of the Thought Lineage of the Victorious Ones were originally taught by the primordial buddha Samantabhadra in his ultimate or dharmakaya (body of reality) form. Through transmission directly from mind to mind with no shape or form, Samantabhadra passed these teachings to buddhas who appear in glorious, nonphysical bodies (sambhogakaya), such as Vajrasattva (Diamond Being). In relation to this style of teaching, Tulku Thondup explains:

> Just by the realization of the meaning of the Tantras by the Teacher, the Buddha, the retinue of disciples, Buddhas who are manifestations of himself, also have the realization; just as when the moon in the sky is reflected in buckets of water, the reflection will be the same in each bucket. This is "the transmission of the identity of the mind of teaching and disciples."[16]

Through the Sign Lineage transmission, by means of nonverbal gestures and symbols, the sambhogakaya buddhas then passed the teaching to the human realm to the realized human beings (nirmanakaya). Tulku Thondup writes:

> [This is] the transmission from a Rig-dzin [Vidyadhara] or knowledge-holding teacher who has attained the Body of the Primordial Wisdom of Tantra to Bodhisattva disciples whose minds are fully ripened to receive the teachings. The teacher focuses his mind, the Primordial Awareness Wisdom, and merely gives the indication by gesture (mudra) and sacred syllables (mantra); whereupon the disciple instantaneously comprehends the complete meaning of the Tantras.[17]

In the Hearing Lineage of the Individuals, the teachings, in the form of words, are then passed on from nirmanakayas, such as Shakyamuni Buddha, to disciples who in turn pass them on, initiating a lineage of unbroken transmission. These texts are contained in the *Nyingma Gyübum,* a collection of tantras from the early spreading in thirty-three volumes.

In relation to the three lineages, Tulku Thondup remarks:

> Most teachers transmit teaching to their disciples through Hearing Transmission. . . . Beginning with Padmasambhava, Vimalamitra and other teachers, the Hearing Transmission was started in Tibet and it has continued until the present day. The

FIGURE 5.1 *Samantabhadra, the primordial Dharmakaya buddha according to the Nyingma school.*

Mind Transmission and [Sign] Transmission also still exist among teachers of high Tantric meditational attainment. All of these systems of transmission are very important because according to the Tantric teaching it is necessary to receive the proper transmission in order to practice. Tantric meditation practiced without receiving the proper transmission is dangerous and unbeneficial.[18]

Trungpa Rinpoche remarks that the Thought Lineage, the most subtle and ultimate of the three, occurs when the teacher transmits the awakened state directly to the mind of the disciple, without the mediation of signs or words. In the Sign Lineage, the teacher communicates through an often abrupt and unexpected gesture. As an example of the sign lineage, Tilopa, the Indian siddha who founded the Kagyü lineage, one day unexpectedly and abruptly hit his disciple Naropa in the face with a shoe; in that instant, Naropa's eyes were opened and he realized the inmost nature of reality. And in the Hearing Lineage, the teachings are conveyed through ordinary words and writing.

THE NINE YANAS

The Nyingma path is structured according to the "nine yanas," arranged in order of ascending ultimacy. Tulku Urgyen comments, "That is why the Buddha said about the nine vehicles, 'My teachings are a gradual progression from the beginning up to the highest perfection, like the steps on a staircase which extend from the lowest to the highest, or like a newborn infant who slowly grows up.' "[19] In one sense, the nine yanas show the progression of human spiritual development up to its highest attainment. At the same time, however, not everyone will begin at the lowest yanas and progress to the highest in this lifetime. Different people, depending on their spiritual preferences and maturity, will naturally be suited to the practice of different yanas. The nine yanas, then, listed from lowest to highest are as shown in table 5.1.

The goal of each of the nine yanas in the Nyingma path is the same: the attainment of ultimate enlightenment. However, the general formulation, symbolism, and means differ. The first non-tantric yanas of the Hinayana and Mahayana, as mentioned, are called "vehicles of cause" because, through purifying negative karma and developing antidotes to obstacles, they seek to generate the causes that will advance one toward buddhahood. Through the Hinayana, one takes refuge in the Buddha, dharma, and sangha and then follows the three trainings of shila (ethical conduct), samadhi (meditation), and prajna (wisdom), seeking to attain liberation for oneself. In the Mahayana, one takes the vow to attain enlightenment for the benefit of all sentient beings and follows the bodhisattva path, developing wisdom and compassion for others.

The six tantric yanas, as we saw, are known as the "yanas of result" because they take the goal of enlightenment or the awakened state as the basis of the path. How is this done? It will be recalled that the fully realized state, the dharmakaya, is held to be actually present within each sentient being although it is covered over with obscurations. In the tantric path, various methods, including ritual, visualization, and the direct pointing out of mind, are used to enable one to experience and develop familiarity with the enlightenment within.

Each of the tantric yanas represents a progressively fuller and more complete identification with the awakened state. In kriyayoga, for example, buddhahood is visualized as a deity outside of oneself, an exalted being to whom one is in relation as a servant. In upayoga, buddhahood is seen still as an external entity, but more on the level of a friend and helper. Yogayana is typified by two stages. In the first, the development stage, one visualizes oneself as the deity, the imagined representation of buddhahood, and then invites the inner essence of that deity to descend into the visualization, enlivening and empowering it. In the second, the completion stage, one meditates directly on the *tathata,* suchness, the essential nature of the deities.

Although the Nyingma path is structured according to the nine yanas, in actual fact practitioners will usually first go for refuge, take lay or monastic vows, and learn how to meditate. Next, at a later time suggested by their teacher, they will take the bodhisattva vow and learn the basic Mahayana practices. Having integrated the Mahayana teachings and perspectives, in the next stage, under the direction of their

TABLE 5.1

THE NINE YANAS OF NYINGMA TRADITION

YANAS OF CAUSE			
	Yana	Main Teachings	Relation to the Deity
Hinayana	1. Shravaka-yana	Four noble truths	
	2. Pratyekabuddha-yana	Karma or causality	
Mahayana	3. Bodhisattva-yana	Emptiness and compassion	
YANAS OF RESULT			
Vajrayana			
Outer yanas	In the Outer Tantras, the distinction between the two truths is maintained, divinities are not visualized with their female consorts, the five meats are not taken, and one does not attain the final result in this lifetime.[1]		
	4. Kriyayoga-yana	Purification of the practitioners' body, speech, and mind. Within absolute truth, all things are equal; within relative truth, deity is master, practitioner is servant.	The deity is visualized as exterior to oneself and is worshiped. Deity as master, practitioner as servant.
	5. Charyayoga-yana	Same view as Kriyayoga-yana.	The deity is still external, but more nearly on a level with the practitioner, as friend and helper.
	6. Yoga-yana	Absolute truth: all phenomena are free of concept, empty, and luminous. Relative truth: all phenomena are the mandala of deities.	One visualizes oneself as the deity. Deity is seen in conventional way without consorts and nonwrathful. Rituals are performed as offerings to the deity.

[1] Tulku Thondup, *Buddhist Civilization in Tibet*, 20.

Inner yanas	In the Inner Tantras the two truths are held to be inseparable, all phenomena are equal, the five meats and the five nectars are taken, the divinities are visualized with their consorts, and the final result can be attained in this lifetime. The tantras of these yanas are the special and distinctive Nyingma practices.[2]		
	7. Mahayoga-yana (masculine principle)	"Within absolute truth all things are accepted as the essence of the mind and the Dharmakaya. All manifestation, thoughts, and appearances are considered to be the sacred aspects of the divinities within relative truth."[3]	Emphasis on the visualization of one-self as the deity with female consort. All phenomena are seen as the essence of the deities.
	8. Anuyoga-yana (feminine principle)	Emphasis on the "dissolution phase" of meditation; emphasis on the perfection of bliss, clarity, and nonthought. Practice of the "inner yogas" of the winds (prana), channels (nadi), and drops (bindu).	The visualization of the deities is not so much emphasized in this yana.
	9. Atiyoga-yana (nonduality of masculine and feminine principles)	"All appearances or apparent phenomena are illusions of the deluded mind. They are false because in reality their nature is free from conceptualizations. In nature all existents are the same and they are pure in the Dharmakaya. In practice there is no acceptance or rejection, rather all existents are accepted as manifestations of the nature, Dharmata."[4]	

[2] Ibid., 20–21.; [3] Ibid.; [4] Ibid.

123

teacher, they will usually skip over the lower tantras and begin the practice of the higher tantras in an order and manner suited to their own situation, needs, and capacities.

The inner or higher tantras represent the quintessence of the Nyingma transmission and are understood as a radical and direct path to enlightenment. They are more unconventional in their approach than the lower or outer tantras: the divinities are visualized with their consorts, the sacredness and equality of all phenomena are emphasized, and it is said that full realization can be attained in the present lifetime.

Mahayoga-yana is associated with the masculine principle and is for those whose primary defilement is aggression. In Mahayoga, one visualizes oneself as the divinity with consort. "All manifestation, thoughts and appearances are considered to be the sacred aspects of the divinities within relative truth," in the words of Tulku Thondup.[20] By visualizing all phenomena as the deities of the mandala of buddhahood, in the development stage, all appearances are purified.

One particular keynote of mahayoga-yana has to do with the use of visualization. In the Vajrayana in general, one visualizes oneself as a buddha, thus giving external form to the enlightenment within. Likewise, one visualizes the external world as pure and sacred, thus undercutting the usual practice of taking things as impure and defiled. In mahayoga, one comes to the realization that actually all of our everyday experience is a visualization. Just as we can visualize ourselves as a buddha and the world as pure, so we can visualize ourselves as an existent ego and the world as defiled. Realizing that all of our images and conceptions of reality are in fact complex visualizations, we gain a unique entry into the underpinnings of the conventional world and gain a certain kind of unparalleled leverage over it. This is reflected in the mahayoga-yana teaching of the "eight cosmic commands," eight kinds of ways to intervene in the operation of the conventional world and alter its momentum for the benefit of others.

Anuyoga-yana is associated with the feminine principle and is for those whose principal obstacle is passion. In anuyoga the emphasis shifts away from external visualization toward the completion stage, in which one meditates on the inner or subtle body with its primary energy centers (*chakras*), and its *prana* (winds or subtle energies), *nadis* (the inner pathways along which one's energy travels), and *bindu* (the consciousness). In anuyoga, all appearances are seen as the three great mandalas, and reality is understood as the deities and their pure lands.

A keynote of anuyoga-yana is the perception of the entire world as governed by passion, understood here not as sexual passion so much as desire, thirst, and longing to unite with our experience. When we turn on a light switch, we do so out of a desire for light. When we see a masterful painting or hear beautiful music, we are charged with passion to merge with that beauty. When we love another person, it reflects our appreciation of qualities we see in them and our longing to be one with those. In fact, in the anuyoga perspective, every move we make is an expression of passion. Moreover, this passion is not ultimately ego-based, but rooted in our very state of being, our buddha-nature.

For a person operating from ego, this endless expression of passion is drawn into the territorial game of manipulation and possession. We desire to have control over that which we feel deep appreciation for. But from an enlightened perspective, to see the entire world as a burning inferno of passion brings liberation. Because the fire of longing is everywhere and uncontrollable, it is seen clearly as primordial warmth and selfless love, rather than an invitation for possession and self-aggrandizement. In such a context, there are no "objects" to own and personal territoriality has no meaning. In this perspective, passion is the literal "fire" of life and an utmost and completely egoless expression of the awakened state.

Atiyoga-yana, containing the teachings of dzokchen, transcends both masculine and feminine and is said to be for people whose principal defilement is delusion. This lineage was transmitted from the sambhogakaya deity Vajrasattva to the human founder of dzokchen, Garab Dorje. His lineage, as we saw, passed eventually to Padmasambhava, Vimalamitra, and Vairochana, who transmitted them to Tibetan disciples.

Ati or dzokchen stresses the closeness of enlightenment—that it is already concealed within our most intimate and immediate experience. Moreover, the awakened state is all-pervading—it lies within every moment of our lives, however painful or pleasurable, however elevated or debased. In that sense, we are never away from it, and it is always available and accessible to us. In the dzokchen perspective, all the phenomena of samsara and nirvana are thus referred to as *kadak,* primordially pure.

The ever-present, all-pervading enlightenment is covered over and hidden by conceptual mind. Conceptual mind refers not only to actual thinking, but also to the way in which we continually solidify our perceptions of ourselves, others, and the world at large. Through the dzokchen practices, conceptual mind—the overlay that conceals the enlightenment within—begins to become more and more transparent and insubstantial. Our reference points, the familiarity we impose upon our experience, our subtle defense mechanisms to avoid the emptiness and groundlessness of existence—all begin to dissolve. Experience begins to become increasingly vivid, but also more and more ungraspable and empty of anything solid. Rather than working toward enlightenment from the outside in, by seeing ultimate reality as something external to be gained, dzokchen empowers our own wakefulness so that it eats through ego, from the inside out, so to speak. This brings us to see that that primordial wakefulness has been with us from the very beginning. Tulku Thondup epitomizes dzokchen as follows:

> Dzogchenpas assert that all the appearances or apparent phenomena are illusions of the deluded mind. They are false because in reality their nature is free from conceptualizations. In the nature all existents are the same and they are pure in the Dharmakaya. In practice there is no acceptance or rejection, rather all existents are accepted as manifestations of the nature, Dharmata.[21]

Dzokchen texts are divided into three categories, which reflect three somewhat distinct types of teaching: the category of mind, the category of space, and the category of oral instructions. Through the category of mind (*sem-de*), one abandons the conceptual mind, including philosophical pondering and religious thinking, as worthless. One develops an attitude that is open and free from care. In the category of space (*long-de*), all experience is realized as an expression of the space or emptiness of enlightenment. The category of oral instruction (*me-ngag-de*), is itself divided into four subgroupings, outer, inner, secret, and innermost esoteric cycle. In this category the final weapons of ego are at last laid down for good. At the conclusion of the dzokchen journey, all phenomena, everything that had previously been thought to have a solid and objectifiable existence dissolves into the vast expanse of dharmata and is seen as the play of energy and wisdom, points and patterns of light without any substance or graspability. This state of being is considered the ultimate attainment of the buddhas of the three times, and the highest expression of wisdom and selfless compassion that can be reached.*

CONCLUSION

When Nyingmapas look back on their own history, they see it falling into two periods. First is that of the early spreading when the foundations of the Ancient School were laid by Padmasambhava, Vimalamitra, Manjushrimitra, Vairochana, and others. Second is the period beginning with Longchenpa and continuing down to the present, when the Nyingma school carried on the early Kama lineages and gave birth to an unending succession of tertöns, beginning with Longchenpa, who maintained the freshness and purity of Nyingma spirituality.

There are three Nyingma masters from this second period who are considered unequaled in their wisdom and compassion, unrivaled in their scholarly and meditative accomplishment, and unmatched as guides to liberation. The first is, of course, Longchenpa; the other two are Jigme Lingpa (1730–1798) and Ju Mipham Rinpoche (1848–1912). Jigme Lingpa was born amidst poverty and, when he entered a monastery near his home, acted as the servant of others, with no tutor and no chance to study dharma. Owing to his innate brilliance, however, and drawing on texts he was able to procure and study at night and on discussions with his monastic friends, he was able to educate himself to

*Atiyoga, considered by the Nyingmapas as the epitome of Buddha Shakyamuni's dharma, is discussed in Reginald A. Ray, *Secret of the Vajra World,* chap. 13.

a high level. Eventually his depth and brilliance were noticed, and he began to receive the formal training he so fervently sought. Decisive in his life were a series of visions of masters of the early spreading, Guru Rinpoche and Manjushrimitra, and then a definitive revelation in which Longchenpa conferred on him the Longchen Nyingthik cycle, the teachings on the innermost essence of Longchenpa's teaching, that subsequently became so central to Nyingma tradition. Ju Mipham was a brilliant polymath who mastered vast sections of Indian and Tibetan religious literature. He wrote thoroughly informed commentaries unexcelled for their brilliance and learning on philosophy, meditation, medicine, astrology, poetry, mythology, and other topics. Even today, Mipham's works continue to be consulted by scholars of all the Tibetan schools. The lives of both Jigme Lingpa and Ju Mipham are summarized in chapter 9, on the Ri-me movement.

The Buddhist traditions that began to be brought freshly to Tibet in the tenth and following centuries criticized the already existing lineages on two points. First, they were antiquated, less pure, or even corrupt because of their much greater historical distance from their Indian origin; and second, they were largely nonmonastic traditions and thus lacked the institutional strength and the virtues of monasticism. As we saw, the emergence of the New Translation schools and their criticism of the already existing lineages led these Old Translation traditions to begin to think of themselves as, in some way, forming a particular orientation vis-à-vis the new schools. Thus the Nyingma, as one of the four "schools" of Tibetan Buddhism, was born.

The Nyingmapas could counter the criticisms of the new schools on several fronts. For one thing, the antiquity of the Nyingma lineages indicated the strength and maturity of their spirituality and their rootedness in the Tibetan soil. In addition, the fact that the Nyingmapas were primarily nonmonastic could be seen as a virtue. The tantric traditions, which were the specialty of the Nyingmapas, had originally existed in predominantly nonmonastic circles and thus the Nyingmapas reproduced the original Indian setting of the tantric traditions more faithfully than the New Translation schools. Further, institutionalized monasticism in Tibet, as elsewhere in the Buddhist world, tends to become involved in competition for patrons and donations and to enter the arena of politics, vying for political power and for favoritism from the powers-that-be. This shifts the emphasis away from individual inspiration and practice to institutional survival and aggrandizement. In support of this point, it may be pointed out that all three of the New Translation schools—the Sakya, the Kagyü, and the Geluk—at one time or another have sought and maintained political power, struggled sometimes militarily with one another, and in some measure used their "worldly" power against their rivals. The Nyingmapas, by contrast, have always been the least political of the four schools in this sense and have been able to focus their attention on maintaining the integrity of their spirituality, their connection with their spiritual foundations, and the living quality of their lineages. In all these ways, then, the Nyingmapas have faithfully retained the spirituality of their origins.

At the same time, the Nyingmapas everywhere reflect the ongoing creativity of their historical evolution. Their terma traditions, although seen as having originated in the early spreading as revelations hidden by Padmasambhava, reflect concerns of a subsequent time and faithfully meet the needs of later generations. Moreover, each generation of saints and scholars has been energetic and inventive in meeting the new challenges of successive ages and in seeing to the preservation of the practice and correct understanding of Nyingma spirituality. The Nyingma school as its exists today is also, of course, quite different from the configuration of Buddhism that existed during the first spreading, owing to the fact that it is "a school" and has a shape, a hierarchy, and a more or less distinct identity within the overall framework of Tibetan Buddhism. In chapter 9, more will be said of the Nyingma, particularly in modern times.

6

The Later Spreading

KADAM AND SAKYA

THE LINEAGES OF THE KADAMPAS AND THE SAKYAPAS both originated in the eleventh century, the first through the work of Atisha, the second through that of Drogmi. At first glance, these two traditions appear to have very different roots, for Atisha was a conventional Mahayanist monk, while Drogmi had received the lineage of the Indian siddha Virupa. However, both the Kadam and the Sakya became established in Tibet from the very beginning as strong, monastic traditions, and in this way they are parallel and comparable schools.

KADAM

When Buddhism made its way to Tibet during the early spreading, the classical monastic tradition in India was defined by conventional Mahayana teachings, such as in Shantarakshita's and Kamalashila's teachings on the gradual path. During this period, Tantric Buddhism seems to have existed entirely outside of the monastic context among yogins and lay practitioners. It was this model—in which monasticism carried the conventional Mahayana, while the Vajrayana existed in non-monastic settings—that was adopted during the early spreading in Tibet.

In the hundred and fifty years from the end of the early spreading to the beginning of the later spreading, the situation in India had changed dramatically. During this interim period, Tantric Buddhism had become much better known and was more widely accepted: the Pala dynasty in northeastern India openly espoused the tantra, monasteries with

SOME DATES OF KADAM HISTORY

982–1054	Atisha
1042	Atisha arrives in Tibet
1008–1064	Dromtön, primary disciple of Atisha
1056	Reting monastery founded by Dromdön; center of Kadam order
11th CENTURY	Gampopa becomes Kadam monk (Kadam practice lineage thereby enters into the Kagyü)

a tantric bent were built, and certain forms of Tantric Buddhism were practiced in monasteries by monks and nuns following the Vinaya. When the Tibetans came to India during this period, Indian monasticism thus included the tantra, and it was assumed that the well-trained monk was versed in all three yanas, Hinayana, Mahayana, and Vajrayana. The Tibetans of the later spreading emulated this model in their monastic lineages in Tibet.

During the early spreading, both streams of Indian Buddhism—the monastic and the nonmonastic—made their way to Tibet. Buddhist monasticism, in the form of the conventional Mahayana (the way of the sutras) had arrived chiefly with the founding of Samye monastery and with the teachings of Shantarakshita and Kamalashila. With the assassination of Ralpachan, the monastic presence in Tibet was largely eliminated. When Buddhism was reintroduced during the later spreading, if Buddhism was to survive with an institutional dimension—and this had been critical to its Indian survival and strength—this time monasticism would have to be founded on a firmer, better supported, and more widespread basis.

Atisha

This important task was initially undertaken by the great Indian master Atisha (982–1054), founder of the Kadam lineage, which, centuries later, through Tsongkhapa's reform, became the Geluk school.

FIGURE 6.1 *Atisha, the Indian scholar who founded the Kadam school of Tibetan Buddhism in the eleventh century.*

Atisha was a deeply and intently religious person who, in the course of his life, went through several major phases of development. As a youth, he had a vision of the goddess Tara and he remained devoted to her as his tutelary deity. After a period of study and practice of the Vajrayana, he had a vision of Shakyamuni Buddha, who enjoined him to enter the monastic way. This he did at twenty-nine at the Bodhgaya monastery, and thenceforth he devoted himself to study, mainly of the Vinaya, Prajnaparamita, and the tantras. He pursued his studies and taught at other Indian monasteries, attaining particular renown at Nalanda. He eventually went to Sumatra to study Mahayana philosophy (Madhyamaka) with the great scholar Dharmakirti. He then returned to India and became abbot of Vikramashila. It was from here that he went to Tibet in 1042.

When Atisha arrived in Tibet, he was already sixty years old. The year of his arrival was two hundred years after the murder of Langdarma, marking the effective end of institutionalized Buddhism in the Land of Snow. As mentioned, while Buddhist teachings, practices, and lineages continued among individual families, small groups of practitioners and yogins, the monastic tradition did not survive in tact. Even in Atisha's day, it had only just begun to reappear. Atisha took it as his primary aim to reintroduce the monastic way of life and monastic discipline in as pure a form as possible.

In fact, after his vision of Shakyamuni, Atisha came to view monastic life as the centerpiece of Buddhist spirituality. By this, the master understood taking the monastic ordinations and living a simple, unpretentious life, following the Vinaya and engaging in study and meditation. Although Atisha himself was trained in tantra and made a place for it in his system, he taught that the highest form of religious life is to be a celibate Mahayanist monk who adheres to the Vinaya, studies the sacred texts, and follows the conventional Mahayana way of the gradual path to enlightenment, working for the welfare of beings. Tantra has a role to play, but primarily in its support of this ideal. It is this orientation that was later adopted by the Gelukpas and marks their approach today.

Those Tibetans whom Atisha accepted as disciples were required in particular to follow four rules: to abstain from marriage, intoxicants, travel, and possession of money. These rules made for a life of religious poverty and extreme simplicity. Tulku Urgyen summarizes the modesty and humility that characterizes Atisha's approach:

> Atisha told us to "keep a low seat," meaning a low profile. Don't strive to be high and important. Wear simple clothing, not fancy, expensive garments; wear whatever you come by. . . . Don't let your mind become preoccupied with food, clothing, fame and importance.[1]

In support of his mission of monastic reform, Atisha accepted monastic disciples and composed works on the Buddhist path, including the renowned *Bodhi-patha-pradipa*. This latter work became the basis of the Geluk founder Tsongkhapa's *lamrim* ("stages of the path") teachings. Atisha was a devotee of the simple yet profound wisdom of the Prajnaparamita. And he emphasized the importance of the guru, enjoining practitioners to request acceptance by a teacher and then to follow that teacher with complete obedience and devotion for the rest of their lives.

Atisha learned to speak and read Tibetan fluently, a mark of his devotion to his mission and a factor no doubt contributing to his success. He accepted as his primary disciple the Tibetan Dromtön, who founded Reting monastery (later important for the Gelukpas) and followed the life of purity and simplicity taught by his master. Atisha appreciated the Tibetan people well enough, finding their literal and rugged character both irritating and endearing. A story is told that when Atisha came to Tibet, he brought with him a Bengali tea boy as an attendant, who was as difficult and irascible an individual as one could find. Atisha later remarked that he had brought this person with him so that he could practice the paramita of patience but that after meeting the wild and unruly Tibetans, he realized that he no longer required the services of this worthy.

Atisha had planned to stay in Tibet three years. He ended up spending the rest of his life there, dying in 1054 at the age of seventy-two. By the time of his death, he had accomplished his mission and more, founding the first enduring monastic order in Tibet. Moreover, it was one with such clarity, purity, and integrity, that it would provide a model not only for Tsongkhapa's Geluk order but also for the other monastic lineages in the Tibetan tradition, down to the present day.

The Kadam order, along with the Geluk, into which it was later absorbed, contains the primary heritage of Atisha. In fact, the Kadam lineage also survives in the Kagyü. In order to understand the reason for this, one must recall that Atisha's own training reflects both scholarly study and meditation practice. Each of these two dimensions of Atisha's training has spawned a somewhat distinct lineage. First is the practice of contemplation and, in particular, of the Mahayana type of meditation called *lojong,* or "training the mind." Second is the scholarly lineage of study, dialectics, and debate. Trungpa Rinpoche remarks, "There is what is known as the contemplative Kadam school and the intellectual Kadam school." In relation to the contemplative school, he says, "The Kagyüpas received these instruction on the proper practice of Mahayana Buddhism through Gampopa, who studied with Milarepa as well as with Kadam teachers. . . . The Gelukpas specialized in dialectics and took a more philosophical approach to understanding the Kadam tradition."[2] In a broader sense, as mentioned, it is also accurate to say that Atisha's Kadam school, in its teachings on the importance of a pure monastic life, continues to provide inspiration to the monastic way in all of its various Tibetan manifestations.

The Kadampas' Approach to Dharma

Something of the spirituality of Atisha's teaching can be felt in his instruction of the so-called "four aims," as summarized by Tulku Urgyen Rinpoche:

1. "Aim your mind at the Dharma." This means your final aim should be directed at what is true and meaningful rather than at mundane attainment. . . .
2. "Aim your Dharma practice at simple living," not great wealth. It is easier to pursue the teachings if we are simple practitioners. . . .

3. Aim at simple living for your entire life," not just for a short while. . . . Aim at remaining a simple practitioner for your entire life, until the time of death. . . .

4. Finally, Atisha said, "Aim your death at solitude." This means decide to die alone and friendless in a retreat hermitage or un-peopled place, without being surrounded by attendants and companions.

For Tulku Urgyen, Atisha serves as an example for all practitioners: "The great master Atisha lived by these principles, and achieved great accomplishment. We should try our best to apply as much as we can of his advice."[3]

As a principal transmitter of the New Translation traditions, Atisha had a way of understanding the tantras that was in some respects different from that of the Old Translation approach of the Nyingma. The system of classification used by Atisha and the other New Translation traditions was that of the "four orders of tantra." Since this system became a central feature of Tibetan Buddhism and is the one most often encountered today, a few words of explanation are in order.

In its earlier days in India, the various traditions that we now think of as comprising Tantric Buddhism existed in the form of many individual lineages—perhaps numbering in the hundreds or even thousands—passed on from master to disciple. Each of these was in some sense distinctive and the differences among them could be considerable. At this time, there certainly was no attempt—or even any context for an attempt—to sort out these differences in a comprehensive way or set these many lineages into general types or categories.

However, as Tantric Buddhism became better known, just such an endeavor was undertaken. During the time of the early spreading, the scheme that was later to become the nine yanas of the Nyingma was apparently in development in India. As will be recalled, as part of this system, all tantras were classified into six categories, those of the three lower or outer tantras and those of the three higher or inner tantras. By the time of the later spreading, the Indians had developed a related but somewhat different arrangement, a grand scheme according to which the more prominent tantric traditions were arranged into four orders of tantra. This method of classification was accepted and adopted by all the later-spreading schools of Tibetan Buddhism. When Tibetans discuss a particular tantric text or initiation, if the text is a Nyingma tantra, they will locate it within the nine yanas; if it is a New Translation tantra, they will tell you which of the four orders of tantra it belongs to.

The four orders of tantra, in ascending order of sophistication and ultimacy are:

1. Kriya tantra, ritual texts compatible with conventional Mahayana practice. They are distinguished as tantras that emphasize purification.

2. Charya tantra, a second group of ritual texts also compatible with conventional Mahayana. They are distinguished from the previous category as tantras that emphasize the worship of one of the classical Mahayana deities as an external entity.

3. Yoga tantra, texts that enable practitioners to identify with "the supremely divine form representing the goal of buddhahood."[4] As with the kriya and charya tantras, the methods, symbolism, and deities of the yoga tantra are compatible with conventional Mahayana and are thus able to be practiced by ordained monks and nuns within the monastic context. It was the yoga tantras that were taken to China and Japan during the eighth and ninth centuries. The first three orders of tantra are often considered to be equivalent to the three outer tantras of the Nyingma system.

4. Anuttara-yoga tantra, texts that are devoted to meditation upon the great yidams such as Guhyasamaja, Hevajra, Chakrasamvara, and Vajrayogini. In their Indian origins, these are distinguished by practice in cremation grounds, solitary retreats, and other strictly nonmonastic contexts, and the injunction to various unconventional behaviors. It was the anuttara-yoga tantras that were practiced by the great siddhas of India and by the Tibetan siddhas. Sometimes this category is divided into father tantras (e.g., *Guhyasamaja Tantra*), mother tantras (*Chakrasamvara Tantra*), and nondual tantras (*Kalachakra Tantra*). It is sometimes

maintained that the anuttara-yoga category, with its three subdivisions, roughly corresponds to the three inner tantras of mahayoga, anuyoga, and atiyoga in the Nyingma system.

The first three orders of tantra were, as mentioned, quite conventional in their approach and their methods, and compatible with life in the north Indian monasteries during the time of the later spreading. In contrast, the fourth order, that of the anuttara-yoga tantras, required attitudes, behaviors, and methods incompatible with conventional monastic life and were therefore practiced primarily outside of the monastic context during this period. It was this order of tantra that eventually came to be prominent in Tibet, and most of the New Translation tantras that one hears about nowadays belong to this order, such as the *Guhyasamaja, Hevajra, Chakrasamvara,* and *Kalachakra* tantras.

To what extent the subdivisions of the anuttara-yoga tantra and the inner tantras of mahayoga-, anuyoga-, and atiyoga-yana are fundamentally equivalent is a matter of debate. This issue probably depends on one's point of view. Certainly on a general level, these can be seen at least to be parallel, yet there are important differences of central deity, basic perspective, teachings, text, and practice. Another related question is the extent to which mahamudra (the culmination of the anuttara-yoga tantra) and dzokchen (the culmination of the nine-yana journey) are two different terms for the same thing. Most contemporary Tibetan masters say that they are, for all intents and purposes, equivalent realizations. At the same time, however, it is important to acknowledge that their lineages, texts, style of transmission, oral instructions, and practices may differ on important points.[5]

SAKYA

The Sakya lineage played a critical role in the importation of Buddhism to Tibet during the later spreading in the eleventh and twelfth centuries and was politically the most powerful tradition during the thirteenth and fourteenth centuries when the Mongols made the Sakyapas rulers of Tibet. The Sakya maintains a distinctive set of traditions received from India, including a unique balance of both conventional monastic and esoteric Vajrayana teachings. Although their political fortunes waned after the fourteenth century, the lineage has continued to produce great scholars, practitioners, and saints. In spite of its past and present importance, the Sakya is the least known of the four schools of Tibetan Buddhism. This is due to a variety of factors, including both Western scholarly neglect and an interest by the Sakyapas themselves to protect their teachings from the sometimes predatory intentions of modern scholarship and of consumeristic culture in general.[6]

Indian Origins

The Sakya school, like the Kagyü, emerges from the teachings of the Indian siddhas. The Indian progenitor of the Sakya is the master Virupa, known in Tibet as Birwapa, one of the eighty-four Indian mahasiddhas. Although, like others of the eighty-four siddhas, Virupa's date is uncertain, he probably lived sometime during the eighth to the tenth centuries. His traditional biography reports that he was born into a royal family in the eastern part of India. At a young age, he took ordination and became a monk at Nalanda University, where he was known as Shri Dharmapala. Virupa quickly proved himself a brilliant student and attained mastery of the various branches of Buddhist learning. Eventually, in recognition of his extraordinary scholarly abilities, he was made an abbot and senior teacher at Nalanda.

While he was a monk at Nalanda—fairly late in his life, apparently—Virupa received tantric initiation into the anuttara-yoga tantra. Virupa's tantric practice necessitated secrecy, for the unconventional practice of the anuttara-yoga was quite incompatible with the routines and customs of Nalanda's community. Thus it was that Virupa remained a monk, participating in the regular monastic activities of study and debate during the day, but pursuing his tantric practice secretly at night. Thus by day he would teach Hinayana and Mahayana subjects to his monastic disciples, while at night he would forgo sleep to pursue his Vajrayana meditation.

Over a period of many years, Virupa recited Vajravarahi's mantra,

SOME DATES OF SAKYA HISTORY

ca. 8th–10th CENTURY	Indian Mahasiddha Virupa
993–1077	Drogmi (Tibetan founder of Sakya order)
1034–1102	Könchok Gyalpo (disciple of Drogmi)
1073	Founding of head monastery of Sakya order, by member of Khön family, Jönchog (1034–1102), student of Drogmi.
1092–1158	Sakyapa Künga Nyingpo The lamdre teachings of the *Hevajra Tantra,* deriving ultimately from the Mahasiddha Virupa, are adopted by Sakyapa Künga Nyingpo. Sakya gompa is center of Sakya lineage.
1182–1251	Sakya Pandita Tibetan chiefs forced to submit to Genghis Khan.
1235–1280	Phakpa
1249	Sakya Pandita is appointed Tibetan viceroy by the Mongols.
1260	Phakpa, who succeeded Sakya Pandita in 1253, is made viceroy of Tibet by Kublai Khan.
1354	Fighting between Sakyapas and Kagyüpas; former defeated; end of Sakya political hegemony; beginning of Phagmotrupa in power.
1358	Changchub Gyaltsen takes over power.

twice accomplishing a cycle of ten million recitations. In spite of this achievement, no signs of success appeared, even in his dreams. In addition, Virupa was experiencing many bad omens and physical and psychological obstacles. Finally, at the age of seventy-one, despairing of ever gaining attainment, he threw his rosary into the communal privy and determined to return to the Hinayana and Mahayana meditation that he had previously practiced. However, in the evening of that same

day, the female buddha Vajravarahi bestowed teachings, empowerments, and blessings on him. She told him to abandon all concepts and
look directly at the primordial state. On subsequent evenings, she appeared to Virupa repeatedly, leading him through various teachings and
instructions. By the end of this visionary journey, Virupa had attained
the exalted sixth stage, or bhumi, of a bodhisattva.

Now that Virupa had arrived at this level of awakening, ordinary
monastic life revealed itself a rather small container for the majesty of
the siddha. For a while, Virupa remained within the monastery, following its usual routines. It was inevitable, however, that his tantric practice
and his realization would eventually come to light. One day, the pigeons
of the monastery that usually received offerings from the monks turned
up missing. It was discovered that Virupa was in his room eating the
flesh of the pigeons—having apparently killed them—and drinking
wine. The consumption of meat and liquor is, of course, part of tantric
liturgy and the ritual nature of his meal need not be doubted. Having
broken two important monastic rules, not to kill and not to consume
liquor, Virupa was summarily and publicly ordered to leave the monastery. In accordance with custom, he went before the central image of
the monastery, returned his begging bowl and monastic garments to the
Buddha, made a prostration, and prepared to set out for parts unknown.

Before Virupa left, in order to quell the pride of the monks who had
expelled him, he exhibited his realization and power in two miracles. In
front of the monastery was a large lake filled with lotuses, and Virupa
walked across the lotus leaves as if they were dry land. He next took
the bones and wings of the pigeons he appeared to have killed and
eaten, snapped his fingers, and returned them to life. Then they
bounded up into the sky and flew away. He demonstrated in the first
miracle that reality is not always what it seems and in the second that
what had seemed like an immoral action was in fact an illusion from
the start. The monks now realized that the apparently immoral monk
was in fact a realized siddha and they begged Virupa to stay. His course
was determined, however, and the monastic phase of Virupa's career
had ended. He now took up the life of a wandering siddha, and from
this time on he expressed his realization in songs, miracles, and uncon-

ventional behavior, training disciples and teaching and converting beings. Among Virupa's most important teachings were those that came to be known in Tibet as *lamdre,* the "path and fruition" teachings associated with the *Hevajra Tantra* of the anuttara-yoga class.

The essence of Virupa's attainment is contained in a text known as the *Vajragatha,* or "vajra songs," covering only twelve Tibetan folios. This composition represents the first statement of the lamdre teachings, and it outlines the entire Buddhist path, beginning with a person's first entry into the buddha-dharma and extending up to the point of full and perfect enlightenment. It includes, in a condensed fashion, all the teachings of Buddhist schools of the three vehicles, Hinayana, Mahayana, and Vajrayana. In subsequent commentarial tradition, it became customary to divide this teaching into two broad sections: the "three visions," containing teaching common to Hinayana and Mahayana, and the "three tantras," outlining the stages and practices of the Vajrayana, both of which are considered below. It is this comprehensive body of instruction that is known as the lamdre, "path with its result," the essential teaching of the Sakya lineage.

Development in Tibet

Virupa's teachings were passed through four successive Indian masters, finally making their way to Drogmi (993–1077), a Tibetan who traveled to India and Nepal in search of the Buddhist dharma. After studying Sanskrit in Nepal for a year, Drogmi traveled to India to the famous North Indian monastery of Vikramashila, where he became a student of the renowned Mahayana scholar Shantipa (who later became a siddha), with whom he studied, among other things, the *Hevajra Tantra.* For eighteen years, Drogmi pursued a study that included the basic texts of the Hinayana and Mahayana as well as many of the most important tantras of his day. During this period, the great tantric teacher Viravajra transmitted to Drogmi the lineage of Virupa, including the cycle of the three tantras of the *Hevajra Tantra* and the instructions on the lamdre. His studies completed, Drogmi returned to Tibet and gathered many disciples, teaching them the scholarly and practice traditions that he had learned in India. At the core of these was the lamdre teaching with the instructions on the three tantras.

Like the originator of the lamdre, Virupa, and like his own teacher Shantipa, Drogmi embodied an education that involved many years of conventional monastic training in the scholarly texts of Indian Buddhism. For Drogmi, as for Virupa and Shantipa, this rigorous training was then followed by initiation into the anuttara-yoga tantra. In this particular configuration, the scholarly study of Hinayana and Mahayana textual tradition plays the chief role, with tantric practice being seen as appropriately coming after the scholarly foundation has been laid. This great emphasis on thorough training in Buddhist scholarship with the practice of tantra standing in the background as a later and more advanced stage was to characterize the Sakya lineage throughout its history in Tibet.

One of Drogmi's disciples was Könchok Gyalpo (1034–1102), who actually founded the Sakya lineage in Tibet. Könchok Gyalpo was a member of the Khön, a family of hereditary lamas. Tradition relates that the Khön had been devotees of the Nyingma school since the eighth century, when Lu'i Wangpo and other Khön family members had been disciples of Padmasambhava. However, by the time of the eleventh century, the Nyingma teachings had declined in the part of the Tsang province where the Khön family lived. At the same time, the new inspiration of the later spreading was beginning to be felt. The Khön decided that the time had come for a change of allegiance, and Könchok Gyalpo was accordingly sent to find a teacher to transmit to him the new tantras. Könchok Gyalpo eventually found the master, Drogmi, who gave him a thorough training, including transmission of what was to become the central tantric teaching of the Sakya, the *Hevajra Tantra* cycle.

Virupa, as we have seen, had been a scholastically trained monk for most of his life, entering tantric practice only after this basic foundation in conventional study and practice had been laid. This approach was passed down through the lineal generations to Drogmi who, again as we saw, engaged in extensive study of the sutras and commentaries before he took up the study and practice of tantra. Under Drogmi, Könchok Gyalpo similarly received a thorough grounding in the scholarly sutra traditions, followed by training in the tantra. In fact, he was so accomplished in his study that, by the age of forty, he was considered one of the most brilliant and informed Buddhist scholars of his day. In the relatively great emphasis on his monastic scholarly training and attainment, Könchok Gyalpo was moving in the direction of the more conventional, academic Mahayana approach, and away from the unconventional, noninstitutional tantric style of the Nyingmapas. The tantric practice connected with the deity Hevajra, as found in the *Hevajra Tantra,* remained important, but as a more esoteric and inner dimension of the Sakya lineage.

It was at this point, in 1073, that Könchok Gyalpo built a monastery in south-central Tibet, in the Tsang province. This monastery, known as Sakya, or "Gray Earth," after the appearance of the site, became the primary institutional home of the Sakya lineage and an important center for the study, practice, and spread of the tantras of the later spreading, as well as for the Mahayana teachings of ethics, philosophy, metaphysics, logic, and the other major areas of Buddhist and Indian learning. It is interesting that although the Khön family thus distanced itself from the Nyingmapas, they still retained connections with their traditions, and the Nyingma yidam Vajrakilaya, in particular, continued to be important to them in later times.

Könchok Gyalpo's son, Sakyapa Künga Nyingpo (1092–1158), became his spiritual successor and was the first Khön-family lama to adopt the lamdre teachings. It was one of Künga Nyingpo's primary accomplishments to bring together and systematize the teachings received from his father, including the various sutra and tantra instructions, along with their commentaries. Like his father, Künga Nyingpo was an accomplished scholar. In his training, he had studied the Abhidharma, epistemology, Madhyamaka, the "five dharmas of Maitreya," medicine, sutras, and tantra. His tantra instruction included the *Hevajra Tantra* and the lamdre. A gifted author, he wrote eleven commentaries on various aspects of the teachings. Under Künga Nyingpo, the Sakya monastery rapidly became one of the major monastic centers in Tibet, renowned for the opportunity for monastic and scholarly training that it provided. Künga Nyingpo's third son, Jetsun Dagpa Gyaltshen, continued this writing activity in numerous extensive commentaries and explanations of the lamdre.

The form of succession that developed among the Sakya involved hereditary transmission, so that the lineage remained within the Khön family, as it does to this day. In the first few generations of Sakya hierarchs, a celibate lama was often the religious head of the order. When the time came for him to step down, the position was then passed to the son of one of his married brothers. In later times, the head of the Sakya order was often married. The Sakya monastery itself became renowned as a monastic university where monks could devote themselves to the preservation, study, and debate of the scholarly and academic traditions of Indian Buddhism, now coming to Tibet in the later spreading of the dharma.

Sakya Pandita, Künga Gyaltsen

One of the most important and influential masters of the tradition was the renowned scholar Sakya Pandita, Künga Gyaltsen (1182–1251), born to the fourth son of Künga Nyingpo. His birth and early life proclaim his remarkable academic capabilities and attainments. At birth, according to his biography, he began to speak Sanskrit, and as an infant he was able to write the Sanskrit letters. As a child, he could memorize and understand any dharma that he heard. He was ordained as a monk in his youth, and thereafter until the day he died, he followed the prescriptions in the Vinaya with great devotion and purity. In his monastic training, Sakya Pandita's studies ranged far and wide, and he became expert in the whole range of Buddhist literature available to him. In recognition of his unique academic talents, he was sent to many of the greatest scholars of his day to develop his knowledge as well as his analytical and debating skills. During his studies, he had numerous dreams in which the great Indian luminaries of Buddhist philosophy gave him direct transmissions of their teachings. Vasubandhu appeared in one dream and conferred knowledge of the Abhidharma, Dignaga passed to him the teachings on logic and epistemology, and so on.

In his scholarly work, Sakya Pandita attained a prominence unequaled by anyone else in his day. His specialties were logic and the theory of perception, and he wrote a textbook on this topic that is still respected. Samuel remarks, "Many of his writings have a strong flavor of controversy and logical disputation. His usual targets are the Nyingmapa and the Kagyüpa, both of whom he accuses of carrying on the rejected and morally suspect 'Chinese' tradition and of running the risk of omitting the necessary moral foundation of bodhicitta."[7] Unparalleled scholar that he was, Sakya Pandita was considered an emanation of Manjushri, the celestial bodhisattva of wisdom, and is depicted in the Tibetan painted scrolls known as *thangkas* with this deity's symbols, the sword of prajna and the text of the *Prajnaparamita*.

It was through Sakya Pandita that the Sakyapa formed an alliance with the Mongols and became the first monastic order to rule Tibet politically. In the thirteenth century, the Mongols were threatening to invade Tibet and in fact had already sacked several monasteries. An envoy was clearly needed to try to negotiate some kind of settlement. At the same time, the Mongol leader Godan heard of Sakya Pandita's reputation and summoned him to his court. Thus the lama journeyed to Godan's court, made full submission, and wrote a letter to the lamas, lords, and people of Tibet, praising Godan and expressing the hope for good relations. In 1260, Kublai Khan, who had become ruler of the Mongols and of China, made Sakya Pandita's nephew and successor, Phakpa (1235–1280), vassal ruler of all of Tibet. This arrangement, in which the Sakyapa were religious rulers of Tibet backed up by the Mongols, lasted until 1358, when—Mongol power having weakened—the Kagyü lama Changchub Gyaltsen, head of the Phagmotru lineage, seized power from the Sakya. From this time forward, until this century, one or another of the New Translation schools, backed by local or foreign power, stood in the position of religious rulers of Tibet. This arrangement had the obvious merit of enabling Buddhism to flourish in Tibet in a unique way. Under what other political system could such a high percentage of people (perhaps 20 percent) have participated in the monastic way of life or Buddhism have permeated the life of the culture so thoroughly? At the same time, this theocratic system was not without its drawbacks. In modern times, the absolute control of religion over the affairs of state was certainly one factor in keeping Tibet in its extreme isolation. This, in turn, made the Chinese takeover of Tibet in the 1950s relatively easy and without much political risk.

The Sakya Presentation of the Path: Lamdre

Lamdre means "path and fruition." The path (*lam*) consists of the practices that one carries out to advance toward enlightenment, while fruition (*dre*) is the state of enlightenment itself. In the Sakya system, particular emphasis is placed upon the inseparability of the path and the fruition. The underlying cause of buddhahood is the buddha-nature or the enlightenment within that is covered over by the defilements of ego. The purpose of the path is to remove these defilements, thus laying bare the brilliance of the innate inner wisdom. Thus the cause of buddhahood and its fruition are one, and the practitioner discovers this through the path. The path is inseparable from the fruition because it is inspired and driven onward by the cause, which is itself the fruition as it lies hidden within us.

As mentioned above, the lamdre teachings are divided into two broad categories: the three visions contain teaching common to Hinayana and Mahayana, while the three tantras outline the stages and practices of the Vajrayana path. Victoria Scott provides the following overview of the lamdre:

> The lam-dre system is derived from the *Hevajra Root Tantra.*
> It presents the essence of the tripartite Buddhist canon: ethical discipline (vinaya), discourses of the Buddha (sutra), and psychology/cosmology (abhidharma). The lam-dre is a complete and harmonious system of exoteric (sutric) and esoteric (tantric) methods. Its teachings have been passed down with special emphasis on the "four authenticities": authentic teachers, direct experiences, scriptures, and treatises. Central to the lam-dre system is its unique and profound view of "the non-differentiation of samsara and nirvana, within which perfect enlightenment, or buddhahood, is to be realized. There the nature of mind is

explained as "the root of samsara and nirvana," and "the union of luminosity and emptiness."[8]

THE THREE VISIONS

The *Vajragatha* states the three visions in the following verse:

> For sentient beings with afflictions
> is the impure vision.
> For the meditator with trance absorption
> is the vision of experience.
> For the ornamental wheel of the Sugata's*
> inexhaustible body, voice and mind
> is the pure vision.

This set of verses, then, and its classical commentary by Ngorchen Konchog Lhundrub, *The Beautiful Ornament of the Three Visions,* divides all sentient beings into three categories according to their level of spiritual maturation. According to Lhundrub, the first verse gives us a picture of ordinary sentient beings trapped within the six realms of samsara and points to the endless suffering they endure. This verse also confronts us with the reality and uncertainty of the time of death and reminds us that human life provides a unique opportunity to practice the dharma. Finally, this section explains teachings on karma, that one's present condition is a result of former actions and that one's present actions will determine one's future condition. Section one, then, presents a version of the well-known Tibetan teaching on the "four reminders," discussed in chapter 10 of this book.

The commentary on the second verse speaks about the Buddhist path, dividing it into two general sections. First is the common path, which describes the commitments of the buddha-dharma, including the taking of the bodhisattva vow, the generation of *bodhichitta* (mind of enlightenment), actions based on compassion, and the meditation of *shamatha* (development of peace) and *vipashyana* (insight). These are the practices

---

Sugata means "One Gone to Bliss," i.e., the Buddha.

148

engaged in by practitioners at the Hinayana and Mahayana level of the path (described in chapters 10–13). The second verse of the "vision of experience" outlines the extraordinary teachings and practices of the Vajrayana. It enjoins practitioners to seek out a qualified teacher, to request tantric empowerments and their accompanying oral instructions, and—having received them—to carry out the practices diligently until realization is attained.

The commentary on the "pure vision" depicts the final goal of the Buddhist path, the complete enlightenment of a buddha. Here is discussed the enlightened body, speech, and mind of a fully realized one.

THE THREE TANTRAS

The three tantras represent a particular presentation of the *Hevajra Tantra,* the root tantra of the Sakya tradition. The teachings are divided into three categories, the causal tantra, the path tantra, and the fruition (or result) tantra.

The *causal tantra* teachings point to the fact that the buddha-nature within lacks inherent existence. Any idea that we may have of it is invalid. Any quality that we may attribute to it is merely our projection. In fact, it stands beyond any and all conceptualization as that which cannot be known by ordinary knowledge. Lama Yuthok notes:

> This involves an initiation which reveals to us that our mind has always been pure and untainted. We have simply failed to recognise this in the past. We try to recognise the true self, which is not the way it appears. The self which appears is not the self. But there is a mode of existence of the self which is incomprehensible.[9]

The teachings on buddha-nature are discussed in chapter 16.

Through the path tantra, we are given Vajrayana initiations, methods, and practices that enable us to gain access to this incomprehensible self within. Lama Yuthok comments:

> That incomprehensible self is articulated in the form of deities, using gestures and symbolism to help us identity with this ideal

self. We try to meditate in that form, rather than as the ordinary self.

We assume the role of a Buddha, who can express different moods and shapes, hold different implements and express divine enlightened qualities. Therefore we do not meditate on the "nihilistic" concept of emptiness which focuses on non-existence. We employ a creative concept of emptiness, which makes everything possible. We create a world, a celestial mansion. The meditator himself is the Buddha. The whole process becomes an expression of the ideal self, which is no different from the universal consciousness of all enlightened beings.[10]

Through the methods of tantric meditation, one's usual, habitual, ego-centered patterns of body, speech, and mind are temporarily replaced by patterns of non-ego or enlightened body, speech, and mind of a buddha. This destabilizes our ego's mechanisms. The ego's usual "total lock" on experience is disrupted. One begins to become more and more uncertain about who one is or what one is doing. This provides gaps in the ego's shell, and the buddha-nature can begin to shine through. The more it shines through, the more shaky and impotent the ego becomes. The more the ego-centered consciousness begins to dissolve, the stronger the light of buddha-nature becomes. It is a process that accelerates the further along it goes.[11]

The fruition or result tantra is understood as mahamudra.[12] Lama Choedak Yuthok comments as follows:

When a person reaches this level, which is enlightenment, he will see all beings as Buddhas and Bodhisattvas. This is also known as resultant Mahamudra. Within the Sakya tradition we use the term Mahamudra only when discussing ultimate realisation. At this stage, there is nothing to think. No language, no matter how eloquent, could express this state. It is better not expressed. It transcends all knowledge. It is not knowledge, it cannot be shared. It is so deep that one cannot see its beginning. It does not cease. It is permanent. It is like the sky. It is self-cognisant. There is no feeling of omniscience in the enlightened person, because there is no knowable thing outside of himself. Self-cognisant means self-realising. The realised person knows that the knowing of anything is the knowing of self. The world is no other than self. The self is no other than the world . . . There is no output, there is no input. It is just as it is. But it is flexible. It can play. It can manifest anything.[13]

Conclusion

The Sakya, then, represents a lineage in which an attempt is made to integrate and balance the exoteric scholarly monastic path with the esoteric path of the tantras. Lobsang Dagpa and Jay Goldberg comment that "throughout its history, members of the Sakya tradition who have been considered masters have been those who brought the aspects of study and practice into a proper balance."[14] In terms of scholarship, the Sakyapas have produced many generations of eminent scholar-monks and have maintained a tradition of rigorous intellectual training from which the Gelukpas were later to draw a great deal. Through their tantric lineages, they have produced many realized masters, including the great nineteenth-century yogin-scholar Jamyang Khyenste Wangpo, one of the founders and propagators of the Ri-me movement.

7
The Later Spreading
KAGYÜ

WHEREAS BOTH THE KADAM AND SAKYA SCHOOLS WERE inspired and shaped largely by conventional Indian monasticism, the Kagyü order originated from strictly tantric roots, at least for the first few generations of teachers and disciples. Again, while the Kadampas and Sakyapas were institutionalized from the outset, for several generations, the Kagyü lineage was passed on from master to disciple, only beginning to take its present institutional, monastic shape with Gampopa and the early Karmapas. The following briefly summarizes the lives of the Kagyü founders as a way of typifying the lineage and illustrating its particular qualities of unconventionality, meditation, and the devotion of disciple for master.

TILOPA: HUMAN FOUNDER OF THE KAGYÜ LINEAGE

Tilopa is born a brahman (member of the priestly caste) and, as a young man, renounces the world and takes monastic ordination, living in a monastery presided over by his uncle. After a short period, however, he has a vision of a dakini who gives him tantric initiation and instruction and sets him to meditating. She tells him, "Now speak like a madman and, after throwing off your monk's robes, practice in secret."[1] Then abruptly she disappears. Like other tantric practitioners, through abandoning the monastic life, appearing to be mad, and practicing in secret,

SOME DATES OF KAGYÜ HISTORY

988–1069	Tilopa (human founder of the Kagyü)
1016–1100	Naropa (Tilopa's primary disciple, guru of Marpa)
11th CENTURY	Maitripa (teacher of Marpa)
1012–1096	Marpa (Tibetan founder of the Kagyü)
1040–1123	Milarepa (disciple of Marpa)
1079	Gampopa born 1110 Gampopa becomes disciple of Milarepa
1110–1193	Tüsum Khyenpa

1175–1189	Monasteries of some of the Kagyü subsects founded
	
	  1158 Phagmotrupa founds monastery of Thil
	  1175 Monastery of Tshal founded
	  1179 Drigung monastery founded
	  1189 Tsurphu monastery founded by Karmapa
	     Tüsum Khyenpa (1110–1193)

1284–1339	Rangjung Dorje, third Karmapa
1354	Fighting between Sakyapas and Kagyüpas; former defeated; end of Sakya hegemony; beginning of Phagmotrupa rule
1358	Changchub Gyaltsen takes over power.

Tilopa is enjoined to separate himself from conventional values and pursuits. In particular, by acting crazy, he puts himself in the category of outcaste, living beyond the pale of Hindu society, reviled and abused by others. All of this is to enable him to separate himself from the deceptive comforts and security of egoic existence within society.

Tilopa follows the dakini's instructions, wandering from place to place and meditating. Encountering obstacles, he seeks out and receives instruction from several gurus, all of them siddhas. Eventually, he is instructed to go to Bengal and to carry out his practice while pounding sesame seeds by day and acting as the servant of a prostitute by night. In these circumstances, defiling in the extreme for a brahman, he meditates, some sources say for twelve years. Having completed this phase of his practice, Tilopa realizes that he needs to withdraw completely from the provocations of ordinary life. He goes to Bengal and enters into retreat, in a tiny grass hut that he builds for himself. There, finally, he comes face-to-face with reality, in the person of the celestial buddha Vajradhara in the highest celestial realm. He later remarks, "I have no human guru. My guru is the Omniscient One. I have conversed directly with the Buddha."

Following his realization, Tilopa wanders about, bringing others onto the path and instructing them in the Vajrayana way. He becomes renowned as a powerful and unpredictable master, who in the service of the dharma, like other siddhas, often performs actions considered shocking or scandalous in a conventional setting. He spends much of his time in cremation grounds, practicing and teaching, as is common for the other siddhas. When debating with non-Buddhists, he often makes his points by means of miracles rather than discursive argument.

Although Tilopa had several human teachers, his role as progenitor of the Kagyü lineage stems from his having met the celestial buddha Vajradhara face-to-face and received teachings directly from him. Tilopa's lineage includes teachings on mahamudra received directly from Vajradhara; practices of inner yoga that make up the "six yogas of Naropa"; and anuttara-yoga tantra transmissions including father, mother, and nondual tantras.

NAROPA: SCHOLAR TURNED SIDDHA

Naropa, Tilopa's primary disciple, is born in wealthy circumstances, the favored son of a kshatriya (ruling caste in India) family. At seventeen, he is compelled by his parents to marry. After eight years of marriage, however, he announces his intention to renounce the world. He and his wife agree to a divorce, and Naropa, like Tilopa, takes ordination into the monastic way. Unlike Tilopa, however, Naropa invests many years

FIGURE 7.1 *Naropa, an Indian mahasiddha whose teaching reached Tibet through his Tibetan student Marpa. The tantric practices associated with Naropa are central to the Kagyü school.*

in intensive study, mastering the major branches and varieties of Buddhist texts, including the Vinaya, Sutras, and Abhidharma of the Hinayana, the Prajnaparamita of the Mahayana, and the tantras. Eventually, he rises to the top of his religious profession, becoming first a high-ranking scholar at Nalanda and then its supreme abbot. His fame as a scholar spreads everywhere, and he is considered unexcelled in his understanding of Buddhist doctrine.

One day, in one of the many courtyards of Nalanda, Naropa is sitting with his back to the sun studying texts on grammar, logic, and other topics. Suddenly, a terrifying shadow falls over him. He turns to see an old woman, dark blue in color, with red, sunken eyes, a yellow beard, a distorted gaping mouth, and rotten teeth. She is leaning on a cane, wheezing and panting. She asks Naropa, "What are you looking into?" When Naropa enumerates the texts he is studying, the old woman asks him whether he understands the words or the inner meaning. When he replies that he understands the words, the old woman is delighted, rocking with laughter, and she begins to dance, waving her cane in the air.

Naropa, to make her even more happy, adds, "And I also understand the inner meaning." At this, the old woman begins to tremble and weep, hurling down her cane. When Naropa questions her about this sudden change in mood, she replies, "When you, a great scholar, admitted that you understand only the words of the dharma, you told the truth, and this made me happy. But then you lied, saying that you also understand the inner meaning, which you do not. This made me sad."

Naropa, initially shocked and speechless, then takes the plunge that will change his life. He asks the old crone, "Who understands the inner meaning and how can I come to the same understanding?" She directs him to her "brother" and, without specifying who her brother is or where he may be found, adds, "Go yourself, pay your respects to him, and beg him that you may come to grasp the inner meaning." Then this dakini—for that is what she is—disappears, "like a rainbow in the sky."[2]

Perhaps many of us would reject such an experience as too bizarre to be taken seriously. Particularly those of us with some accomplishments under our belt and some reputation to protect would find it much easier to revert back to our achievements and to quickly forget about the "nightmare" we had had. It is to Naropa's credit, and a mark of his devotion to something beyond ego, that he takes a different tack. He goes before the assembly of monks at Nalanda and announces his intention to seek the "brother" of the dakini, whose identity and name he does not know and whose location he has not been told.

The monks at Nalanda think that Naropa has gone crazy. They point out to him that the monastic way, with its study and ethical behavior, represents the epitome of Buddhism and that to abandon this path would be a great sin against the true dharma. They recall to him the years he has spent studying and the investment he has made in his learning. They beg him not to throw away the illustrious position he has attained in such a precipitous and ill-considered fashion. They also remind him that the king of the region, the patron and protector of Nalanda, will be most displeased with Naropa's actions. They warn that if he goes ahead with his intention, his reputation will be forever ruined. However, Naropa will not be dissuaded from his mad and perilous quest: he throws away all of his texts, on which he has spent so many years, takes his begging bowl and staff, and heads off in an easterly direction, into the jungles, in search of his guru.

Naropa searches for Tilopa "in the east," in jungles and deserts, in mountains and valleys, in villages and uninhabited regions. He finds this quest trying, confusing, and agonizing, for he has many strange experiences that he rejects as irrelevant to his search, only to discover with each of them in retrospect that they were marked by Tilopa's presence. As he wanders, Naropa experiences over and over his own obstacles: an overly conceptual understanding of the dharma; a thick and unyielding pride accumulated from so many years of study; and the scholar's arrogance of thinking he knows what things are. Eventually, Naropa becomes exhausted over his failure to find Tilopa—and exasperated by his own mind—and falls into deep depression. He despairs that he has thrown away his former life yet cannot find any new one. Unable to go back to who he was, he seems prevented by his own obstacles from going forward to who he feels he must be. Believing that his own karma is so negative that he will never find his destined guru in this life, he determines to kill himself. He takes a knife and prepares to cut open his veins.

At this moment, Tilopa appears, a blue-black man dressed in cotton trousers, with a topknot and bulging bloodshot eyes. He declares that ever since Naropa formed the intention to seek him, Tilopa has not been separate from him and that it was only Naropa's defilements that blinded him to this fact. He tells Naropa that he is a worthy vessel, will indeed be able to receive the deepest teachings, and that he will accept him as a disciple.

For the next twelve years, Naropa is Tilopa's disciple, undergoing a most demanding tutelage. He suffers immensely through all kinds of physical, psychological, and spiritual trials, torments, and tribulations. The rigor of his training is in direct measure, he understands, to the karmic accretions and obscurations that he has accumulated in his previous lives. Each of Tilopa's teachings is a catastrophe for Naropa's sense of personal identity, and in each instance he believes himself to have been irreparably and mortally harmed. In each case Tilopa reveals a deeper level of Naropa's being, one that is open, clear, and resplendent, independent of the life and death of ego. Throughout this period, Tilopa says very little, and Naropa's instruction occurs in nonverbal ways, through his own pain and through symbolic gestures that he must assimilate. No security and certainly no confirmation is ever given, and Naropa is able to persevere out of complete devotion to Tilopa and his conviction that he has no other options.

After twelve years of training, one day Naropa is standing with Tilopa on a barren plane. Tilopa remarks that the time has now come for him to offer Naropa the much-sought-after oral instructions, the transmission of dharma. When Tilopa demands an offering, Naropa, who has nothing, offers his own fingers and blood. As Lama Taranatha recounts the event:

> Then Tilopa, having collected the fingers of Naropa, hit him in the face with a dirty sandal and Naropa instantly lost consciousness. When he regained consciousness, he directly perceived the ultimate truth, the suchness of all reality, and his fingers were

restored. He was now granted the complete primary and subsidiary oral instructions. Thereupon, Naropa became a lord of
yogins.[3]

From Tilopa, Naropa receives the transmissions of mahamudra, the
six inner yogas, and the anuttara-yoga tantras, and himself becomes a
realized siddha in the tradition of his master. Naropa is subsequently
seen sometimes roaming through the jungles, sometimes defeating here-
tics, sometimes in male-female aspect (that is, in union with his consort,
a mark of his realization), hunting deer with a pack of hounds, at other
times performing magical feats, at still other times acting like a small
child, playing, laughing, and weeping. As a realized master, he accepts
disciples, and through all of his activities, however benign or unconventional and shocking they may be, he reveals the awakened state beyond
thought, imbued with wisdom, compassion, and power. He is also a
prolific author whose previous scholarly training enables him to be an
eloquent writer on Vajrayana topics, evidenced by his works surviving
in the Tenjur.

Naropa is a pivotal figure in the evolution of the Kagyü lineage for
the way in which he joins tantric practice and more traditional scholarship, unreasoning devotion and the rationality of intellect. Through
him, Tilopa's profound and untamed lineage is brought out of the jungles of east India and given a form which the Tibetan householder
Marpa can receive.

MARPA: HOUSEHOLDER-YOGIN

The biographies of Tilopa and Naropa reveal the intense, committed,
and uncompromising spirituality of these Indian founders of the Kagyü
lineage. These qualities subsequently remain features of the Kagyü,
which, among the four schools of Tibetan Buddhism, as mentioned, is
known for its particular emphasis on the devotion of disciple for teacher
and for intensive meditation in retreat.

Tilopa and Naropa represent rather different kinds of people, the
former being an anonymous yogin roaming like a specter through the

FIGURE 7.2 *Marpa, the Tibetan householder-yogin who was the Tibetan founder of the Kagyü lineage.*

jungles of Northeast India, the latter a world-renowned scholar who abandoned what most people would consider an extraordinarily favorable situation. Marpa, the Tibetan founder of the Kagyü lineage, represents yet another type of person. Born in 1012 of relatively prosperous parents in southern Tibet, as a young boy Marpa is depicted as possessing a fearsome temper and a violent and stubborn disposition. He is what one might call a holy terror, and while he is still young his parents send him off to be trained in the dharma with a variety of teachers. Marpa soon realizes that one has to make a lot of offerings in order to receive even basic teachings, let alone more advanced ones. Moreover, Tibetan teachers often guard their transmissions jealously, and Marpa is repeatedly rebuffed when he seeks the higher initiations. Eventually, he comes to the conclusion that to receive the full measure of dharma instruction, he will have to journey to India. His parents capitulate, and Marpa sets off over the Himalayas on a long, tedious, and dangerous journey to India, the first of three trips he will make to the holy land.

While staying in Nepal before descending to the Indian plains, Marpa hears of the siddha Naropa. His biography states, "A connection from a former life was reawakened in Marpa and he felt immeasurable yearning."[4] While many of his Tibetan contemporaries arrived in India and went straight to one or another of the great Indian monasteries for tantric instruction, Marpa takes a different course, bypassing the monastic scene, seeking for his yogin teacher in the forest. Marpa eventually finds Naropa, is accepted as a disciple, and receives extensive instruction and initiation from him. For twelve years, Marpa studies with Naropa and also with other siddhas to whom Naropa sends him. The most important of these is Maitripa from whom Marpa receives instructions on mahamudra. At the end of this time, he returns to Tibet, marries a spiritually gifted Tibetan woman named Damema, begins to teach, and establishes himself as a well-to-do farmer. Subsequently, Marpa returns to India a second time, on this occasion studying with Naropa for six years. At the end of his visit, at Naropa's request, Marpa promises to return yet one more time to India to complete his training. When Marpa arrives back in Tibet, he gathers around him a number of close disciples, including Milarepa, to whom he will eventually entrust the full transmission of his dharma. Finally, although well into middle age and over the strenuous objections of his family, Marpa sets off for his third and final journey to India.

In previous journeys his relationship with his guru had gone relatively smoothly. Now, however, when he arrives in India, Marpa finds a very different situation, one that plunges him into experiences of agony, searching, and aloneness that are so often characteristic of tantric students in their relation to their teachers. Marpa searches high and low for Naropa and cannot find him. He is informed by one of Naropa's disciples that the master, like other siddhas before him, has disappeared into the jungles to follow a hidden and anonymous path and that there is no hope whatever that Marpa will find him. After more searching, Marpa abandons all hope of ever seeing Naropa again. At this moment, Naropa appears and the disciple is able to communicate with his master without the barriers that had formerly existed between them. After three years of further study, Marpa returns to Tibet to continue his teaching.

Now, however, tragedy strikes. Marpa has seven sons, but only one possesses special gifts for helping others. Marpa greatly loves this one son, named Tarma Dode, and fixes all his hopes on him for carrying on his spiritual lineage. Naropa had predicted that there would be a serious obstacle and said that Tarma Dode would have to do a strict retreat and complete a certain number of mantra recitations. Tarma Dode undertakes this retreat but, in the middle, learns that there is a great festival in the area with many people going. He thinks to himself that his retreat is boring and lonely, and that he does not want to waste his youth in this way. He breaks off his retreat and, taking a horse, gallops off to join the fun. As he is riding with others of Marpa's disciples, suddenly a partridge flies up from the bushes and Tarma Dode's startled horse bolts, causing the young man to fall. Catching his foot in the stirrup, he is dragged along the ground and his skull is broken.

Milarepa catches up with the horse and, freeing Tarma Dode's foot, holds his friend's shattered head in his lap, weeping. The other disciples arrive, and Tarma Dode's unconscious body is carried back to Marpa's house. His father and mother, seeing that he is mortally injured, hold him with terrible grief as his life ebbs away. The son regains consciousness briefly and expresses his own sorrow that now he will not only be unable to repay the kindnesses of his parents, but will cause them further suffering. Tarma Dode now performs the practice known as *phowa,* the ejection of the consciousness at death. Transferring his consciousness to the body of a pigeon, he dies. At his cremation, his mother, beside herself with anguish, attempts to throw herself into the funeral pyre, but is prevented by the disciples.

Marpa's biography tells us that the pigeon flies to India, where its consciousness enters the body of a newly dead brahman boy. This youth, by the name of Tiphupa, suddenly comes back to life and reveals his true identity to his startled parents. When Milarepa's disciple Rechungpa goes to India, he is said to meet and study with Tiphupa. In subsequent years, Marpa continues to teach and transmit his lineage to his four chief disciples. Among these is Milarepa, who, since Marpa's son had been killed, now becomes his primary dharma heir.

Marpa's biography recounts his passing:

> After teaching and working solely for the benefit of beings his entire life, on the fifteenth day of the Horse month in the Bird year (1093), as the sun dawned over the mountain peaks, Marpa, eighty-eight years old, was free from sickness in body and joyful in mind. A rainbow appeared in the sky and various flowers rained down. There arose sounds of various kinds of music ravishing to the mind and immeasurable kinds of delightful scents. Smiling, Marpa shed tears, joined his palms together, closed his eyes, bowed his head again, and performed the sevenfold service.[5]

When asked by a disciple what is happening, he replies, "Prepare excellent offerings. Glorious Naropa surrounded by immeasurable hosts of dakas and dakinis has arrived to escort me as he promised. Now I must go to the celestial realm as his attendant."[6] Then Marpa passed away.

Marpa's biographer remarks, "Marpa was the sun of the Buddha's teaching, and in particular, he dispelled the darkness in the Land of Snow and was the life tree of the teachings of the secret mantra." Marpa was so extraordinary because he appeared so ordinary, as a farmer with a large family, heavy worldly responsibilities, and a temper to boot. At the same time, he was a realized being, a person who had "achieved inner luminosity and mastered prana and mind."

> Even though he had completely realized the immeasurable virtues of the transference of consciousness, miracles, higher perceptions, and the like, he lived in a hidden manner. Appearing to share the outlook of ordinary people, he enjoyed the five qualities that please the senses and the eight worldly dharmas. Thus he benefitted many worthy vessels.[7]

Marpa's attainment can be seen clearly in the devotion and accomplishments of his disciples, primary among whom was Milarepa.

Marpa lived at a time when Buddhism was just beginning to be reimported from India, and he is remembered for playing a principal role in these early days of the later spreading. He is known as "Marpa the Translator, in recognition of his work rendering important Indian texts into Tibetan. Marpa also introduced into Tibet a new kind of religious poetry, the *dohas,* or songs of realization of the Indian Vajrayana, a form subsequently developed and made famous by Milarepa. His most important accomplishment, however, was receiving the lineage of Tilopa and Naropa, bringing it to Tibet and, through his training of Milarepa, acting as the Tibetan forefather of the Kagyü lineage.

Marpa trained in the dharma not as a yogin or a monk, but rather as a layperson. He lived an ordinary life in the world, experiencing the joys and sorrows of household life, and these became vehicles of his path and expressions of his realization. In this, he harked back to the style of many of the greatest Indian siddhas who were householders when they met their gurus, while they were in training, and after they had achieved realization. Marpa is noteworthy in the modern context because he provides a model of the lay tantric practitioner that, unlike those of the hermit, the wandering yogin, or the monastic person, may be feasible for the majority of Buddhist practitioners in the contemporary world.

MILAREPA: TIBET'S GREATEST YOGIN

Most biographies of Tibetan saints present their subjects in an idealized fashion, as if, from the very beginning of their lives, they were already far above the ordinary human condition. In these accounts, the saints are born amid wonders, recognized from birth as destined for greatness, and portrayed as exceptional at each stage of life. Their enlightenment is a kind of obvious conclusion to everything preceding. This kind of presentation can be inspiring and elicit devotion on the part of followers, but it does create the impression that full realization is not something that most of us can aspire to, at least in the present lifetime.

The life of Milarepa provides a striking exception to this general trend. We find in Milarepa's life a person who, in his early years, is about as confused, self-destructive, and misguided as anyone could possibly be. And yet, through perseverance and great devotion to his teacher, he attains complete enlightenment in one life. Milarepa's biography shows how any ordinary person can aspire to the highest goal. It is perhaps for this reason that the life of Milarepa, told in the first person, is one of the best-loved and best-known of all sacred biographies of Tibet.

Milarepa is born in southern Tibet, in a place called Kya Ngatsa, near Gungthang in the Tsangpo River valley. In his early childhood, he enjoys a warm and prosperous family life. However, his father dies while he is still a small boy. Following this tragedy, through a poorly conceived will, Milarepa's aunt and uncle take custodial control of all of the family's considerable property and wealth. Within the arrangement, Milarepa, his sister, Peta, and his mother are turned into virtual slaves in their own house. Milarepa comments, "In summer, at the time for work in the fields, we were the servants of the uncle. In winter, while working with wool, we were servants of the aunt. Our food was fit for dogs, our work for donkeys. For clothes, some strips of rags were thrown over our shoulders and held together with a rope of grass. Working without rest, our limbs became raw and sore. Due to bad food and poor clothing we became pale and emaciated."[8] When, as specified in the will, the time comes for the return of the family wealth to Milarepa's mother, Mila, and his sister, the uncle and aunt falsify the original document, claiming that all the family's possessions belong to them.

FIGURE 7.3 *Milarepa, Marpa's main disciple and Tibet's most beloved yogin.*

Milarepa's mother is by now obsessed with hatred and vindictive rage against the uncle and aunt, and communicates this to her children. She eventually conceives a plan to take revenge, sending Mila to study with a lama skilled in spells that can bring ruin upon these enemies. Milarepa, the dutiful and unquestioning son, leaves home to do his mother's bidding. He finds a lama to instruct him and, after more than a year of study, is given the destructive practices that he seeks. Building a small ritual house on the ridge of a mountain, he calls on the protector deities to destroy the uncle and aunt. After fourteen days, signs of success appear: "The loyal deities . . . brought us what we had asked for: the heads and the bleeding hearts of thirty-five people."[9] Only two are left alive, and when they ask Milarepa if these too should be killed, he replies, "Let them live so they may know my vengeance and my justice."[10] Later, Milarepa learns that there had been a wedding feast of the uncle's eldest son in the family house. When all the people were gathered, the horses in the stable below the living quarters went mad and pulled the house down. Thirty-five people were killed, but the two who were allowed to live were none other than the uncle and aunt. Nevertheless, the vengeance is satisfying to Milarepa's mother, and she publicly rejoices in the carnage that has occurred.

The karmic retribution for this crime begins immediately. Villagers plot to kill Milarepa, who is hated and feared for what he has done. He is able to fend off their aggression only by threatening further destruction. He is stalked as a murderer, but one that is too dangerous to confront directly. Milarepa begins to realize what he has done and the terrible karmic consequences that he has brought upon himself through his actions. He knows that retribution for murder is rebirth in hell, with aeons of terrible suffering, and he has killed not one but thirty-five people. Milarepa's teacher expresses regret at what has happened and declares his intention to seek the dharma to save himself from whatever evil consequences he has incurred. Milarepa realizes that, for himself also, the only alternative to a fearful, lower rebirth is to seek purification through sincere practice.

Milarepa wanders about the Tibetan countryside, looking for a teacher to help him. He meets a Nyingma lama, who indicates his inability to help but suggests a master by the name of Marpa the Translator. Milarepa tells us, "Hardly had I heard the name of Marpa the Translator than I was filled with ineffable happiness. In my joy, every hair on my body vibrated. I sobbed with fervent adoration. Locking my whole mind with a single thought, I set out with provisions and a book.

Without being distracted by any other thoughts, I ceaselessly repeated to myself, 'When? When will I see the lama face-to-face?' "[11]

Milarepa eventually finds Marpa plowing a field near his house. He and his wife, Damema, have both had dreams about the arrival of an important disciple, and Marpa is in fact waiting for Milarepa. But he lets on none of this. When Milarepa confesses the evil he has done through his black magic and begs Marpa for teachings, Marpa sets him to work as a menial laborer, as a preliminary to his receiving instruction. Marpa's treatment of "the Great Magician," as he now called Milarepa, is demanding, seemingly unreasonable, and harsh. The work escalates until, eventually, Milarepa is commanded to build a watchtower for Marpa. When this tower is completed, Marpa seems to change his mind and demands that Milarepa tear it down and build another tower in a different location. This happens four times. As each previous tower is torn down and Milarepa is ordered to build another one, Marpa promises that if the next project is completed, he will surely give Milarepa the desired teachings. Yet, each time, Marpa reneges at the last moment.

Months turn into years, and still the desired empowerments and instructions are not forthcoming. In the meantime, other disciples studying with Marpa seem to be freely receiving the very teachings that Milarepa covets. Milarepa is lost, confused, and beside himself with frustration. Yet he stays with Marpa and tries to fulfill each new demand. Milarepa's great suffering is illustrated by the following typical example. On one occasion, Marpa is giving a Chakrasamvara initiation to a group of people. Milarepa, who has just completed the fourth tower at Marpa's command, tells us:

> In my heart I thought, "Now that I have built this tower. . . . I am going to receive the initiation." Then, after having greeted the lama, I sat down with the others. The lama called to me, "Great Magician, what gift do you bring me?" I answered, "I rendered you homage by building the tower. . . . You promised to give me initiation and instruction. That is why I am here."
>
> "You made a little tower which isn't even as thick as my arm. It is hardly worth the Doctrine which I, with great difficulty,

brought all the way from India. If you have the price of my teaching, give it to me. Otherwise do not stay here among the initiates of the secret teaching." Speaking thus, the lama slapped me, grabbed me by the hair, and threw me out. I wanted to die and I wept the whole night. The lama's wife came to console me.[12]

Yet, in spite of his agonies, Milarepa's devotion to his teacher never wanes. On another occasion, Mila attempts to receive teachings by offering as a gift a turquoise given him by Damema. Marpa responds by beating him and throwing him out of the assembly. The next morning, the lama sends for Mila and asks, "Are you not dissatisfied by my refusal to teach you? Do you not have evil thoughts?"

"I have faith in the lama," I answered, "and I have not uttered a single word of rebellion. On the contrary, I believe that I am in darkness on account of my sins. I am the author of my own misery." I wept. And he continued, "What do you expect to gain from me by these tears? Get out!"[13]

As time goes by and Marpa's demands on Milarepa seem more and more excessive and unreasonable, Milarepa's frustration turns into desperation and eventually black despair. He attempts to run away from Marpa several times, each time returning because he realizes that he has nowhere else to go. The only saving grace in the situation seems to be Marpa's wife, Damema, who expresses a steady kindness and love toward Milarepa. Finally, Milarepa can bear no more. He decides that his karma in this life is so black that he will never be able to receive the teachings he desires. He determines that his only remaining course is to kill himself and hope that in a future rebirth his fortunes will be better. Marpa's other disciples restrain him, but Milarepa has given up all hope and cannot be consoled. Still, they stay with him, fearful that he will fulfill his desire to die.

Marpa, well aware of Milarepa's sufferings, has often enough secretly shed tears before his wife and expressed his love for Great Magician. On this occasion, again, he weeps and says to Damema, "Disciples of the secret path must be such as these." He now extends an invitation to all of his students to appear before him. Although included in the invitation, Milarepa cannot bring himself to go, thinking that on this occasion again, Marpa will verbally attack him and beat him. Informed, Marpa replied, "In the past, he would have been right. But today, I shall not do the same as before. Great Magician is to be the principal guest. Let the mistress go and fetch him!"

Milarepa comes but is filled with apprehension lest this be yet another trick and that further suffering lie in store for him. Instead, Marpa, for the first time, speaks openly about Milarepa's path and his own devotion and love for his student.

> If everything is carefully examined, not one of us is to be blamed. I have merely tested Great Magician to purify him of his sins. If the work on the tower had been intended for my own gain, I would have been gentle in the giving of orders. Therefore I was sincere. Being a woman, the mistress was also right not to be able to bear the situation. . . . Great Magician was burning with desire for religion, and he was right to use any means to obtain it. . . . his great sins have been erased. . . . Now, I receive you and will give you my teaching, which is as dear to me as my own heart. I will help you with provisions and let you meditate and be happy.[14]

Milarepa tells us:

> As he was saying these words I wondered, Is this a dream or am I awake? If it is a dream, I wish never to awaken. At this thought my happiness was boundless. Shedding tears of joy, I prostrated myself. The mistress . . . and the others thought, "What skillful means and power the lama has when he wants to accept a disciple! The lama himself is a Living Buddha." And their faith grew still more. Out of love for me they all cheerfully prostrated themselves before the lama.[15]

On this occasion, Marpa tells Milarepa, "My son, from the very first moment, I knew you were a disciple capable of receiving the teaching.

The night before you came here I learned from a dream that you were destined to serve the teaching of Buddha. . . . In this way, my lama and the guardian deity sent you do me as a disciple."[16]

Milarepa now receives the teachings that he has desired for so many years and enters retreat to practice them. His only habitation is whatever isolated cave in the mountains he is able to find. His only garment is a cloth of white cotton, hence his name, Mila the *repa* ("cotton-cloth one"). During his retreats, he eats whatever he has been able to beg in the villages ahead of time, and often he subsists only on a tea brewed from nettles that grow wild in the mountains. In the winter months, the heavy snows cut off his retreat places from all human contact for months.

As Milarepa's fame grows, more and more people come to visit him. Among these are sometimes local monastic prelates and scholars who, following the very different lifestyle of settled monasticism, are suspicious of Milarepa and jealous of the veneration he receives from his disciples and from the devoted laity. Some of these monks attempt to discredit and even to harm him; others find love for and connection to him, renounce the monastic life, and became yogin disciples.

Over time, a circle of devoted disciples gather around Milarepa. Like their master, they renounce the world, donning a cotton cloth as their only garment, begging their food in the villages, and spending most of their time in retreat, meditating. By the time of his passing, Milarepa has a small circle of close disciples who will carry on his teachings, including the yogin Rechungpa and the monk Gampopa.

Until his death at eighty-four, Milarepa lives in remote places, practicing meditation throughout the day and most of each night. His biography (*The Life of Milarepa*) and collections of his songs (*The Hundred Thousand Songs of Milarepa, Drinking the Mountain Stream,* and *The Miraculous Journey*) give a vivid and inspiring account of his life in retreat, showing the rigors and trials of such an existence, and also its joys and fulfillments.

It is hard to understand how a gentle and understated if persevering meditator like Milarepa who spent most of his adult life in mountain retreats could be the source of teachings so powerful that they would affect an entire culture. And yet this is exactly what happened. In subsequent times, Milarepa's lineage developed into the Kagyü school which, in its four great and eight lesser branches, was one of Tibet's most important and influential Buddhist traditions, giving rise to generations of accomplished masters. Milarepa himself became Tibet's most beloved yogin, and his life story was known to every Tibetan. His songs established a new genre in Tibetan expression and were known and loved not only by those who carried on his lineage in mountain retreats but by others as well.

THE DHARMA HEIRS RECHUNGPA AND GAMPOPA, AND THE SUBSEQUENT LINEAGE

Milarepa receives a prophecy that he will have two primary disciples, Rechungpa, who will be like the moon, and Gampopa, who will be like the sun.

Rechungpa

While Rechungpa is a young boy, his father dies, causing him and his family great suffering. Rechungpa is quite adept at reading and goes around reciting texts for people in exchange for offerings. One day, when he is eleven years old, he notices people gathering at a cave in the valley. Going to the cave, he finds Milarepa inside, singing a song of realization. Rechungpa feels himself strongly drawn to the master and tells him of his own sorrow and hardships. Milarepa speaks kindly to him, telling of his own early pain, of meeting Marpa, and of his joy in the practice of dharma. Rechungpa sees in Milarepa his spiritual mentor, father, and guide. He does not return home but stays with Milarepa and studies under him, taking refuge and bodhisattva vows, then receiving Vajrayana empowerment and beginning the practice.

Rechungpa's uncle and mother are extremely angry at this apprenticeship and one day kidnap him, tying him up and dragging him back to their home. Since he cannot be trusted to recite texts, they said, he will have to work in the fields. This work is terrible for such a young boy, and he contracts leprosy. His mother and uncle eventually throw him out of the house and tell him to go and make his living elsewhere. Rechungpa returns to Milarepa's cave and begins to study with him in earnest.

Some Indian yogins once come to visit Milarepa. When they see that Rechungpa has leprosy, they advise him that in India there exists a teacher who can give him a practice to cure his disease. Rechungpa asks Milarepa for permission to make the long journey to receive these teachings. When Milarepa agrees, Rechungpa sets off to India. Although he is very sick on this trek, he eventually arrives and finds one Balichandra, the guru recommended by the yogins. Receiving the empowerment of Vajrapani and undertaking the practice, Rechungpa finds the cure that he had been looking for. He returns to Tibet and goes again to Milarepa. He now resolves to stay with his master until he attains realization. His mother and uncle once again attempt to intervene but are scared off by Milarepa's threat to cast a spell on them. Rechungpa engages the practice with a whole heart.

He now takes up the life of meditation in wild and remote places. In order to obtain provisions for his retreats, he carries out the "begging practice of one taste." This means seeking alms and regarding all treatment by prospective donors, whether generous or abusive, with the same attitude. Thrangu Rinpoche explains:

> Sometimes he would do the particular practice of one taste which meant going begging for food in which one might find a good donor and get very nice food and be asked to give dharma teachings with a nice seat and a nice place to stay. Another time one might go begging and the person might say, "Why are you always coming around here begging for food?" and tell you off and hit you. In the practice of one taste, whatever happens, whether good or bad, has the same flavor, so one develops equanimity in both good and bad situations. So with this practice, one can develop realization through begging.[17]

Although Rechungpa is sometimes the devoted practitioner, he also suffers from the typical ups and downs of the ardent meditator. Sometimes his experiences lead him to spiritual inflation and pride. On one occasion, Milarepa attempts to warn Rechungpa about potential obstacles in his practice and the danger of falling into a samsaric state of mind. Rechungpa replies, "I am like a garuda flying in the sky and there is no danger of my falling to the ground. I'm like fish in the water and so there is no danger from waves. With these instructions meditating in solitary places in the mountains with the yogins, there is no danger of any obstacles to me."[18] Milarepa, recognizing in this expression of spiritual arrogance a most serious impediment, laments Rechungpa's bull-headedness and tells him the obstacles this will cause to his realization.

Rechungpa also experiences confusion about what is most important on his spiritual path. When Milarepa is attacked by monastic scholars, Rechungpa is upset that his guru does not know the forms of logical debate and cannot overcome the scholars on their own terms. At one point, he decides that he should go to India to study logic and debate in a monastic setting so that he can return and vanquish his guru's detractors. Although this aspiration is well intentioned, from Milarepa's perspective it misses the point entirely. Milarepa responds, "Don't go to India to study logic. . . . This is just worldly thinking and you can never know it all . . . It will not lead to Buddhahood. The best thing for you to do is just to stay here and practice and meditate."[19] Milarepa eventually gives Rechungpa permission to travel again to India but not to study logic. Instead, he sends him to find certain tantric teachings that would fill out and complete the teachings he received from Marpa.

Finally, although Rechungpa is a devoted student, he also experiences periods when his devotion seems to evaporate. On one occasion, returning from India with some important tantric texts, he sees Milarepa coming to meet him. He feels very proud of what he has accomplished and wonders if his guru will show him special honor and will prostrate to him. Milarepa, ever the selfless and devoted teacher, perceives this pride and provides a shock to Rechunga's system: when Rechungpa is away from their retreat place, the master appears to burn Rechungpa's texts.

This plunges Rechungpa into anger and resentment toward his teacher from which he will not be dislodged. It is only later, after Milarepa's compassion, attainment, and love for his disciple can no longer be denied, that Rechungpa relents.

Through these ups and downs, Rechungpa perseveres in his practice and gains many realizations. Eventually, with the permission of Milarepa, he goes to Central Tibet, to the Yarlung Valley, where he spends his time meditating in caves, giving teachings and empowerments, and gradually gathering disciples. One day, Rechungpa comes upon a gathering of people among whom is a very fine, well-dressed monk. This person says to Rechungpa, "You are obviously a serious practitioner. But it is a shame that you go about in such ragged clothing and live such a hard life. It would be much better if you would become a monk." In Thrangu Rinpoche's words, "Rechungpa sang him a song in which he said that he was very kind with his compassion towards him, but he was a yogin and pupil of Milarepa, so he just spent his time meditating. If he were to become a monk, it would be just a superficial image. So it was much better that he be just as he really was, dressing in whatever he had, and doing whatever came about." The monk saw the evident realization of this disheveled yogin and asked him for teachings. Rechungpa replied with a summary of the dharma he had learned from his master:

> Rechungpa said that to practice the dharma, one needed first to find a good lama, to seek out a good teacher. When one had found a good teacher, the next thing to do was to receive all of the teachings that he or she had. Having received them, one should then practice them properly. If one could do all of these three things, then one could achieve Buddhahood in one lifetime. This monk became a very good dharma practitioner, great meditator, and siddha.[20]

By now the fame of Milarepa has spread through Central and southern Tibet. Among the people of the region, along with Milarepa, there is also talk of Rechungpa, known as Milarepa's primary disciple. Rechungpa now and then meets people who, not knowing who he is, articulate the aspiration to meet the famous Milarepa and his disciple Rechungpa. Sometimes Rechungpa reveals his identity, while at others he wants to avoid the fame and attention that would follow him if others knew who he was. Rechungpa's primary objective, like his master's, is to continue his practice of meditation in retreat with a minimum of distraction. Nevertheless, during his time in Central Tibet, Rechungpa meets many donors, some who treat him with respect and others who try to manipulate and control him, even to the point of criticizing and beating him when he does not conform to their expectations.

Like his guru, Rechungpa has difficulties with conventional monastics who disapprove of his lifestyle and his dharma. Once when he is visiting Lhasa, many people come to receive teachings from him. As Thrangu Rinpoche tells the story,

> the monks living in Lhasa became very jealous of him. They said, "He doesn't keep any monastic vows like we do, so there really isn't any point for people to receive teachings from him. He shouldn't be teaching them!" Rechungpa replied to them, "This is how people without vows go walking," and he began walking on the water, just like he was walking on land. Then he said, "I just sleep in a state of complete stupor and this is how I go in and out of the house." And then he simply walked through the walls of the house. After he had performed these miracles, the monks developed great faith in him and received teachings from him and did retreats and were able to develop very good realization.[21]

Rechungpa also criticizes Buddhist yogins who look at the dharma as an opportunity to wander about, gather alms, and enjoy a life of ease. Once, when he is making a pilgrimage to various sacred places to practice there, some yogins come to join him.

> They said they liked the unrestricted yogi's life where they could eat what they liked [and] do what they pleased. Rechungpa then said, "Yes, a yogi's life is a happy one, but the yogi also has

to practice the dharma. If one becomes distracted from practice, then being a yogi is pointless. So one has to practice the dharma very carefully to keep one's commitments. If one takes it too easy, one will find out that a yogi's life in the end is not really an easy life."[22]

Rechungpa's experiences in Central Tibet purify much of the karma of the obstacles that separate him from Milarepa. He eventually returns to Milarepa and now finds, in Thrangu Rinpoche's words, "very stable love and compassion and faith."[23] Now Milarepa confers on him the final teachings he has to give. He further tells his disciple that since all the teachings have been given, Rechungpa should not remain with the master but should wander from place to place, putting the teachings into practice in retreat. Milarepa tells him that it is in this way that he will be of most benefit to beings.

Rechungpa now asks Milarepa who is going to hold his lineage. Milarepa replies that he has many good disciples, some of whom have attained buddhahood, some of whom have achieved the bodhisattva bhumis, and some of whom have only made a connection with the dharma. From among all of his disciples, Gampopa will have a certain preeminence as a lineage holder, and so will Rechungpa. Rechungpa himself will attain complete realization and will go directly to the buddha realms without leaving a body behind. Likewise, his yogin disciples will reach the same exalted attainment.[24] Although Rechungpa wants to stay with Milarepa, the master tells him that he must wander forth for the good of others.

The master now informs Rechungpa that there is one special teaching that he has not yet given him. As they walk to the place where he will present this instruction, Rechungpa wonders what it could possibly be. When they arrive, "Milarepa lifted up his robe to show Rechungpa his bottom. Because he had been practicing so much sitting on a stone, all of the skin on his bottom had become very thick and hardened. And he said, 'This is how you should practice. You need this kind of diligence.' "[25]

Rechungpa wanders through Central and northern Tibet, meditating and teaching. He gains many close disciples who will carry on his lineage. When he dies, as prophesied, he does not leave a physical body behind but disappears into the "rainbow body," a reflection of his very great attainment.[26] His lineage is the noninstitutionalized one of the yogin and is known as "the lineage of the oral instructions of Rechungpa." Among his disciples are thirteen special spiritual heirs. One of the most accomplished is a woman who practiced diligently and, at death, did not leave her physical body behind.[27] His lineage in Tibet continued down to the time of the Chinese invasion in 1949. Rechungpa was specifically connected with the tradition of *togdenmas,* female yogic practitioners and women of extraordinary power and attainment. These yoginis followed methods developed specifically for female practitioners by Rechungpa, and they looked back to him as the founder of their specific lineage.[28]

Gampopa

In terms of the institutional continuity of the Kagyü lineage, Gampopa was Milarepa's most influential disciple. He was born in 1079 in the region of Takpo and is hence also known as Takpo Lhaje (the Doctor from Takpo). His biography tells us that, as a young man, he marries and has one child. However, while he is still in his mid-twenties, a plague sweeps through the region, and both his wife and child die. Disconsolate, with a new and vivid understanding of death, he realizes that seeking ordinary happiness in the world makes no sense and is doomed to failure. From this realization comes his decision, at the age of twenty-five, to renounce the world and enter monastic life.

Gampopa enters the Kadam tradition of Atisha and pursues a life defined by following the monastic Vinaya, studying the main scholarly traditions of Buddhism, and practicing meditation. His support is provided by some land that he continues to own. One spring, he has entered retreat in a hut built near the monastery. On a certain day, having come out of retreat and walking in the monastic grounds, he hears three beggars talking. The first expresses a desire for plentiful food and drink, while the second says he would like to be a king like Tsede of Tibet.

FIGURE 7.4 *Gampopa, Milarepa's most influential disciple, who integrated the Kadam tradition of scholarship with the Kagyü training in meditation.*

The third, however, comments, "Even Tsede will one day die, so his happiness is not lasting. As long as you are going to wish, wish to become a great yogin like Milarepa who needs no clothing or human food. He is fed nectar by the Dakinis, rides atop a white snow lion, and flies in the sky. Now that would be truly wondrous."[29]

"Merely by hearing the name of Milarepa the hair of Gampopa's body stood on end, tears came to his eyes and a special devotion, unlike he had ever felt before, emerged in his mind."[30] Initially, his upsurge of feeling paralyzes him, and he is unable to move. When he eventually returns to his retreat hut, he is unable to meditate but keeps thinking constantly and obsessively about Milarepa. He returns to the monastery, locates the three beggars, and questions them about the person, the teachings, and the location of Milarepa. They direct him to a mountainous region in western Tibet where Milarepa is in retreat. Selling his land for four ounces of gold, Gampopa sets off to find his master.

Kalu Rinpoche tells the following story of the meeting of Milarepa and Gampopa. While Gampopa was journeying toward western Tibet,

> Milarepa was giving teachings in the mountains, surrounded by a number of disciples. He said to them, "In a few days, an excellent monk who is a real bodhisattva is going to come from the south to meet me. If a few of you could help him, it would be very good and greatly help your progress toward enlightenment."
>
> Soon after that, Gampopa arrived in the region where Milarepa lived. He met one of his disciples who had heard the prediction and said to her, "I have come from the south looking for Milarepa the yogi. Would you know where he is?" And the woman said, "You come from the south, you are a monk . . . you must be the great bodhisattva who Milarepa said would come. I will help you meet him. He wanted us to."
>
> Gampopa thought, "I must be very special for the great Milarepa to make such a prediction." He swelled with pride. When the woman led him to Milarepa, the yogi could see his state of mind because of his extraordinary knowledge, and he wouldn't give Gampopa an audience for [two weeks], even though he was a noble monk. The waiting deflated Gampopa, and, finally, seated in his hermitage, Milarepa called him. As he entered, Gampopa respectfully prostrated three times. Then Milarepa invited him to sit down. "Welcome! Here, drink!" he said, of-

fering him a skull full of alcohol. Disconcerted, Gampopa hesitated. On the one hand, he couldn't refuse what was offered him by the person he came to receive teachings from. But on the other hand, a good monk cannot drink alcohol. What a terrible dilemma. Milarepa insisted. "Don't hesitate. Drink!" So, stopping all thought, Gampopa drank in one gulp the entire skull of alcohol. "Excellent! What a great sign of your capacity to assimilate all the teachings of the lineage!"

Kalu Rinpoche concludes: "Gampopa remained for a very long time with Milarepa. He received the teachings, practiced them, developed deep understanding, and arrived at enlightenment."[31]

Gampopa's path included the strict disciplinary and scholarly training of the monk as well as the meditation of the yogin in solitary retreat. In his person and in the teachings he gave, Gampopa expressed the integrated combination of these two strands, something that was unusual in Tibet at that time. This integration is laid out in his *Jewel Ornament of Liberation,* a work on the stages of the path that has enjoyed great fame throughout Tibetan Buddhist history and is still popular today. It was Gampopa's mission to institutionalize this integration of his Kadam and Kagyü training. In fulfillment of this, he built a monastery and ordained his main disciples. According to his biography, almost all of his primary disciples were ordained monks, following the Vinaya.[32]

The Subsequent Lineage

One of Gampopa's primary disciples was Tüsum Khyenpa (1110–1193), who received monastic ordination and carried on the monastic lineage. Tüsum Khyenpa built three Kagyü monasteries: Tsurphu near Lhasa, and Karma Gon and Kampo Nenang, both in Kham. These three institutions became the foundation of the Karma Kamtsang, one of the most important branches of the Kagyü lineage.

Tüsum Khyenpa's main disciple had a student by the name of Karma Pakshi. This person was recognized as a reincarnation of Tüsum Khyenpa, who was retroactively recognized as the first Karmapa, with Karma Pakshi being seen as the second. Karma Pakshi is generally understood as the first reincarnation, or *tulku,* to be recognized in Tibet.[33] It was under this second Karmapa that the Karma Kagyü lineage gained in power and stature, owing partly to his close relation with the Mongols and his becoming the guru first of Mongka Khan and later of Kublai Khan.

The third Karmapa, Rangjung Dorje (1284–1339), is notable for his practice and integration of the mahamudra traditions of the Kagyü and the dzokchen teachings of the Nyingma. In addition to receiving the mahamudra instructions deriving from Milarepa and Gampopa, this master also studied with Rigdzin Kumaradza, the foremost dzokchen teacher of his day and guru of the great Nyingma lama Longchenpa. Rangjung Dorje's synthesis of mahamudra and dzokchen has been reinvigorated by each generation of masters and has remained a hallmark of the Kagyü lineage down to the present day. The lineage of Karmapas continues down to the present, the sixteenth Karmapa having died in 1981.[34] The seventeenth Karmapa is now in his teens and undergoing the traditional training of a tulku.[35]

In addition to Tüsum Khyenpa, the first Karmapa and progenitor of the Karma Kamtsang, Gampopa had several other important disciples, from whom the other three of the four original schools arose: in addition to the Karma Kamtsang, there were the Phaktru Kagyü, founded by Phagmotrupa (1100–?), and the Tsalpa and Barom Kagyü. From these, eight subbranches developed. All together, these were known as "four great and lesser" lineages of the Kagyü. Although most of these twelve have not survived as independent traditions, there are four that are particularly important today. The first is the Karma Kamtsang, while the other three—the Drigung Kagyü, Taglung Kagyü, and Drukpa Kagyü—all derive as subbranches of the Phaktru Kagyü. The Drigung Kagyü was founded by a student of Phagmotrupa's, Kyura Rinpoche, a highly respected monk and scholar. This lineage has particular strength in Ladakh. The initiator of the Taglung Kagyü was another disciple of Phagmotrupa, Tralung Thangpa Tashi Pal. And the Drukpa Kagyü was begun by Phagmotrupa's highly realized yogic disciple Lingrepa (late eleventh to twelfth century). The school subsequently divided into three branches, the most successful of which migrated to Bhutan, where it is important today.

The "four great" and "eight lesser" lineages deriving from Gampopa are all known as Takpo Kagyü (i.e., deriving from Gampopa, "the Physician of Takpo"). There are also Kagyü lineages that do not derive from Gampopa but rather run through other lines. Already mentioned are the traditions deriving from Milarepa's other main disciple, Rechungpa. In addition, also considered a Kagyü subschool is the Shangpa Kagyü. Originally an independent lineage, the Shangpa was established by the accomplished yogin Khyungpo Naljor (or Naljorpa, 978–1079). This master studied in India with some of the great siddhas of his day and received transmission in a vision from Niguma, the tantric consort of Naropa. Subsequently, the lineage was brought into the Kagyü orbit and is now considered Kagyü. One of the most well-known representatives of the Shangpa Kagyü is the late Ven. Kalu Rinpoche, quoted frequently in this book, a master who spent much of his life in retreat and, at the request of the sixteenth Karmapa, taught meditation widely in the West.

Although in the diaspora the sixteenth Karmapa was considered the "head" of the Kagyü lineage, in Tibet the situation was more decentralized. In spite of the titular role of the Karmapa, even in exile the various surviving Kagyü subschools maintain a high degree of independence and autonomy.

Sorting out the various schools, subschools, and attendant lineages and traditions of the Kagyü, as for any of the other main Tibetan sects, can be a complex and confusing task. The reason is that it is not the institutional entity that ultimately defines a lineage but rather the line of teachings passed on from teacher to disciple. For example, a given teacher, as a hierarch in one particular monastery, would receive the primary teaching lineages passed down in that institutional context. But, at the same time, he might be a personal student of several different masters, some of whom might be closely aligned with his own lineage, but others of whom might belong to a different sect or school altogether. Thus the teacher might be a holder of many different lineages of teachings, only some of which might be associated with his institutional seat. In the next generation, things become even more complex because that teacher would typically pass his different lineages on to different disciples, who, in turn, would each carry lineages from the individual configuration of teachers with whom they had personally studied. In any generation, particularly gifted disciples along with their own students might become the center of a newly forming sublineage, likely with an attendant institutional component. While in the very brief historical overview that we are attempting here there can be no question of seriously engaging the full complexity of Tibetan lineage histories, it is important for the reader to be aware of their general texture and the characteristic way in which they unfold.

Like other New Translation schools, the Kagyü specializes in various anuttara-yoga tantras such as the *Chakrasamvara, Hevajra,* and *Vajrayogini* tantras. Central to the Kagyü transmissions is the instruction on mahamudra, originally received by Marpa from the siddha Maitripa. The six yogas of Naropa are another central teaching of the Kagyü, practiced by yogins in the strict confines of retreat. These include the practice of inner heat (*tummo;* Skt. *chandali*), the illusory body (*gyulu*), dream yoga (*milam*), the practice of luminosity (*ösel*), *bardo* meditation, and the ejection of consciousness (*phowa*). The generally stated purpose of these yogas is, among other things, to clear away karmic obscurations to a very deep level and thus to provide stabilization and clarity of the experience of mahamudra.

CONCLUSION

The Kadam (later Geluk), Sakya, and Kagyü lineages represent the three principal Tibetan Buddhist schools of the later spreading. Together with the Nyingma, they make up the so-called "four schools" of Tibetan Buddhism. Sometimes the Bonpo is mentioned as a fifth school of dharma, although it is not explicitly Buddhist. It is important to realize, however, that there were other traditions and lineages that arose during the later spreading that did not survive as independent lineages.

Among the more important of these are the Shije, the Chö, and the Jonang.

Shije means "pacification" and refers to teachings that bring suffering to an end. The Shije lineage was founded in eleventh-century Tibet by the great South Indian saint, Phadampa Sangye. This master visited Tibet five separate times, the last in 1098, and also traveled elsewhere in North Asia, including China. The Shije, based on the Prajnaparamita and the teaching of Nagarjuna, is known for its distinctive way of paci- fying suffering. As Tulku Thondup mentions, in most traditions, the defilements that give rise to suffering are first purified, and this leads naturally to the abatement of suffering. However, in the Shije, suffering itself becomes the focus of practice: "In this method the suffering is first purified and then the defilements which are its cause are eliminated."[36]

The Chö teachings and practices were also taught by Phadampa San- gye but in Tibet are considered to constitute a separate lineage from Shije. *Chö* means "cut off" and refers to the cutting off of ego and the defilements that support it. Of the two distinct Chö lineages, the mascu- line Chö (Pho Chö) and the feminine Chö (Mo Chö), the Mo Chö is by far the most well known and practiced. The Mo Chö was transmitted from a principal student of Phadampa to the realized dakini Machik Labdrönma (1031–1124). Machik is loved and respected throughout Ti- betan Buddhism as a wisdom dakini—a fully realized being in human form. Through her teaching, the Chö teachings spread widely in Tibet, becoming part of all the Tibetan schools and being found in every re- gion. Many texts derive from Machik, including some terma hidden by her. Machik spent her entire life as a yogini and passed the last years of her life in a cave in southern Tibet. Like the Shije, the Chö teachings are based on the Prajnaparamita. Through the practice, one cuts ego at the root by offering one's body, mind, and all one's attachments to the most hungry and fearful beings in samsara. To do so, the practitioner meditates in charnel grounds in the dead of night, inviting all the fear- some spirits that lurk there to come and partake of the feast. The Chö has not continued as an independent school, but its transmissions are kept alive in the various lineages and are particularly practiced by the

Nyingmapas and the Kagyüpas. Tulku Thondup quotes the following lines from Machik:

> To travel to dangerous and solitary places is the Outer-Chod [Chö],
> To transform the body as food for demons is the Inner-Chod,
> To cut off the single thing (grasping) from the root is the
>   Actual-Chod,
> Whoever practices these three Chods is a yogi.[37]

Finally to be mentioned is the Jonang school, founded in western Tibet by the twelfth- to thirteenth-century siddha Yumo Mikyö Dorje, a disciple of the Kashmiri pandit Chandranatha.[38] The Jonangpas became renowned in Tibet for their advocacy of the teaching of *shentong,* or "emptiness of other," an interpretation of *shunyata* particularly congruent with tantric practice. According to tradition, Yumo was practicing the *Kalachakra Tantra* at Mount Kailash. When he reached the "fourth empowerment" in the liturgy, the teaching of shentong suddenly appeared in his mind. The shentong lineage of Yumo was first passed through his own family line, then through several generations of masters and disciples. In the fourteenth century, the then-holder of Yumo's lineage[39] founded the Jonang monastery, and from this time forward the school became known as the Jonang. The master Dolpopa Sherab Gyaltsen (1292–1361), the tenth holder of the lineage, for the first time gave written expression to the shentong doctrine, systematizing the teaching and composing texts that articulated it in detail. A particularly great shentong master was Lama Taranatha (1575–?), one of the greatest historians and authors in Tibetan history.

The essential teaching of the Jonangpas, then, concerns the shentong, or "emptiness of other" doctrine." This philosophical view is based on the third turning of the wheel of dharma and holds this teaching as the Buddha's ultimate and final promulgation. According to the Jonangpas, within each human being is the essence of enlightenment, in the form of the buddha-nature. As it exists in ordinary beings, this awakened mind is covered over by the adventitious defilements of passion, aggression, and delusion. Through the path, these defilements are gradually removed, revealing the immaculate enlightenment within. This realization consists in the inseparability of emptiness and clarity; that is, while there is no solid reality to be found, there is the luminous and self-cognizant quality of awareness. (For further discussion see chapter 16.)

The Jonang lineage flourished for some three hundred years and had a powerful influence on Tibetan Buddhism. Although eventually eliminated throughout most of Tibet, the Jonang continued to exist in the east down to the Chinese invasion. Tulku Thondup comments that the Shar Dzamthang monastery built by Kashipa Rinchenpal, a great disciple of Dolpopa Sherab Gyaltsen in Golok province, functioned as the primary center of Jonang in recent centuries.[40] In addition, the Jonang lineage has also continued to be transmitted by lamas within the Nyingma, Kagyü, and Sakya schools and continues to have an important impact on Tibetan philosophy and practice.

The later spreading of Buddhism from India to Tibet began at the end of the tenth century and continued until the beginning of the thirteenth when, through a combination of cultural forces within India and Muslim invasions from the outside, institutionalized Buddhism largely disappeared from the Indian subcontinent. From the thirteenth century onward, Tibetans could no longer travel to India to study the dharma at the feet of Indian masters but were forced to rely on their own resources. The roughly two hundred years of the later spreading, however, was a period of great activity and creativity, and by the end of this period the major institutional patterns that would characterize Tibetan Buddhism had been developed and were in place. Of particular importance, by the close of the later spreading, the four major lineages that together would make up the classical Tibetan Buddhist landscape had been founded and were assuming their classical form. All four continued to be enriched by incorporating the teachings and lineages of one another and of other traditions such as Shije, Chö, and Jonang.

Equally important, the model of classical Indian monasticism had finally been transplanted successfully to Tibet. Now the primary schools of the later spreading, the Kadam/Geluk, the Sakya, and the Kagyü—later to be followed by the Nyingma—all developed strong systems of monasteries that provided a power base, institutional focus, and context for the preservation particularly of the scholarly and disciplinary teachings. In addition, monasteries functioned as the primary players in the world of Tibetan government and politics. Finally, monasteries also supported yogic practice through providing caves and hermitages, as well as material support, for those monks particularly wanting to enter into strict retreat.

By the end of the later spreading, parallel and sometimes in tandem with the different monastic centers housing conventional monks, were a variety of nonmonastic practitioners following mainly the tantric teachings. Some, like Milarepa, kept the eremitical traditions alive and pursued the radical and unconventional lifestyle of the wandering and meditating yogin. Others followed the model of the Nyingma lay practitioners, who practiced tantra as people in the world, with families and ordinary occupations. By the thirteenth century, these three approaches to the dharma—that of monasticism, nonmonastic meditation, and lay yogic practice—appear to have been flourishing, each in its own unique way. As mentioned above, it was this mix of approaches, and the relationships among them that have made Tibetan Buddhism the creative and dynamic phenomenon that it was down to this present century.

8
Modern Traditions
GELUK

TIBETAN BUDDHISM, AS WE KNOW IT TODAY, IS COM-
posed of two primary orientations or approaches, embodied most clearly
in the Geluk, or "virtuous school," on the one hand, and the nineteenth-
century Ri-me, or "nonsectarian movement," on the other.¹ The Geluk
school, founded in the fourteenth century by the great scholar Tsongkhapa (1357–1419), represents a reformulation and reinvigoration of the
old Kadam tradition of Atisha. For this reason, the Gelukpas are sometimes known as the "new Kadam" and carry forward Atisha's emphasis
on monastic discipline and scholarship as central components of the
path. In contrast to the Geluk, the Ri-me movement is not a coherent
school but rather a loose grouping of like-minded people. It was given
impetus in the eighteenth century by the Nyingma yogin-scholar Jigme
Lingpa (1730–1798) and represents a consolidation of the contemplative
traditions and schools of Tibet, emphasizing meditation and retreat
practice as the foundations of the spiritual life. The primary seat of the
Geluk was in the provinces of Ü and Tsang in central and west-central
Tibet, and the school maintained its institutional base there. The Ri-me,
by contrast, evolved primarily in East Tibet, in Kham and Amdo, and
continued to be located there up to the Chinese invasion.

The Geluk and Ri-me each represent modern expressions of Buddhist trends that go back to the origin of Indian Buddhism. As we saw
above, the Indian tradition originated in the forest tradition of the Buddha and, from the beginning, included two renunciant orientations, that
of the yogin living in the wilds and meditating, aiming at realization in
this life, and that of the settled monastic living within monasteries and

following the more gradual path of monastic discipline and textual scholarship. We also saw that the vitality of the Indian tradition could, in large measure, be ascribed to the relationship and mutual interaction of these two approaches to the dharma. In a very real sense, the Geluk and the Ri-me represent the modern Tibetan expression of these two ancient Buddhist ideals.

As in ancient India, so in Tibet, these two ways of approaching the dharma were not mutually exclusive. Thus, although the Geluk emphasized the path of the monastic scholar, it also acknowledged the importance of meditation and allowed its most senior scholars to pursue the path of tantric practice. Similarly, although the Ri-me found in meditation the ultimate method of spiritual transformation, study and intellectual understanding were considered important parts of the path, and many of the most important Ri-me masters were not only accomplished meditators but also great scholars. Thus both Geluk and Ri-me give a place in the path to study and scholarship as well as to meditation. In addition, both Geluk and Ri-me included both institutional monastic and noninstitutional aspects. In spite of this shared ground, however, the two schools do have different and distinctive approaches: the Geluk clearly embodies and champions the way of classical monasticism, while the Ri-me represent a modern version of "yogic Buddhism" with its emphasis on practice and realization.

The Geluk and Ri-me orientations are classical in both a typological and a historical sense. They are classical in the sense that they embody, in a particularly clear and typical form, the two trends that characterize Tibetan Buddhism since the eighth century. Historically, the Geluk dates from the fourteenth century and has become the most important "monastic synthesis" since that time. The Ri-me, although existing as such only since the nineteenth century, in its basic orientation also traces its lineage from the fourteenth century, from the time of Longchen Rabjam (1308–1363), who was himself drawing on earlier traditions.

Relations between representatives of the Geluk and Ri-me orientations have varied. At one end of the spectrum, they have been cordial and respectful, and sometimes mutually supportive. The present Dalai Lama, for example, is a Geluk monk trained in its perspectives and

SOME DATES OF GELUK HISTORY

1357–1419	Tsongkhapa
	1397 Tsongkhapa joins Reting monastery.
	1408 Establishes Mönlam New Year festival
1391–1475	Gendün Druppa, disciple of Tsongkhapa, is retrospectively recognized as first Dalai Lama.
1408	Emperor Yung-lo invites Tsongkhapa to China; a disciple is sent.
1409–1447	Founding of principal Geluk monasteries
	1409 Ganden
	1416 Drepung
	1419 Sera
	1437 Chamdo in Kham
	1447 Tashilhünpo in Tsang
late 15th CENTURY	Schools struggle with one another; political conflicts.
late 15th, 16th CENTURIES	Second to fourth Dalai Lamas
	[2] Gendün Gyatso
	[3] Sönam Gyatso
	[4] Great-grandson of Altan Khan
1578	Sönam Gyatso, the third Dalai Lama, is given the title Dalai Lama by Mongol leader Altan Khan.
1617	Birth of fifth Dalai Lama, Ngawang Losang Gyatso
1617–1682	Fifth Dalai Lama, Ngawang Losang Gyatso
1641	King of Tsang is defeated by Mongols; fifth Dalai Lama given political control of Tibet.
1642–1659	Consolidation of the Tibetan theocracy under Geluk rule
1876–1920	Thirteenth Dalai Lama
1934	Fourteenth Dalai Lama is born (enthroned in 1940).

traditions. At the same time, he receives teachings from all the major sects and subsects and is deeply practiced in a variety of traditions, including both Geluk and Ri-me. Although officially belonging to the Geluk, as political leader of Tibet in exile he has made the survival, well-being, and spread of all of the Tibetan lineages, including the heterodox Bön tradition, his particular responsibility.

Still, there has often been an underlying tension between those representing the Geluk and Ri-me orientations, a tension sometimes fanned into open conflict by a number of factors. Most important, the Geluk and the Ri-me exhibit quite different trends not only in history, doctrine, and practice but also in their classical monastic versus more yogically oriented approaches. In addition, in spite of the "unity" of Tibetan culture, the fact that Geluk and Ri-me are seated in different parts of Tibet is significant. Certainly, the attendant differences between Lhasa and Central Tibet on the one hand and Kham and Amdo on the other in matters of dialect, social customs, and culture provide challenges to mutual understanding. Finally, the involvement of the Tibetan Buddhist schools—at least those of the New Translation period—in seeking, winning, and maintaining political power has been a source of considerable conflict. Unfortunately, persecution by those in power has not been unknown in Tibetan history. Many examples of conflict between the orientations, whether doctrinal, social, legal, or even military, can be traced to this factor.

TSONGKHAPA

Tsongkhapa, the founder of the Geluk school, was born in 1357 in the Tsongkha Valley in Amdo province, in northeastern Tibet. His traditional biography tells us that his birth was heralded by a number of auspicious signs. His father, in particular, dreamed that a young monk came to him from Wu T'ai Shan in China, the sacred mountain of Manjushri, the bodhisattva of wisdom. This represented a foreshadowing of the fact that Tsongkhapa would be a great scholar and would be understood as an emanation of Manjushri.

Figure 8.1 *Tsongkhapa, the great scholar who founded the Geluk school by reforming the Kadam tradition of Atisha.*

Tsongkhapa was ordained at the age of three by the fourth Karmapa, Rölpe Dorje (1340–1383), and received novice vows at the age of seven. It is said that even at this young age he was already showing an extraordinary aptitude for scholarship. Early on, Tsongkhapa began traveling throughout Tibet, studying with some of the greatest masters at the most renowned monasteries. At this time, his studies included the *Abhidharmakosha* of Vasubandhu, the treatises on logic and epistemology of Dharmakirti, Asanga's *Abhidharma-samucchaya,* Chandrakirti's *Madhyamakavatara,* as well as texts on monastic discipline. Through all of this study, Tsongkhapa was consistently able to memorize vast quantities and to understand quickly whatever was presented to him. He was, moreover, an accomplished and formidable debater. The level of Tsongkhapa's scholarly thoroughness and attainment is revealed in the fact that his commentary on Maitreya's *Abhisamaya-alankara* utilizes all twenty-one Indian commentaries. Tsongkhapa's biography stresses that he was also an accomplished practitioner, that he kept the rules of monastic discipline impeccably, and that he was humble and free of arrogance.

At the age of thirty-three, over the objections of his primary teacher, Rendawa, Tsongkhapa gave up his scholarly studies, entered retreat, and turned to the practice of tantra. At this time, he carried out Heruka practice of the Kagyüpa, the six yogas of Naropa, the tantric practices of Niguma, and the *Kalachakra Tantra,* this latter of which remains important to the Gelukpas today. In the following years, he received a series of revelations from Manjushri, guiding both his study and his practice. In 1398, at the age of forty-one, after having a dream in which he was blessed by the Indian Prasangika founder, Buddhapalita, Tsongkhapa attained realization.

When Tsongkhapa, looking from the vantage point of his attainment, surveyed the dharma traditions that existed in the Tibet of his time, he saw a need for purification and reform. He felt, in particular, that those following the monastic life had fallen into laziness and laxity, and that study and scholarship had become sloppy and confused. Tsongkhapa wanted to make his life work the rectification of this situation. As the master set about his work, several themes came to the fore.

1. A clear statement that the way of the fully ordained monk is the highest Buddhist practice. Tsongkhapa was particularly concerned to reestablish the integrity of the monastic ideal and to insist on the necessity of a full and careful adherence to the Vinaya, the rules of monastic restraint.

2. A reaffirmation of the importance of study, scholarship, and debate as critical elements of the Buddhist path. The master felt that Buddhist philosophy was in a state of decline and wanted to again place it at the center of religious life and reinvigorate it with more rigorous standards. Drawing again on the traditions of Atisha and reflecting his own study, Tsongkhapa set up a curriculum of study and debate that came to include five topics. These reflect the topics that were important in the great North Indian monasteries flourishing at the time of the early and later spreadings. The curriculum of the Geluk monasteries, then, came to include:

1. Paramita, study of the *Prajnaparamita* and other Mahayana sutras;
2. Madhyamaka philosophy, the Prasangika approach of Chandrakirti;
3. Pramana, logic, epistemology;
4. Abhidharma, Buddhist psychology; and
5. Vinaya

These same five topics were also adopted for use in the monastic colleges (*shedra*) of the other schools, although of course the actual texts studied differed.

3. A reform of tantric practice so that it would be protected against excesses and abuses. As we have seen, the practice of tantra was an important element in Tsongkhapa's own Buddhist training. In addition to the traditions mentioned, he particularly valued the *Vajrabhairava, Guhyasamaja,* and *Chakrasamvara* tantras, and these remain the most important for the Gelukpas. At the same time, however, Tsongkhapa was particularly sensitive to the challenges presented by the practice of tantra, and most especially to its dangers. He felt that those who were not sufficiently prepared for tantric practice ran the risk of misunderstanding it and bringing great harm on themselves and others. How could one be properly prepared? First, Tsongkhapa held that the tantra could only be properly practiced by fully ordained monks. In addition, one's motivation of bodhichitta, one's bodhisattva commitment, had to

reach a certain level of maturity. Finally, even as a fully ordained monk who was a good bodhisattva, one should only enter tantra after having passed through a most demanding course of scholarly studies carried out over many years. Samuel summarizes the matter nicely: "The message is clear: Tantric practice is dangerous and it should be left to the great lama-meditators with their decades of prior discipline and academic training. . . . The Gelukpa system was to produce a small minority of intensively trained scholastics and a smaller elite of Tantric adepts, while the vast majority fell out at some point early in the academic training."[2]

Tsongkhapa was a prolific author, and, by the end of his life, he had composed 210 texts collected in twenty volumes. His most important work is perhaps his *Lamrim Chenmo* (Stages of the Buddhist Path), a summary of the path that distinguishes three main levels of spiritual development. This text, reflecting Tsongkhapa's respect for Atisha's teachings, is a kind of commentary on Atisha's *Bodhipathapradipa,* itself an outline of the Mahayana path. According to the *Lamrim Chenmo,* at the first stage, that of the ordinary layperson, one is preoccupied with gaining happiness for oneself in terms of a better rebirth. Here one performs meritorious actions to bring about that result. Second is the level of the Hinayanist, in which one practices the threefold training of shila, samadhi, and prajna. At this level, one's motivation is to attain liberation from samsara, but for oneself alone.

The third and highest stage of the path, according to Tsongkhapa, is that of the Mahayana. Here one generates the bodhichitta, both ultimate and relative (discussed in chapter 12), and takes the bodhisattva vow. One's practice consists of the six paramitas. The last two, *dhyana* (meditation) and *prajna* (transcendental knowledge), are identified as shamatha and vipashyana. *Shamatha* has roughly the same meaning as that discussed above, namely the meditative stabilizing of the mind in one-pointed attention. Vipashyana, however, is seen by Tsongkhapa in a way different from the brief description given in chapter 3. There it was defined as spontaneous, egoless insight arising from within shamatha. By contrast, Tsongkhapa interprets it as, in Samuel's words, "the point-by-point contemplation of the logical arguments of the teachings, culminating in those for the voidness of self and all phenomena."[3] Tsongkhapa's interpretation of vipashyana, it should be noted, has ancient roots within Indian Buddhism as one of the two major ways in which vipashyana was understood in early tradition, his rendition aligning itself with a more scholarly slant, while the one given in chapter 3 is more yogic. (Further discussion of shamatha and vipashyana occurs in chapter 11.)

Tsongkhapa's understanding of vipashyana represents an affirmation of philosophical study and debate as powerful elements of transformation. In Robert Thurman's words, "Philosophy is thus vindicated as a complete path of liberation and transformation; the conclusively reasonable mind is esteemed as completely capable of transcending the unreasonable prejudiced mentality trapped in the vicious circle of inconclusive realization. One should therefore resist the temptation to discard critical reason and relapse into experiential confirmation of mundane intuition."[4]

Another important work of Tsongkhapa is his summary of the tantras known as the *Ngag-rim Chenmo* (Stages of the Path of Tantra). In this work, Tsongkhapa insists that the philosophical viewpoint of tantric practice must be that of the Madhyamaka school of Mahayana Buddhism and, more specifically, that of the Prasangika Madhyamaka. This philosophical tradition mobilizes a battery of logical arguments to refute any "views" that the practitioner may hold concerning the nature of ultimate reality. Thus Tsongkhapa says that one can only practice tantra if one has purified oneself, through study, of any views, opinions, or thoughts about what is ultimately real (see chapter 15).

An important part of his approach involved an evaluation of the other, non-Geluk schools. It has already been mentioned that he found the existing schools, both New Translation and Old, deficient in monastic discipline, scholarly study, and pure tantric practice. He also followed the later-spreading traditions by disputing the authenticity of texts of the first turning, and this meant particularly those important to the Nyingma. Tsongkhapa adhered to the prevailing later-spreading view that only texts brought to Tibet during the later spreading that could be proved to be translations of Indian originals should be considered legitimate. All other texts, whether deriving from the first turning or from non-Indian influences, should be avoided.

THE CONSOLIDATION OF THE GELUK

Tsongkhapa had two principal disciples, Gyaltsap Tarma Rinchen (1364–1432) and Khedrup Gelek Belsangpo (1385–1438), who became known as Gyaltsap and Khedrubje. Tsongkhapa's meeting with Gyaltsap is instructive. Once when Tsongkhapa was about to give teachings, Gyaltsap, an accomplished but arrogant scholar, blatantly challenged the master by ascending the teaching throne from which Tsongkhapa was to deliver his lecture. This was Gyaltsap's way of declaring his own scholarly superiority and of throwing the insult publicly into the master's face. However, when Tsongkhapa simply began to teach, Gyaltsap immediately realized that he was in the presence of one far his superior, offered three prostrations to the master, and humbly took his place among the other monks in the assembly.

Tsongkhapa finally gave definitive institutional form to the school he had founded by building Ganden monstery in 1410 acting as its first head. After his death, the abbatial seat passed to his first close disciple, Gyaltsap, and then, when he died, to his other main disciple, Khedrupje. Since that time, the "throne holder" of Ganden, the Ganden Tripa, has functioned as the head of the Geluk order.

In addition to Gyaltsap and Khedrupje, another disciple of Tsongkhapa, Gendün Druppa, played an important role in the founding of the Geluk school, for it was he who was retrospectively recognized as the first Dalai Lama. Gendün Druppa founded Tashilhünpo monastery and proved a powerful and competent leader. After his death, in accordance with the practice that had already developed among the Kagyupas, a reincarnation, or *tulku,* was located. The successor, Gandun Gyatso, was thus considered the rebirth of Gendün Druppa and inherited his institutional and lineage role. Thus Gendün Druppa became the second tulku in what became the Dalai Lama line of incarnations. Sönam Gyatso was the third in the series. Up until this time, in these first generations after the death of Tsongkhapa, the Geluk order was relatively uninvolved with politics and grew largely as a result of its reputation for monastic purity and accomplished scholarship.

Sönam Gyatso, however, took a step that changed this situation. He accepted an invitation to visit the Mongol prince Altan Khan and the two met in northeastern Tibet near Kokonor. This visit resulted in the formation of strong ties between the Mongols and the Gelukpas, and it was at this time that the Khan conferred the title of Dalai Lama on Sönam Gyatso. This title was henceforward used to designate the line of tulkus that now included Gendün Druppa as the first Dalai Lama, Gendün Gyatso as the second, and Sönam Gyatso as the third. The connection between Gelukpas and Mongols was further enhanced when the fourth Dalai Lama was discovered to be the great-grandson of Altan Khan.

Gelukpa religious and political power in Tibet was further consolidated under the reign of the fifth Dalai Lama, Ngawang Losang Gyatso (1617–1682), known as the Great Fifth. Prior to the time of the fifth Dalai Lama, since the end of Mongol overlordship (fourteenth century), Tibet had been ruled by different powerful families in alliance with one or another of the religious sects of the time. This political pattern was marked by frequent conflicts between these various family-sect alliances. Through the work of the fifth Dalai Lama, this pattern changed. The Great Fifth further cultivated the relationship with the Mongols that had been begun by the third Dalai Lama and enhanced at the time of the fourth. Gushri Khan, a Mongol chieftain and supporter of the fifth Dalai Lama, using his own military power, set the Geluk in place as the ruling religious and political authorities not only over both Ü and Tsang, but also over portions of eastern and western Tibet. From that time until the Chinese takeover, the Gelukpas were, in effect, the primary ruling power in the land, with the Dalai Lama being the head of the government.

From the time of Tsongkhapa, the Geluk underwent steady growth, reflected in the development of many large, well-endowed monasteries, often on trade routes or near important towns and cities. At the center of their monastic system were three very large gompas near Lhasa: Ganden, Sera, and Drepung. Two other equally sizable monasteries—Tashilhünpo, southwest of Lhasa, and Kumbum, in Amdo—have also played central roles in Geluk history. The oldest of these is Ganden, built by Tsongkhapa himself in 1409 and located about twenty-five miles from Lhasa. Its four thousand monks studied in two primary colleges, devoted respectively to the study of sutra and tantra. Drepung monastery was built by one of Tsongkhapa's disciples, Jamyang Chöje, in 1416, three miles west of Lhasa. Its nine thousand monks studied in three colleges for sutra and one for tantra. Sera monastery was constructed by another of Tsongkhapa's disciples, Cham Chan Chöje, in 1419. It housed seven thousand monks and had two colleges, one for sutra, the other for tantra. In Lhasa itself were two monasteries devoted exclusively to tantric studies, Gyü-me Tratsang, Lower Tantric College, and Gyütö Tratsang, Upper Tantric College, housing five hundred and nine hundred tantric *bhikshus,* or fully ordained monks, respectively.

Important in eastern Tibet was Kumbum monastery in Amdo, located at the birthplace of Tsongkhapa and built at the time of the third Dalai Lama (sixteenth century). It housed thirty-seven hundred monks who studied in three colleges, one for medicine, one for sutra, and one for tantra. Tashilhünpo monastery is located about 130 miles southwest of Lhasa near Shigatse. Built by the first Dalai Lama in 1447, it accommodated four thousand monks who studied in three sutra colleges and one tantra college. In the seventeenth century it became the seat of the first Panchen Lama, the reincarnation of a former close disciple of the third Dalai Lama.

The conventional Mahayana perspectives and practices advocated by the Gelukpas are discussed in chapters 12 and 13; the second turning of the wheel of dharma, their preferred philosophical position, is outlined in chapter 15; and mahamudra, the meditation lineage associated with the Geluk, as with the other New Translations schools, is summarized in my book *Secret of the Vajra World,* chapter 7.

GELUK MONASTIC TRAINING[5]

To be a monk means to commit oneself to the strict behavioral standards of the rules of monastic deportment found in the Vinaya and to pursue rigorous study of the dharma by following the demanding scholarly curriculum outlined in the Geluk order. Through submitting oneself to the Vinaya, one is undergoing a process of purification: the Vinaya rules leave little room for the impulsiveness of ego and force one continually to rein in one's desire to seek gratification and aggrandizement in one's actions. For monks truly devoted to the Vinaya, the outcome is gentleness and humility, and a pure heart with plenty of room for care and concern for others. While following the Vinaya puts one through a purification through reining in one's body and speech (one's external actions), the philosophical study of the monastic curriculum brings purification by addressing the mind—both *what* one thinks about reality and *how* one goes about thinking. The end point of both following the Vinaya and philosophical study, and the justification for the life of the monk, is the fruition of enlightenment.

In the Geluk order, as in the other Tibetan monastic traditions, one becomes a monk in stages, first becoming a novice (*getsül*), later taking full ordination as a *gelong*. Although theoretically a man can enter the monastic order at any age, in common practice one entered the monastic life as a child, usually at the behest of parents or relatives. The novice undertakes to follow a life rule of ten vows, including not killing, stealing, lying, engaging in sexual activity, or taking intoxicants. After a certain period of time, but not before the age of twenty, he can apply for full ordination. In the ordination ceremony, one undertakes to follow the two hundred and fifty or so rules of the Mulasarvastivadin Vinaya that is followed in Tibet.

Having entered into the Geluk order, monks are then in a position, at least theoretically, to pursue the scholarly curriculum. In fact, according to Donald Lopez, even in Tibet's large teaching monasteries, as few as 10 percent of the monks are actually able to undertake the study of philosophy.[6] Students begin with the study of logic and proceed to an examination of the *lörik*, or study of the various ways of knowing or types of knowledge. Following this, they take up the study of texts exemplifying the five areas of study mentioned above. The student engages each area in turn and must successfully complete it before being allowed to move on to the next. In the order in which they are studied, these five, along with the primary texts studied in each, include:

1. Prajnaparamita
   Primary Text: *Abhisamaya-alankara* (Ornament of Clear Realization) by Maitreya
2. Madhyamaka
   Primary Text: *Madhyamakavatara* (Entry into the Middle Way) by Chandrakirti
3. Pramana
   Primary Text: *Commentary on "Compendium of Valid Cognition"* (of Dignaga) by Dharmakirti
4. Abhidharma
   Primary Text: *Abhidharma-kosha* (Treasury of Abhidharma) by Vasubandhu
5. Vinaya
   Primary Text: *Vinaya Sutra* by Gunaprabha

Although the root texts of these five main areas are all Indian works, it is equally true that the interpretations followed are exclusively those of Tsongkhapa, his disciples, and later Geluk commentators. This means that in order to be competent within the Geluk scholarly arena, one has to read and know in detail the various commentaries of the school that are considered to be definitive.

The pedagogical method is twofold: memorization and debate. Lopez describes the process as it existed in old Tibet, "It was customary for a monk over the course of his study to memorize the five Indian texts, his college's textbooks on the Indian texts, and Tsongkhapa's major philosophical writings; it was not uncommon for an accomplished scholar to have several thousand pages of Tibetan text committed to memory." Lopez describes the debate process as follows:

> Debate took place in a highly structured format in which one monk defended a position (often a memorized definition of a term or an interpretation of a passage of scripture) that was systematically attacked by his opponent. Skill in debate was essential to progress to the highest rank of academic scholarship, and was greatly admired. Particular fame was attained by those monks who were able to hold the position of one of the lower

schools in the doxographical hierarchy against the higher. These debates were often quite spirited, and certain debates between highly skilled opponents are remembered with an affection not unlike that which some attach to important sporting events in the West. It was commonly the case that a monk, adept at the skills of memorization and debate, would achieve prominence as a scholar without ever publishing a single word.[7]

In Western accounts of Tibetan Buddhism, emphasis is often placed both on the tremendous amounts of textual material that monastic scholars routinely committed to memory and on the importance in debate of knowing the various positions, arguments, counter-arguments, and refutations of the various philosophical schools. This could leave the impression of a conservative, rigid, and arid scholastic enterprise. However, as Lopez' comments begin to suggest, memorization and command of received knowledge provided only the foundation for the open, dynamic, and creative process that was the goal of debate. Lobsang Gyatso, an accomplished Geluk scholar, teacher, and school administrator who died in 1997, tells us that an excessive and timid literalism was not held in high regard among the scholars. In relating his experiences at Drepung monastery, where he was trained, he comments:

> Monks who insisted on a close reading of what a text literally said and who were scared to venture afield into the realms of thought that followed naturally from an apprehension of the essence of a topic were not only not valued particularly highly but could even be hauled up by the older monks. The abbot might tell them to stop being so literal-minded and to look deeper for the meaning.[8]

The ultimate purpose of the debate process was thus not to exhibit knowledge and defend received positions, but to open up the mind, to free it of its unconscious assumptions and disclose the depth, the vitality, and the vastness of reality itself. When a scholar engaged in debate was able to lead the process to this expanding horizon, he met with respect and won the esteem of others. Lobsang Gyatso:

Even if a debater was off a bit from what a sacred text said, still, if his debate was based on some contact with a reality which was authentic, then he would be admired, even praised for his honest attempt to find meaning. Even if he was in opposition to an accepted position of the monastic textbook, his straightforward and honest intellect would be praised. Who cared if a person was not following the party line if his position was one which opened up a view of reality? Since that was what we were drawn to, we naturally felt admiration when it became opened to us.[9]

The quest for the discovery of deeper meaning that guided the debate process was also reflected in the way in which teachers and students worked together in the monastic colleges. Lobsang Gyatso:

It was because of this search for meaning that the more important topics might be taught to a student not just once but two or three times, while there were other topics which should have been learned, but which were skipped over and not taught in any depth at all. Those less important parts might be taught in a day. One might be in a class where the teacher read quickly through fifteen or twenty pages of a text when it was not a crucial part, and then at another time one would not get through a page even in an hour and a half. At another time one would be stuck on two lines for a day or more. The lines might occasion a whole series of investigations such that when the class next met, the teacher would be stuck right there and another whole class would be spent dealing with the ramifications, going through the argument with the responses and counter-responses, the lines of ideas which led to dead ends or which led to greater and clearer vistas of the vast and profound. The teachers would be happy on account of such occurrences, not irritated that they were not able to go quickly on.[10]

In Tibet, once a monk had successfully completed each of the five areas, he might have continued to more advanced studies and competed for the honored degree of *geshe*. In order to qualify for this opportunity, one had to be either a novice or a fully ordained monk, at least twenty-five years old, and trained at one of the seven major Geluk monastic training centers (Ganden, Sera, Depung, etc.). The course of study for this degree was long and extremely demanding, and students typically spent from fifteen to twenty-five years working toward it. At each stage in the process, they studied a body of textual material until they felt confident that they had mastered it. They then proceeded to the examination process, which was conducted as an oral debate. In this debate, students were expected to be able to prevail against their opponents, articulating, defending, and critiquing a wide variety of philosophical positions and views.

In order to be granted the degree of geshe, students first had to pass examinations in their own monastery or monastic college. If they succeeded there, they then went for examinations at the monastic university with which their own monastery or college was affiliated. Those who successfully completed these examinations were few, the great majority of aspirants for the geshe degree having dropped out or been eliminated somewhere along the way. Those who passed all of the examinations could compete for the highest academic degree of all, the *geshe lharampa*. These faced the most difficult examination of all, going to the Potala, the residence of the Dalai Lama, and being examined by the most accomplished scholars in the Geluk school. Having passed these examinations, they attended a final round of examinations at the time of the new year festival, when monks from the three main Geluk monasteries came together at the Jokhang temple in Lhasa. There, the geshe lharampa candidates had to answer questions put to them, showing a thorough and detailed knowledge of the Buddhist scriptures, a quick, flexible, and penetrating intelligence in responding to the questions, and surpassing debating skill.

Those who attained the degree of geshe were permitted to enter fully into tantric practice. In practice, it was common for those who had become geshes to accomplish a long meditation retreat. This practice followed Atisha's view, developed and reaffirmed by Tsongkhapa and his followers, that before one can hope to meditate with success, a thorough knowledge of the Buddhist sutras and commentaries, as well as skill in analysis and debate, are necessary. Following their retreat, geshes then could have elected to pursue tantric studies at one of the Geluk tantric colleges in Lhasa and elsewhere.

9
Modern Traditions
THE RI-ME (NONSECTARIAN) MOVEMENT

RI-ME LITERALLY MEANS "WITHOUT BOUNDARIES" AND
refers to the nonsectarian or nonpartisan movement that arose in Eastern Tibet in the nineteenth century. Ri-me cannot really be called a
school and thus is not strictly parallel to the Geluk or any other school
in this sense. It is, rather, a particular outlook or orientation held by
practitioners belonging to a variety of different lineages. Ri-me represents an appreciation for the multiplicity of authentic Tibetan practice
traditions in all their diversity and a commitment to work for their
survival. While remaining firmly rooted in their own lineal traditions
and maintaining primary allegiance to their own monastery, order, and
lineage, the Ri-me adherents studied and received teachings from one
another in a nonsectarian way. In addition, they worked cooperatively
together to preserve the various authentic practice traditions that existed
in their day but were beginning to disappear under the pressures of sectarianism and persecution.

Ringu Tulku comments that the "nonsectarian" approach for the Ri-
me actually harks back to the original teaching of the Buddha that
sentient beings have differing capacities, propensities, and needs.[1] In response to this situation, the Buddha gave eighty-four thousand different
dharmas or types of instruction to address the various situations of beings. Thus Buddhism from its earliest days acknowledges the necessity
of a multiplicity of authentic doctrines and teachings. According to
Ringu Tulku, the essence of the dharma is thus the opposite of sectarianism, in which people claim that their own school, lineage, or doctrine
is the only correct one and that all the others are somehow misguided,

inadequate, or wrong. The Ri-me contends that there are many authentic teachings within the buddha-dharma. All of these teachings and lineages arose because of a certain need, and it is important that all of them be preserved so that the full resources of the dharma may be available to future generations. The Ri-me masters thus did not consider themselves limited by sectarian identity or the orthodoxy of this or that school. In consequence, they were able to affirm spiritual authenticity even in traditions that were not their own, and to criticize posturing and superficiality even in their own schools.

Namkhai Norbu points out that although masters of various schools participated in the Ri-me movement, the orientation of dzokchen plays a particularly important role.[2] Dzokchen seeks a direct relationship to reality, not limited, governed, or controlled by a particular sectarian belief or philosophical standpoint. This does not mean that dzokchen is without any viewpoint, but rather that its aim is to move beyond any stricture of conceptual thought.[3] Namkhai Norbu comments, "In Dzogchen, you have to integrate everything. You have to remove this barrier of you and me, and understand the real condition *as it is*. This is called *ji-shin-wa,* in which there is not any barrier."[4] This approach shows the possibility of a direct and unmediated experience and appreciation of the wisdom found in living spiritual traditions, whatever their sectarian affiliation may be.[5]

PRECURSORS OF THE RI-ME

Tsongkhapa and the Gelukpas drew their inspiration from the work of Atisha and, standing behind him, the great Indian monastic universities and their traditions of textual scholarship. The basis of their lineages was conventional Mahayana Buddhism. By contrast, the core of the Ri-me movement was tantric and looked back to the yogins and lay practitioners mainly of the Nyingma, but also of the Kagyü and other practice traditions. Beyond that, the Ri-me found its ultimate origins in the Indian siddhas with their emphasis on Vajrayana practice and the attainment of enlightenment in this life. In the fourteenth century these various strands were gathered together in the person of the great Nyingma scholar and practitioner Longchenpa. As we saw, this master articulated a synthesis of the various Nyingma practices and, moreover, set them within a comprehensive philosophical and doctrinal frame. In a very real sense, Longchenpa and Atisha are comparable figures, each having provided the practical and philosophical foundations upon which later tradition could build, Atisha doing so for the Gelukpa, Longchenpa for the Ri-me.

From the fourteenth to the seventeenth century in Tibet, as mentioned, the Vajrayana traditions of the Nyingma and other practice traditions were passed on from one generation to the next, usually in the contexts of families and practitioners living in small hermitages. The essence of their dharma centered on daily tantric practice when they were not in retreat, and on solitary retreats, sometimes many years in length, when possible. All of this contemplative activity produced a tradition of deep spirituality and, occasionally, some very remarkable saints. Terma revelations continued to appear to tertons and reflected the lively and vigorous nature of these meditative schools.

Although the heart of the activity and creativity of these contemplative traditions lay in the arenas of meditation, ritual, and retreat, they also had their share of accomplished yogin-scholars. Beginning with Longchenpa, the fourteenth to seventeenth centuries also saw the development of a scholarly tradition that provided a doctrinal foundation for the later Ri-me. In addition to Longchenpa, the third Karmapa, Ranjung Dorje (1284–1339), the eighth Karmapa, Mikyö Dorje (1507–1554), the great Drukpa Kagyü master Pema Karpo (1527–1592), the Jonang scholar Taranatha (1575–?), and others composed works that articulated, clarified, and justified the view that corresponded to the kinds of practices that they were doing. The need for this kind of scholarly activity was twofold. First, a coherent and thorough philosophical view is a necessary analogue to meditation. Second, the contemplative schools were increasingly being challenged in the doctrinal sphere by the Gelukpas, and a clear and effective defense against the Geluk critiques became necessary. This became increasingly the case as the Geluk challenges spread to the political arena.

The essence of the doctrinal disagreement between the Geluk and the Ri-me lay in the interpretation of ultimate reality. The Geluk followed the second turning of the wheel of dharma in which the ultimate is seen as emptiness, defined as the absence of self-nature (see chapter 15). In contrast, the Ri-me generally followed an integration of the second and third turnings, in which the ultimate is seen as empty of self-nature—the second turning—but as inseparability with cognizance and buddha qualities—the third (see chapter 16). These two different ways of talking about the ultimate are rooted in the different kinds of dharma practiced by the two orientations: emptiness as the absence of self-nature corresponds well with a path of study, scholarship, and debate; emptiness as resplendent with luminosity accords more with the realization of the meditating yogin.

The forebears of the Ri-me were quite different from the Gelukpas in the manner of their institutional configuration. The Gelukpas, as we saw, were based in a series of very large monasteries in Lhasa and beyond. By contrast, the Nyingmapas, among the primary transmitters of what later became the Ri-me and typifying the movement, tended to prefer less centralized contexts. This institutional decentralization was reflected in the fact that schools later included in the Ri-me orbit tended to be defined by many different, individual cycles of teaching and practice. In many cases, these were cycles that had been revealed by one of the great tertons. Each was held by a particular retreat center or small gompa, or by a lay-practitioner family. Each usually formed a self-sufficient and complete set of teachings.

Seen from the point of view of the large monastic universities of Central Tibet, this kind of diversity and decentralization could be viewed as a weakness. It certainly did not allow the development of the kind of powerful, standardized, scholarly machine represented by Gelukpa training. It also made the formulation of a single, all-inclusive system of the Buddhist teachings difficult and inhibited any attempt to create a single and coherent "orthodoxy." Finally, it did not provide a sufficient institutional base for attracting large donations, for the rapid growth of monasteries, or for gaining and exercising political power. From another point of view, however, the decentralization of the Nyingmapa traditions could be seen as a strength in that it placed spirituality to the fore, made ample room for individual creativity, and was eminently flexible, allowing the various traditions to grow and evolve each in its own way.

This is not to say that the schools and lineages comprised by the Ri-me movement were not institutionally seated in Tibet. The Sakya and Kagyü were both fully institutionalized in the monasteries that formed their base. And, as we have seen, in the centuries leading up to the nineteenth, the Nyingma had also built a series of relatively large gompas. At these places, monks were trained, scholars were able to become versed in the most important scholarly traditions, and the lineages were able to ensure the integrity of the training received by the next generation of tulkus, scholars, and ordinary monks. For the various traditions considered Ri-me, then, the monastic way of life offered a needed focus providing definition, continuity, and a sense of identity. Nevertheless, among the Ri-me schools, one finds less single-minded focus on the monastery as the locus of the dharma, and more of an emphasis on the contexts of the yogin and lay practitioner as also having unique roles to play.

Among some of the trends flowing into the Ri-me, indeed, one sometimes finds a somewhat anti-institutional approach. Among the Indian siddhas, for example, one finds a pointed critique of the monastic way, fueled not by the way itself but by the pretensions and ambitions that periodically arose among those who followed it. In Milarepa's songs, as we have seen, one reads of encounters between the mountain yogin and conventional scholars from the Kadam monasteries down in the valley. Invariably Milarepa calls into question the spiritual efficacy of the monks' dharma of study and debate and instead points them in the direction of meditation and true realization. In the fourteenth to seventeenth centuries, a steady stream of "mad saints" appears in the contemplative schools, and these figures are particularly eloquent in their espousal of a dharma of practice as opposed to a dharma that is involved with other pursuits. This strong inspiration of these "crazy yogins" lies at the origin of the Ri-me and continues to invigorate it today.

A good example is provided by the Kagyü yogin Tsangnyön Heruka (1452–1507), "the mad (*nyön*) enlightened one (*heruka*) from the province of Tsang."[6] Born in a village lama family, Tsangnyön was ordained a novice at the age of seven. When he was eighteen, a vision urged him to make a pilgrimage to the sacred mountain of Tsari. During this journey, he met his guru, Shara Rapjampa, who sent him into retreat to practice. Afterward, again on the instructions of his guru, Tsangnyön entered a Sakya monastery at Gyantse, where he engaged in study of the Vajrayana. However, he aspired for the full realization of the teachings that he was studying and could see that the monastic way would not enable him to attain this longed-for goal.

At this time, he began to behave in a very strange manner, laughing and talking without cause. His odd behavior came to a climax during a visit of the prince of Gyantse, whom he insulted and ridiculed. After this incident, he left the monastery for good and gave up the monastic way. From then on, Tsangnyön followed the lifestyle of Milarepa, living and meditating in caves, and wandering through the villages teaching and seeking alms. He traveled extensively throughout Tibet and also Nepal, spending a great deal of time in western Tibet, particularly in the sacred caves where Milarepa had meditated.

Tsangnyön compiled a number of influential works, including his renowned life of Milarepa and collection of his "hundred thousand songs," both of which have been translated into English. This work as well as Tsangnyön's hermit lifestyle and preference for meditation in the very same places frequented by Milarepa show his great devotion to the "cotton-clad yogin." He also composed other texts, including a life of Marpa, and in these compositions originated a new style of Tibetan biography that emphasizes the humanity and ordinariness of its subjects.

Tsangnyön could always be counted on for an insightful, sometimes humorous critique of the religious establishment of the day. He himself was not celibate but took a female consort. Interestingly enough, he and his disciples did not trace their lineage back to Gampopa, the monastic disciple of Milarepa, but rather to Milarepa's other main disciple, the yogin Rechungpa. Tsangnyön also seems to have been opposed to the rigid hierarchies developing in his time that placed the great tulkus, or incarnate lamas, as the elite, at the top of the religious scale, with ordinary monks and hermits far down on the ladder, and the laity beneath them.

RI-ME FOUNDATIONS: JIGME LINGPA (1730–1798)

Initial impetus that would later nurture the Ri-me movement may be found at the end of the eighteenth century in the person of the Nyingma yogin Jigme Lingpa.[7] This master was born in a village in south-central Tibet to parents of simple means. Later he commented that the humbleness of his origins allowed him to follow his own spiritual inspiration rather than having his life planned out for him, as was usually the case of the nobility and aristocracy. Jigme Lingpa's biography depicted him as an unusual child—alert, kind, and courageous. Later in life, he recalled memories that pointed to lifetimes as various teachers and siddhas of India and Tibet.

When he was six, Jigme Lingpa was ordained as a novice and entered a monastery near his home. From the age of six until he was thirteen, owing to the poverty of his family, he lived as a novice of the lowest status. Because he could not provide his own support, he served others and was unable to have a tutor and study the dharma. Nevertheless, he possessed intelligence, feeling, and sensitivity. Although outwardly he seemed an insignificant little peasant boy, inwardly he felt great devotion to Guru Rinpoche and yearned to study and practice the dharma. During this time, he had many spiritual experiences and visions. In his monastic environment, he was able to receive various transmissions and empowerments, and this provided some satisfaction. In terms of his study, he was very quick and able to learn a great deal on his own, listening to the conversations of his socially more fortunate peers and readings texts that he was able to obtain: "By nature, I felt very happy when I was able to study [any subject such as] language, secular writings, canonical scriptures and their commentaries, or the Vajra[yana] teachings on the ultimate nature. I would study them with great respect, both by daylight and lamplight. But I hardly had the opportunity to develop the knowledge by studying with a master, even for a single day."[8]

At the age of thirteen, Jigme Lingpa met the tertön Thukchok Dorje and experienced a very strong sense of connection with and devotion toward him. From this point onward, this master became Jigme Lingpa's root guru and transmitted to him the essential Mahamudra instructions and other teachings. The close relationship of master and disciple continued even after Thukchok's death, for Jigme Lingpa continued to receive blessings and transmissions from him in visions. From this point onward, he met and studied with a variety of other gurus, deepening his understanding of the Nyingma lineage.

Jigme Lingpa had had a strong yearning for meditation since his childhood and had received practice instructions from an early age. At twenty-eight, he began a three-year retreat, taking a number of vows to maintain the simplicity and solitude of his practice. He meditated on the teachings that he had previously been given and read works composed by Longchenpa, with whom he felt a strong connection. He perfected both visualization and formless meditation, and experienced many visions of divinities and former teachers, such as Guru Rinpoche and his Tibetan consort, Yeshe Tsogyal. During this retreat, Jigme Lingpa also trained in the inner yogas of the winds (pranas), channels (nadis), consciousness (bindu), and psychic centers (chakras).[9] This purification of his inner being released his perception, intelligence, and creativity, and he found himself able to see the natural beauty and purity of the world and to express his experiences effortlessly in speech and writing. During this time, he received a series of visions of masters of the first spreading, including Guru Rinpoche and Manjushrimitra, an important early Nyingma founder. After this, he abandoned his maroon monastic robes and his monastic identity. He now put on the simple white robes of the ascetic and let his hair grow long, binding it up into a topknot, yogin style.

At twenty-eight, Jigme Lingpa received the decisive revelation of his life, the Longchen Nyingthik cycle, on "the innermost essence of Longchenpa's teaching." One night, after he had gone to bed, Jigme Lingpa was filled with longing for Guru Rinpoche and was resting in the clarity of unconditioned awareness. Abruptly, he found himself soaring through the sky, riding a white lion. He eventually arrived at what he later identified as the Bodhnath stupa, one of the most sacred Buddhist monuments in Nepal. A wisdom dakini gave him a wooden casket, and inside he found five scrolls. Following the instructions of another dakini, he swallowed the five scrolls, and immediately there appeared in his mind the complete teachings of the Longchen Nyingthik cycle, the summary and epitome of the dzokchen teachings destined for Jigme Lingpa's age. Tulku Thondup says that he found the words of this cycle in his mind "as if they were imprinted there."[10] Thus, the Longchen Nyingthik teachings and realization, which were entrusted and concealed by Guru Rinpoche many centuries earlier, were awakened, and Jigme Lingpa became a tertön. He gradually transcribed the teachings of the Longchen Nyingthik, starting with the *Nechang Thukkyi Drombu.*

At the age of thirty-one, Jigme Lingpa entered another three-year retreat. During his practice, he had three visions of Longchenpa and attained realization of dzokchen. In the first vision of Longchenpa's enlightened body, Jigme Lingpa received the transmission of Longchenpa's teachings in their words and their inner meaning. In the second vision of the master's enlightened speech, he received the injunction to maintain and propagate Longchenpa's teachings as his representative. And in the third vision of the guru's enlightened mind, he experienced the power of Longchenpa's innate awareness entering into his own being. He subsequently received a number of other transmissions of the Vima Nyingthik (the innermost essence of Vimalamitra's instructions) and other teachings.

Up until this point, Jigme Lingpa had kept his experiences and terma discoveries secret from everyone. Now, however, he began to teach, conferring empowerments of the Longchen Nyingthik on his own disciples and giving elaborations and explanations. In a short period of time, the word spread of the extraordinary teachings that the master was giving, and people came from far and wide to receive them. Tulku Thondup comments that "the Longchen Nyingthik teachings reached every corner of the Nyingma world, and they became the heart core of meditation instructions for many realized meditators and for ceremonial liturgies to this day."[11]

Jigme Lingpa now moved to the Chöngye Valley in southern Tibet and built a hermitage and meditation school there named Tsering Jong. Although, like Longchenpa before him, he could have attracted the funds to build a monastery and found a large institution, he avoided such an option and remained a simple hermit. As he himself said, quoting Longchenpa:

> To assemble numerous associates by various means,
> To have a monastery with comfortable accommodations—
> If you try, it will come about for a while, but it distracts the mind.
> So my advice from the heart is to remain alone.[12]

Jigme Lingpa remained at the Tsering Jong hermitage for the rest of his life, meditating, teaching disciples, and composing texts. A person of childlike nature, he said, "My perceptions have become like those of a baby. I even enjoy playing with children." He was known particularly for his kindness and compassion, and he frequently ransomed the lives of animals from the hunters and butchers who were going to kill them. At the same time, he was also an uncompromising master and would reflect people's deceits and posturing back, as he says, "in their faces, even if they are respected spiritual leaders or generous Dharma patrons."[13] He thus sums up the priority of his spiritual life: "In every action of sitting, walking, sleeping, or eating, I secure my mind [in the state that is] never dissociated from the brilliance of the ultimate nature."[14]

THE FLOWERING OF THE RI-ME MOVEMENT

Jigme Lingpa's life and teaching reflect what became the basic themes of the nineteenth-century Ri-me movement. These include the simple, nonaristocratic origins of many of its greatest masters and a religious life driven not by institutional concerns but by a personal, sometimes fervent spiritual quest. Devotion to Guru Rinpoche and the close bond of teacher and disciple were also important Ri-me features. As in Jigme Lingpa's life, the Vajrayana stood at the center of Ri-me spirituality, and a great emphasis was placed on meditation and retreat practice. In the biographies of the Ri-me masters, spiritual experiences, visions, and revelations take center stage. The fresh infusions of terma continue to occur throughout the Ri-me period, invigorating the movement. As in the case of Jigme Lingpa, the Ri-me movement also produced a number of accomplished scholars who gave birth to formulations and reformulations of the "view" of tantric practice. Again like him, it was common for the Ri-me teachers to avoid institution building and to prefer the simple, unadorned, rugged life of the hermit.

Jigme Lingpa's work established the foundations of Ri-me in several more specific respects. For one thing, the Longchen Nyingthik provided one of the most important transmissions of the Ri-me, giving it life and direction. In addition, his teaching provided the intellectual basis of the orientation, particularly in its third-turning emphasis on the positive, open, and dynamic aspects of enlightenment.[15] Finally, his three incarnations—Do Khyentse Yeshe Dorje (1800–1866), Paltrül Rinpoche (1808–1887), and Jamyang Khyentse Wangpo (1820–1892)—were among the founders and most important leaders of the Ri-me movement.

Jigme Lingpa lived in Central Tibet, but his influence quickly spread eastward to Kham and greater East Tibet. The principal heirs to his teaching were the first Dodrup Chen Rinpoche, Jigme Trinle Öser (1745–1821) and Jigme Gyalwe Nyugu (1765–1843). Jigme Lingpa's three incarnations, became principal transmitters of the Longchen Nyingthik and, as mentioned, influential figures in the Ri-me movement. Other important Ri-me lamas inspired by Jigme Lingpa's work included Jamgön Kongtrül the Great (1813–1899), Choggyur Lingpa (1829–1870), and Shalu Losel Tenkyong (nineteenth century).

The Ri-me movement embodied the nonsectarian understanding of Buddhism in Tibet described above. To restate, the dharma is universal and can be found in many different lineages and traditions. For Ri-me, a person ought to be evaluated not according to the school or sect to which he or she belongs, but by the quality of his or her awakening. A tradition ought to be judged not by its sectarian identity but by its spiritual potency and efficacy. Every authentic spiritual tradition possesses a measure of truth, but no one lineage can claim exclusive access to it. Each has something vital to give the others. Given the variety of human temperaments and needs, a rich array of diverse teachings, empowerments, and meditative approaches is a necessity. Thus it is that a practitioner of dharma must relate with other lineages in a context of mutual respect, dialogue, and interaction.

Along with this general outlook was a specific project of preservation and this arose directly out of the general Ri-me orientation. In order to understand this aspect, some historical background is necessary. In the period of time leading up to the inception of the Ri-me, sectarianism (*sho-ri*) had increasingly begun to rear its head in Tibet. Parallel to increasing political centralization and advancing institutionalization among the various traditions, schools and lineages were falling into the posture of proclaiming their own superiority and denigrating others. More and more, schools were claiming that their teachings were better than those of others, that they were the only correct and legitimate ones. Some went so far as to prohibit their members from visiting the monasteries of other lineages and receiving instruction from other teachers, threatening severe punishment to anyone violating this prohibition. Beyond this, schools holding political power in the different regions—and from the seventeenth century onward this meant primarily the Geluk—were engaging in open persecution.

The Ri-me leaders were aware of the many powerful and authentic spiritual traditions of their day, both Buddhist and non-Buddhist, that had survived from earlier times and were scattered throughout Tibet. In particular, the Ri-me teachers identified "eight great contemplative schools" as representing the pinnacle of the dharma in Tibet. According to these masters, any of the eight great schools could enable one to attain complete enlightenment. These eight schools, as given in Dudjom Rinpoche's history of the Nyingma lineage, are as follows:

1. the Nyingma;
2. the Kadam (including both the old Kadam as taught by Atisha and the new Kadam, i.e., the Geluk);
3. the Sakya (Path and Fruit);
4. the Marpa Kagyü (through Milarepa and Gampopa);
5. the Shangpa Kagyü (deriving from Khyungpo Naljorpa);
6. the Kalachakra;
7. Shije and Chö from the master Phadampa Sanggye and his Tibetan disciple Machik Labdrönma; and
8. the Uddiyana Tradition of Service and Attainment.[16]

Within these traditions and also outside of them, there were many lineages of authenticity and power that had been helpful to practitioners in the past and could be helpful in the future. Under the pressure of the increasing sectarianism and persecution, many of the lesser-known and institutionally less powerful traditions were in the process of disappearing. And the general sectarian trend posed a potential threat in the future even to the existence of the more established lineages.

The Ri-me masters viewed the accelerating destruction particularly of so many non-Gelukpa traditions in their day as a tragedy in the making. Two in particular—Jamyang Khyentse Wangpo, a Sakya lama, and Jamgön Kongtrül the Great, a Kagyü lama—wandered throughout Tibet, gathering tantric transmissions, liturgical texts, and practice commentaries of the Nyingma, Kagyü, Sakya, Kadam, Jonang, and other lesser-known lines.

Jamgön Kongtrül the Great, for example, had been raised in a Bönpo family and exhibited a preference for the Nyingma. However, at an early age he was kidnapped by the Kagyü leader Palpung Situ and held virtually as a hostage, an event he bitterly resented. This unfortunate incident shows that vulgar behavior in Tibet was not restricted to any one sect.

After receiving an education in both the practices and the scholarly traditions of the Kagyü and after studying with other masters, Kongtrül took up the Ri-me banner, traveling around Tibet, visiting gompas, hermitages, and teachers in search of tantric initiations and oral instructions that had accumulated in Tibet since the time of the first spreading. Jamgön Kongtrül—and in this he was joined by his colleague Jamyang Khyentse—went about his travels receiving empowerments, texts, and oral instructions. Kongtrül compiled the teachings he received in five large anthologies and collections, principal among which are the sixty-three-volume *Rinchen Terdzö* and the ten-volume *Damngak Dzö*. He was also a brilliant scholar whose *Sheja Kunkhyap* represents a comprehensive overview of Buddhism in its various philosophical traditions and schools.

Each Ri-me master was, as mentioned, firmly rooted within a particular school and tradition. It was this that defined his essential role and lineage identification, and it was this that he practiced and passed on to his disciples. Ringu Tulku remarks that Jamgön Kongtrül was a Kagyüpa and held his own lineage firmly, while Jamyang Khyentse "was very Sakya, his monastery was Sakya, he was a major Khenpo within the tradition, and he held his Sakya seat very strongly." At the same time, the various Ri-me proponents—as part of their endeavor of preserving the contemplative traditions—studied with one another and exchanged teachings and practice instructions. And they sent their disciples and students to do the same. This kind of deep and mutual interchange proved to be a most powerful element within the Ri-me movement. By receiving teachings of other lineages, the Ri-me masters were able to see that the same level of wisdom, compassion, and power was transmitted through different forms. This counteracted any tendency to solidify any one approach as superior to all others. Through studying with one another, the Ri-me teachers were also able to see how different traditions emphasized particular aspects of enlightenment and provided a variety of avenues to its attainment. Ringu Tulku remarks that through becoming acquainted with different approaches, one gains fresh and unexpected insights into one's own tradition and finds new depths and subtleties. In these ways, then, the endeavor of preserving the teachings of the authentic contemplative traditions was a critical element in the innermost spiritual lives of those holding the Ri-me outlook.

Important impetus to the Ri-me movement was given by the opening of a body of texts that had previously been unavailable. By way of background, in the seventeenth century, the Geluk tradition, under the leadership of the fifth Dalai Lama, had been engaged in conflict with the princes of Shigatse for control over central Tibet. It was this conflict that resulted in the intervention of the Altan Khan and the establishment of the Gelukpas as religious and political rulers of Tibet. The Karma Kagyü and the Jonang schools were closely tied with the Shigatse princes and therefore incurred the special enmity of the Geluk. Part of the ill-will directed at the Jonangpa, in particular, may have stemmed from their adherence to the shentong, "emptiness of other" doctrine that was strongly at variance with the Geluk view. Taking the third-turning teachings in a rather more literal way than the Geluk, the shentong doctrine held, as mentioned in chapter 7, that while ultimate reality is empty of self-nature, as stated in the second turning, it is not empty of its own qualities of wisdom and compassion. In this sense, the ultimate is empty only of that which it is not—hence shentong, emptiness of other.

The fifth Dalai Lama, after being given religious and secular control over Tibet by the Khan, forcibly closed down the Jonang order. Many of its monasteries were converted to Geluk institutions, an action that he also applied to some monasteries of the Kagyü and also of the Bönpo. Most of the Jonang texts were burned, but the library of the main Jonang gompa was merely sealed rather than its contents being destroyed. In the nineteenth century, some two centuries after this occurrence, an important Ri-me master, Shalu Losel Tenkyong, was able to convince the then-reigning Dalai Lama to remove the ban on the Jonang texts and to open the library. This occurred and the various major Ri-me scholars began to read the Jonang texts, finding in them most helpful syntheses of scholarship and meditation. In various ways, the Jonang literature supported and enhanced aspects of Ri-me thinking and provided an important source of inspiration and ideas for many of its masters.

In spite of the emphasis on meditation, as mentioned, among Ri-me masters appeared scholars of very considerable accomplishment. Perhaps the most remarkable was Ju Mipham Rinpoche (1848–1912), a brilliant Nyingma scholar.[17] Born in East Tibet, Mipham began learning to read and write at the age of six. In that same year, apparently, he memorized a text on the *Domsum,* or three vows of Hinayana, Mahayana, and Vajrayana. When he was twelve, Mipham went to study at one of the branch monasteries of Shechen monastery. The scholars at Shechen quickly recognized Mipham's extraordinary talents and began to make their learning available to him. After three years of study, at the age of fifteen, he went into retreat for eighteen months, carrying out the practice of Manjushri, the bodhisattva of wisdom and "patron saint" of scholars. At this time, Mipham had a vision of Manjushri and, subsequently, found that he was able to understand any topic that he approached. From this time on, he was known as Jamgön Mipham, "Jamgön" being an epithet of Manjushri.

After his retreat, Mipham began his studies in earnest, training under some of the most learned and accomplished masters of his day. He studied Sanskrit and Tibetan medicine under Jamgön Kongtrül the Great, "valid cognition" under Pönlop Loter Wangpo, the *Bodhicharyavatara* under Dza Paltrül Rinpoche, dzokchen from Khyentse Wangpo, the five dharmas of Maitreya under one Sölpön Pema, and so on, accomplishing his lessons with astonishing speed, depth, and clarity. The following story illustrates something of Mipham's astounding acumen. Once, while living in a hermitage above Riwoche monastery, Mipham asked his attendant to bring him ten volumes from the monastery's collection of the Kanjur, texts containing the sutras and tantras preached by the Buddha. Each of these volumes contained between four and six hundred pages. Mipham went quickly through the ten volumes and then asked for a second set of ten. In a few hours, he had finished going through the second set and asked for a third. This process continued until his attendant, tired from carrying this sizable burden of volumes between monastery and hermitage, up and down the mountain, inquired into Mipham's activities. Was the Rinpoche, perhaps, looking for something, some passage or quotation and, if so, could the scholars in the monastery down below not assist in the process so that all these books did not have to be carried up and down all day long? Mipham replied that, actually, he needed to read through each of these volumes.

His attendant asked how this was possible, as Mipham was turning the pages as fast as he could. But Mipham insisted, with this admission, however: "Mind you, I am not memorizing what I am reading, but I am reading everything and comprehending everything I am reading." Mipham continued until he had been through the entire Kanjur collection with its tens of thousands of pages.

Mipham Rinpoche's writings themselves fill thirty-two Tibetan volumes. Moreover, all of this was original writing, not anthologies or collections of other people's work. It is remarkable that this writing is consistently profound, clear, and comprehensive. What is even more remarkable is that Mipham actually spent most of his time not writing but occupied with continuous meditation, day and night. During his lunch and tea breaks, he would put a pot of ink in his lap and write with his pen in his right hand. With his left, he would continue to count the beads of his mala (rosary), marking the mantras he was reciting while he was composing his scholarly texts. The quality of Mipham's composition was uniformly superior, irrespective of his age or his external circumstances. For example, when Mipham was much older, he came upon a text outlining his view of the Madhyamaka orientation of Nagarjuna and Chandrakirti that he had composed in a few days while he was in his twenties. After reading through it, he remarked that he found it correct and accurate in every respect and that he would not want to change even a word.

The extraordinary manner in which Mipham was able to compose his texts, as well as the extraordinary results, led some to regard Mipham's compositions virtually as terma. In other words, they gave the impression of having existed, in their complete and perfect form, in the limitless space of mind, having come through Mipham as the open and unobstructed vessel of transmission.

The Ri-me adherents had a particular understanding of the practice of tantra that was quite different from that of the Gelukpas. In the monasteries of the various schools involved in Ri-me, people were able to take up the practice of tantra at a fairly early age. In addition, they did not have to be fully ordained monks to do so. Nonordained yogins and noncelibate lay practitioners were able to receive tantric empowerments and enter into the practice as easily as fully ordained monastics. The gate to tantric practice was thus a broad one, and an individual might be accepted as a disciple and initiate not because of his or her formal training or credentials, but because of demonstrating the openness of mind and discipline that are required for success in the practice of tantra.

The Ri-me movement never became a single, organized school with its own monasteries, its own hierarchy, and its own orthodoxy. As Ringu Tulku comments, there was never any lama who was known as a Ri-me lama; instead, each had a particular lineage seat and identification. Diversity, decentralization, and absence of dogmatism remained key elements in the Ri-me approach. It is typical that even the emphasis on the third turning of the wheel of dharma and the shentong, which characterizes most Ri-me teachers, is by no means adhered to by all. In fact, Mipham identified himself as a Prasangika Madhyamika and held that this, and not shentong, was the highest philosophical position.

As is obvious, then, the Ri-me masters represented a diverse group of people, and this is also true of their ways of life. Some were monastics and others were yogins or lay practitioners. Many important Ri-me leaders were not celibate but married. As in other matters, the important point here was not to set one particular lifestyle, e.g., that of the monk, yogin, or layperson, above the others, but rather to appreciate how each, in the right circumstances and with the right commitment to practice, could become a vehicle to the highest realization.

CONCLUSION

Ringu Tulku observes that it is natural for Buddhist adherents to say, "I received such and such a teaching from my teacher, I have full confidence in it, and I don't need anything else." It is certainly essential for a practitioner to have full confidence in his or her own lineage, lama, and practice. However, when one goes further and contends that "my school is the best and all the others are inadequate," then sectarianism is born and the problems start.

The Ri-me proponents showed that one can have this kind of confidence in one's own tradition and, at the same time, realize that it is appropriate for others to have the same kind of confidence in other lineages and other teachers. It is further necessary to acknowledge that just as one can gain full realization through devoted practice within one's own tradition, so others can gain that very same realization through devoted practice within theirs.

Ringu Tulku comments that sectarianism can only flourish in an environment of ignorance, where those maintaining the superiority of their own school do not actually know what others are saying or how they view things. Sectarianism developed in Tibet as the different institutional traditions became stronger, more self-contained, more isolated from one another, and more ignorant of what the others were doing. It was quite possible in Tibet to live in one's monastery for one's whole life, to study and practice the teachings of one's own lineage, and to remain uninformed about what was going on elsewhere.

Ringu Tulku also remarks that while in Tibet it was often possible to remain isolated from other lineages, in the modern world we have an entirely different situation. Here, not only do the adherents of the different Tibetan lineages rub shoulders with one another on a continual basis, but they also find themselves interacting with practitioners of Zen, Theravada, and Pure Land Buddhism. Here, a Ri-me outlook would appear absolutely necessary. In our present environment, in order to avoid misunderstanding, conflict, and mutual harm, it is critical that Tibetan Buddhists—whether of Western or Asian origin—take an active interest in gaining some real appreciation of Buddhist lineages that are not their own. This could begin with a general Ri-me attitude, with the realization that while one lineage may be best suited for one person, another may be most suitable for someone else. This attitude also involves the recognition that these different lineages may, in fact, lead different individuals to the same ultimate and unsurpassable goal. On a more practical level, while remaining firmly rooted within one's own lineage and set of teachings and practices, one might read about other lineages and seek out dialogue with their members. A full Ri-me approach, however, should not stop here. Beyond this, it would seem indicated to receive teachings from masters representing other traditions. Without this, how can one understand what the others are saying and what their teachings and practices actually involve?

PART THREE

Core Teachings

IN THE MODERN WORLD, AND PARTICULARLY IN THE West, religion and spirituality are often equated with doctrine, philosophy, and belief. Many of us assume that the spiritual path is paved with more and more sophisticated thinking. This assumption has produced a multimillion-dollar sector of the publishing industry in the United States, with each month seeing the appearance of new and ever more novel and inventive books on the spiritual life. Tibetan Buddhism has to some extent capitalized on this trend. Over the past thirty years, publications on Tibetan Buddhism have numbered in the hundreds if not thousands. From the viewpoint of Tibetan teachers, this publishing phenomenon has benefit, for it enables a great many people to become informed about Tibet and also provides the means for important texts and bodies of oral instruction to be preserved for the future.

What may be lost sight of in this situation, however, is that Tibetan Buddhism is ultimately not so much about having the right ideas as it is about ongoing spiritual practice and the transformation it brings about. This perspective is illustrated by the well-known analogy, given by the Buddha, of a man dying from the wound inflicted by a poisoned arrow. In that critical situation, what one needs is the practical knowledge of how to extract the arrow and treat the dying man. All other knowledge is not only extraneous; it is actually harmful because it creates diversion and wastes precious time. We are all that dying man, and what we need is practical knowledge of how to address our situation, not lofty ideas of how things could be.

Still, as even the casual observer will know, doctrine and philosophy play quite a prominent role in Tibetan Buddhism as exemplified, again, by all the books. This raises the important question of what the role of doctrines and ideas is in Tibetan tradition, and what it has to do with practice and transformation. An answer is provided in a teaching that is frequently given by Tibetan teachers, that of the three kinds of prajna, or understanding. These show us how to work with the ideas of Buddhism, beginning from the stage where we know nothing about the dharma whatsoever, up to the point of realization.

THE THREE PRAJNAS

Everything that we do, however simple and nonconceptual it may seem, always implies some kind of conceptual understanding or belief. Even brushing our teeth implies certain ideas about what teeth are and how we should care for them. It also implies certain beliefs about ourselves, for sometimes, when one is very depressed, even brushing one's teeth seems impossible.

By way of another example, most of us believe in the existence of a solid, enduring "self" that is oneself, "myself," "me," that needs to be constantly looked after, protected, and built up. This belief leads us to spend a great deal of time and energy on actions in the service of this supposed "self." Because of this belief, if we begin to feel shaky or weak or even nonexistent, we will think that something "bad" has happened and we will panic. We might run to the self-help section of our local bookstore or to our therapist or to the refrigerator or to the gym or, if we are a workaholic, back to the computer to do some more work. Or maybe, if we are so inclined, we will have a drink, take some drugs, or call a friend. Based on our belief in a self, if someone appears to ignore us or insult us, we will consider that person an "enemy" and will mobilize all the feelings, attitudes, and actions that we consider appropriate to someone who is "against" us. It takes a lot of work to maintain an ego, but most of us are more than up for it and take this as our primary life project.

Beliefs are very powerful, because what we do with every moment of our lives is guided by them. If our beliefs about reality are accurate, our lives will be fruitful and fulfilling. But if they are false, we will be building our lives on a foundation that has no substance, no strength and, in fact, no reality. Sooner or later—and probably sooner—the foundation will cave in and our lives will collapse. Look around. It happens all the time. It eventually happens to all of us when we meet our own death. The belief in a solid, substantial "self" is an example of a "wrong view." In other words, it is a belief that, however much we may be invested in it, is incorrect, inaccurate, and not in keeping with how things actually are.

The first step on the spiritual path is to call into question the various beliefs that we carry around. For many of us, this questioning is provoked by some event in our lives, something that has caused us pain or confusion or frustration. At a certain point we see that our concepts, our expectations about reality, not only are not being fulfilled but are actually creating a lot of problems for us and for those we are close to.

It is at this point that one might begin to take a serious interest in Buddhism. We might begin to see it as a possible resource helping us to look more deeply into ourselves and begin to sort our lives out. To explore this possibility, we might begin to read some books, talk to friends, or go to hear a Buddhist teacher. The first thing that Buddhism presents us with is the need to gain a more accurate understanding—and this means a more accurate conceptual understanding—of who we are and what life is. We need to begin to shed our "wrong views" and come to "right views"—that is, an understanding that accurately reflects, as much as words and ideas can, the nature of things as they are. It is only on the basis of such a "right view" that any kind of genuine spiritual practice such as meditation is possible.

For it is a fact that no one who is 100 percent committed to the existence and aggrandizement of his or her ego would ever meditate. Why? Because meditation involves looking into one's own experience. Ego is basically a bad idea with no future; and this kind of looking spells the death-knell of ego. The first thing one begins to notice is that things are not as solid and substantial as they previously seemed. There are gaps in one's thoughts and feelings; things appear somewhat random; one may see things about oneself not previously noticed, perhaps one's pretensions or unkindness. Meditation is definitely not healthy for the ego. It is not possible to meditate unless you are more interested in finding out what is going on than in maintaining a particular idea of who you are.

The ground of meditation, then, is developing a conceptual understanding that is more or less accurate ("right view") and that will allow us to sit down on the meditation cushion and begin to take a look at ourselves. The path from where we are now to full understanding goes through the three phases of hearing, contemplating, and meditating.

The first step on the Buddhist path is hearing and learning the teachings. In Tibet and in Tibetan Buddhism today, there are two ways to do this, either through the oral accounts, the stories, and explanations of a living teacher; or through studying the sacred texts. The texts provide the classical accounts, often with elaborate and well-structured arguments and examples. Since they originated in a different time and place, sometimes their contents are difficult to assimilate. We often need a teacher's commentary or some previous training to be able to make sense out of them and use them.

The oral teaching that we might hear from our teacher, on the other hand, usually addresses our situation more directly and is spoken in a way that is much easier for us to hear and comprehend. Often the oral teaching is rooted in the textual tradition but has been adapted and interpreted for us by the teacher. When you go to hear a talk by a Tibetan lama, often there will be elements of both textual presentation and oral teaching. For example, the lama might teach from a particular text, quoting line after line, and then give his or her own explanation.

The first prajna involves simply finding out what the tradition says about something. It does not really involve critical reflection or assessment. In relation to oral teaching, it means just knowing what one's teacher said about a given topic. In relation to textual learning, it means knowing the literal content of the text, including its logic, its line of argument, and its examples.

In reference to hearing, Sakyong Mipham Rinpoche tells us:

> It is said that if you are of the first quality, which usually means you have a karmic predisposition, you only need to hear the words once. If you are stupid like the rest of us, you need to hear them at least twenty or thirty times. . . . Khenpo Namdrol [a well-known Nyingma scholar] is regarded as one of the greatest khenpos alive right now, and every time I hear him it

is "bombs away!" His teachings go on for months. Talk about
lists! And not just lists, but also the profundity of his explanations. He told me that he used to go over whatever he had
learned on a particular day ten times. . . . And he is a pretty
smart guy! He told me that it takes a while to really understand
the teachings.[1]

The second prajna or kind of understanding is contemplation or reflection. Simply having heard or learned a particular Buddhist teaching
does not mean that we agree with it or see that it is true. The second
prajna requires us to take what we have learned and look into it closely,
asking ourselves questions. What is the actual meaning of this teaching?
What is it trying to point to? Does it reflect the actual condition of my
life as I experience it? Does it make sense in terms of what I see in the
lives of others around me? This kind of contemplation doesn't just
involve determining whether a certain teaching is true or not. On a
much deeper level, it provides a vehicle to begin to inquire into how
things actually are for us.

For example, the first thing Buddha Shakyamuni taught his students
was the first noble truth, that life is suffering. The first prajna is to know
the basic idea and teaching on suffering, that life is always somehow
incomplete and finally unsatisfying. The second prajna involves actually
looking closely at one's life moment by moment to see whether, in fact,
the first noble truth pans out. Through the second prajna, one aims to
find out whether the truth of suffering is true and to discover the extent
and manner of its truth.

Sakyong Mipham Rinpoche explains how contemplation works. Taking the example just mentioned, when we *contemplate* suffering, in the
beginning it is just an idea. Eventually, however, through the practice
we come face-to-face with its concrete reality: we find ourselves looking
straight at it.

It's a relief and it's much easier, because usually we avoid looking
at it. So when we sit down and just look straight at [suffering],
there can be a quality of profound shock, profound emotion,
just as when somebody dies and we realize the truth of death.

That kind of experience affects how we see our body and mind, our emotional state, how we look at the rest of our life.[2]

When we contemplate the truth of suffering and see it reflected in our lives, this can have a profound effect on our general state of being. We find ourselves slowing down, becoming more rooted and grounded, and our mind becomes more settled, stable, and strong.

Rinpoche continues by indicating the importance of the contemplation for the practice of meditation.

If we're to move along the path, at a certain point we have to sit down and [through contemplation] incorporate the reality of the human condition into our inner being in a steady way. That understanding has to become part of our nature. Then when we get up and we see an old person, a sick person, or a dead person, the continuum of our mind does not change. We know that we understand death; death is real and we have incorporated it. When our death finally comes, it will hopefully be a relatively smooth transition.[3]

This stability and strength developed through the second prajna, contemplation, then, provides a most needed and necessary foundation for the third prajna, the practice of *meditation*.

Sakyong Mipham Rinpoche remarks, "When we get to the stage of meditating, the stages of hearing and contemplating have already been established; the foundation is there. When we meditate, we are discovering our mind."[4] In the third prajna, meditation, the Buddhist teachings are ultimately tested and one is able to make their truth completely one's own. In meditation, one looks directly at one's mind, one's experience, to see how and what it really is, apart from expectations, fear, and wishful thinking. One looks to see just how reality appears.

Many people interested in spirituality in the West have resistance to the first prajna. They may want to skip over it and get on to contemplation and meditation, to get at the "real meaning" of the teaching. Their resistance is understandable, for all of us have grown up in a culture in which "learning," particularly in the formative years prior to college (and, sadly enough, too often also at the college level) is largely rote. Moreover, what is memorized and "regurgitated" all too often has little or nothing to do with the actual concerns, inspiration, or life of the student. For many of us, the mere thought of the kind of literal learning that takes place in the first prajna causes us to freeze up or lose interest.

Yet, according to Buddhism, knowing just what our teacher has taught or what the texts actually say is necessary. Why? For one thing, Buddhists teachings, while initially seeming "other," have emerged out of countless generations of meditators and point us to our most inner, subtle, and personal experience. In addition, the first prajna provides us with something reliable to reflect upon in the second prajna. If we don't know what the teachings say, we will simply fall back upon our preconceptions and patterns of habitual thought, which have gotten us into so much trouble in the first place.

It may be asked, "Why do I have to study and reflect—as in the first two prajnas? Why can't I just sit down and meditate without the extra baggage?" Unfortunately, even when we sit down to "just meditate," subtle thoughts accompany us and have an enormous effect on what we see. If one has not, to some extent, understood the Buddhist teachings on egolessness, chances are that his or her meditation will be directed toward the subtle perpetuation of ego, through trying to escape discomfort or to produce some state of mind the person considers "worthy" and "valuable."

The first two prajnas are important for another reason: we will need what we have learned to fall back on later, as we progress along the path. Trungpa Rinpoche required his students to study and even memorize the teachings that he gave. In my own case, I must say that a very great deal of what he taught went right over my head. And yet how frequent has been my experience, say in retreat many years later, that something he had said suddenly appeared in my mind just when I was in difficulty and in need of clarification or guidance. It would be hard to overestimate how helpful one's learning can be when one is meditating, simply trying to locate and rest in "the nature of mind."

On the path, the three prajnas are used sequentially, as I have described them here, and they are also employed in a more back-and-forth way. For example, having reflected on the teachings and come to a deeper understanding of their relevance for our experience, we may be inspired to go back to study the texts more thoroughly. Or, having meditated, we may find ourselves with many questions to bring to our teacher or to our study of the texts, wanting to know what they say about what we have experienced in our practice.

In traditional Tibet, a tremendous amount of emphasis was placed upon studying, memorizing, and being able to repeat the contents of the literal teaching. Tibetan lamas, particularly if they have not had a great deal of experience teaching Westerners, will often stay close to the traditional style of teaching, simply expounding this or that text, with a minimum of commentary. Western students sometimes find this approach frustrating and look for something more adapted to their situation, their way of thinking, and their problems.

In this context, it can be helpful to realize that as Tibetan Buddhism moves to the West, a major journey of translation needs to be accomplished, so that the dharma, far from being in any way alien, becomes a language that directly gives voice to our most intimate experience as Westerners. Tibetan teachers have accomplished much of this translation, coming to the West and presenting the teachings as they do; and a few extraordinary ones have met us far more than halfway. But whatever distance there may be left is up to us Westerners to cover, through our own study, contemplation, and meditation.

THE THREE YANAS

Often in our Western religious traditions, as mentioned, we find an emphasis on correct doctrine and unquestioning belief. This leads to the idea that spiritual truth has one and only one correct formulation. The religious person is then left with no real alternative but to accept that one formulation, whether or not it has any relationship to his or her actual experience or understanding.

Buddhism understands spiritual teaching as *upaya,* or skillful means.

No formulation of the truth has value in and of itself, independently of the person to whom it is addressed. Instead, a particular formulation is to be judged according to its ability to open our eyes to a deeper experience of reality. In fact, at different stages of our own spiritual journey, we see reality in different ways and need teachings that are appropriate to our situation at that moment.

One might ask, what about when one has attained enlightenment? At that time, isn't there a teaching that is no longer relative to the individual's situation, but absolute? The answer is no. It is said that when a person has attained the complete realization of buddhahood, then he or she sits in beatific silence, contemplating the wondrous universes as they come into being and die, and expressing the perfection of that experience in love for others. In a strange paradox, the Buddha actually never utters a word, never narrows his realization down in any manner. Yet, by some miracle, we sentient beings "hear" the plenitude of his silence in various ways and perceive him speaking in words that articulate what we need to learn. In other words, the Buddha's silence is the only ultimate teaching there is.

On the relative level, it is said that the Buddha gave eighty-four thousand dharmas or different kinds of instruction. Each of these is appropriate to a specific kind of human situation and to a particular level of spiritual development. The eighty-four thousand dharmas reflect the vast array of Buddhist teachings that developed in India. This array is arranged, in Tibetan tradition, into the three yanas, or vehicles. The three yanas are three general levels of spiritual understanding that each Tibetan Buddhist goes through on the journey to full enlightenment. They include the Hinayana, or basic vehicle; the Mahayana, or great vehicle; and the Vajrayana, or indestructible vehicle. Each yana is not just a level of understanding but also a set of doctrines and practices appropriate to a person at that stage.

According to Tibetan tradition, the teachings of the three vehicles were given by the Buddha during his lifetime, on specific occasions and to particular audiences. Each vehicle has its own "view," "practice," and "result." Kalu Rinpoche expresses the traditional formulation:

The Hinayana approach involves maintaining perfect discipline and ceasing to behave in a way that causes harm to oneself and others. This protects the practitioner from obstacles and distractions and allows for single-pointed meditation.

The Mahayana approach involves practicing compassion toward all beings as well as meditating on profound emptiness. These two are done simultaneously. On the basis of the altruistic state of mind, or bodhicitta, we practice the six perfections: giving, morality, patience, enthusiastic perseverance, meditation, and wisdom.

The Vajrayana approach is a way of transmutation that purifies all activities—emotions, impure illusions—and allows us to quickly reach enlightenment through the Generation and Completion Stage meditation.[5]

In Tibetan tradition, the three yanas are viewed in two different ways. First is the "three yanas of the school," in which they are a way to understand and organize the various historical Buddhist schools. In this rendition, the eighteen schools of nikaya Buddhism, such as the Sarvastivada and the Theravada, belong to the Hinayana; traditions emphasizing the practice of the six paramitas belong to the Mahayana; and the various tantra schools belong to the Vajrayana.

In Tibet, the three yanas have also functioned as a way to classify people's various levels of spiritual development, known as the "three yanas of the person." Thus an individual practitioner may be said to be at the Hinayana, Mahayana, or Vajrayana level of maturity. Even within classical Tibetan tradition, it was realized that to identify a person with a particular yana does not really tell us what school he or she is following. Each school, whether classified as Hinayana, Mahayana, or Vajrayana, has practitioners at all levels of understanding. For example, one can be a member of a Hinayana school yet have a Vajrayana level of maturation, or follow a Vajrayana school with a Mahayana level of understanding. And, as Ringu Tulku points out, one can even belong to a Mahayana school and not be practicing Buddhism at all! Trungpa Rinpoche once expressed the view that within the Theravadin tradition over the course of its history, there were undoubtedly realized people who reflected a Mahayana and even a Vajrayana orientation. He also commented that within the historical Theravada there were probably realized siddhas (the Tantric Buddhist enlightened ideal).

This somewhat complex way of talking about schools and practitioners makes a simple but important point. The school or sect that a person belongs to does not really tell us about his or her level of understanding, maturation, or attainment. A practitioner is to be evaluated strictly according to the degree of humility, insight, and compassion. A Vajrayana practitioner who thinks that he or she is automatically at a higher level than a Theravadin completely misunderstands the matter.

To classify the schools in this way also does not mean that everything in them can be reduced to one or another yana. According to Ringu Tulku, each of the schools contains all three yanas. The schools are identified with one or another of the yanas depending upon which teachings are more prominent and explicit in them. Ringu Tulku observes that when one reads Hinayana texts alone, one may not find the Mahayana or Vajrayana teachings in them. However, when one has a living understanding of the Mahayana or Vajrayana, one can then go back to the Hinayana sutras and find both the Mahayana and Vajrayana contained implicitly therein.

Within Tibetan tradition, then, each practitioner follows a path that is defined by the three yanas. The practitioner begins his or her spiritual journey with the Hinayana, then takes up the Mahayana, and finally enters into the Vajrayana. When a person is ready, he or she enters a particular yana and practices it until there is some attainment. This indicates readiness to move to the next yana. There is no sense that one has to have the full attainment of each yana before moving on, but rather that there has to be enough study, practice, and understanding to enable one to progress to the next level. In this section, we consider the Hinayana and Mahayana stages of the journey as defining the basis of Tibetan spirituality. (I examine the Vajrayana in my book *Secret of the Vajra World*.)

The preceding discussion raises an important question touched upon in chapter 3: what is the relation between the "Hinayana" as the first step on the Tibetan Buddhist path and the Buddhist traditions that existed prior to the appearance of the Mahayana, and especially the Theravada, which is so important in Southeast Asia today. Sometimes people think that they are the same thing and refer to the Theravada as a "Hinayana" tradition. This is an error, something certainly revealed by the strong negative reactions many Theravadins feel when labeled "Hinayanists."

In fact, as we shall see presently, "Hinayana" refers to a critical but strictly limited set of views, practices, and results. The pre-Mahayana historical traditions such as the Theravada are far richer, more complex, and more profound than the definition of "Hinayana" would allow. For example, the Theravadin sacred scriptures, the Pali canon, include texts on emptiness and compassion, neither of which fit the classical definition of Hinayana. Within the Theravada, there are also trends that remind one of the Vajrayana. Moreover, in the Theravada today there are monastic traditions that seem to reflect a Hinayana orientation, but there are also those of forest renunciation whose realized saints are reminiscent of tantric siddhas and appear very different from the definitions found of the Hinayana. The term "Hinayana" is thus a stereotype that is useful in talking about a particular stage on the Tibetan Buddhist path, but it is really not appropriate to assume that the Tibetan definition of Hinayana identifies a venerable living tradition such as the Theravada or any other historical school.

10

Hinayana
The View

The so-called Hinayana provides a foundation for both the Mahayana and Vajrayana. Thus in Tibetan Buddhism, the Hinayana outlines the fundamental Buddhist ideas of suffering, karma, and non-ego that will be refined in the two higher vehicles. It also describes the basic Buddhist meditation practice of tranquillity (shamatha) and insight (vipashyana) which, again, are taken up and refined in Mahayana and Vajrayana. And it articulates the goals of renunciation and surrender that form the basis of Buddhist spirituality throughout. Within Tibetan tradition, the Hinayana is understood not so much as a "lower" path that is later transcended but rather as a foundation which, if well laid, makes the journey through the further yanas possible.

The Hinayana teachings were given by the Buddha in the Deer Park at Benares, shortly after his enlightenment, to his five former renunciant companions, who became his first disciples. On this occasion, according to the early texts, the Buddha preached the four noble truths, which include the [1] truth of suffering, [2] the truth of the origin of suffering, [3] the truth of the cessation of suffering, and [4] the truth of the path. Alternatively, Tibetan tradition typically organizes the Buddha's early and later teachings into the three categories of the view, the practice, and the result. *View* refers to the conceptual understanding that provides orientation to the practice. *Practice* outlines the concrete methodologies of transformation. And *result* points to what is attained through the practice. This raises the interesting question of how the four noble truths are to be divided into the more typically Tibetan format of view, practice, and result. For readers more familiar with the four noble truths, the correlations in table 10.1 may be helpful.

TABLE 10.1

HINAYANA: VIEW, PRACTICE, AND RESULT

VIEW, PRACTICE, AND RESULT	SANSKRIT	NOBLE TRUTH	FOUR REMINDERS
View of Hinayana	Duhkha	1. Truth of suffering	2. Impermanence 4. Defects of samsara
	Samudaya	2. Truth of the origin of suffering	2. Karma
		Implications of the view of Hinayana	1. Precious human birth
Practice of Hinayana	Marga	4. Truth of the path	
Result of Hinayana	Nirodha	3. Truth of the cessation of suffering	

In Tibet, the four noble truths are most often presented in terms of "four reminders." These are literally "four thoughts that turn the mind" (*lo dok nam shi*). The four reminders attempt to provide antidotes for certain basic, habitual delusions that we all carry around. For example, we all tend to take our lives for granted; to counteract this, the first reminder, the preciousness of human birth, is taught. We also tend to disregard our own mortality; to redress this, the second reminder, that of impermanence, is given. Further, we tend to think that, apart from actually breaking the law, we can act with impunity; to dispel this illusion, the third reminder, karma, is presented. Finally, we have convinced ourselves that we can be happy by following this or that course of mundane action; to correct this most harmful wishful thinking, the fourth reminder is taught, the defects of samsara.

How are these four reminders correlated with the four noble truths? As table 10.1 indicates, the truth of suffering is elaborated in reminders number 2 and 4, impermanence and the defects of samsara; and the truth of the origin of suffering is treated in reminder number 3, karma. Reminder number 1, precious human birth, articulates the impact of having understood the first two noble truths: since suffering and death are real and unavoidable and our future is determined by karma, we should make the most of the opportunities that we have as human beings.

PRECIOUS HUMAN BIRTH

In the Tibetan view, as mentioned, our human state is only one among many possible modes of being. Like the vast majority of other human cultures, the Tibetans teach that our current human existence is one brief moment in a long spiritual journey composed of millions of lives. We may be human beings at the moment, but since beginningless time, we have been trapped within the prison of samsara and have been cycling through its various types of existence. Within Tibetan tradition, samsara is seen as being composed of six realms, the three lower realms including those of the hell-beings, the hungry ghosts, and the animals, and the three higher realms, those of humans, demigods, and gods. Chagdud Tulku remarks that among all the possible samsaric states that we could be born into, the human one is among the most rare. It is said that hell-beings are as numerous as dust particles in the entire universe, hungry ghosts are as plentiful as grains of sand in the river Ganges, and animal life teems in every drop of water or particle of earth. Even the gods may be compared to the number of snowflakes in a blizzard. In contrast, those endowed with a blessed human life are as rare as stars in the noonday sky.[1]

Tibetan teachers never tire of telling us not only that human birth is a rare occurrence but that, of all the six realms of being, it is the most fortunate. This is so because it is only here that spiritual practice can be undertaken. Chagdud Tulku remarks:

> The three lower realms allow no opportunity to hear or understand the teachings of dharma. Beings there lack leisure or other supportive circumstances to aid or encourage practice: they experience too much suffering. On the other hand, the god realms provide no incentive to practice. Beings in these realms are so infatuated with and intoxicated by sensual pleasure and bliss

that the thought of escaping from this or any other state of cyclic existence never occurs to them. . . . In the human realms, however, we taste both sweet and sour. We know enough about suffering to want change, yet the suffering isn't so acute that we can't do anything about it. . . . Precious human birth provides a freedom and a leisure to practice that cannot be found in other realms of experience, either the three lower realms . . . with their immense suffering, or the nonhuman higher realms . . . with their false contentment.[2]

We must not take our human life for granted in another way. There are many people living now on the planet who are suffering and confused yet have no access to spiritual teachings to help them grow and make sense of their lives. Tibetan Buddhism mentions four obstacles that prevent human beings from practicing the dharma:

1. *Wrong view,* such as believing that a purely materialistic approach to life will bring happiness or that killing animals or harming other people will have no consequences for oneself.
2. *Skepticism,* in Chagdud Tulku's words, being "skeptical about spirituality and religion. Mere intellectual sophistication or scholarly learning doesn't enable one to acquire or maintain spiritual faith. Clever but cynical people find it difficult to put their trust in anything and thus don't have the openness and receptivity necessary to look for a spiritual practice."[3]
3. *Being born in a dark age,* a time and place where the dharma is not available.
4. *Having a beleaguered life,* as through extreme mental or physical illness, economic deprivation, social degradation, or political oppression, such that one cannot even begin to think about spirituality.

If our lives are not impeded and bogged down by any of these obstacles, then not only will we have a precious human birth, but we will also enjoy a human birth that is "free and well favored." If this is our situation and if we are in a condition and frame of mind where spiritual practice is actually a possibility, we are urged to appreciate the rare opportunity that this provides and encouraged not to waste it.

In relation to a free and well-favored birth, a story is told of His Holiness the sixteenth Karmapa, Rikpe Dorje, when he visited Hong Kong for the first time. Night had already fallen when he was taken to his suite at the top of a luxury hotel. As it was already dark, he was immediately led out on the balcony to see the city below. Having lived in Tibet and Sikkim all his life, he had never seen such a sight, and at first he responded to the spectacular lights of Hong Kong at night with great interest and delight. But almost at once he began to weep uncontrollably and had to be helped back to the suite inside. Later he said that he had been overcome by grief that here were these millions of people trying desperately to be happy, and yet the vast majority of them had never heard even the least mention of the dharma.

IMPERMANENCE

The second reminder concerns the impermanence of our lives. When we are young and as we grow into adulthood, particularly in modern cultures, we are conditioned not to think about or even notice death. Our cultural obsession with youth, beauty, and materialism, driven as it is by advertising and modern economies of consumption, leads us to the view that serious disease and old age, not to speak of death, are not parts of our own future. Death is sequestered and hidden from sight, trivialized, or turned into adrenaline-producing entertainment that merely feeds the devouring demon of consumerism.

Yet the fact remains that all of us are right now facing the specter of death. Chagdud Tulku advises us to contemplate that all people will soon die, no matter how powerful, famous, or wealthy they may now be. All of them will die, and none will be able to take anything of what they are, what they own, or what they have accomplished with them. Little more than a century from now, everyone currently living on the planet will be gone. In our own personal case, there will definitely come a day—and for some of us it is not far off—when we will take our last breath. After we die, people will quickly forget about us, and in a short period of time no one will even remember that we ever existed. And sometime later, not long in cosmic terms, even our earth will perish and life will cease to exist here altogether.

But how can we know this not just intellectually—which has very little impact—but in our bones? Tulku Urgyen suggests that we contemplate the following analogy from Padmasambhava's *Karling Shitro:*

> Imagine that you are standing on a half-inch-wide ledge on a sheer cliff overlooking an almost bottomless abyss, with a roaring river raging below. You cannot bear to look down. Only your toes can rest on the ledge, while your hands grasp two handfuls of grass the size of a goat's beard. You are hanging onto these two handfuls of scrub-grass that represent your life span and life force. At the same time, impermanence, in the form of two rats . . . gnaws away the grass you are clinging to, piece by piece. Once the grass is consumed, there will be nothing left to hold onto. There is only one way to go: to plunge into the nearly bottomless abyss and the raging river. . . . So you hang on while the rats eat up the grass, blade by blade. You have no chance of survival whatsoever. This is our current situation.[4]

Why is awareness of death so important? Because it leads us to examine our own lives and priorities. When we are unaware of our own mortality, when we are under the impression that we have "all the time in the world," we tend simply to follow our habitual patterns, drifting along and finding gratification, confirmation, and material well-being where we may. But when death is staring us in the face, then we begin to see what is really important in our lives.

What kind of an impact can awareness of the reality of death have on a person? With the reader's permission, I would like to report a personal experience. Several years ago, over a course of a few months, I gradually became increasingly ill until I was eventually more or less incapacitated. My trusted physician of many years ran one series of tests and then a second, more complex set. When the results were back, she urgently called me into her office and told me that she was quite certain that I had a relatively rare form of cancer that was fast-acting and basically untreatable. She sent me to the best oncologist in the area, and, after reviewing the tests and my symptoms, he confirmed the hypothesis and ordered some more tests that would give an indication of exactly how long I had to live. When I asked him, "Do you have any doubt whatsoever that I have this form of cancer?" he replied, "None whatever." He added that death—and it would be a painful one—could come in a matter of months. He concluded by saying, "My only question is, have you made out your will?"

The following week, while the tests were being processed, was an intense time for me and for my wife and children. We spent our time asking all the questions one asks in those situations. I wondered how I could face my own death. How could my wife and children live without me? How could the family survive on just my wife's income? How would the children fare without a father? Most of all, I realized how I had wasted so much of my life. I became aware that I had spent far too much of my time doing things that were reflections of how I and others thought I should act but were not expressions of who I really was. I am a college teacher and I saw how I had expended my energy trying to fulfill external academic expectations rather than giving the students the best of myself. I had spent long hours reading and writing but little time with my family, the people in this world—I realized—who mattered the most to me. In interactions with colleagues and administrators, I had played it safe rather than contributing the sometimes unconventional ideas and perspectives that were mine to offer. And though I followed a spiritual path, I did so too often by rote and acted as if I had all the time in the world.

I was a person who had certainly thought about death over the course of my life, but I had not actually realized that it could and would happen to me. When I was actually confronted with the prospect of imminent death, I began to see my life in an entirely new perspective. I said to myself over and over, "If only I had realized, I would have lived my life in a different way. If only I had my life still to live, I would do things differently. I would live more in terms of who I am and what really calls me." In talking to others about my situation, I realized that those few I met who were similarly facing their own imminent death were right on my page, and that those who had not had death staring them in the face in this way had no idea what I was talking about. They thought they understood, but they had no idea. An experience like this opens one's eyes, and one begins to see others who do not have this immediate awareness of death as living in a dream world.

The end of the story is that when the final test results came in, the ones that were going to determine just how long I had to live, they turned out to be negative. I did not, the doctor reported, seem to have the dreaded form of cancer, or at least he could not find it. He was somewhat incredulous and reported that he had gone down to the lab to look into the microscope himself. My reaction to the news was interesting. Of course my family and I were, on one level, relieved, to say the least. But the horror that we had been through could never be undone. I found myself unable to enjoy life as I had before, taking the kind of naive satisfaction in things that I used to. I now felt like a prisoner living under a sentence of death; I had won a reprieve, but it was only temporary; and at some point sooner or later, I was going to be right back in that doctor's office (figuratively speaking) and this time, the results would not be negative. I felt strongly that the life I used to live and to love was ruined, gone forever.

As the saying goes, something was lost, but something was gained. I was able to make some important changes in my life. Although I still do many of the same things I used to, I now realize that they are better understood not as ends in themselves but as vehicles to something else, a connectedness with people and an exchange that transcends roles. I also have more awareness of the limited value of external accomplishments, and I take my spiritual practice and teaching more seriously. But now, several years later, the trauma of that experience has somewhat faded, and I have to work to keep the reality of death before me; there is such a strong human tendency to want to forget about it. Frankly, I wouldn't wish my experience on anyone. Or would I? I am grateful that it happened to me—I certainly needed something like this—and I am glad that I was forced to look more closely at my life. I find myself with tremendous respect—and that is really an understatement—for those with terminal diseases and others whose death is imminent and who have no hope of surviving. They live in a situation of monumental power and potential spiritual transformation. My experience taught me that the Tibetans are right: there is no teacher nearly as powerful as awareness of one's own mortality.

It is sometimes quite startling how in young people today, there is often a strong awareness of death. Each fall I teach an introductory Buddhism class at the University of Colorado in Boulder. Most of the students who enroll in this course know little about Buddhism, but they do have some idea that it presents a different perspective on life and death. On the first day, I ask each student what brought him or her to sign up for this class. I find that an extraordinarily high percentage of them report having had to face death or the prospect of death in some way. Some students have themselves faced life-threatening illnesses; some are still ill; others have been in serious accidents; some are still recovering; others have lost a parent, a sibling, a close friend, or a mate; and so on. For most of these young people, their encounter with death has dropped out of a clear blue sky and caught them completely unawares. These experiences have been transformative, making them realize that their lives are not a guaranteed thing. For some, the attitudes and values that had previously carried them have literally evaporated before their eyes. This, in turn, has led them to begin to look deeply and critically—usually for the first time—at who they are and what their life is about. They have found their way to my class on Buddhism as part of this endeavor.

Tulku Urgyen describes an analogy illustrating the effect that an awareness of death can have on a practitioner. Suppose, he tells us, that you are sentenced to death and have been dragged before the executioner. Your head lies on the chopping block and the executioner raises his ax in the air above your neck and is about to bring it down. At this moment, someone steps up to you and offers you a beautiful consort, a magnificent palace, and countless luxuries and enjoyable experiences. Knowing that you are about to die, would these offers have any appeal to you whatsoever? Even if someone offered you a taste of delicious wine or food, right in your mouth at this moment, would this be of any interest whatsoever? This analogy, Tulku Urgyen says, illustrates in a very vivid way how futile are attempts to gratify oneself in light of the reality of death. Do we really think such gratification has any meaning? "Practitioners," he urges, "combine the metaphor with the meaning!" In other words, take it to heart!

The great Ri-me master and yogin Paltrül Rinpoche has similar advice:

> Meditate single-mindedly on death, all the time and in every circumstance. While standing up, sitting or lying down, tell yourself: "This is my last act in this world," and meditate on it with utter conviction. On your way to wherever you might be going, say to yourself: "Maybe I will die there. There is no certainty that I will ever come back." Wherever you are, you should wonder if this might be where you die. At night, when you lie down, ask yourself whether you might die in bed during the night or whether you can be sure that you are going to get up in the morning. When you rise, ask yourself whether you might die sometime during the day, and reflect that there is no certainty at all that you will be going to bed in the evening. Meditate only on death, earnestly and from the core of your being. Meditate like the Kadampa Geshes of old, who were always thinking about death at every moment. At night, they would turn their bowls upside down [only done when a person died]; and thinking how the next day there might be no need to light a fire [because they had died], they would never cover the embers for the night.[5]

Does this sound arcane or impractical? A Zen roshi, a teacher who is a respected friend and mentor, once told me, "Every morning when I wake up, I am surprised that I am still alive" and it was clear that awareness of the fragility of his own existence ran through his life and guided everything that he did.

Tulku Urgyen says that the more one progresses along the path of meditation, the more acutely one feels the impermanence and urgency of one's own life. In illustration, he tells the following story about Longchen Rabjam, the great Nyingma teacher of the fourteenth century whose life was discussed in chapter 5.

Longchen Rabjam meditated for many years in a place called Gang-ri Tokar, White Skull Snow Mountain, where he even lacked a proper cave. He took shelter for three years under a cliff overhang. His only possession, in terms of bedding and clothing, was hemp-cloth sack bedding. This single scrap of sackcloth also served as his seat during meditation sessions. At the entrance to this rock overhang grew a huge thorn bush. Whenever he had to go out and relieve himself, the thorns pierced his body in numerous places. When he was urinating outside, he would think, "It's really uncomfortable having to push past this thorn bush every day. I should hack it down!" Then, on his way back in, he would think, "On the other hand, maybe this is the last day of my life. Why should I spend it cutting down a bush. That's meaningless—I'd rather do something that has real significance, like train myself in the view, meditation, and conduct. If this is my last day, I should spend it practicing. One never knows how much time one has left in life." So, he would forget about cutting down the bush and go back inside to continue his practice session. This went on day after day, and after three years he attained complete realization. And he never cut down the thorn bush. This is an example of how the reflection on impermanence can manifest itself in a great realized master like Longchenpa.[6]

As I myself had discovered, there is an acute sadness and sense of loss in the recognition that all life is destined for death. But such an awareness brings with it a sense of immediacy and also freedom. Since one realizes that the future really is uncertain, the present moment takes on increased importance. One sees that this moment is, in fact, all that one has or ever can have. The rest is just empty speculation. And since everything that one is and does is one day going to come to nothing, one is free to be whatever and do whatever exists in one's heart to be and do. This is exactly what the spiritual path is about—to live increasingly in the present and, in this present, to become fully and completely who we are, the person that it is our fate to become, the person already written in our heart of hearts. Thus it is that awareness of death leads us powerfully to the practice of dharma and, thereby, to the discovery of our true being. As one of the Kadam masters of old put it, "At first meditation on impermanence . . . leads you to search for the Dharma; in the middle it inspires you to practise; in the end, it helps you attain the goal."[7]

The transformative power of awareness of death is illustrated by a final example. Many years ago, I was close with a young woman whose mother was dying of cancer. The mother was still in the prime of life, in her forties, and her story was a sad one. Her own mother had died when she was a young child and she had never recovered from the loss. On some level, she remained an emotionally starved and neglected little three-year-old, who spent the rest of her life calling out for the mother who had been taken from her. Throughout her youth and adulthood, her entire existence had been focused upon trying to find the love and nourishment that she been deprived of as a child. She had been a thoroughly self-centered and self-absorbed person, fixated on each situation in terms of what she could get out of it for herself, unable to appreciate the needs of others or to care for anyone else. She had not been a mother in any real sense to her children, and my friend used to joke that, throughout her childhood, she had had to be a mother to her own mother and to expect nothing from her.

As my friend's mother progressed through her illness, going gradually downhill with no real hope for recovery, for the first time in her life, she began to change. I vividly remember the last time we saw her, lying in her hospital bed with tubes running out of her nose, being fed in both arms with intravenous drips. We asked her how she was doing and whether she was in much pain. She did not respond to these questions but proceeded to look intently at us as if trying to see something. She wanted to know how we were, what we were doing, how things were going for us. I could see that at that moment, our happiness and our pain were the most important thing in the world for her. We talked for a while, and at a certain point she said, "You know, this experience has changed me. I feel that I have finally found myself and become myself. I can finally care for others. I am happy now, for the first time in my life. I am very grateful—more than anyone can ever know—that his has happened to me." This was not the woman that I had known before. She had clearly undergone some fundamental transformation. Here was a person who had come into her own fullness, who, through going through the process of dying, had come to a profound realization of her human life. She died a short time afterward, but the gift of herself that she left will always stay with me.

KARMA

The third reminder is karma. A Sanskrit word meaning "action," karma refers to the basic principle that everything we do in life has some kind of result that comes back upon us. It is expressed in the popular saying "What goes around comes around": whatever I put out will eventually come back on me. What the impact on me will be depends upon my motivation when I perform the action. If I act in a self-serving and aggressive way, harming others, then the result will be a negative one, involving suffering and confusion. If I give of myself to others, the result will be positive.

In Buddhism, there are two especially important kinds of karma. First, there is the karma of result, referring to the fact that the past and present circumstances of my life are the results of actions performed at a previous time. Everything that we are and that has happened to us up to this moment is the result of these prior actions. The fact that we are human beings points to a great deal of very positive karma from the past. But, within this life, our situation is mixed and we experience a considerable amount of negative circumstances. These are the result of prior negative actions.

The second kind of karma is the karma of cause, referring to the actions I perform now which will condition my own future. If I use others and harm them for my own ends, I will be sowing the seeds of future obstacles, negative circumstances, and sorrow for myself. If I act in a positive way, respecting others and trying to help them, I will sow seeds of good opportunity and happiness.

Sometimes the karmic retribution is immediate. If I shout angrily at others or pull at them in a grasping manner, their response is likely to be quick. If I am so preoccupied with myself that I forget to put gas in the car when it is empty, I will directly run out of gas. If I exhaust myself with overwork and do not heed the warning signs, I may well become sick in body or mind. Consequences such as these may be painful, but they also represent the speedy ripening of negative karma and therefore need to be respected. It is the karmic retribution that does not occur at once that is the most cause for concern, for it festers and will often appear in a way and a form that makes it harder to deal with. At the same time, actions are complex and produce many levels of karmic imprint, and even immediate retribution does not necessarily exhaust all of the karmic seeds of a deed.

Sometimes virtually all of the karmic retribution is deferred. We often see people in our society, perhaps in the business world, operating on the boundary of the law or using their power to harm others in a most open and flagrant way. In the educational world, one may sometimes observe teachers, whose responsibility is to help and guide their students, ignoring the real needs of their charges and aggressively inflicting on them the same kind of pointless, dehumanizing, and depressing knowledge that they themselves have experienced. Sometimes we see parents acting in the most vicious or mindless way toward their children, creating scars that may never heal, at least in this life. At the time, it often appears that such people "get away" with their actions. All of us, in fact, try to get away with things all the time. In the Buddhist perspective, however, no one ever gets away with anything. We will be held accountable for every negative thing that we ever do, and we will be credited with every positive action as well.

This raises a critical question. If Buddhism is nontheistic in that there is no overarching God or god keeping track of everything we do, then how are we held accountable for negative actions and credited with positive ones? The answer is that everything we do is written in our own bodies and minds. When we are angry about something that happened at work and speak aggressively to our small child, the impact of what we did registers in our own being and remains there. When we go beyond our own limits in helping someone, that action is likewise written in our hearts.

Our state of being includes many layers and levels of awareness. The "I" or person that we are conscious of right now represents only a gross, walled-off fragment of our overall intelligence, sensitivity, and awareness. Our "ego" is not very sensitive or intelligent, but beneath it—and, for most of us, generally unconscious—are deeper and more subtle levels of awareness, all the way down to our buddha-nature. The deeper we go, the more completely open and aware is our state of being. Nothing that we ever do is lost on these deeper levels of ourselves. And it is from these deeper levels that our emotions, reactions, and habitual patterns emerge, all of those many things about ourselves that arise outside of the control of our centralized ego. If we continually poison the deep wells of our being with negative actions, of course the water that rises to the surface will be foul and repulsive. But if we continually strive to be kind to others and restrain our own egomania, then this is like purifying the deep well of our being.

So far I have been speaking in strictly inner, psychological language. I have been saying that our karma is written in our hearts. So far, I have been conforming to the modern Western habit of separating the inner and the outer worlds, as if the inner world of myself and the outer world of everything else are two completely different and separate entities. I have left unquestioned the assumption that my inner psychological world has intelligence and can register karma, but the outer world is unintelligent and dead, and is irrelevant in this discussion.

Tibetan Buddhism would seek to correct this approach in the following way. At the most superficial level of our awareness, our ego consciousness, we do seem to be completely separate from other people and from the world around us. "I" and "other" seem to be the way things are. However, at deeper levels of our being, the separation of I and other begins to break down. The more we begin to gain access to these deeper levels through meditation, the more we begin to see in a vivid and unmistakable way that the realm of the "outer" or "other," including the entire animate and inanimate world, is alive, intelligent, and responsive to the very same degree and in just the same way as our own state of being. In fact, at a certain point, you really cannot separate the two. Our karma is recorded at this deep level, where the division of "inner" and "outer," of "I" and "other," does not pertain. Thus it is that karmic retribution occurs in the form either of my own feelings, emotions, and dispositions, or of things that happen to me in my life, seeming to occur randomly, coming from the "outside." We will examine this perspective in more detail in chapter 14.

When we die, according to Tibetan tradition, we undergo a "life review," quite similar in many respects to the review that is sometimes reported in modern near-death experiences. At this time, Yama, the Lord of Death, holds up a mirror. In the mirror, we see exactly what we have done with our lives, all of the actions both positive and negative, down to the smallest details. In this "judgment," in fact, we are our own judge. At this moment, we are deprived of the defenses and self-justifications of ego, stripped of our conventional clothing and our masks. During our lives, these have hidden just how base and self-serving our intentions have been. Now that they have been torn away, we have no choice but to see exactly what is what, and to accept the joy of actions well performed and the sorrow and anguish of all of our selfishness, aggression, and unkindness to others.

This kind of naked revelation of karma is the substance of Charles Dickens's tale *A Christmas Carol,* in which Ebenezer Scrooge has a horrifying encounter with his former partner Jacob Marley, now deceased, who exists in a nonmaterial form as a ghost. Weighed down with the massive chain of his own misdeeds, Marley lives in a nether world of torment. As he tells Scrooge, each person is given a human life with the power to love others, to help them at each step, to share with them their sorrows, and to feel the joy that results from selfless action. Those who fail to fulfill these possibilities in life, at death are held accountable and are condemned to wander throughout the world; they see and acutely feel the human need all around them, but, being impotent to address it, they are tortured by the boundless opportunity of the human life that they have wasted. Through these and other encounters with the implacability of karma, Scrooge finds his own life laid bare, and his awareness awakens him to an entirely different approach to life.

Why is karma a reminder? Like the other reminders, this one calls us to wake up from our self-deception and wishful thinking. The first reminder is taught because we do not realize the preciousness of our human situation. The second is given because we do not really see our own mortality. The third reminder comes to awaken us to the very real consequences of how we live and what we do.

An understanding of karma is essential if one wants to pursue the dharma and follow the path of meditation. One may ignore the teachings on karma and, without modifying one's behavior, try to meditate. You may try this, and you may find that you can only get so far. Perhaps your external situation is such that you cannot devote much time or energy to meditation. Perhaps your internal situation is so turbulent or obstacle-ridden that when you do try to meditate, you become too angry or distracted, or you continually fall asleep. Perhaps you cannot find a suitable teacher or locate teachings that are really helpful to you. Perhaps in meditation you continually find yourself getting off on sidetracks, for hours, days, or even years. Perhaps you feel that you are unable to make any progress no matter how hard you try.

All of these impediments are karmic situations. None of them can be addressed simply by trying harder to meditate properly. They can only be addressed by looking at one's entire life and beginning to generate positive karma. Through such efforts, one will begin to sow seeds that will produce more positive circumstances in the future. This takes a tremendous amount of patience and is often difficult in a culture where results are expected on demand. However, according to Buddhism, there is no other avenue to enlightenment than this. Through generating positive karma by means of meritorious actions, our overall life situation will gradually begin to show signs of improvement, gaining greater balance, healthiness, and spiritual meaning. And we may be confident that we are creating the right kind of circumstances for following a spiritual path in the future and into future lives.

The teachings on karma not only show us how to create the right conditions for pursuing a spiritual path, but also provide a certain perspective for working with hardship and suffering in this life. Tibetans believe that the form of suffering that we experience now indicates the kind of negative action that was performed in a former life. In addition, and more important, the present suffering is not to be seen as negative, but as an opportunity to clear one's karmic debt for the past misdeed. Paltrül Rinpoche explains:

> If you are falsely accused and criticized now, it is the effect of your having told lies in the past. Instead of getting angry and hurling insults at people who say such things about you, be grateful to them for helping you to exhaust the effects of many negative actions. You should feel happy. Rigdzin Jigme Lingpa says:
>
> > An enemy repaying your good with bad makes you
> > progress along in your practice.
> > His unjust accusations are a whip that steers you
> > toward virtue.
> > He's the teacher who destroys all your attachment
> > and desires.
> > Look at his great kindness that you can never repay![8]

Chagdud Tulku tells a story that illustrates just the attitude advised by Paltrül Rinoche and Jigme Lingpa. The story is about his own sister, the very remarkable yogini Thinley Wangmo, and recounts an incident that occurred during the Chinese invasion.

> As she was riding her horse along the road, she was seized and brutally beaten by the highest Chinese official in the region. He used as his weapon the thick branch of a thorn tree. She was not angry as he beat her, for she recognized the beating as karmic purification. In that tumultuous moment, she made a prayer that, by her suffering, others might be spared.

Chagdud Tulku continues the story, illustrating the extraordinary impact that reversing one's usual attitude toward suffering can have:

> When he thought he had beaten her to the brink of death, the official let her fall to the ground. To his amazement, she re-

mounted her horse and, with the wild, triumphant yell that Khampas emit, she galloped away. The official jumped on his own horse and overtook her. He was amazed to see that the wounds had already healed. He invited her to stay at his house, and the next morning gave her six hundred yuan before sending her on her way, asking that she pray for him when he died.

The karmic link that Thinley Wangmo had forged with the Chinese official by her actions was evidently a strong one.

As it happened, the Chinese [government officials] later summoned her to the regional capital and upon arrival, as she was walking to their offices, she passed a funeral procession. "Who is that?" she asked. "That is the governor of this region, who just died," she was told. Thinley Wangmo began to pray, happy to be able to fulfill his request.[9]

Sometimes a realized person puts others through difficult situations in order to purify their karma. Chagdud Tulku tells another story about his sister. After Chagdud Tulku had left Tibet, his stepfather, Sodga, himself a lama, stayed at his own monastery along with his daughter Thinley Wangmo. Owing to her own remarkable qualities as a yogini, he told his daughter that she would never have to marry and live an ordinary life. Sometime later, against her father's strong objections, Thinley Wangmo married a man known to have killed two people. Later he killed two more, in efforts to retrieve a lama's stolen horse. Sodga could not abide the new son-in-law and kept his distance through three decades of their marriage.

One day she entered his house in a rage, smashed every cup and dish he owned and left without explanation. A friend visited him shortly after and, surveying the wreckage, asked what had happened. "Thinley Wangmo has done me a great service today," Sodga replied. Later that day he received from the Chinese a summons to appear before a tribunal; the next day he received a second letter informing him that there was no need to appear. In demolishing his crockery Thinley Wangmo had purified the last vestiges of his karma to have to undergo such an ordeal.[10]

The importance of an understanding of the teaching on karma for the practice of dharma is illustrated by the following story of Milarepa, recounted by Paltrül Rinpoche:

> [Milarepa's] disciples said to him one day: "Jetsun, all the deeds that we see you doing are beyond the understanding of ordinary beings. Precious Jetsun, were you not an incarnation of Vajradhara, or of a Buddha or Bodhisattva right from the start?" "If you take me for an incarnation of Vajradhara, or of a Buddha or Bodhisattva," the Jetsun replied, "it shows you have faith in me—but you could hardly have a more mistaken view of the Dharma! I started out by heaping up extremely negative acts, using spells and making hail. I soon realized that there was no way that I would not be reborn in hell. So I practised the Dharma with relentless zeal. Thanks to the profound methods of the Secret Mantrayana, I have developed exceptional qualities in myself. Now, if you cannot develop any real determination to practise the Dharma, it is because you do not really believe in the principle of cause and effect. Anyone with a bit of determination could develop courage like mine if they had that true and heartfelt confidence in the effects of their actions. Then they would develop the same accomplishments—and people will think that they too are manifestations of Vajradhara, or of a Buddha or Bodhisattva."[11]

THE DEFECTS OF SAMSARA

In the Buddhist view, it is a feature of the human state to be continually looking for happiness. Each of us has his or her own collection of ideas of how to accomplish this end, and these are always changing. But the fact of having some version of how to be happy characterizes all of us.

When we are young, we seek our parents' approval, a new toy, or a favorite treat. But as we get older, things don't change that much, and we may crave socially acceptable credentials, material possessions, or the enjoyment of physical comforts of food, drink, or habitation. The fourth reminder points out that, while short-term gratification is sometimes possible, no long-term solution to our desire to be happy can occur as long as we remain within samsara.

Samsara means the condition of going around and around. In Tibetan Buddhism, it refers to the cycling from one of the six realms of existence to another that sentient beings undergo in accordance with their karma. In the absence of the dharma and of liberation, this cycling, which is beginningless, is also endless. The driving force of this cycling is thirst for happiness, satisfaction, security, fulfillment, contentment. That thirst is called *trishna* and is said to be the defilement that we need to eliminate to be free.

People in the modern world obviously do not share the cosmology of traditional Buddhism and are not necessarily willing to accept the idea of the six realms or even the notion of rebirth. Tibetan teachers having contact with Westerners have responded in a variety of ways to this lack of acceptance. Some continue to emphasize the traditional presentation that rebirth is a literal reality for everyone and that each of us will, after death, be born in one of the six realms. Other lamas—most often those living and teaching in the West—while not denying the traditional view, tend to give more experiential and psychological interpretations. Chögyam Trungpa, for example, presented the endless cycling of samsara as the experience of being trapped in one's own habitual patterns. Samsara, then, is finding oneself responding to new situations with the same set of self-defeating, neurotic behaviors. Many Western students who come to Buddhism have some degree of psychological sophistication and have found an engaging relevance in this kind of interpretation.

Trungpa Rinpoche also gave a similar reading to the teaching on the six realms. While affirming their objective reality, he tended to present them to his students primarily as states of mind that human beings can experience and that predominate in different kinds of people. The six realms became, then, a kind of typology of six different human types, each characterized by the psychology of one or another of the realms. Trungpa Rinpoche was not the innovator of this interpretation, for it is found within Vajrayana Buddhism in the teaching of the Buddha families. But he was among the first Tibetan lamas to bring this interpretation to Westerners and it remains uniquely developed in his writing. For Trungpa Rinpoche, then, the way to communicate the defects of samsara was to point to the neurotic, repetitive, and ultimately self-defeating aspects of the psychology of each of the six realms understood as human types. The following discussion of the fourth reminder presents the six realms as both objective states existing in their own right, and as possibilities of experience for those born in the human realm.

The Three Lower Realms

THE HELL REALM

The hell realm (*naraka-loka*), the lowest and most unfortunate of the six realms, extends downward beneath Mount Meru and contains eighteen subdivisions. Included in these are eight hot hells, neighboring hells, the eight cold hells, and the ephemeral hells. Beings are reborn in the hells as the result of hatred, anger, and aggression toward other beings, in which they saw others as mortal enemies and tried to harm or kill them in any way they could. The texts describe the intense suffering that one undergoes as a resident of one or another of the eighteen hells.[12] In speaking of the hot hells, for example, Paltrül Rinpoche remarks:

> These eight hells lie one above the other like the storeys of a building, from the Reviving Hell on top, down to the Hell of Ultimate Torment at the bottom. In each the ground and perimeter are like the white-hot iron of a smith—there is nowhere at all where you could safely put your foot. Everything is a searingly hot expanse of blazing, fiery flame.[13]

> [The] suffering is tremendous. Apart from the cries of distress, there is no longer any indication of the presence of actual bodies. They constantly long to escape, but it never happens. Some-

times there is a small gap in the fire and they think they can get out, but . . . they are subjected to all the agonies of the seven previous hells, such as having molten bronze poured into their mouths. Life span there is a whole intermediate *kalpa*.[14]

In the cold hells, according to Paltrül Rinpoche,

the environment is entirely composed of snow mountains and glaciers, perpetually enveloped in snowy blizzards The beings there, all completely naked, are tormented by the cold. In the Hell of Blisters, the cold makes blisters erupt on their bodies. In the Hell of Burst Blisters, the blisters burst open. In the Hell of Chattering Teeth, the biting cold is intolerable and the teeth of the beings there chatter. In the Hell of Lamentations, their lamenting never ends. In the Hell of Groans their voices are cracked and long groans escape from their lips. In the Hell of Utpala-like Cracks, their skin turns blue and splits into four petal-like pieces. In the Hell of Lotus-like Cracks, their red raw flesh becomes visible, and the cold makes it split into eight pieces. Lastly, in the Hell of Great Lotus-like Cracks, their skin turns dark red and splits into sixteen, thirty-two, and then innumerable pieces. Worms penetrate the cracked flesh and devour it with metal beaks.[15]

This description intends to evoke a particular state of mind or kind of experience that characterizes the objective realm and also human beings who experience its psychology. The particular experience or psychological profile of the hellish state is oriented to anger and aggression. Trungpa Rinpoche remarks:

Experiences in the hell realm are quite terrifying and horrific . . . the hallucinations of Hell are generated from an environment of claustrophobia and aggression. There is a feeling of being trapped in a small space with no air to breathe and no room in which to move about . . . [the hell-being] even attempts to kill himself in order to escape the excruciating and continuous pain. But he cannot really kill himself, and his suicide attempts only intensify his torture. The more [he] struggles to destroy or control the walls, the more solid and oppressive they become.[16]

We may regard a hell realm as an actual place somewhere in the cosmos where we might literally incarnate as a hell-being in some future existence, or we may understand it as an interior mental state that we might experience in this very human lifetime; nevertheless, in both cases a hell realm is a projection of our own mind as a result of our own actions (karma), and therefore it can be said that we have created it and we maintain it, although we are generally not consciously aware of doing so. Like any other of the six realms of samsara, the hell realm represents a particular way in which beings attempt to be real, solid, and definite. For the hell-being, the apparent solidity of the realm is—strangely enough—more attractive than the ever-present possibility of open space.

Most people have probably entered the psychological hell realm numerous times in their lives. For example, conflict and argument are parts of any intimate relationship. Sometimes we may find ourselves in a heated exchange with a partner. As the heat increases, we may find our own position becoming more and more extreme, more and more unreasonable. If we find ourselves hurting the person we love, the pain can be unbearable, truly a hellish torture. Yet we feel powerless to halt or even alter the momentum of the escalating insanity. This is a taste of the psychology of the hot hells.

Again, out of our arrogance, anger, and pride, we may have a habitual pattern of pushing others away and refusing love. At the same time, on some level, we feel isolated and cut off, and deeply yearn for human connection, interchange, and mutual affection. Sometimes, in halting and inept ways, we may reach out in some way to make contact with others. Yet, when they respond, particularly when they are inviting toward us and begin to come close, we find ourselves lashing out in self-protection. We drive them away, hurt them beyond their ability to forgive, and annihilate any possibility of closeness. Part of this is hatred toward ourselves, toward the tender parts of our being that yearn for connection. This state of mind is intensely hellish in its frozen isolation. This is a glimpse of the psychology of the cold hells.

THE HUNGRY GHOST REALM

The hungry ghost realm (*preta-loka*) lies beneath Jambudvipa but above the hell realms.[17] It is most generally understood as the abode of the dead and is ruled over by Yama. One is said to be born in the preta realm as the result of stinginess and lack of generosity to others. There are two major groupings of pretas, which appear rather different from each other. First are those ghosts who closely resemble human beings and live together in misery. These pretas are particularly tormented by intense hunger and thirst that can never be satisfied. They are depicted with bloated bodies, signifying starvation and terrible thirst; large, slack mouths, distorted with pain, showing tremendous need; and a thin, needlelike neck through which virtually nothing can pass. Unable to ingest what they need, these pretas are beside themselves with want. "Centuries pass without their even hearing any mention of water. Constantly obsessed with food and drink, they search for them endlessly, without ever finding even the tiniest trace. . . . Their sensations torture them terribly."[18] Part of the pain felt by the preta is that he or she continually sees the possibility of food and drink in the distance but can never obtain them. These pretas are generally shown as being pitiful and powerless beings.

The second grouping of pretas includes various kinds of demons and malevolent spirits such as the general categories of *yakshas* (demons) and *bhutas* (ghosts), as well as the *tsen, gyalpo, mamo, rakshasas, pishachas,* and other similar beings mentioned in chapter 1.

> All of [these] live out their lives in constant terror and hallucination. Thinking of nothing but evil, they always do whatever they can to bring harm to others, and many of them fall into even lower realms such as the hells as soon as they die. In particular, every week they relive all the pain of their preceding death

from sickness, weapons, strangulation, or whatever it was. What they want to do is to offload their pain onto others, so wherever they go, they do nothing but harm. But they still fail to do themselves any good by it. Even when they happily visit their former friends and loved ones, they only bring them sickness, insanity and other unwelcome sufferings.[19]

Whether we are speaking of those reborn in the preta realm or of human beings experiencing a preta mind-state; the mark of a hungry ghost is the passion of insatiable hunger and unquenchable thirst. He or she can never get enough of what is needed. As human beings, we have all felt this kind of hunger, and so we recognize what it is like to roam the earth consumed by our need, always unfulfilled, always alone. It is as if we are walking through a frigid winter night, lost and alone, looking for shelter, warmth, food, and companionship. We pass house after house, looking in the windows and seeing others rejoicing in the warmth of a blazing hearth and a table laid with a feast, surrounded by faces ruddy with happiness and love. Yet every door is barred to us. Finding no entry, we must wander on, tortured by our unfulfilled desires. Part of our pain is the generation of endless fantasies of how we might fulfill our hunger, fantasies that always turn out to be unreachable. It is important to realize that the preta realm, like the other realms, is ultimately defined by a particular psychology and mind-state. Whether one lives in the actual preta realm or is a human experiencing a preta mind-state, one has a particular style of fixation, an obsession that becomes one's security and identity.

> So the pain and hunger of the *Preta* Loka, as with the aggression of the Hell Realm and the preoccupations of the other realms, provide the being with something exciting to occupy himself with, something solid to relate to, something to make him feel secure that he exists as a real person. He is afraid to give up this security and entertainment, afraid to venture out into the unknown world of open space. He would rather stay in his familiar prison, no matter how painful and oppressive it might be.[20]

THE ANIMAL REALM

Unlike the inhabitants of the other lower realms, animals are part of our tangible, everyday experience: they occupy our physical world and we can see and interact with them. Paltrül Rinpoche describes the tremendous sufferings undergone by animals, from the tiniest insects to the greatest sea beasts. In the oceans, the smaller animals are devoured by the larger ones, and the larger ones have the smaller ones burrowing into their flesh and eating them from the inside out. Wild animals are hunted by one another and by humans, who snare, spear, trap, shoot, and beat them, with no concern for their suffering. Domestic animals are

> milked, loaded down, castrated, pierced through the nose and yoked to the plough. . . . Horses and other beasts of burden continue to be loaded and ridden even when their backs are nothing but one big sore. When they can go no further, they are whipped and pelted with stones. The fact that they could be in distress or ill never seems to cross their owners' minds.[21]

The animal realm (*pashu-* or *tiryag-loka*) is the highest of the lower realms, but it still represents an unfortunate rebirth because of the suffering and exploitation that animals suffer, particularly at the hands of human beings.

Animals are marked by a relative fixity of habitual patterns, dictated by the limitations of their nervous systems and physical bodies. According to Tibetan tradition, the animal-realm mentality is characterized by dullness, stupidity, and delusion. Animals are driven in their actions by a kind of blind instinct that lacks openness or flexibility. A human who exhibits an animal-realm mentality deliberately plays deaf and dumb, sticking to habitual ways of doing things. The animal quality is one of purely looking directly ahead, ignoring what is to the left, right, behind, above, or below. One's behavior is regimented and routinized, approaching every situation with the same limited set of possible responses. One is stubborn, fixed, and dumb in clinging to familiar ways of seeing and acting. The animal-realm psychology refuses to relate to uncertainty, ambiguity, or newness. Such a psychology is overly serious and lacking in a sense of humor.

Trungpa Rinpoche indicates how even socially lauded ways of being may reflect an animal realm mentality:

> One could develop this by believing in a certain religious framework, theological or philosophical conclusions, or by just simply remaining secure, practical, and solid. Such a person could be very efficient, very good and consistent at work, and quite contented. It is like a . . . family man whose life is very happy, predictable and secure, with no areas of mystery involved at all. If he buys a new gadget there are always directions for using it. If there is any problem he can go to lawyers or priests or policemen, all sorts of professional people who are also secure and comfortable in their professions. It is utterly sensible and predictable, and highly mechanical at the same time.
>
> What is lacking is that if any unknown, unpredictable situation occurs, there is a feeling of paranoia, of being threatened. If there are people who do not work, who look different, whose whole life-style is irregular, then the very existence of such people is in itself threatening. Anything unpredictable fundamentally threatens the basic pattern.[22]

The Three Higher Realms

THE HUMAN REALM

The human realm (*nara-loka*) is the first of the three "higher realms" and stands between the higher realms of the gods and jealous gods and the lower realms of the animals, hungry ghosts, and hell beings. The human birth is considered the most auspicious one for spiritual development because of its intermediate location. As mentioned, there is enough pain to motivate one to practice on the path, but not so much that one is wholly preoccupied with suffering and paralyzed by it.

The human state is marked by three kinds of suffering. First is the "suffering of change," the pain we feel when we are suddenly thrown into a state of misery. Such a change may be as dramatic as a sudden illness, the loss of a loved one, or some other major turn of fortune. It may also be as ordinary as going to a fine restaurant with the expectation of a delicious meal, only to find our salad limp, our vegetables over-cooked and tasteless, our meat tough, and our waitperson resentful and hostile.

"Suffering upon suffering," number two, refers to the pain that comes upon us when we are already in a state of unhappiness. In Paltrül Rinpoche's example, "we get leprosy, and then we break out in boils, too; and then as well as breaking out in boils, we get injured."[23]

The third kind of suffering, "suffering in the making," is the most subtle and provocative of the three.[24] This refers to the fact that all of samsaric life, as such, is permeated and saturated by suffering. Paltrül Rinpoche gives the example of the simple happiness of having a sip of tea. In Tibet, that tea came from a farming process in which countless small creatures were killed; the tea was traded for the skins and meat of animals that were themselves killed; it was carried in huge loads on the backs of suffering porters and animals; and it was finally sold in a climate of greed and deception. In our culture, we could point to the fact that most of the comforts and possessions of "the good life" have been made in third world countries by children, penal laborers, or others in poverty—and that our Western economies to a very real extent rely upon the servitude of the rest of the world.

The third kind of suffering may also be translated as "the suffering of conditioned states." This rendering points to a more subtle interpretation: merely to approach things in a samsaric way—that is, with thirst and self-serving intent—is itself ultimately excruciatingly painful, the more so the more aware one is. Even the way we perceive things, with "hungry eyes," destroys their integrity and their beauty, reducing the experience of them to our own petty ideas and preconceptions. For example, when we look at a tree, to a large extent, we do not see the tree itself, but rather what we have been conditioned to see. Our expectations will largely limit what we can perceive. Again, a bigoted person, when looking at someone from a social underclass, will not see an individual in his or her full humanity and possibility, but will see a despicable person. The suffering discussed here comes from the fact that our initial and natural perception of things is pure and unbounded. Then, before we are aware of it, we grasp on to our perceptions with our want, narrow them down, and produce a tiny, concept-bound world that we think of as real. For people of attainment, this transition is the most painful suffering of all. (This matter will be discussed from a philosophical point of view in chapter 16 and in the context of meditation in chapters 12 and 13 of my book *Secret of the Vajra World*.)

The psychology of the human realm is based upon desire or discriminating passion. Because of our position midway between states of great pain and great pleasure, and because of our relative freedom, we human beings are engaged in an endless pursuit to maximize pleasure and minimize pain. Our minds are geared toward every conceivable strategy to increase our pleasure. The pleasure we continually seek may be physical (a good meal, sex, the feeling of physical well-being), emotional (pleasant emotions rather than fear, anxiety, depression, etc.), social (the approval or praise of others), intellectual (a pleasing and convincing belief or concept), or spiritual (peace or bliss). The characteristic activity of the human is discriminating, selective grasping, trying to draw what is desirable toward oneself. Human psychology is also inherently comparative and competitive. We continually compare one thing with another to see which will yield more for us, we compare our situation with that of others, and so on. For these reasons, hope and fear play a central role in the psychology of the human realm: hope for further pleasure, possessions, and security, and fear of losing what we have and of experiencing greater suffering. And, for these reasons, discursive thinking runs rampant in the human realm, the constant thinking, strategizing, and angling to improve one's situation. Trungpa Rinpoche remarks that in the human realm, "You are stuck in an absolute traffic jam of discursive thoughts. It is extremely busy. There is no end to it."[25]

Inherent in this process is obviously a great deal of suffering. What happiness we may achieve is always fragile and in danger of disintegrating. Our efforts to achieve happiness are frequently overwhelmed by the painful situations that occur in our lives. We never feel that we have completely achieved happiness, and there is always some intimation of misery at the margins of whatever good feeling we may have managed to obtain.

It is interesting to realize the extent to which the human realm, while seeming to some extent sealed off and separate from the other realms, is in fact dependent upon them. As we have seen, there are experiences of the other realms within the human one, windows to the other realms, and even glimpses of spheres that are entirely outside of samsara. Our subliminal awareness of these other possibilities of existence undergirds our human world, contributes to it, and helps make it what it is. In other words, our flat world cannot be explained on its own terms. The reason we have this particular flat, human world—and the reason that we hang onto it so tenaciously and deny the existence of other possibilities—is because of what lies underneath it, above it, and outside of it. To put it in a nutshell, maintenance of our human realm depends on a large-scale denial of reality as a whole.

THE JEALOUS GOD REALM

The inhabitants of the jealous god realm (*asura-loka*)—the asuras—match the gods in strength, pleasure, and abundance but are their inferiors in merit. In previous lifetimes, they indulged in ambition, envy, quarreling, and fighting. As a result of these demeritorious actions, the moment they take asura form, they experience jealousy and paranoia. The *Abhidharmakosha* depicts them as dwelling in the ocean surrounding Mount Meru, presiding over sometimes vast territories and provinces. There they are constantly fighting among themselves. When they look upward to the realm of the gods, they are stricken with unbearable envy and resentment at the gods' superior situation. The asuras immediately put on their armor and set off to make war with the gods. However, the gods, owing to their superior stature and weapons, are always victorious. This of course makes the jealous gods even more resentful and envious than before, feeding the psychology of their realm.[26]

The character of the asura is revealed by a story in the *Dighanikaya,* or Long Discourses of the Buddha, concerning the asura Rahula, who ruled over a vast city in the northern ocean. One day he became angry that the thirty-three gods and the sun and moon were continually passing above his realm, so he went to battle with Indra, Lord of the Gods, and, in a completely futile manner, threatened to make earrings of the sun and the moon.[27]

The psychology of the asura is based on ambition, jealousy, and paranoia. Trungpa Rinpoche remarks about the asura personality:

> His version of heaven may be the acquisition of extreme wealth or power or fame—whatever it is he would like his world to be, and he becomes preoccupied with achievement and competition. . . . [He is] always trying to be better than everyone else. . . . But his preoccupation with always being best, with always being master of the situation, makes him insecure and anxious. He must always struggle to control his territory, overcoming all threats to his achievements. He is always fighting for mastery of this world.[28]

This realm typifies the tendency

> to look back and suspect your own shadow, whether it is a real shadow or someone's strategy. Paranoia is a kind of radar system, the most efficient radar system the ego could have. It picks up all sorts of faint and tiny objects, suspecting each one of them, and every experience in life is regarded as something threatening.
>
> This is known as the realm of jealousy or envy, but it is not envy or jealousy as we generally think of them. It is something extremely fundamental, based on survival and winning. Unlike the human or animal, the purpose of this realm of the jealous gods is purely to function within the realm of intrigue; that is all there is, it is both occupation and entertainment. It is as if a person were born as a diplomat, raised as a diplomat, and died as a diplomat. Intrigue and relationship are his life-style and his whole livelihood.[29]

THE GOD REALM

The realm of the gods (*deva-loka*) begins on the slopes of Mount Meru and extends upward through many, increasingly ethereal heavens to the highest pinnacle of samsara. Compared to inhabitants of the other five realms, the gods (at least those that have forms at all!) are physically bigger and more beautiful, they have immense power, and they have every pleasure and enjoyment imaginable at their beck and call. In fact, they may gratify any desire simply by wishing for it. In addition, the life span of the gods is enormously long and some of them live for a kalpa, which by one definition lasts for eight billion years.[30] Beings are born into the god realm as a result of meritorious actions performed in previous lifetimes. In any case, rebirth among the gods is not to be sneered at!

The god realms have many levels and sublevels to accommodate the tremendous variety of divine beings that were known in India at the time of the Buddha. On the slopes of Mount Meru dwell the four great kings, beings who are guardians of the world. On the summit live the "thirty-three gods" led by Indra, all of whom are deities known and worshiped in the *Rigveda,* the ancient scripture of Hinduism. These deities and others who dwell in four levels above Mount Meru belong to the realm of desire, indicating that they have wants and desires much as humans do. At each successive level, however, the gratification of passion becomes more subtle. Above them dwell the deities of the four levels of the realm of form, whose state of being is defined by the fact that they have a form like the lower deities, but they do not share our gross materialism and they are no longer driven by desire for gratification. These deities share a freedom from passion and experience more and more subtle states of mind in each higher level. In the first level, the freedom from passion is experienced; in the second, freedom from discursive thought; in the third, the elimination of gross joy in meditation, leaving only sublime delight; in the fourth, freedom even from delight. Above these are the four levels of the realm of formlessness, whose inhabitants have transcended form altogether and have no bodies or forms at all. Here deities experience successively even more subtle states of mind: the infinity of space, the infinity of consciousness, "nothing at all," and neither perception nor nonperception.

These states can certainly appear enormously attractive from our human point of view. In fact, they correspond to what many think religious practice is all about—attaining some kind of heaven or some sort of tranquillity or bliss. But from the Buddhist viewpoint, the sublimity even of these states is not a worthy ultimate goal. One may ask, "What can possibly be wrong with such attainments?"

It is important to remember that the divine states of the desire realm, the form realm, and the formless realm, like all the other states known in the other five realms, are still part of samsara and subject to karma, impermanence, and suffering. In spite of the relative exaltation of their way of being, there comes a day for every god when he or she begins to feel the signs of impending death. The intoxication of the godly state gives way to sadness, pain, fear, and finally terror, and this is followed by death and rebirth in a lower realm.

In addition, the gods have one enormous liability: precisely because of their power, longevity, and intoxication, they are unable to hear the dharma with its teachings about duhkha, the first noble truth. They, like the inhabitants of all the other nonhuman realms, are victims of their karma and are unable to practice a spiritual path to gain liberation. In this respect, Paltrül Rinpoche remarks:

> The gods enjoy perfect health, comfort, wealth and happiness all their lives. However, they spend their time in diversions and the idea of practising the Dharma never occurs to them. Throughout their lives, which may last a whole *kalpa,* they do not have that thought even for an instant. Then, having wasted their whole life in distraction, they are suddenly confronted with death.[31]

The state of mind of one in the god realm is characterized by intoxication and pride. Those in the realm of desire are intoxicated by gross pleasure; those in the form realm by the purity of their existence; and those in the formless realms by the various levels of infinitude that they experience. Along with this positive mind-state there is pride that one has achieved such a thing. Once in the god realm, one wishes to maintain one's pleasure, delight, or tranquil vastness at whatever cost.

Human beings can experience the godlike state as they can the psychology of the other realms. The realm of desire may be experienced by those who have attained great power, wealth, or fame. Through those attainments, they experience a temporary freedom from the limitations that the rest of us experience—people idolize them, they can have any material object or diversion they wish, they can implement ambitions with a word, and they are often insulated from negativity. They can block out and avoid suffering in a way that others cannot.

The realms of form and of formlessness are also accessible to human beings, but only to advanced meditators. According to Indian tradition, on the night on which the Buddha attained enlightenment, he experienced successively the four levels of the realm of form, then the four levels of the formless realm. Meditators of high attainment have the same ability to experience the levels of the form and formless realms as shown in the Buddha's story, and the capacity to experience at least the four levels of the form realm is considered essential for the attainment of enlightenment. These levels of the realm of form are called the four *dhyanas,* or concentrations, while those of the formless realm are called the four *samapattis,* or attainments. Like the external god realms to which they correspond, the four dhyanas and four samapattis remain within the realm of samsara. They are considered of potential value on the spiritual path because they develop within the practitioner greater and greater subtlety and sensitivity of experience. Emerging from any of these sublime states, meditators find themselves increasingly sensitive to the usually invisible underpinnings of samsara and its subtle machinations. And the path to full enlightenment is traveled only through a progressively deeper and more complete understanding of what samsara is and how it works. Nevertheless, as among the gods, so among humans experiencing the god-realm psychology, the absorption of this state brings dangers. The intoxication of the very rich, famous, and powerful often leads—if we are to believe the newspapers—to sudden and dramatic falls. And meditators can get stuck, sometimes for long periods, in one or another of the trance states.

TABLE 10.2

THE SIX REALMS OF SAMSARA

REALM	SANSKRIT	LOCATION	LIFE SPAN	DOMINANT DEFILEMENT (KLESHA)	TYPE OF SUFFERING
THE HIGHER REALMS					
God Realm	Deva-loka	On and above Mt. Meru	Up to a kalpa	Pride, delusion	Dullness and stupidity of intoxication and continual pleasure
Jealous God Realm	Asura-loka	Lower flanks of Mt. Meru or in the oceans surrounding		Jealousy, paranoia	Constantly struggling and fighting with competitors
Human Realm	Nara-loka	On Jambudvipa		Passion	Suffering of change; Suffering upon suffering; Suffering in the making
THE LOWER REALMS					
Animal Realm	Pashu-loka	On Jambudvipa		Delusion	Being exploited, tortured, devoured by others
Hungry Ghost Realm	Preta-loka	Below Mt. Meru, above the hell realms		Passion, hunger	Intense, insatiable hunger, thirst; poverty mentality
Hell Realm	Naraka-loka	Beneath the hungry ghost realm; Cold hells Hot hells	An entire intermediate kalpa	Anger, aggression	Intense, inescapable, searing cold Intense, inescapable, claustrophobic heat

The impact of the fourth reminder with its teaching on the six realms (table 10.2), whether understood as objective states or types of human experience, is twofold. First, it shows the various ways in which beings are engaged in maintaining themselves. Second, it illustrates the repetitive, self-defeating quality of each realm and each type of psychology. The result aimed for is a clear view that, from top to bottom, the samsaric approach is a bad job. It is guilty of false advertising: it does not and cannot produce the desired results and should be abandoned. The only hope one has for any kind of human fulfillment is to renounce samsaric values and goals, and to strive for the liberation of enlightenment.

THE IMPACT OF THE FOUR REMINDERS

Our attitude toward our life and what we think about it more or less completely determine what interest we may have in a spiritual path and our ability to commit ourselves to it. If we take our lives for granted, do not realize our mortality, ignore the repercussions of our actions, and think we can make ourselves happy through mundane activities, it will be very difficult indeed to pass up the quest for immediate gratification and nearly impossible for us to meditate or follow a spiritual path. But if we are willing to hold up the mirror of the four reminders and allow ourselves to be confronted with the realities of our lives, then meditation practice becomes the most natural activity in the world—in fact, the only thing to do. That is how important the four reminders are. This is why Chagdud Tulku says, "contemplation of the four [reminders] upholds our practice, just as a foundation holds up a building."[32]

The purpose of the four reminders, and of the view of Hinayana in general, is to help establish the kind of psychological climate in which one will be motivated to enter the path of spiritual practice. These are not teachings that are to be read through or heard just once. In order to bring about the needed effect, one must reflect on them constantly. If approached in this manner, gradually, they will begin to become integrated into one's view of life. In terms of the first reminder, the time we can find for daily meditation, teachings we are able to receive from accomplished teachers, dharma books we come across, occasions when we can do periods of intensive practice—these are opportunities that the vast majority of people on the planet simply do not have, bringing home the preciousness of human birth.

In a similar way, the impermanence of life and the ever-present possibility of death become more and more a dimension of our ongoing awareness rather than abstract and occasionally remembered concepts. An illustration is provided by a medical doctor who worked in the emergency room of a children's hospital and daily saw his young patients in conditions of harrowing suffering and disease, sometimes dying as he held them. When asked what impact, if any, this had on his personal life, he responded that his work was difficult for him and brought him into a constant state of painful awareness. He had two young children whom he loved dearly, and each morning when he said goodbye to them, he was acutely aware that he might never see them again. The pain of this awareness was difficult, but he also said that it made him appreciate each moment he had with them and enabled him to love them in a total and unconditional way that would otherwise not have been possible.

The first two reminders each counter the habitual laziness of our samsaric minds, which cruise along in blissful ignorance, taking everything for granted and never doubting that our existence is endless. The third, the teaching on karma, provides the same kind of wake-up call, but from a different angle. It points, first, to the fragility of any happiness that we may have and, second, to the fact that how we conduct each moment of our lives will have a direct impact on our future state. Dilgo Khyentse Rinpoche comments that the third reminder thus leads us to increased mindfulness of this very moment and calls us to pay attention to everything we do. The third reminder not only calls us to perform actions now that will have a positive effect on our future but also opens up the opportunity to purify whatever negative actions we have already performed. Khyentse Rinpoche says, "However heavy our negative actions may be, they can be purified. There is nothing that cannot be purified."[33]

The teaching on the suffering of samsara, reminder number four, often sounds like pessimism or nihilism to modern Western ears. It seems to say that life is miserable and that we can never be happy, and raises the question of why anyone would want to cultivate such a negative attitude. In fact, from a certain point of view, the Buddhist teaching of suffering is the most positive and optimistic that one could imagine. The fourth reminder is saying that *within samsara* there is no lasting happiness. The call here is not to enter into an existence of permanent misery but rather, on the contrary, to abandon the ego game and enter the one way that actually leads to unconditioned joy and fulfillment. Khyentse Rinpoche summarizes the impact of the four reminders as follows:

> The real point of these preliminaries is to appreciate that this human life offers a real opportunity for one to achieve liberation, to realize the urgency of doing so, to generate a strong conviction that the ordinary samsaric condition produces only suffering, and to realize that suffering comes about through karma, and is the effect of negative actions. When we have a genuine understanding of these four points, [their] main point has been realized. You should not merely think about them, but experience them in your very being.[34]

11

Hinayana
THE PRACTICE AND RESULT

THE PRACTICE

IN RELATION TO THE IMPACT OF THE FOUR REMINDERS, Chagdud Tulku says:

> We know that our contemplation of the four [reminders] has been effective if we begin to see through our samsaric experience, to understand that it lacks essence, that nothing within it is reliable and unchanging. What, then, can we count on? Where will we find true heart, true essence? Only in the sacred dharma, the spiritual path, will we discover something of lasting value.[1]

The view provided by the four reminders opens our eyes and makes our hearts more tender. At the same time, the four reminders only provide the foundation of the spiritual path and do not in and of themselves lead to radical transformation. In order to accomplish that, one must put the teachings into practice. This means [1] entering into the Hinayana stage of the path by taking refuge, [2] adopting a life of positive behavior, and [3] committing oneself to the regular discipline of meditation.

Refuge

How, then, does one step onto the path? In Tibetan Buddhism, the way to do so is to take refuge in the "three jewels": the Buddha, as the human example who shows a spiritual life is possible; the dharma, as the collection of theoretical and practical instructions on how to live such a life; and the sangha, as the community of like-minded others who are also following this path and can provide feedback and companionship.

In keeping with the nontheistic approach of Buddhism, the three jewels of Buddha, dharma, and sangha should not be understood as purely external. In fact, they are external representations of awakened qualities that lie within. As Dzigar Kongtrül Rinpoche explains:

> We take refuge in the Buddha as guide not so much in his form, but more in the awakened state of Buddha's mind, which inspires us to be awake. We take refuge in the dharma more in the meaning of dharma which inspires us to be awakened. We take refuge in the sangha more in the sense of sharing the same kind of intention to be awakened, which inspires us to be awakened. But ultimately, one's own mind is one's true refuge. The awakened state of mind in which we take refuge has to be within one's own mind. Likewise the meaning of dharma . . . and sangha has to be within one's own mind.[2]

One takes refuge in a ceremony that, in its essentials, goes all the way back to the time of the Buddha. Through the refuge ceremony, one acknowledges that one does not expect to find happiness within samsara and affirms the desire to place sole reliance on the spiritual path, as embodied in the lineage of the Buddha. In the ceremony, one makes a commitment—or, perhaps more properly put, a vow—that, for the rest of one's life, one will seek to emulate the Buddha's example through study and practice of the dharma.

The actual refuge liturgy is a simple one. In a typical ceremony as performed in the Karma Kagyü tradition in the West, after a talk on the meaning of refuge by the preceptor, those seeking refuge make three prostrations to the shrine. The prostrations symbolize their humility and openness, while the shrine represents the presence of Buddha Shakyamuni and the lineage of awakened ones. Then aspirants repeat the refuge vow three times: "I take refuge in the Buddha; I take refuge in the dharma; I take refuge in the sangha." At the conclusion of the third repetition of the threefold refuge, the preceptor will snap his or her fingers and with that, the energy of the lineage is believed to enter the top of the head and become part of one's system. Following this, those who have taken refuge are given a Buddhist name that expresses their particular character or qualities as a person on the path.

The refuge vow functions as the official point of entry into the Buddhist religion. Particularly for Westerners, taking refuge often marks a very dramatic change in identity; one now is "Buddhist" rather than Christian, Jewish, agnostic, or any of the other more familiar Western identifications. At the same time, however, particularly to Westerners, Tibetan teachers typically emphasize that taking refuge is essentially making a commitment to oneself to find out, through meditation, who one most fundamentally is and to express this innermost nature in one's activities in the world. This is, of course, a way of expressing in contemporary language the age-old goal of Tibetan Buddhism of uncovering the buddha-nature within, with its dual components of wisdom (finding out who one is) and compassion (expressing this in one's life).

The refuge vow marks the moment when the dharma becomes fully personal and an integrated part of one's life. Dzigar Kongtrül Rinpoche clarifies this point:

> Taking refuge is the first step of entering the path. We could study the dharma and practice the dharma on our own without fully taking refuge in it, but if one is serious about the path of dharma, taking refuge in the Three Jewels would make it complete. It also brings forth the blessings into one's study and practice. In addition, it brings a sense of meaning of the practice in one's life. . . . For myself, the meaning of the practice is strictly to work with my mind and to be able to have a sense of awakened clarity, an unconfused state of mind, and, from there, to be able to benefit others.[3]

Within Tibetan Buddhism, vows such as refuge play an extremely important role on the path. When one takes refuge, the vow is said to become part of one's karmic situation in a most literal and fundamental way, imprinting itself in one's mental and physical person down to (as we might say today) the cellular level. This brings about a permanent transformation in one's state of being with important implications for one's practice. Tibetan teachers say that if you keep your vow, your progress on the path will be greatly accelerated. But if you break your vow, you will encounter all kinds of obstacles and will be haunted by the fact of having turned away from yourself. The refuge vow is thus a weighty commitment. As one progresses along the path to the Mahayana and then the Vajrayana, the weight of one's vows, along with the potential benefits and liabilities, increases proportionately.

Shila: Life Rule of Discipline

The ultimate reality that Tibetan Buddhists seek to realize is beyond all karma, beyond all conditionality. Yet our human situation is one of karmic causes and conditions. Since beginningless time, through the way we have acted in the relative world, through actions based on passion, aggression, and delusion, we have created layer upon layer of obscurations over our original enlightened nature. We have done so because we did not know better. Now we need to remove these obscurations so that we may realize the resplendent buddha-nature within and so that it may shine forth in compassion for others. The way to do this is through what is called in Tibetan Buddhism, the accumulation of merit and wisdom.

In the Hinayana, the accumulation of wisdom refers to the direct experience of the non-existence of one's "self" or ego. The accumulation of merit refers to creating, through meritorious actions, a more positive karmic environment without which the accumulation of wisdom is not possible. Specifically, as mentioned in the previous chapter, one seeks to generate in this life the conditions for successful dharma practice and in the future a human birth in which dharma practice will be possible.

How does one go about accumulating merit? Most basically, one needs to avoid harming others and to act kindly toward them. In Tibetan Buddhism, as in Buddhism in general, it is felt that this instruction, in order to be effective, needs to be given much more specificity in particular behavioral principles and vows that one can take on and follow. It is the function of shila to enumerate particular actions that should be avoided and other actions that should be performed.

Shila, literally "conduct" or "discipline," refers to a particular code of behavior that a Buddhist follows as part of his or her spiritual path. In Tibetan Buddhism, there are shilas in the form of general behavioral guidelines that are understood to apply to everyone, such as the ten unvirtuous actions to be avoided. These include injunctions against such unwholesome actions as killing, stealing, lying, and sexual misconduct. There are also more specific shilas, derived from the general guidelines, that are taken by individuals as particular vows. Exactly what these are depends upon the kind of life that one is following, whether that of a layperson, a monastic, or a yogin. While many of the elements of shila are found in other religious traditions, the understanding, interpretation, and use of these elements is more or less specific to Buddhism.

In relation to the specific shilas, Kalu Rinpoche says:

> The Hinayana offers different vows for individual liberation which help us to maintain right moral discipline. There is: major monastic ordination, with the vows of a *bhikshu* or fully ordained monk; minor monastic ordination of a *shramanera* or novice monk or nun, with fewer vows; and the *upasaka* vows, or the layperson's vows. If we do not take the monk's vows, we can take the lay vows, or at least we can take the refuge vow, which involves abandoning the ten negative actions and cultivating the ten positive actions as much as possible.
>
> These vows are important as a way of closing the door on negative tendencies: they greatly facilitate abandoning harmfulness and taking positive actions. In fact, if we are not able to abstain from killing, stealing, or sexual misconduct in the ordinary context, the vows provide the strength to do so, as well as the ability to restrain negative acts of body, speech and mind.[4]

THE TEN UNVIRTUOUS ACTIONS AND THE TEN MERITORIOUS ACTIONS

The ten unvirtuous actions provide general behavioral guidelines for all Buddhists in Tibet. While these are not usually taken as specific vows, everyone is under the obligation to try to avoid these actions. In relation to these, Kalu Rinpoche remarks:

> Negative activity, or bad karma, is made up of acts and their results which harm others and oneself or attitudes of body, speech, and mind produced by self-cherishing tendencies and afflicted behaviors that lead to desire, anger, pride, and so forth. These kinds of activities stimulate and in turn reinforce self-cherishing and afflicted tendencies, contributing to the perpetuation of samsara and the delusions that maintain it. Briefly, negative karma comes from the ten negative actions: three of body, four of speech, and three of mind.[5]

BODY

1. *Killing any sentient being.* As Chagdud Tulku explains, any non-virtuous act, to produce the full karma of that act, requires the object of the action, the intention, the act, and the result. The karma of killing necessitates a living being to be killed; the intention to kill; the act of killing; and the result of the death of that being.[6] If any one of these is missing, then one does not accumulate the karma of having killed a sentient being. Nevertheless, the karma incurred in such a case can still be very serious. Suppose there is a person, the intention to kill the person, and the firing of a gun. If we do not succeed in killing the other, although we have not accumulated the karma of murder, still the karma of our attempt will entail grave consequences.
2. *Stealing.* "Stealing means taking something that hasn't been given to you. It includes taking something without the owner knowing it, overpowering a person in order to appropriate

something, or using a position of power and authority to seize something from another in order to benefit oneself."[7] This definition is obviously much broader than the Western idea that there is no stealing involved as long as one takes something that does not legally belong to another.

3. *Sexual misconduct.* "Sexual misconduct involves sexual activity with someone underage, with someone who is sick, or when such activity will cause mental or emotional distress, or the breaking of one's own or another's vows or commitment to a sexual partner."[8] The phrase "when such activity will cause mental or emotional distress" is interesting, because it suggests that even if two people are married, sexual conduct may still be unvirtuous. By this standard, sex used for one's gratification alone, to gain or exert power over another, or as a way of demeaning or humiliating the other would all qualify as sexual misconduct.

SPEECH

4. *Lying.* Misrepresenting situations.
5. *Slander.* Using speech to sow discord and cause divisions among people.
6. *Abusive speech.* Using speech as a vehicle of one's aggression.
7. *Idle chatter and gossip.* Wasting time, diverting awareness through mindless and pointless speech.

MIND

8. *Covetousness.* Being preoccupied with coveting something that someone else has.
9. *Thoughts of wanting to cause harm to others.*
10. *Wrong view.* Chagdud Tulku: "Having wrong view means thinking in very contrary ways, as opposed to doubting and questioning, which is a healthy component of spiritual contemplation. Believing that it's good to be bad, or bad to be good, is an example of wrong view. So is disbelieving in the illusory nature of experience because we can't prove it and thus denying

the basic truth that will ultimately produce liberation from suffering."[9]

Like any of the Buddhist *shilas,* the ten nonvirtuous actions to be abandoned are not behavioral absolutes but rather guidelines. In Buddhism, it is always finally one's *intention* and the *impact for good or for ill on sentient beings* that finally determine whether an action is virtuous or not. In illustration of this point, Kalu Rinpoche tells the following story.

> In one of his previous lives, Buddha was captain of a ship. One day, as the ship was transporting five hundred merchants, a pirate came on board, intending to kill everyone in order to seize their riches. Overcome by great compassion for the pirate and for the merchants, and thinking that if the pirate actually followed through on his plan he would have to suffer for innumerable eons in hell, the captain decided, with an altruistic and compassionate motivation, to kill the pirate, thus saving the lives of the five hundred merchants. While he himself committed a murder, his sincerely altruistic and detached motivation was the source of enormous positive karma, because the action was beneficial. A lie can also be positive in certain cases; for example, to save a life. If a murderer is looking for someone who he wants to kill and asks where that person is, to give him the wrong directions in order to save the person's life is good.[10]

The ten unvirtuous actions are based on egocentricity and selfishness, and produce negative karma. The ten meritorious actions, by contrast, "proceed from the transcendence of self-cherishing attitudes and are based on feelings of love, compassion, goodness, and so forth."[11] These actions produce positive karma. The ten meritorious actions to be cultivated are summarized by Chagdud Tulku:

> Saving and protecting life, for example, creates tremendous virtue. All beings are equal in that they all seek happiness, don't want to suffer, and value their lives as much as we do [our own].

To save the life of an insect or an animal is extremely virtuous and, when the merit is dedicated, creates great benefit not only for that animal but for all beings. Merit dedicated to the long life of others, for example, can be of immense benefit to those who are sick. Generosity, no matter how seemingly insignificant—even giving a bit of food or water to a hungry bird—produces great virtue. Maintaining discipline in sexual relationships, telling the truth, using speech to create harmony, to help another's mind, and to create temporary and ultimate benefit for oneself and others—these, too, are virtues, as are rejoicing in the happiness of others, generating helpful and kind thoughts, and learning correct view.[12]

Specific Codes for Laypeople, Monastics, and Yogins

A specific code of five precepts, taken formally as vows, is particularly recommended to laypeople in Tibet, including abstention from killing, stealing, lying, sexual misconduct, and taking intoxicants that cloud the mind. At any given time, one may swear to one, two, up to all five precepts. In one typical tradition, one takes the vows only for one day. If someone wants to carry the practice to the next day, he or she will take the vow again the next morning, and it will remain in force for that day. The daily taking of the precepts is important. They are specific, and one's commitment to them needs to be renewed frequently to keep one's intention and investment fresh.

One usually initially takes the vow from a preceptor, an authorized teacher, and thenceforth one is able to take the precepts on any day that one wishes. The understanding of the force of the vow is similar to that of the refuge vow: if one keeps the vow, it produces good karma and accelerates one's progress on the path; however, if one breaks the vow, it creates particularly negative karma (far more than if one performed the same action without having taken the vow), and it generates obstacles to one's path. Sometimes, on special holy days, laypeople may take the five precepts and some additional vows as ways of producing particularly good karma.

Most Buddhists in Tibet were laypeople. However, a relatively large percentage of the population lived as renunciants, either as monks or, more rarely, yogins. The shila of monastic people is defined by the two primary levels of ordination in Tibet, the novice (*shramanera*) and full (*bhikshu*) ordinations. Men could aspire after both ordinations; however, because the lineage of the full ordination of women did not survive in Tibet, women could only take the novice vows. In the case of men, in order to advance to full ordination, some period spent as a novice was necessary. However, many monks took only the first ordination and, like the women, lived out their lives in the status of novice.

Monastic rules, whether those of the novice or the fully ordained monk, are considerably more demanding than the five precepts of the laity. The novices, for example, take ten precepts. The first five are the same as the five lay precepts except that the sexual prohibition calls for avoiding alcohol entirely as well as all sexual activity. The other five precepts include not eating after noon; not adorning or beautifying oneself; avoiding dancing, singing, and attending entertainments; not sleeping on a high bed; and not handling money.

The precepts for fully ordained monks, following the Mulasarvastivadin tradition, number some 258 rules of restraint and range all the way from grave offenses requiring expulsion from the monastic community to matters of decorum with no particular punishment for their infraction. Thus one will be permanently separated from the monastic life for four offenses: sexual intercourse; committing the crime of robbery; killing a human being; or falsely claiming supernatural attainments. A considerable number of the precepts involve various prohibitions against sexual or potentially sexual contact or encounters with women, indicating the danger to both monk and monastery of relationships with the opposite sex that could under any circumstances become sexual or be construed as sexual. Other precepts address behaviors considered appropriate to the monastic life (concerning food, clothing, dwelling, and possessions); the relationship of monks to the laity, to one another, and to the monastery; the handling of money; and matters of etiquette relating to dress, eating, general behavior, and so on.

At any given time in any Tibetan generation, a small number of people were engaged in strict retreat practice. Fully ordained monks, novices, and laypeople could all take up the yogic or retreatant life. The path of the yogin was considered the highest and most direct of all, and it was the way followed by those intent upon realizing enlightenment in the present lifetime. People pursuing this path would typically receive empowerment from their teacher and then enter retreat to carry out the associated practices. Retreats would typically range from a few months in length to three years or more. Upon entering retreat, one would usually take a vow to remain for a certain period of time. Occasionally, yogins would take a "life vow" that they would remain in their retreat until they died. In such cases, the wall of the cave where they would carry out their meditation was often sealed with rocks and mortar, with a small opening for food to be passed in and slops to be taken away. This is solitary confinement, with no term and no reprieve.

A good friend of mine at Naropa University, a prominent psychiatrist, psychoanalyst, and author, left his job a number of years ago to undertake a three-year retreat. At the end of this period, he decided that he wanted to spend the rest of his life in retreat, and he wrote us informing us that he would no longer return to the world and that we would never see him again. I saw pictures of his retreat place, a tiny cabin in France, surrounded by a small yard and fenced in by a high enclosure. Each of his days is exactly the same: he rises and meditates until breakfast. After breakfast he meditates until lunch. After lunch he meditates until dinner. After dinner, he meditates until bedtime. From the worldly point of view, this kind of life would be a nightmare. Ego would be screaming for relief after the first day. I have an idea, however, that my friend may see it differently.

In this context, one is reminded of a comment made by the great siddha Saraha, who was similarly engaged in a life of meditation and nothing else. Someone happened by his retreat place and suggested he might like to see the sights of the world. He replied, in essence, that in his body and in his mind was contained the entire universe. His visitor pressed the matter, saying that surely Saraha would like to see the great sacred sites of his land. Saraha replied that even the great rivers of the Ganges and the Yamuna were contained within his body, and he had

S H A M B H A L A

The World Soul (1617)
by Robert Fludd, from
Ego and Archetype
(Shambhala 1992).
Öffentliche Bibliothek
der Universität Basel,
Color version © 1990
by Roberta Weir.

S H A M B H A L A

If you wish to receive a copy of the latest Shambhala Publications catalogue of books and to be placed on our mailing list, please send us this card—or send us an e-mail at info@shambhala.com

Please print

BOOK IN WHICH THIS CARD WAS FOUND ....

NAME ....

ADDRESS ....

CITY .... STATE ....

ZIP OR POSTAL CODE ....

COUNTRY (*if outside U.S.A.*) ....

Detach bookmark before mailing card.

Shambhala Publications, Inc.

Mailing List
P.O. Box 308, Back Bay Annex
Boston, Massachusetts   02117-0308

Elementum

Aquæ et Terræ

Artes Liberaliores

Mineralia

Vegetabilia

Animalia

SHAMBHALA

no need to go wandering abroad. I have an idea that my retreatant friend finds in his little hut and enclosure a world that is far vaster and more beautiful than anything one would find outside.

Like laypeople and monastics, yogins take certain vows and observe certain conventions. There are twelve that are most famous in classical tradition, known as the *dhuta-guna,* conventions of the ascetic life. These pertain to what one eats (restricted to one bowl or one meal), where one lives (in the wilds), what one wears (only a garment made from cast-away rags is allowed), and how one sleeps (one must sleep while seated upright, meditating, not lying down during the night). Retreatants usually take some number of these vows. In addition, they may take additional vows such as not eating meat or perhaps not eating at all for periods of time. It is also common for retreatants to take a vow of total silence, sometimes for years or for their entire lives, such that the few contacts with the outside world over food, water, needed supplies, illness, or whatever may arise, are communicated only by writing. All of these vows have the same purpose: they create and protect the retreat environment and inconvenience the ego in such a systematic way that insight into its own folly will come more easily.

THE PURPOSES OF SHILA

On the most general level, as mentioned, the purpose of shila is to show the kind of behavior most conducive to the accumulation of merit—in other words, the production of positive karma. Shila has more specific purposes on the path itself that may be considered under the categories of ground, path, and fruition.

Ground

The heart of the Buddhist path is meditation. However, meditation can only be successfully practiced in the context of a relatively stable, settled, and ethical life. One develops such a life through not harming others and through practicing kindness toward them. It is the purpose of the various shilas to show us how to live in such a way.

The teaching on shila is often a difficult one for Westerners to accept.

In our individualistic culture, there is often the assumption that spirituality is purely a personal thing and that how we relate with other people is another, separate, and unrelated matter. They often raise the question of how the practice of *shila* promotes the kind of life in which meditation not only is possible but can flourish.

One may look initially at the immediate and personal psychological impact of negative actions, or actions in which one's self-serving behavior harms others. For example, if in a relationship one engages in lying and deception, one will feel a considerable amount of continual mental agitation. If one lives by stealing from others, this will produce a mind that is characterized by greed, paranoia, and enmity. Engaging in a livelihood that directly harms others likewise results in feelings of guilt and continual self-justification. If one tries to sit down and meditate in any of these states of mind, one will likely encounter only one's own mental confusion, anxiety, and chaos. The whole process of meditation is about softening up, opening, and surrendering to the deeper aspects of one's own being, aspects that are not self-centered. Negative actions, if persisted in, lead us in the opposite direction by making us hard, selfish, insensitive, and defensive. The more one tries to sit, the more the enormity of one's actions will assert itself. This kind of logic works in the short term and also in the long term: a life lived largely to help and benefit others results in an inner peace and confidence that open the way for quick progress in meditation.

It is important to realize that this psychologically oriented presentation, perhaps relatively understandable and even acceptable in the contemporary West, would not normally be used in a traditional Tibetan context. If one were a Tibetan listening to a dharma discourse, one would be told that meritorious action in accordance with the elements of shila produces good karma. This good karma manifests itself in the appearance in one's life of conditions favorable to dharma practice. One may have opportunities to practice the dharma now, but there are always limitations and obstacles. Moreover, the conditions of our lives are always uncertain. One never knows when past negative actions may come to fruition and make it impossible for us to practice. Shila helps us purify past negative deeds and generate further opportunities for dharma practice. And finally, while at this time we have a fortunate human birth and can practice the dharma, there is no guarantee that in the future we may not be reborn in a situation where this is impossible. Here again, shila provides a way to maximize the chances that future births will be conducive to our pursuit of the path. For these reasons, Tibetans in general, whether simple laypeople, learned monks, or realized saints, invest a considerable amount of care, attention, and energy in avoiding demeritorious actions and performing those which are meritorious.

The following example illustrates this point. At the Rocky Mountain Shambhala Center (RMSC), a Tibetan Buddhist contemplative center in Red Feather Lakes, Colorado, a *stupa,* or sacred reliquary, has been under construction for many years. It is large, 108 feet high, and costly for the small community that is building it. During one summer, as in previous years, a fundraising event was held, presided over by Tenga Rinpoche, a Tibetan lama of the Kagyü lineage. For the week prior to "stupa day," Rinpoche gave teachings for which he received a teaching gift. On the fundraising day, he talked about the good karma that is generated through giving gifts toward the support of dharma teachers and dharma centers, and toward the construction of sacred monuments such as the RMSC stupa. At the end of the day, as the event was drawing to a close, Rinpoche donated his entire teaching gift to the stupa construction. It was clear that this was not a donation made for effect but represented a genuine expression of the Rinpoche's path, a watering of the field of karma for present and future lives, positive merit that he then dedicated to the welfare of all sentient beings.

Path

Shila is not about "being good" simply for its own sake. Rather, as we have seen, it is a functional practice. One adheres to meritorious behavior because of the concrete effects that are produced thereby. The practical importance of shila is seen further in that it not only brings about positive conditions necessary as the foundation of the path, but it also has direct and immediate functions on the path itself.

For example, committing oneself to adhere to a particular shila restricts and simplifies one's behavior in certain ways, facilitating settled-ness and clarity. Thus laypeople may vow for a certain specified period, not to drink liquor or engage in sexual conduct. In the contemporary West, Buddhists will sometimes commit themselves to shilas that, while not mentioned in the Buddhist texts, are pertinent to their modern lives. This might include abstaining for a specific time, from watching televi-sion or reading magazines and newspapers. How often we turn to a drink or to sexuality, or these days to television or the magazines and newspapers to fill up our time, alleviate our anxiety, or counteract our boredom. Removing these engaging activities from our lives for periods of time can have a profound effect. Having removed such options as possibilities, one finds that one's life has been greatly simplified. And simplicity produces insight and peace.

A friend recently took a vow to abstain from television and print media for a month. She told me that previously, when she came home from work each day, she would turn on the television and watch for an hour or two, leafing through magazines and newspapers when the pro-gram became too boring. Having taken her vow, now when she came home from work, she would come into her house and immediately no-tice a silence and peace she had not noticed before. Its interior space even seemed less "junky" and cluttered. Then she would sit in her living room, amid the plants she loves, and enjoy the afternoon sun as it flooded in through the windows. She said that after a few days of this practice, a feeling of deep peace and well-being began to fill her, and she began to look forward all day to this time. After her month was up, she did not renew her vow, but she did sell her television and cancel most of her many magazine subscriptions.

In close connection with its role of simplifying one's life, shila also performs another critical function on the path. By placing restrictions on our behavior, it encourages insight into our own self-serving machi-nations and sheds light into the dark corners of our self-deception. How does this occur? Let us consider the shila of not lying and let us suppose that I am a layperson and, for a certain period of time, each morning take the vow not to lie. As I try to keep this vow, I may begin to notice that while I am successful in avoiding out-and-out lies, there is a more subtle level. I may begin to notice that every time I talk to someone, I am promoting some angle, shading my presentation so that it will benefit me in some way. If I am talking to a colleague about a project I am involved in, I may present it in overly positive terms, in order to elicit the good opinion of my hearer. Or, wanting that person's sympathy, I may present it in overly negative terms. If my boss asks me what I think about an idea of his, my answer may not have very much to do with what I really think, and may be instead tailored to improving my relationship with my boss. Having taken the vow not to lie, I begin to discover, in short, how very often in my interactions with others I do not tell the truth. This insight, painful as it is, represents an increase in awareness and provides a fresh opportunity to let go of the ego's habit of grasping at situations.

This example shows us something important about the practice of shila in Tibetan Buddhism. The fundamental goal in taking on various shilas is not to do them perfectly. Indeed, as in this example, such perfection is not a possibility for any but a realized person. Rather, the aim is to create a context in which, through our attempts to keep the shila, we diminish the harm we do to others, simplify our life, and gain deeper insight into who we are and how things work. Properly understood, then, shila is the farthest thing from self-righteous moralism. Rather, it creates a situation in which we realize more deeply our own limitations, which can only lead us to renewed humility.

Fully ordained monastic people, as we have seen, are beholden to a great many more shilas than lay people. What is true of shila for the laity is even truer of the monastic person. The many shilas of the monastic life, in their function of embodying an attitude of respect toward others and of not harming them, are considered to provide an exceptionally meritorious ground for one's dharma practice. Similarly, in the present context of the path, the monastic shilas effect a tremendous and (since monastic vows are normally for life) ongoing simplification of one's existence. This generates a feeling of contentment and well-being and provides many opportunities to unmask the ego, to see how ravenous for entertainment and distraction we are, and, because so few opportunities are provided, to let those tendencies go.

Westerners presented with the full extent of the shilas of the fully ordained monastic life sometimes express disbelief that anyone would want to adopt such a restricted and "uptight" lifestyle, forgoing so many options for personal gratification. In quite some contrast, then, are the feelings about shila of many monastic people, not only Tibetan, but also Western. These are epitomized by the point of view of a friend who has been a fully ordained nun for some fifteen years. She remarks that the monastic shila is the greatest gift ever given to her by her teacher. In giving her "permission" to simplify her life to such a radical degree, it has brought about a situation in which she has learned to be content, just "to be," rather than filling her life with diversions and distractions as she used to. And, the radical simplicity of the monastic way nourishes her meditation practice, providing an unceasing flow of insights and ever deepening understanding of her life. In addition, by restricting her opportunities to treat others in unvirtuous ways, as objects to be manipulated for some end or other, she finds many more possibilities for genuine warmth toward those with whom she interacts.

Fruition

Finally, at the fruition level, shila is not a set of precepts that one is asked to follow, but rather a description of the natural and unpremeditated behavior of an enlightened person. Taking the ten meritorious actions as an example, a realized person saves the lives of sentient beings, is endlessly generous to them, relates to sexuality with the utmost integrity and compassion, and speaks with words that are transparent to the truth, using speech to bring peace, harmony, and understanding, and so on. Seen from this viewpoint, the spiritual path involves imitating the behavior of a realized person until, through the accumulation of merit and wisdom produced thereby, one becomes oneself realized.

Samadhi: Meditation

In Tibetan Buddhism, at the Hinayana stage of the journey, one is primarily engaged in laying a foundation for the spiritual path. Based on

FIGURE 11.1 *The Buddha in meditation—the heart of Buddhist practice.*

the view provided by the four reminders, one engages the path: through taking refuge, one makes a commitment to practice the dharma. Then, through the practice of shila, one addresses the need to accumulate merit through virtuous action. All of this is only a preliminary, however, to the heart of Buddhism, which in Tibet as elsewhere is the practice of meditation. In Tibetan tradition, meditation practice in Hinayana, Mahayana, and Vajrayana is described in terms of two stages: shamatha, or quieting the mind, and vipashyana, developing insight. As one progresses through the yanas, these stages are developed and refined to ever deeper and more subtle levels.

SHAMATHA: TRANQUILLITY MEDITATION

On the three-yana journey, most of the emphasis at the Hinayana level of meditation is on shamatha, taming and quieting the mind. This is because a practitioner, at the initial stages of his or her journey, is usually afflicted by a mind that is excessively discursive and uncontrollably active. Such a mind cannot easily give birth to insight, or vipashyana. Through the practice of shamatha, then, the mind can begin to slow down and become less wild and distracted.

Shamatha requires setting aside periods of time for the formal practice of sitting meditation in daily life and, as possible, in periods of intensive group practice and in retreat. Shamatha involves placing one's attention on a chosen object and resting it there. In Tibetan tradition, as we shall see, a number of different objects are used. At the beginning stages of practice, it is the breath that is most commonly chosen. One is instructed to focus on one's breathing, usually attending to the breath at the tip of the nose. One is to pay attention to the sensations of the breath entering the nostrils on the in-breath and exiting the nostrils on the out-breath. One's awareness is to be tethered to this precise point and held there as one breathes in and out. If the mind wanders, as it is likely to do, one is to bring it back gently but firmly to the sensation of the breath.

Through carrying out this practice with diligence as a daily part of one's ongoing life, the character of one's mental activity will gradually begin to change. In the initial stages, one will find oneself forcibly taken over by thoughts, emotions, and fantasies. In fact, one may be distracted, forgetting to pay attention to the breathing, for long periods of time. Then, all of a sudden, one will realize that one has been thinking or daydreaming, and one will "come back" and begin again to practice the mindfulness of breathing. In the beginning, the pattern of trying to pay attention to the breath, being pulled away, and then coming back can be painful, frustrating, and exhausting. However, one may also feel periods of surprising lightness and peace. Both the difficulty of the mindfulness and the occasional moments of relief are signs that the practice is evolving.

Through this process, one cultivates greater and greater attentiveness or mindfulness of one's breathing. Sakyong Mipham Rinpoche describes the progressive development of this mindfulness.[13] First, one becomes familiar with (in this case) one's breathing. In the beginning, we cannot find the breath. We do not know what it is, from a strictly perceptual viewpoint. Through the practice, we become more and more acquainted with the breath, what it feels like, the different moods that it takes on when we are excited or depressed, and so on. The second stage is called "not forgetting" and refers to maintaining a placement of the attention on the breathing. Just as the mind of a hungry person is fixed on the feast placed before him or just as the mind of a lover never strays from the thought of her beloved, so the mind of the meditator is always turned toward the breathing and attentive to it. The third stage is called nondistraction, in which one is able to rest one's mind on the breathing without being distracted at all.

As one's practice of shamatha evolves, so does the technique that one employs. The following summary of major stages in the evolution of a practitioner's shamatha technique, while not literally reproducing a traditional Tibetan list, should serve to provide the reader with a general idea of how the practice develops. Let us take the mindfulness of breathing as an example.

[1] In the beginning, when one's mind is in endless turmoil, one needs to focus one's attention on the in-breath and the out-breath. The actual practice might go something like this. Focus attention on the in-breath and the out-breath as described, perhaps for nine, fifteen, or twenty-one breaths. Each in-breath and out-breath count as one. Counting each breath is a further aid to maintaining mindfulness. During each series, focus your attention as if you were hanging on to the edge of a cliff with your fingernails. If you let your attention wander, you will fall into the abyss. After you have completed, say, nine breaths, relax and let your mind rest for a bit. At this time, leave your mind relaxed and open, aware of the space around you, being aware of sights, sounds, physical sensations, thoughts. Then do another series of nine breaths, or whatever number you are using.

[2] Eventually, at certain points, the mind will begin to become somewhat less rabid and will begin to slow down. As the mind begins to slow and become more tranquil, as you feel more openness and peace, it will become obvious that it is neither necessary nor appropriate to focus quite so heavily and intensely on the in-breath and the out-breath. At this time, lighten your attention on your breathing. Your attention is still on the in-breath and the out-breath, but it is much lighter, perhaps like a Ping-Pong ball floating on water. As you lightly focus your attention in this way, you will find yourself naturally aware of your environment, sights, sounds, smells, thoughts, and so on. At this time, perhaps 25 percent of your attention is on your breathing and 75 percent is on the space around you. If, while doing this practice, the mind begins to be stirred up again, simply return to the first technique until the mind again slows down and you can again lighten your attention on your breathing.

[3] As the mind becomes more relaxed, peaceful, and open, begin to let go of your attention on your in-breath entirely, so that you are lightly resting your attention only on your out-breath. At this time, let your mind go out with your out-breath and, with your out-breath, dissolve in space. On the in-breath, simply let your mind rest in the space around you. At this time, your mind is at rest, open, free. Then, as you again begin to breathe out, once more lightly place your attention on your out-breath and ride with the breath, letting your mind dissolve at the end of the out-breath. Trungpa Rinpoche provides the following instructions for this third type of shamatha:

> You identify with the breath, particularly with the out-breath. The in-breath is just a gap, a space. During the in-breath you just wait. So you breathe out and then you dissolve and then there is a gap. Breath out . . . dissolve . . . gap. An openness, an expansion, can take place constantly that way.[14]

There is a traditional story that Buddha told an accomplished musician that he should relate to controlling his mind by keeping it not too tight and not too loose. He should keep his mind at the right level of attention. . . . We should put 25 percent of our attention on the breathing. . . . The rest of our mental activities should be let loose, left open.[15]

Why does the attention need to be this light and open?

When you tell somebody to keep a high level of concentration, to concentrate 100 percent and not make any mistakes, that person becomes stupid and is liable to make more mistakes because he's so concentrated on what he's doing. There's no gap. There is no room to open himself, no room to relate with the back-and-forth play between the reference point of the object and the reference point of the subject. So the Buddha quite wisely advised that you put only tentative attention on your technique. . . . So you keep just on the verge of your technique, with just 25 percent of your attention.[16]

It is interesting and informative to pay special attention to the moment after the out-breath dissolves in space. Look. What do you see? What happens in that gap between the end of the out-breath and the beginning of the in-breath? Try to rest your mind in that place.

It is likely, during what we may call shamatha number two and shamatha number three, that the discursive mind will kick up again, and one will find oneself suddenly engaged in thinking. It may be light-handed thoughts that have suddenly entered the picture, and one may also find oneself abruptly taken over by some heavy fantasy or aggressive stream of thoughts. This occurrence is neither a problem nor is it a sign that one's practice has degenerated. It is simply a reflection of the fact that, because the mind is uncharacteristically open, deeper levels of one's own karmic propensities have surfaced. If this occurs, look at what arises and see what it is. Wait to see whether it is a momentary eruption or if the mental speed has picked up. If the agitation continues, simply return to shamatha number one, focusing quite intently on both in-breath and out-breath, until the heavy-handed discursiveness has diminished.

[4] It sometimes happens that one's discursive thinking will subside and one will find that even resting one's attention lightly on the out-breath is more technique than one needs. It will feel like something "extra," too strained and effortful. At this time, simply let go of all technique and take the space, the peace, the pregnant silence of consciousness itself—whatever you want to call it—as your object of meditation. Beyond this, "no object" can be your object of meditation.

If pursued far enough, the pacification process of *shamatha* can lead one to enter one or another of the four dhyanas or "form trances" or even the four "formless attainments," mentioned above. In these, as we saw, discursive thinking, emotions, and even joy and peace are gradually abandoned and one comes upon the experience of space, consciousness itself, and so on. These various states of mind are, again, high levels of *shamatha* attainment, usually experienced only by yogins in retreat. Sometimes, however, people meditating "in the world" can come upon one or more of them, unexpectedly, in the course of their practice. The four form trances and four formless attainments have their value in rendering the mind increasingly subtle, open, and sensitive.

It is natural at the beginning that shamatha becomes the focus of our practice. Moreover, we naturally find something attractive and even compelling about the shamatha experience. Through the practice of mindfulness, if one perseveres, the mind does begin to slow down, sometimes in dramatic ways. Most of us take our incessant thinking for granted; but within the experience of discursiveness there is a considerable amount of discomfort—in our mental speed, aggression, rigidity, tension, and worry. When one experiences the peacefulness of shamatha for the first time, one may feel one is drinking clear, cool water in a burning desert. Most of us will feel powerfully drawn to this experience, for the refreshment, relief, and peace it provides.

At this point it is important to realize that the various levels of shamatha are not ends in themselves. Why is shamatha not an end in itself? Because all of the shamatha states fall within the cycle of samsara. They represent ever more subtle states of mind, but states of mind that are still based on causes and conditions and that do not necessarily imply any insight into the nature of things. If shamatha is limited in this way, why is it a necessary preliminary to vipashyana? Because as long as discursive thinking holds sway within our minds, as long as our field of consciousness is rampant with the chaotic storm of thoughts, it is difficult for us to experience insight. However, once we begin to slow down, then insight can begin to be recognized.

In the shamatha practice, then, one is working with the mind to develop presence and precision (shamatha), in order to connect with the experience of awareness or insight (vipashyana). One relates with the breath in a simple and disciplined way. Rather than peace being our goal, we relate with the breath and, through this, as the mind is slowed and stabilized (shamatha), we find ourselves making a lot of discoveries (vipashyana). The discoveries cause our mind to kick up again, and then we bring ourselves back through shamatha. And so the path unfolds.

Part of the practice is not judging our meditation sessions. It is not that the more peaceful our meditation, the "better" the session was. Sometimes the more vipashyana, the more turbulence. It can happen that the practitioner misuses shamatha as a way to defend him- or herself against painful insights. Shamatha takes us to the verge of opening, of insight, and when we find ourselves on this threshold, we have to be willing to step over.

Tibetan tradition, in fact, alerts us to the natural temptation to bend all of our efforts toward cultivating the peace of shamatha to deeper and deeper levels. Making shamatha an end in itself in this way is viewed as a sidetrack—and potentially a dangerous one. The possible dangers of very advanced shamatha states are illustrated by the following example. Trungpa Rinpoche reported that in Tibet, meditators looking for a remote and isolated cave in which to practice would occasionally come across a very strange phenomenon. They would find people who had developed shamatha to such a high degree that they had gone into one of the formless trances, and entered into a state of mind equivalent to the formless gods, described above. Such meditators would remain in these trances virtually not breathing at all and with pulses that were not detectable, for scores and even hundreds of years. During this time, a minuscule amount of energy would be used up to maintain this state between life and death. This energy would come from the body consuming itself until, in the end, there remained only the semblance of a living human being.

Tulku Urgyen provides the following similar account:

In Bangkok there are some unfortunate examples of meditation gods [meditators stuck in the form or formless realm] who are supposedly called arhats. The bodies of a few monks are preserved in a state in which they are neither dead nor alive; the perfect example of knowing how to meditate but not how to be free. It's been quite a few years since they "passed away" and have remained in a blocked state. They are in a "frozen emptiness," in a state of cessation that is not allowed to dissolve. This state of cessation happens before really passing away. . . . These people are in meditation but not liberation. . . . It is of course a quite impressive state of meditative concentration; but, to stay in one stable thought cannot be called liberation. . . .

Remaining in that state after we have seemingly passed away means that our life span, merit and power have been all used up but we still stick around. If you burn the body you make the bad karma of killing it. It is very difficult to revive such a person; you need a yogi, a real meditator, for that. The best is to perform the transference of consciousness for him. The state of cessation has a time limit and at some point the person wakes up again. Then he thinks, "Oh no! I've been wasting all this time. It was totally pointless. It was no use at all!" He develops wrong views, regret, and anger; and such bitterness can easily "open the door" to a rebirth in hell. "I have used all these years meditating and I have not gotten even a cup of water's worth of benefit!" The duration of this state, dependent on the force and stability behind it, can last for many years.

There were many meditators like that in the eastern part of Tibet. Some Chinese working in the area went into the caves where the bodies trapped in inert [meditation] were sitting. They cut open the stomachs and took out a substance that is used to make gun powder. Some of the bodies' insides were almost like red fresh meat. The heart, the intestines, everything was there. I have heard that in some caves there were five or six of them sitting together. They can remain for a thousand years. They sit, not looking; their eyes are not open. The body remains unmoving, like in hibernation. The state of mind is a kind of stupidity, though. I have not gone there myself, but another tulku in Kham went and told me there are three or four of these dried-up meditators sitting there. He did not know for how long. These Chinese workers cut up many and wrecked them.[17]

This kind of sidetrack is fortunately not a possibility for most of us. It requires, first, believing that the state of peace is a goal worth sacrificing everything for and, second, being able to shut oneself in a cave for the rest of one's life to bring this state about. Stories like these are told in Tibetan tradition not so much because anyone might seek such a path, but rather to illustrate in a vivid and unforgettable way the limitations of shamatha. We need to develop shamatha on the path of meditation, but it finds its real purpose and fruition in vipashyana.

VIPASHYANA: CLEAR SEEING

As the mind becomes more trained, as we begin to slow down and become less discursive, in the context of one's meditation or in the periods between meditation sessions, one may begin to experience momentary glimpses of insight, known as vipashyana, or "clear seeing." Trungpa Rinpoche compares the vipashyana experience to lightning on a dark night. You are sitting on a hillside on a cloudy night, looking out. However, it is so dark that you can see nothing. This is the state of our normal ego existence where we are wrapped in the dark shrouds of ignorance. Abruptly, a bolt of lightning strikes in the sky before you, illuminating the landscape. In this instant, as clearly and sharply as if it were broad daylight, you can see the hills and valleys, with their trees and bushes, their rivers and ponds, spread out before you. The image of lightning illuminating the darkened landscape is the *vipashyana* experience. Trungpa Rinpoche:

Awareness is acknowledging the totality of the whole thing. In the Buddhist tradition, awareness has been described as the first experience of egolessness. . . . Awareness in this case is totality rather than one-sidedness. A person who has achieved awareness or who is working on the discipline of awareness has no direction, no bias in one direction or another. He is just simply aware, totally and completely.[18]

What kind of insight does vipashyana represent? Vipashyana is an experience of the world that stands outside of our expectations and wishful thinking. It is felt as an experience of things "as they are." Moreover, this kind of vipashyana is always situational. One may be talking to someone and there may be an uneasy feeling to the conversation, but one doesn't know why. All of a sudden, like that bolt of lightning, one sees clearly the struggle that is going on—how one is trying to manipulate the conversation in a certain direction, while the other person is trying to push it in another. There is a sense that, for an instant, one stood apart from oneself and saw the true and unmistaken nature of the situation. In vipashyana, then, the world is momentarily glimpsed, not from the standpoint of ego, but—at least in an incipient way—from the standpoint of the buddha-nature.

A striking example of vipashyana was provided by a student of mine in her early twenties who had been meditating for some time. Since her late teens, she has been a devotee of "raves," dance parties held at enormous warehouses in our area, attended by literally thousands of young people. Well-known bands are engaged, the music is loud, alcohol and drugs are sometimes consumed, and the dancing goes on until dawn. The atmosphere is said to be usually "mellow" and fun, and the young folks are drawn back to the parties again and again. My student was attending a rave one Saturday night and, for no apparent reason, wanted to feel the cool, the space, and the silence of the night. She left the huge warehouse where the party was happening and walked across an adjacent field to a hillock beyond. Turning around, she looked at the building, throbbing with music and blazing with light, packed as it was by several thousand ravers. Suddenly, without warning, it was as if her eyes were opened for the first time and she "saw" the party—so she reported—in all its naked reality. She saw the tremendous desperation of the people inside, their loneliness and hunger, how they had all come there seeking to escape from their suffering. She saw how they had all become predators, preying upon one another, in a fruitless search for happiness. It was as an endless game in which, she too, was involved. Overcome by the sorrow and hopelessness of the situation, she broke down and wept. She came to talk to me because, as she said, this experience had shown her something not only about raves, but about life in general, about the many things people do out of their own pain and misery. She told me that she felt, for the first time, the meaning of the first noble truth, the truth of suffering. She saw her experience as a direct product of her meditation practice and her commitment to her spiritual path. Her experience made her realize, again for the first time, that her meditation was the one anchor in her life and that the spiritual journey she had undertaken was about having her eyes opened, in perhaps shocking and painful ways, to the underpinnings of the seemingly normal, everyday world.

The vipashyana experience represents, then, a gap in the process of maintaining oneself and playing out the games of ego. In my student's case, having seen what she did, she could no longer enter into a rave in "the same old way," with the naive expectation that she could banish her suffering and find fulfillment. She understood too much. She still attends raves, but in a more knowing, and also less desperate, way.

The vipashyana experience, while often not occurring when one is engaged in a meditation session, arises based on the practice of sitting meditation and the cultivation of shamatha. Before we began meditating, our minds were so overburdened with discursive thought and were going so fast that the kind of gap represented by vipashyana was unlikely. If, by force of circumstance, such a gap did arise—and such *can* happen to anyone—because the experience is usually so out of context, it may be ignored or dismissed as some kind of "craziness." Because vipashyana represents a threat to ego, people often simply deny what they have seen because they have some instinct that they cannot manage it. Indeed, my student asked me, "If someone not on a spiritual path and without the resource of meditation had the kind of experience that I did, how would they have handled it?" Through shamatha, then, as the mind slows down and the hold of discursive thinking is weakened, the vipashyana experience becomes more frequent. Indeed one begins to suspect that vipashyana really represents gaps in the ego process that are there all the time but generally remain unnoticed.

CONCLUSION

In the traditional context, meditation is understood as a practice that produces great benefit both during life and at the moment of death. During our lives meditation tames us, frees our minds so that things can be more workable, and provides a sense of groundedness and well-being. At death it opens the way for our further journey. Dzigar Kongtrul:

> Meditation helps us in our ordinary life, as we go through our day-to-day experiences. Through the process of working with our thoughts and emotions, through having some detachment in relation to them, everything seems to work much better. In addition, when we practice, we always feel that we are coming back home. When we are not practicing, when we are distracted, when we are gone with our thoughts and emotions and activities, we feel like a child lost in the wide world. But then we practice, and there is a sense of finding ourselves again, finding our home. Meditation also helps us at the time of death. If we have had the experience of working with different emotions and understanding their ultimate nature, then when we die, this will help us tremendously in making a better transition from this life to the next.[19]

THE RESULT

The result of Hinayana, given in the third noble truth, is *cessation*. This refers to the cessation of those defiled states of mind that continue to keep us trapped in samsara. In the Hinayana view, they simply cease to arise anymore. With the ceasing of the defilements, we see the ego as it truly is: an idea, and nothing more than an idea, that has been superimposed on our experience. From the viewpoint of cessation, we see clearly that what we had previously called "myself" is actually a cascade of momentary experiences with no solid core and indeed no ground or fixed reference point at all. This is sometimes referred to as "experience without an experiencer." These momentary events that I have been calling "me" are traditionally grouped into five basic types, "aggregates," or "heaps" (*skandhas*): form (*rupa*), feeling (*vedana*), perception (*samjna*), karmic formations (*samskara*), and consciousness (*vijnana*). See chapter 14 for further discussion.

To see the five skandhas clearly is to unmask the ego, to expose its self-deception. When ego is unmasked, then the five skandhas have nowhere to go: they arise, they fizzle out, and they disappear. They become like a shadow flashing across the sky, or a shooting star, which only proclaims its own impermanence and insubstantiality.

The Hinayana, with its view of the four reminders and its practice of *shila* and the meditation of *shamatha* and *vipashyana*, could be a complete and self-sufficient path unto itself. According to Tibetan tradition, if one were to follow the path of Hinayana all the way out, one would arrive at individual liberation, known in Tibetan as *soso tharpa*. This liberation involves seeing through and relinquishing one's efforts to attain fulfillment in samsara. One would attain freedom from the suffering of samsara and the boundless peace of nirvana.

However, the Hinayana is only the first step on the Tibetan path. In the context of Tibetan Buddhism, one remains a "Hinayana practitioner" only long enough to lay a foundation for the rest of one's journey. This raises the question: What is it that one needs to accomplish through Hinayana practice before moving on to the Mahayana? One needs to see, in a direct and nonconceptual way, that the ordinary pursuit of happiness within samsara is a fruitless enterprise. It means, in addition, that one looks to the spiritual path of dharma as his or her only reliable refuge and, through taking refuge, has made a commitment to that path. It means further that one has recognized the necessity of practice, both in terms of shila, some kind of virtuous discipline in one's life activities, and samadhi, meditation. And it means finally that one has been able to establish some kind of regular meditation practice in one's life and has established some kind of stability in one's state of mind.

At a certain point, the Hinayana phase of one's journey comes to an end. Nevertheless, the Hinayana provides the basic perspectives and tools that, from a certain point of view, are merely refined in the Mahayana and Vajrayana stages. For example, in terms of the view, in the Mahayana and Vajrayana, the four reminders evolve into [1] a view of the sacredness of being, [2] the immanence of death in the midst of life as a blessing, [3] karma as the vehicle for compassion, and [4] suffering as ego's response to the energy of awareness. In relation to the path, the restrictions of shila become the increased restrictions of the bodhisattva vow to help beings with one's every breath and the still greater restrictions of the tantric vows where one's mind itself must not depart from the true nature. In terms of meditation, in Mahayana and Vajrayana, shamatha becomes resting in the buddha-nature and vipashyana becomes insight into its luminosity and emptiness. Finally, in relation to the result, the Hinayana insight into the futility of building up one's ego provides the "groundless ground" without which the experiences of Mahayana and Vajrayana could turn into egomania on a cosmic scale.

12
Mahayana
The View

THERE ARE CERTAIN EXTERNAL CRITERIA THAT SUGGEST the time has come for a person to take the bodhisattva vow and enter the Mahayana discipline. First, of course, one must have taken his or her refuge vows. One must also not only understand, but have integrated the perspectives embodied in the four reminders. In addition, there needs to be a practical knowledge of shila and meditation, and these need to be firmly implanted in one's life. Finally, it is important that one has gained some sense of renunciation—that is, that one has some realization that nothing external is going to provide the ultimate answers to the dilemmas of life. Yet, even given these attainments, something more is needed before one is ready to enter the Mahayana. This additional "something" has to do with a sense of longing to go further that arises from within.

To understand the transition to Mahayana, we need to recall that Buddhism is essentially a method to release the wisdom and compassion of the buddha-nature within. As human beings, we suffer; Buddhism encourages us to look into our suffering. We begin to find that within our pain there are fundamental lessons for us. We are then motivated to look deeper. Buddhism then provides the tools of meditation that enable us to do so. In the course of our practice, we see that we do not have to maintain our ego boundaries so rigidly or put quite so much energy into maintaining our version of reality. Through this process, through learning to relax and to become more alert and present to our lives, we begin to discover a deep source of peace, sanity, and tenderness within ourselves.

It is absolutely natural and organic that, at a certain point, we would want to let down our barriers and boundaries further and to share the living water we have found with other suffering beings. In Tibetan Buddhism, this marks what is called the *birth of bodhichitta*, the heart of enlightenment. Kalu Rinpoche describes this transition in classical terms: "On the Hinayana path, an altruistic motivation develops toward the benefit and happiness of all beings. When the mind of enlightenment, or *bodhichitta,* arises, the Hinayana path becomes the Mahayana path."[1]

Trungpa Rinpoche explains this transition in more detail. He says that at a certain point on the Hinayana path, one begins to feel a sense of accomplishment in one's practice. In particular, one feels growing confidence that one can handle any state of mind, however painful, troubling, or seemingly negative. One knows how to sit down with it and, through meditation, to process it and work through it. This produces a sense of well-being, strength, and confidence.

Yet, at the same time, the very feeling of accomplishment begins to seem almost too perfect. One's life is almost too under control. One begins to detect a subtle but troubling self-satisfaction. The edge seems to be disappearing from one's spiritual life, and somehow things begin to seem a little too predictable and even stale. The Hinayana, which initially had seemed like such a steep challenge, such a "dangerous" enterprise, now is beginning to feel like a suit of clothes that is a little too small.

One now longs to go further, and this longing has two aspects. First, one wants to shed one's Hinayana clothes and to move toward the openness, the space, and the nakedness that is essential to the ongoing path. Second, through Hinayana practice, one has become increasingly sensitive to the larger world and particularly to the suffering of others. Now their plights and pain begin to make a claim on us and we feel called to respond. These feelings come as an inner imperative.

It is similar to what occurs when a couple has their first baby. The cries of the newborn are most compelling. The mother and father are glad to get up at three-thirty in the morning to try to alleviate the pain of their small and helpless charge. They feel relieved to be able to feed their child, wipe a baby bottom, or try to alleviate colic. Normal people who value their sleep and their comfort as much as anyone else suddenly experience the bodhisattva motivation and feel no choice but to act on it. One frequently hears Tibetan teachers comment that, through responding to the incessant demands of being the parent of a small child, a mother is a bodhisattva and is following the bodhisattva path.

When one discovers that others' suffering is, to some extent, one's own concern, this means that the Mahayana motivation has arisen and that the bodhichitta has been born. At this point, the practitioner is ready to take the bodhisattva vow and to enter the Great Vehicle, becoming familiar with its view and entering its meditative and altruistic practice.

MOTIVATION

The Tibetan teachings on the Great Vehicle begin by placing the inspiration to practice the Mahayana within a larger context that includes the motivations of ordinary worldly activities and those of the Hinayana practitioners. Motivation refers to the intention with which one pursues the various activities of one's life, including the dharma. "Motivation" in Tibetan is *künlong,* that which leads you forward and up, which can bring you out of your samsaric slump to enlightenment. Tibetan tradition sees the kind and quality of a practitioner's motivation as the determining element in defining the level at which he or she follows the spiritual path and the results that come about. Sakyong Mipham Rinpoche outlines three distinct and progressive levels of motivation that human beings can have: ordinary, Hinayana, and Mahayana.

Ordinary Motivation

Ordinary motivation is found among those who are driven by the desire for happiness in the world and are not particularly interested in getting out of samsara. It is divided into small, medium, and great levels. The small level of ordinary motivation refers to beings whose focus in life is on being happy and content within their one lifetime, trying to make themselves secure and comfortable. They seek a good family situation, health, an ample income, a fine dwelling, social status, and so on. They think only of this lifetime and are not concerned with what happened before their present life or what will happen later. Beings of this level are not spiritually inclined. They do not practice any particular religion or follow any path.

People of the middle level are interested in both the dharma and worldly means to try to achieve happiness. In their worldly activities, they are like those of the previous level. In the dharma, they find something that brings them satisfaction and understanding about their life. They are not serious spiritual practitioners, but they find a connection with the dharma essential to their sense of well-being and contentment.

Like those with the small and medium levels of ordinary motivation, those possessing the great level do not seek escape from samsara. However, they do want to act in such a way as to provide the conditions for a good rebirth. They believe in the teachings of karma and see their present life in this context. They believe that their present circumstances are the result of actions performed in previous lifetimes and that their future rebirths will depend in large measure on what they do in this life. They think about the six realms and the pitfalls and horrors that lower rebirths can bring. Therefore they engage in dharma practice to sow positive karmic seeds.

Hinayana Motivation

The Hinayana motivation is rooted in a deep understanding of the futility of samsara, a realization that attempting to gain any kind of pure and lasting happiness within the round of birth and death is basically impossible. People of this motivation also understand the cyclical nature of samsara, that one samsaric state of mind leads to another, continuously and without end. They realize that their cycling through the six realms has been going on from beginningless time and will continue into the indefinite future, and that it will never come to an end by itself. They see that the only way to find any kind of permanent relief is to escape from the samsaric cycle. Hinayanist practitioners therefore study and practice the dharma in order to attain personal salvation or liberation. They are not really interested in the plights of other sentient beings and feel that if they can extricate themselves from samsara, their spiritual aspirations will be fulfilled.

Mahayana Motivation

Beings with the Mahayana motivation want liberation not only for themselves but for all sentient beings. They see the welfare of all sentient beings as their own responsibility. According to the traditional analogy, when they see the suffering of others, they are as deeply moved as a mother caring for her only child. For bodhisattvas, helping others is not a matter of choice, it is the essence of who they are. They spend their lives and will endure even death in the service of others. It is said that the bodhisattva can never refuse the request of sentient beings for help. In accomplished Tibetan teachers, one senses the extreme self-giving that is implied by this injunction.

A mundane example is provided by the life of Chögyam Trungpa, shortly after he had come to America. Rocky Mountain Shambhala Center, a mountainous retreat land of some five hundred acres in northern Colorado, had recently been purchased, and Rinpoche had been set up in a tiny one-room trailer on the upper part of the main valley. The person attending him later recounted to me how one particular evening progressed. Rinpoche had not had dinner and was trying to get through a long line of people who had requested interviews with him. The attendant was sitting by the door and could overhear some of the conversations. People were asking Rinpoche everything—about their personal lives, their jobs, their relationships, their hopes and fears, their practice. Hour after hour passed. Rinpoche patiently talked to each person until he or she felt answered. Soon it was midnight and the interviews continued. Finally, at about 3:30 A.M., the attendant, bleary with fatigue and himself famished, overheard the last interviewee saying to Rinpoche,

"Rinpoche, there are two movies in Boulder that I heard about. Which one do you think I should see?" Rinpoche responded in some way or other. To the attendant, this overheard snippet of conversation epitomized Trungpa Rinpoche's endless generosity, patience, and selfless exertion in working with his students.

A more dramatic example of the impact that the bodhisattva motivation can have on people is illustrated by an account given by Glenn Mullin of the death of a personal teacher, a Rinpoche who was the former abbot of the Dalai Lama's monastery in Dharamsala. The Rinpoche, owing to a heart condition, had retired from administration and given up formal teaching. He lived in a small meditation room, practicing meditation and seeing private students. Mullin would go to visit him from time to time. Rinpoche would occasionally mention a particular important teaching that he wanted to give Mullin. "One day, out of the blue he told me, 'For several years I have been promising to give a formal instruction to you. I think the time has now come. If you wish, you can invite some of our friends to attend as well.' " On the appointed day, a small group gathered in Rinpoche's room. Mullin made offerings traditionally presented before a formal teaching, and, as Rinpoche accepted a Buddha statue, Mullin says, "I noticed that as he placed it on the table he gave it a push with the corner of his hand, causing it to fall on its back. He quickly set it straight, but our eyes locked for a moment and he met my confusion with a wonderfully reassuring smile." Unbeknownst to Mullin, the Rinpoche's "special teaching" had begun. Rinpoche began speaking:

> [But] after about fifteen minutes I noticed that although he looked perfect when he himself would speak, even laughing and telling jokes, when he would stop and let the translator talk his face would change color and he would curl up slightly and close his eyes to concentrate on his mantras, turning his rosary rather more quickly than usual. After several minutes had passed I leaned over and asked him if anything was wrong.
>
> "Well," he replied calmly, "I'm having a heart attack." At that moment the translator finished speaking and Rinpoche

straightened himself again and went on with the discourse as though nothing were wrong. When he had paused again to let the translator speak I leaned over and asked him, "Goodness, shouldn't we stop the teaching immediately?" He gave me a long, penetrating look. "As you wish," he replied, "we can either go on now or else finish another time." I quickly called a halt to things and got everyone out of the room. Rinpoche moved over to his bed and sat in meditation, and several of his monks rushed in and began chanting to him in low, deep tones. He sat in meditation that evening without moving. The next day I visited his house. He was not well enough to receive me, but sent me a message. "Rinpoche asks that you remember his teaching," his attendant informed me.

That night the lama sat in meditation and ceased breathing. His heart stopped and bodily functions failed, although he did not manifest the full signs of death. This is the practice of *tuk-dam,* when a yogi retreats to the heart in death meditation. He sat like this for three days without manifesting the signs of death. Then his head fell to one side and the death process was complete. Such is the death of an accomplished yogi.[2]

Even the Rinpoche's own passing was thus presented as a gift to others. His last act was to offer his death as a profound teaching to Mullin and his friends. One can only imagine the depth of bodhisattva motivation that would enable a person in the last moments of life to think so selflessly of others and what would help them.

Sakyong Mipham Rinpoche says that these teachings are important because they tell us that it is one's motivation, rather than the specific traditions that one is following, that determines the result of one's practice. One can be engaged in the most advanced Vajrayana practices the tradition has to offer but, as noted, if one is carrying these out with a self-serving motivation, then it will be as if one were not practicing the dharma at all. If one is practicing the Vajrayana with a Hinayana motivation, to remove one's own suffering, then one gains no more than the Hinayana result. Conversely, one can be sweeping a floor or engaged in business, and, if one's fundamental motivation is compassion for others, the result could be vast, nothing less than buddhahood itself.

BODHICHITTA

Mahayana motivation is born with the arising of bodhichitta. The Sanskrit *bodhichitta* is made up of two words: *bodhi,* enlightenment, and *chitta,* mind or heart; it may be translated as the "mind of enlightenment" or "heart of enlightenment." (The word *chitta* refers to the seat of human intelligence, which is considered to reside in the heart center. Since it includes general awareness as well as affective capacities, *chitta* is actually considerably broader in meaning than the English word *mind.*) It refers to the unconditioned intelligence of a realized buddha, existing within each sentient being.

The birth of bodhichitta is like a clear, fresh spring appearing in a dry desert. The dry desert is the territory of ego, where everything is preplanned, expected, and under control. Nothing can grow in this environment, because the ego itself is nothing more than dry sand. The ego, in fact, is opposed to life as too disturbing to its territoriality. Into this dead environment of ego, we have brought our Hinayana practice. Through this, we have dug down, deep beneath the lifeless desert. Now the miraculous spring of bodhichitta appears, pointing to the enlightened wisdom that exists in a limitless reservoir beneath the desert's surface.

Bodhichitta and its cultivation lie at the very heart of the Mahayana. Chagdud Tulku comments:

> *Bodhichitta* is foundational to all we do, like the root of a medicinal tree whose branches, leaves, and flowers all produce life-enhancing medicine. The quality and purity of our practice depend on its permeating every method we use. With it, everything is assured. Without it, nothing will work.[3]

Relative Bodhichitta

Bodhichitta is usually divided into two aspects, relative and ultimate. Both of these appear spontaneously and unexpectedly in the course of one's Hinayana practice and signal that it is time to move forward. Relative bodhichitta is the softening and the tenderness that begin to develop. This leads first to an increased awareness of the suffering of others and then to feelings of empathy, kindness, and compassion. As Kalu Rinpoche says, "By becoming aware of the suffering of all sentient beings, we begin to feel genuine love and compassion for them."[4]

> The inner attitude of compassion begins . . . when we become aware of the suffering of those near and dear to us. It then gradually extends to universal love. The bodhisattva who practices this way gradually eliminates every self-cherishing attitude and cultivates a state of mind truly oriented toward others. This is relative *bodhichitta*.[5]

Relative bodhichitta is not only the attitude of sympathy toward others and feelings such as loving-kindness and empathy; in addition, as we shall see in the next chapter, it also involves a series of practices. Dzigar Kongtrül Rinpoche explains: "Relative bodhichitta, as a practice, involves the thoughts and emotions—positive thoughts and positive emotions. These have the nature of awakened heart [buddha-nature]. One could say that relative bodhichitta is the essential practice of Mahayana Buddhism."[6] Through its practice, one generates altruistic thoughts and emotions; these lead to the development of a compassionate attitude toward others; and this provides the basis for extending oneself in actions to serve and benefit them.

Ultimate Bodhichitta

Having accomplished some mental tidiness and sanity through our Hinayana practice, as mentioned, we begin to feel that very accomplishment as a burden that needs to be shed. That feeling itself is the expression of ultimate bodhichitta. This appears within our state of mind as a thirst for greater openness and nakedness on the spiritual path.

Ultimate bodhichitta itself has two dimensions or levels. First is the recognition of the illusory nature of things. What we have firmed up and solidified in our minds does not represent things in themselves, but rather, merely our concepts of them. One finds now a growing awareness that what we *think* of reality is nothing more than an idea. It is the painful recognition that what we *conceive* about everything—our ideas of ourselves, our world, even our Hinayana path—is nothing more than our own contrived versions. And our conceptual versions of things have no actual reality, they are like a dream, a mirage, or an echo. They are a facsimile, but not the real thing.

But if our concepts of things are nothing more than our own concocted versions, then what does this say about reality? Is there, then, no such thing as reality at all? Ultimate bodhichitta may reveal the illusory or "empty" nature of our version of the world, but this does not mean that there is nothing there at all. In fact, at a deeper level, ultimate *bodhichitta* is the awareness of a reality that is so intense, so boundless, and so ungraspable that the most accurate way to speak of it is to say nothing at all. Thus, in Tibetan Buddhism, one speaks of the "emptiness" of ultimate reality, which does not mean that it is a total void, but rather that it is utterly beyond our ability to speak or think about it. But, through the path, we can most surely touch it and taste it, although such "experience" does not occur within the framework of ego.

EGOLESSNESS IN THE MAHAYANA

The ego, the self or *atman,* as understood at the Hinayana level, is what we think about ourselves and our gross concepts of who we are. For example, my thoughts of myself as a certain kind of person are part of what Buddhism means by ego. "I am such-and-such; I am good at this; I am not good at that; I fit into the world here and not there." These are all examples of ego as defined in the Hinayana.

In the Mahayana, however, ego also includes solidified, frozen versions of the "self" of other things. For example, my ideas of who my wife is and who my children are, the ideas I have about others wherein I divide them into friends and enemies are also aspects of ego. Beyond this, I have concepts of virtually everything I encounter in my world. All these are part of what is meant by self or ego. "Ego" in the Mahayana sense, then, refers to any solidified, conceptualized "self" that I may attribute to anything.

In the Mahayana, the ego further includes, on a more subtle level, even the way I perceive things with my senses. For example, when I see, hear, smell, taste, or touch something, I am bringing subtle concepts to bear. When I look at a face, before I even formulate the concept "friend" or "enemy," there is an experience of familiarity or unfamiliarity in my very perception. I see a face, and within that very perception is the experience that I know that this person or that person is a stranger. When I hear the song of a bird outside my window, the sound is familiar—I know it to be that of a bird. Even these subtle levels of perception are included in the Mahayana notion of ego.

It may make sense to call my more or less rigid ideas of myself "ego," but why refer to my experience of what is other than myself—other people, things, perceptions—by the same term? The reason is that what I *think* of as other, what I *seem to experience* as other, is in fact only another facet of myself. How can that be? Because when I look at my wife, it is my concept of my wife that I see. When I look at a tree, it is my idea of a tree that I encounter, one that is based on all the experiences I have had of trees throughout my lifetime. Does this mean that there is no such thing as my wife beyond my concept, the tree beyond my concept? No, it does not. But it means that as long as I am operating from the centralized standpoint of ego, as long as I am cycling in samsara, I do not see the real person or the real tree, only my manufactured versions of them.

Egolessness of Self

In order to make sense of these various dimensions of "ego," Tibetan Buddhism, as a Mahayana tradition, talks about "twofold egolessness" and the corresponding "two veils" of our ignorance. First is the "veil of conflicting emotions" that needs to be eliminated leading to the first kind of egolessness, the egolessness of self. Second is the "veil of knowables," the removal of which yields the egolessness of phenomena, or *dharmas*. The Hinayana path is directed toward the removal of the veil

of conflicting emotions that brings about the realization of the egolessness of self. It is the recognition that the "I" or "me" that I have imagined throughout my life, that I have tried to protect, augment, and
aggrandize, in fact does not exist. As Kalu Rinpoche says, it is "the
subject's own experience of the self's nonexistence: the self or 'me' has
no inherent existence."[7] This "self" is driven and maintained through
the three conflicting emotions or "poisons" (*visha*), passion, aggression,
and delusion. Through passion, we attempt to draw into our world
those things that confirm our idea of who we are. In a similar fashion,
through aggression we try to push away and destroy those things that
call our ego into question. Likewise we maintain our egos through ignorance by avoiding or ignoring those things in our environment that do
not directly confirm us or threaten us. Through Hinayana practice, the
cycle of passion, aggression, and delusion is slowed down, and we begin
to glimpse the gaps in our own state of mind and to realize that we do
not exist as a solid and continuous entity. Thus the veil of conflicting
emotions is beginning to fall apart.

Egolessness of Dharmas, or Phenomena

Although we may begin to see and accept our own lack of substantial
existence, we will still look at the world and see it as a familiar place, a
place that more or less accords with our own preconceptions. This apparent familiarity points to the veil of knowables. The earth, the sky,
trees, animals, people, streets, buildings—all appear as things we are
familiar with and know about. This is, as mentioned, a more subtle level
of "self," and it is this level that is specifically addressed in the Mahayana practice. In the Mahayana, one comes to realize the *emptiness* or
egolessness of all of the phenomena that we experience in our lives,
from the most gross to the most minute, including our ideas as well as
our perceptions.

How is emptiness actually experienced? Usually, when we attach labels to things in the world that we perceive, we assume that the labeled
perception is what we have actually experienced at the most basic level.
Again, through the three prajnas, we discover that the matter is not this
simple. Through the first prajna, we are taught that when we perceive

things, we immediately attribute to them an "essence" or "self-nature." This is the basic identity that we "find" when we look at things. For example, when I look at my car, the moment it comes into view, I see it as "my car." However, the texts tell us, the perception of "my car" comes at the end of a complex process that begins with the initial perception and is followed by various mental processes wherein I "identify," literally attributing a particular identity to the perception.

Through the second prajna, contemplation, we reflect upon our lives and notice the many times that we have attributed an inaccurate identity to a perception. Examples might include seeing a person and mistakenly "recognizing" him or her to be someone we know; seeing a colored piece of paper in a field and wrongly identifying it as a brightly colored flower; attributing a motivation to someone, only to find out later how wrong we were.

It is only through the third prajna, meditation, however, that we see definitively that external objects have no "self" or "essence." In meditating upon emptiness, we look right at our perceptions to see how they arise and what they are. When we do so, we find that they exist in a realm that is beyond any kind of identification or concept. They are "empty" of any label we might attach to them. They are, in other words, disjunct from the ideas that we project upon them.

This emptiness, then, is clearly not a mere nothing. In fact, while it dissolves the illusory, conceptualized versions that we all carry around, it brings into view a reality that appears but has no substantial or conceptualizable essence. This is the level of reality that is hidden from ordinary sight. Within the Buddhist context, it is described as the world beyond concept, appearance that is beyond thought. It is sometimes referred to as "pure relative truth" to distinguish it from the apparent but illusory world of conventional reality. It is a world of utter intensity and great power.

COMPASSION

Kalu Rinpoche expresses the central role of compassion in the Mahayana:

Compassion, kindness, and love together form the essential Mahayana attitude. Their foundation is a non-self-cherishing frame of mind oriented toward others, aspiring to the well-being and happiness of all other beings, whether human or nonhuman, friends or enemies.[8]

Compassion for other suffering beings is the natural state of the human. At our heart of hearts, in relation to other beings, we feel connectedness, love, and identification such that their suffering is our own. This natural compassion for other people and for other sentient creatures entails the desire to help them in any way possible and at any cost to ourselves.

Nevertheless, we are not normally aware of this feeling of connectedness and love. Why? The reason is that the heart of each of us, with its boundless and selfless compassion, is covered over with hard scales. These have accumulated as layer upon layer of self-serving thinking, and the driving forces of the three poisons, discussed in the previous section. Through the Mahayana path, we gradually dissolve these scales so that the boundless love of our innermost being, our buddha-nature, is released.

In Tibetan Buddhism, three levels of compassion are described: compassion with reference to beings, compassion with reference to reality, and compassion without any reference points whatsoever. Each of these represents a progressively deeper and more selfless level of compassion.

Compassion with Reference to Beings

Compassion with reference to beings arises when we see the suffering of others. Kalu Rinpoche says:

> It is the first kind of compassion to arise and causes us to strive deeply to do everything we can to help all those who suffer. It emerges when we perceive the pain and suffering of others. This form of compassion is marked by no longer being able to remain unmoved by the suffering of beings and by aspiring to do everything possible to help alleviate their suffering.[9]

This level of compassion is the most accessible to us because it can be elicited by the suffering of sentient beings, something that we all see continually throughout our daily lives.

Compassion with Reference to Reality

The second level of compassion arises through a direct experience of the nature of ignorance and through seeing how it is that beings create their own suffering. Kalu Rinpoche:

> This compassion occurs when we really see how others strive to be happy and avoid suffering but how, not understanding the causes of happiness nor the means of avoiding suffering, they produce more causes of suffering and have no idea how to cultivate the causes of happiness. They are blinded by their ignorance; their motivations and their actions contradict one another.[10]

It is when we see ignorance for what it is, perceiving both its power over sentient beings and also that it is entirely unnecessary, that this deeper level of compassion arises in us. Since this type of compassion is born upon seeing directly the nature of ignorance, it is less accessible than the previous one and develops at a later stage of the path.

Compassion without Reference Points

The deepest level of compassion arises in one who no longer lays concepts on the world, who has no notion of a self, an "other," or an action being performed. It appears in a state of mind that is utterly free and present. This compassion is born out of a realization of emptiness, and it is found in a fully enlightened buddha or a high-level bodhisattva. Kalu Rinpoche says, "There is not longer any reference to a 'me' or an 'other.' This compassion opens naturally and spontaneously."[11]

Within the Mahayana, it is often said that emptiness and compassion are inseparable. Emptiness represents the bodhisattva's freedom from concepts about others. Without such a state of mind, compassion remains self-serving and inaccurate, conditioned by one's own habitual patterns. Thus genuine compassion, driven solely by the needs of the other, requires a mind of emptiness. But emptiness also implies compassion, since to be truly empty means to be without any self-preoccupation, and this expresses itself naturally and spontaneously in warmth toward others. A realization of emptiness in which one is not completely available to others is not a genuine realization. Why? If one is not available to others, then one is holding one's realization as somehow special and separate, somehow a personal attainment or possession. A true realization of emptiness entails the recognition that one has no ground on which to stand and no personal territory to maintain; the natural expression of such a realization is compassionate responsiveness to the needs of others.

THE TWO ACCUMULATIONS OF MERIT AND WISDOM

The Hinayana teaching on the two accumulations is further developed in the Mahayana. These two are cultivated through the basic Mahayana disciplines and practices, the six paramitas, and so on. Kalu Rinpoche tells us:

> All Dharma practice can be categorized as purification and accumulation, that is, the purification of the veils that obscure the mind and the practice of the two accumulations of merit and wisdom. This process can be illustrated with the following image. Veiled or obscured, mind is like a sky darkened by clouds that cover its infinite vastness and brightness. The two accumulations are like the wind that dissipates these clouds, revealing the immensity and clarity of pure mind.[12]

The Accumulation of Merit

The accumulation of merit occurs, as we saw, through activities that are beneficial to ourselves or others. Following the principles of shila—not harming others, not stealing, not lying, and so on—results in the accumulation of merit. Positive activities that result in benefit to others, such as caring for them when they are sick, feeding them when they are hungry, consoling them when they are sorrowful—all result in the accumulation of merit. Chagdud Tulku says, "The act of benefiting is called the *accumulation of merit,* the effortful gathering of virtue. We harness the mind's duality using skillful methods . . . in a conceptual framework to create benefit within the relative dream experience."[13]

Kalu Rinpoche remarks, "For the accumulation of merit, the act itself is important, but the underlying motivation is even more important; any act motivated by love and compassion is therefore a source of great benefit."[14] To illustrate the importance of motivation, he tells the following story, which I paraphrase. A mother and daughter, who loved one another devotedly and selflessly, were crossing a river, holding each other by the hand. Suddenly, a powerful current swept them away. Each could have abandoned the other in the struggle for survival. But the mother thought, "It doesn't matter if I die, but my daughter must be saved." Therefore, as the surging river tried to pull her daughter down, the mother held tight to her hand. The daughter thought, "Please let my mother live, even if I have to die." And she, likewise, would not abandon her mother to the river, but held her hand. The river was fierce and deep, and both mother and daughter drowned. But by the power of their great love for each other and of their selfless wish to save the other's life even at the expense of their own, they gained a vast accumulation of merit.

The accumulation of merit is really another way of talking about karma. Through meritorious actions we create positive karma. The arena of the accumulation of merit is the relative world. It has to do with the actions that we perform in relation to the conditioned, phenomenal world. As we saw, everything that we do in relation to the relative world has consequences, karmic results whose seeds will eventually ripen in our own lives. Nothing that we do—or fail to do—is inconsequential.

The accumulation of merit is critical on the path because through it, we are able to bring about the complex of conditions necessary in order for realization to come about. In other words, through performing meritorious actions, we are working to foster a karmic situation in which wisdom can then take birth. This situation is external: the external conditions necessary for us to follow the path, meditate, and attain realization. It is also internal: the psychological openness, mental stability, and inspiration to meditate and gain insight into reality.

There is a dimension to the accumulation of merit that can only be called magical. We begin to exert ourselves in performing acts of kindness and love toward others. With the help of meditation, we begin to tone down some of our sharper and more aggressive edges. And strangely, the complexion of our world begins to change. We begin to find ourselves softer, more open, and more able to work our way through the extremes of our own self-absorption. And in the external world, we notice doors opening that had seemed firmly shut in the way of time, opportunities, and encouragement for practice. This change cannot be quantified. But it is also undeniable, as if the world had heard our attempts at helping others as itself a call for help; and as if the world responded with its own, much vaster outpouring of love.

The Accumulation of Wisdom

The accumulation of merit does not, in and of itself, represent enlightenment. However, it provides the basis and necessary precondition for the accumulation of wisdom, the experience of full realization. While the accumulation of merit is produced through meritorious deeds, the accumulation of wisdom occurs primarily through meditation practice. While meditation leads directly to realization, it is not enough in and of itself. Thus, if a person is lacking in the accumulation of merit, as we have seen, no matter how much they may meditate, nothing much will happen. Their mind will be too scattered, obstacle-ridden, and distracted.

The mutually necessary and supportive relationship of merit and wisdom is revealed by the Western situation. Not infrequently in our culture, adherents of our conventional Judeo-Christian traditions seek what is equivalent to the accumulation of merit without the accumulation of wisdom. That is, they seek to progress along a spiritual path simply through the accumulation of many good deeds, without a meditative or contemplative discipline that enables them to look directly into their own heart of darkness, their own ego. In such cases, it is difficult to work through the "self" that is invariably involved in and continually attempts to co-opt good deeds. Without the accumulation of wisdom, good deeds can become a vehicle of ego: perhaps we avoid the more gross egotism of self-righteousness and blatant moralism but we think of ourselves as "good people" and look down on others who are not so "good." In such an arena of self-satisfaction, genuine spiritual progress becomes difficult.

On the other hand, sometimes people—particularly those pursuing non-Western religions such as Buddhism—seek the accumulation of wisdom and ignore the accumulation of merit. They enter into meditation thinking that what they do with the rest of their lives doesn't matter. They feel that if they simply meditate, they will make rapid spiritual progress. Confused relationships with society, harmful grasping or aggression in close relationships, a livelihood that involves harming others, or a lifestyle of workaholism or other damaging behavior are considered unconnected to their meditation practice. And yet the relationship of such behavior to their meditation practice is immediate and ongoing. Either such people meditate, sometimes for years, with no real progress being made, or, after a certain amount of meditation, it gradually begins to become evident to them that what they are doing with their lives when they are not meditating is having a major impact on their practice. In such a fortunate case, they see that in order to make any further progress, they will need to pay attention to the dark areas of what they do when they are not on the meditation cushion. In relation to the attitude that meditation alone is enough, Kalu Rinpoche provides the following corrective:

> If the right activity of the accumulation of merit is obvious enough to be applied and practiced by everybody, the accumulation of wisdom is more delicate. It is a subtle practice that demands as much skill from the student as from the teacher. So at first it is useful to concentrate our energies on the accumulation

of merit and thereby prepare the ground for wisdom, which develops later with the meditative experience.[15]

Thus it is that the accumulation of merit and the accumulation of wisdom go hand in hand, mutually supporting one another. Practicing generosity, for example, sets up the conditions for the practice of meditation. And meditating softens one's heart and generates insight, making one more able and inspired to give to others. This generosity in turn provides further conditions for meditation, and so on. Kalu Rinpoche says:

> Meditation is fundamental to Dharma practice, but it should always be done together with the accumulation of merit. One of the accumulations without the other leads to errors and impasses. The two are indispensable: good activities without wisdom cannot lead to perfect enlightenment. Practiced together, the two accumulations facilitate each other, and doing them in conjunction leads to enlightenment. The accumulation of merit is like a traveler's legs, the accumulation of wisdom like eyesight: they are complementary, and both are absolutely necessary to reach buddhahood.[16]

13

Mahayana
THE PRACTICE AND RESULT

PRACTICE

The various Mahayana practices are based on the recognition that ego is engaged in a nonstop effort to maintain and aggrandize itself. A large part of this process involves the manipulation of awareness so that, while we are acutely aware of the least iota of our own discomfort, we remain blissfully unaware of the terrible suffering that may be going on just next door. According to the Mahayana, this kind of ignorance is not the natural condition of the human being. In its natural state, our inherent awareness—our buddha-nature—is in connection with all other beings and sensitive to their least suffering. This awareness is so powerful and accurate that we must expend a tremendous amount of energy to suppress it and block it out. We do this so that we can carry on with the illusion of an independent self. The various Mahayana practices, beginning with the bodhisattva vow, and including the paramitas and the active contemplations such as the four immeasurables and tonglen, "sending and taking," act as antidotes to the deliberate ignorance of ego and as keys that unlock the illimitable stores of love and compassion of the buddha-nature.

The Bodhisattva Vow

At a certain point on the Hinayana path, Trungpa Rinpoche says, one becomes "stuck" and can advance further on one's spiritual journey only by taking the bodhisattva vow and entering the Mahayana. In relation to the power and expansiveness of the vow, he comments further:

Taking the bodhisattva vow has tremendous power for the very reason that it is not something we do just for the pleasure of ego. It is beyond oneself. Taking the vow is like planting the seed of a fast-growing tree, whereas something done for the benefit of ego is like sowing a grain of sand. Planting such a seed as the bodhisattva vow undermines ego and leads to a tremendous expansion of perspective. Such heroism, or bigness of mind, fills all of space completely, utterly, absolutely.[1]

The bodhisattva vow has two aspects: aspiring, in which one comes to see what the bodhisattva commitment entails and forms the aspiration to make it; and entering, in which, through the bodhisattva vow liturgy, one makes the actual commitment.

According to Trungpa Rinpoche, "the bodhisattva vow is the commitment to put others before oneself."[2] It involves an inner willingness to let down the rigid barriers that we usually place around ourselves and, as we move about our lives, to include others' well-being in our thinking. "Taking the bodhisattva vow implies that instead of holding onto our individual territory and defending it tooth and nail, we become open to the world that we are living in. It means we are willing to take on greater responsibility."[3]

We are no longer intent on creating comfort for ourselves; we work with others. This implies working with "our other" as well as the "other other." Our other is our projections and our sense of privacy and longing to make things comfortable for ourselves. The other other is the phenomenal world outside, which is filled with screaming kids, dirty dishes, confused spiritual practitioners, and assorted sentient beings.[4]

The bodhisattva's work means giving up privacy. This means privacy in the physical sense—we do not regard our personal "space" and resources as belonging to us alone but are willing to invite others in to share them. It also means privacy in the psychological sense—that we do not "hide out" and pretend to be other than we are, but that we are willing to share ourselves, as we actually are, with others. Further, it means privacy in terms of our ambitions and projects. We no longer simply work for our own selves or our own ideas of what should be done, but we are responsive to the larger world, to the suffering beings that appear before us. And finally, the bodhisattva vow means giving up the privacy of the human world; we are willing to include all sentient life—not only of the seen but of the unseen worlds—in our commitment, as well as the animate and the inanimate worlds in the largest sense. "Taking this mahayana approach of benevolence means giving up privacy and developing a sense of greater vision. Rather than focusing on our own little projects, we expand our vision immensely to embrace working with the rest of the world, the rest of the galaxies, the rest of the universes."[5]

The bodhisattva's commitment to put others before him—or herself is literal and practical. It means that we are opening ourselves up to the difficulties and the demands of working with other people. "If we are asked for help, we should not refuse; if we are invited to be someone's guest, we should not refuse; if we are invited to be a parent, we should not refuse."[6] Working with others is not easy and it is not painless. Trungpa Rinpoche:

> It requires that we not be completely tired and put off by people's heavy-handed neurosis, ego-dirt, ego-puke, or ego-diarrhea; instead we are appreciative and willing to clean up for them. It is a sense of softness whereby we allow situations to take place in spite of little inconveniences; we allow situations to bother us, to overcrowd us.[7]

> By taking the bodhisattva vow, we actually present ourselves as the property of sentient beings: depending on the situation, we are willing to be a highway, a boat, a floor, or a house. We allow other sentient beings to use us in whatever way they choose. As the earth sustains the atmosphere and outer space accommodates the stars, galaxies, and all the rest, we are willing to carry the burdens of the world.[8]

A keynote of the bodhisattva's commitment is his or her relationships with sentient beings. Now each of those relationships is considered important. We can no longer play up to some people while ignoring others, or cultivate friends while avoiding enemies. Each person that we come across in our life has a claim on us. Every meeting provides an opportunity to be fully present, to open one's heart, to see if there is any way that we can be of service. There is also an awareness of the impermanence of this moment with another: soon this person will be gone from our lives, and this encourages a sense of appreciation and of the timeliness of this meeting.

Trungpa Rinpoche in particular has emphasized the importance, in the bodhisattva's way, of avoiding what he calls "idiot compassion." This occurs when, rather than actually looking into sentient beings' situations deeply to see what is needed, one engages in mindless activity to try to please or pacify them. Idiot compassion can also be self-serving—we "help" beings, indulging them in such a way that they will compliment and like us. Trungpa Rinpoche:

> If we do not work intelligently with sentient beings, quite possibly our help will become addictive rather than beneficial. People will become addicted to our help in the same way they become addicted to sleeping pills. By trying to get more and more help they will become weaker and weaker. So for the benefit of sentient beings, we need to open ourselves with an attitude of fearlessness.[9]

An important part of the bodhisattva's commitment is the willingness to help sentient beings, without reward or even the least thanks. "The work of a bodhisattva is without credentials. We could be beaten, kicked, or just unappreciated, but we remain kind and willing to work with others. It is a totally non-credit situation."[10] Thus the bodhisattva lets go of the ideas of a sentient being, of helping and of the act of service, just at the moment of sacrificing him or herself for others.

The second aspect, *entering* the bodhisattva's path, is the actual liturgy of the vow. The power of the vow is manifold. First, it represents an acknowledgment, opening up, and empowerment of the enlightenment within us. Second, it represents "a complete binding of ourselves with the gentleness and compassion of our inherent wakefulness."[11] Finally, through the vow, we corner ourselves into a situation where we can go only forward, not back. As with the Hinayana vows, once we have made the bodhisattva commitment, it enters into our mind-stream and imprints itself on the cellular level in our bodies. If we keep the vow, it will continually empower us and accelerate our progress along the path. However, if we break it, it will act as an energy drain and result in all kinds of obstacles.

The bodhisattva vow ceremony is an occasion of joy and celebration. At this time, one leaves the Hinayana with its emphasis on individual salvation and enters the family of the buddhas, with its immense aspiration to work for the liberation of all beings. This joy is all the more real because the complete enlightenment of a buddha is already within our hearts as our innermost essence. In fact, the enlightenment within means that "since we have basic generosity and compassion within ourselves, we do not have to borrow from anybody else. Based on that inherent wakefulness, we can act directly, on the spot."[12]

The bodhisattva vow itself is taken in a simple ceremony. The preceptor usually gives a talk on the meaning of the vow and on the particular lineage of transmission. Following this, the prospective bodhisattvas will take one or another form of the vow. For example, they might be asked to repeat the following verses from Gampopa's *Jewel Ornament of Liberation,* containing a general aspiration and the vow itself:

> May the teacher be gracious to me. Just as the former Tathagatas, Arhants, Samyaksambuddhas, exalted ones and bodhisattvas living on a high level of spirituality first developed an attitude directed towards unsurpassable perfect great enlightenment, so also I, (so and so), request the teacher to help me in developing such an attitude.[13]

Then, again from Gampopa's text, follows the actual vow:

> May the buddhas of the ten regions of the world be gracious to me. May the teacher be gracious to me. I (so and so) will practice, and rejoice in so doing, the good which grows from generosity, discipline, and meditation, now and forevermore, thus

emulating the Tathagatas, Arhants, Samyaksambuddhas, exalted ones and bodhisattva mahasattvas living on a high level of spirituality, who in ancient times developed an attitude directed towards unsurpassable, perfect, great enlightenment. From now on until I have become the very quintessence of enlightenment, I will develop an attitude directed towards unsurpassable perfect great enlightenment so that the beings who have not yet crossed over may do so, who have not yet been delivered may be, who have not yet found their breath, may find it, and who have not passed into nirvana may do so.[14]

Following this, each of them receives a name, as in the refuge vow, except that the bodhisattva name is intended to reflect the kind of help that one can provide for others. For example, those with a strong capacity for being generous, whether they show it or mask it with miserliness, might receive a name (in Tibetan) with the word "generosity" in it. The name is intended to act as a reminder to new bodhisattvas of their commitment and their need to release their own gifts to the benefit of others.

The Six Paramitas

One fulfills one's bodhisattva vow through acting to benefit beings. Since this kind of activity runs against the deeply engrained habitual patterns of our usual approach, practices need to be given that unlock our compassion. The most important set of bodhisattva practices are the six paramitas. *Paramita* means "transcendent action" and refers to practices that, in being directed to others, transcend ego. These transcend ego also in the sense that their energy flows ultimately from the selfless buddha-nature within. The six paramitas show us six general areas of selfless activity that, as bodhisattvas, we need to cultivate.

The paramitas need to be understood on three different levels, corresponding to ground, path, and fruition. At the level of the ground, they arise in the form of inspiration to help others. As ground, they present themselves as a kind of thirst or intense inspiration. For example, one might find in oneself a longing to express generosity to others, to give to them without reservation. At the level of path, the paramitas are specific practices that one needs to engage in. As path, they involve actions that are particularly challenging because they reverse the normal logic of ego. Two of the more important of these practices will be discussed below, that of the four immeasurables (cultivating loving-kindness, compassion, sympathetic joy, and equanimity) and that of tonglen, sending and taking, whereby one works to take on the suffering of others. At the fruition level, the paramitas are transcendent actions that are performed by fully realized ones, without the least thought or effort and with natural spontaneity. It is as if, when a situation calls for generosity, with irresistible force, generosity arises.

Beginning bodhisattvas experience the inspiration of the paramitas as the ground and then spend most of their time engaged in one or another of the practices. The bodhisattva disciplines, as mentioned above, do not supersede the Hinayana practices, which always remain the ground of the path of dharma. However, as we shall see, they involve the refinement of practices already given in the Hinayana, and they also direct these more specifically and directly to the benefit of others.

The paramitas are divided into relative and ultimate. The first five paramitas are relative in the sense that they involve a subject-object relation and are carried out through actions performed for others' benefit. The sixth paramita, that of transcendental knowledge, is ultimate because it represents that awareness in which there is no subject-object dualism.

GENEROSITY (DANA-PARAMITA)

Generosity is the most important of the relative paramitas because it is the core inspiration of the bodhisattva and underlies everything he or she does. Trungpa Rinpoche says that generosity is symbolized in the act of giving up privacy and inviting all sentient beings as one's guests. As mentioned, this is the generosity of opening oneself and one's resources to others, taking others' needs as seriously as one's own.

Four kinds of generosity are mentioned in the Tibetan tradition:

1. *Giving material things* to those who are in want. Relieving the suffering caused by hunger, thirst, or homelessness. Starvation, homelessness, and other similar forms of suffering, if left unaddressed, lead sentient beings to sadness, depression, and despair.

2. *Giving protection* to those who need it. This might involve giving refuge to those who are in fear; giving aid to those under attack of illness; working to help those who live in situations of political oppression. An example is provided by a friend who has made it her life task to try to fight child prostitution in Asia. Her one inspiration is to find a way to rescue and protect young girls who are kidnapped or sold into servitude by destitute families. Her one thought, morning, noon, and night, is the young children.

3. *Giving love.* Many people in our world feel no love in their lives and perhaps have never known it. Those who do not know love cannot rest within themselves, cannot experience a moment of well-being or contentment. Such people feel a sadness that knows no bounds and has no end. To such a person, the bodhisattva is called to open up his or her heart with love. Such love can heal even the deepest wounds.

4. *Giving dharma.* To give dharma does not mean to convert someone to your religion or even to pull them into your way of thinking. It means showing them and opening up for them the pathway to their own hearts, their buddha-nature. Literally, giving dharma means giving the truth, what is real, beyond wishful thinking. It is giving them the gift that will take them to their own ultimate human fruition and fulfillment. Of course, in alleviating want, in providing protection, in giving love, one is already giving dharma. This is so because these kinds of actions express a deep respect for the other's worth, indeed their sacredness as a potential enlightened one. Yet the gift of dharma in the sense of the truth is more explicit: it shows people how to take advantage of every experience that comes to them, to deepen their understanding of their lives and to unlock their sanity, compassion, and strength.

Trungpa Rinpoche comments that the *attitude* of generosity is critical. We are not giving to someone who is beneath us. Rather, the other person's need becomes an occasion for open, eye-level communication with that person. In giving, the bodhisattva must go beyond irritation and self-defensiveness, and must open his or her love, respect, and vulnerability to the other. "Generosity is a willingness to give, to open without philosophical or pious or religious motives, just simply doing what is required at any moment in any situation, not being afraid to receive anything."[15]

In the fruition of generosity, like that of the other paramitas, the action is carried out as a natural and spontaneous process. Trungpa Rinpoche says that at this level, generosity and the other paramitas are performed as naturally as breathing. Just as one feels the need to breathe, to drink water when thirsty, to sleep when tired, so the bodhisattva performs the paramitas out of a similar sense of fulfilling something fundamental to his or her very being.

DISCIPLINE (SHILA-PARAMITA)

On one level, the bodhisattva's discipline is understood as keeping the various shilas that one has taken on the Hinayana level. This includes avoiding the ten unvirtuous actions and cultivating the ten virtuous actions and also following the appropriate shilas of layperson or monk or nun, as the case may be. However, now that one has taken the bodhisattva vow, the motivation of one's shila is somewhat different. In the Hinayana, one's shila was a way of accumulating merit and thus laying the ground for our present and future path. Moreover, it helped create an environment of simplicity in which awareness could flourish. These roles of shila continue. But on the Mahayana level, the motivation for following shila is to better help others. We are now less concerned with how the practice of shila can make things better for ourselves, and more concerned with how our practice can be helpful to suffering beings.

Suppose, for example, we are tempted to tell a lie to a close friend, perhaps about some transgression of ours, to avoid the inconvenience that telling the truth would bring. On the Hinayana level, we will be concerned to tell the truth to avoid complicating our lives and to avoid the sowing of negative karmic seeds. It is the success of our own path that we have in mind. On the Mahayana level, however, we realize that when we tell a lie to someone close to us, on some level they know they have been lied to; but on another level, because they trust us, they do not know. Our lie will create subtle inner discord in them, subtle suffering, and cause them to shut down in some way, without knowing it. As bodhisattvas, we cannot lie because we cannot inflict harm on them in this way.

This leads us to the deeper meaning of the discipline paramita: it is ultimately not deviating from whatever it is that will help another person. The bodhisattva cultivates the discipline to do whatever is needed for the other and is not put off by whatever inconvenience and difficulties this may bring. In the Hinayana, there was a kind of literal quality to the shilas—either you act in accordance with this or that rule, in which case you have kept that particular shila, or you don't. In the Mahayana, you cannot keep shila by following literal rules, but only by doing something that actually helps another. For example, you might have to break one of the Hinayana shilas in order to be of help, as in the previously mentioned story of the Buddha in a former life as a ship's captain, who killed a pirate who would have killed all the passengers.

At the fruition level of discipline, the bodhisattva acts naturally in accordance with his or her bodhisattva vow.

> If a bodhisattva is completely selfless, a completely open person, then he will act according to openness, will not have to follow rules. . . . It is impossible for the bodhisattva to destroy or harm other people. . . . If someone were observing the bodhisattva, he always appears to act correctly, always seems to do the right thing at the right time . . . his mind is so precise, so accurate that he never makes mistakes. . . . If we are completely open, not watching ourselves at all, being completely open and communicating with situations as they are, then action is pure, absolute, superior.[16]

PATIENCE (KSHANTI-PARAMITA)

The paramita of patience involves not reacting to situations out of irritation, frustration, or fear. Three kinds of patience are mentioned in the tradition: in Chagdud Tulku's words, "forbearance [1] in the face of threats or harm from others, [2] in accepting and dealing with the hardships of spiritual practice, and [3] in accepting and relating without fear to the profound implication of the true nature of reality."[17]

The first type of patience is directed to the suffering that we experience as a result of others' actions. In life, people may resent and hate us, attempt to undermine and cut us down, constantly say mean and untrue things about us, and try to bring us various kinds of harm. Rather than retaliating, the bodhisattva patiently endures such aggression. In relation to this first type of patience, Trungpa Rinpoche comments:

> The practice of patience means not returning threats, anger, attacks, or insults. But this does not mean being purely passive. Instead we use the other person's energy, as in judo. Since we have related to our own aggression through the practice of meditation, we are not threatened by the other person's aggression, nor do we need to respond impulsively or aggressively. . . . We do not return such a person's threat, and at the same time, we prevent further aggression by allowing the other person's own energy to undercut itself.[18]

The second type of patience involves forbearing in the face of the hardships of spiritual practice, hardships that come in many forms. Having made a commitment to the dharma, we might feel tremendous pain at not having the time or energy to study or practice as we feel we need to. Or we might feel desolation at not being able to be with our teacher. In addition, practice often accelerates the ripening of karma, and our lives may suddenly become far more painful and difficult than before. Our practice may become a source of ridicule from others or, conversely, a resource that makes others attempt to feed off us. Patience is being willing to live with these situations, knowing that this is how the spiritual path is and it cannot be otherwise.

The third type of patience entails, in traditional terms, "forbearance in the face of dharmas that fail to be produced." "Non-production" means that whatever arises in our lives never makes it to the point of becoming a true and solidified phenomenon. As Mahayanists, we can never come to definite conclusions about anything. There is always something intangible, ungraspable, and empty about whatever we experience. In other words, things are never quite what they seem or what we want them to be. Nothing ever matches our expectations. We are always waiting for a train that never comes. What does show up at the station platform, however, is not a train, but an ostrich. And this ostrich wakes us up to the fact that the station platform was just our dream and that we are actually out in the middle of a wilderness somewhere. And yet, this place doesn't quite make it as a wilderness either. When things are so manifestly not what we want, expect, or think, this could cause great irritation, impatience, and anger. Instead, as bodhisattvas we know that the nature of reality never matches our concepts about it, and this enables us to rest in an unconditioned patience, one without conditions or limitations.

There is something more to patience, something more creative. The bodhisattva can practice patience because of an unconditional trust in whatever occurs. This trust is unconditional because it is not based on past experience. It is trust in the unfolding karma of situations, a confidence that whatever occurs is right, fitting, and an expression of the order of things. For this reason, situations are accurate and they are headed somewhere. The bodhisattva is patient because he knows that only by allowing situations to unfold in their own way, to grow and reach maturation as they need to, can gentleness, kindness, and insight occur.

Thus the fruition of patience is living without expectations, without hope or fear. It is being present without a whole battery of ideas locked in place. Because the bodhisattva is without expectation, then when things occur, he or she has no basis for irritation or impatience. Trungpa Rinpoche comments on the fruition of patience:

> Patience also feels space. It never fears new situations, because nothing can surprise the bodhisattva—nothing. Whatever

comes—be it destructive, chaotic, creative, welcoming, or inviting—the bodhisattva is never disturbed, never shocked, because he is aware of the space between the situation and himself. Once one is aware of the space between the situation and oneself, then anything can happen in that space. . . . Therefore transcendental patience means that we have a flowing relationship with the world, that we do not fight anything.[19]

EXERTION (VIRYA-PARAMITA)

The paramita of exertion means being willing to apply oneself with diligence to the bodhisattva's commitments. Kalu Rinpoche comments that when we follow the bodhisattva path, we need great exertion to persevere along the way.[20] Our dharma practice puts us in a situation where we must go ahead rather than seeking our own personal comfort and security. The *paramita* of exertion is needed to enable us to continue on. The way is long, and there will be opportunities and temptations to give up. Through the energy of exertion, we persevere. The way of the bodhisattva is painful; exertion provides the strength to step into our pain and take advantage of it rather than try to avoid it.

It is critical to realize that exertion is not manufactured like the energy we sometimes feel from being a workaholic, being distraught, or taking stimulants. Exertion is not the mindless speed and aggression that mark much of modern life. This may be illustrated by the following example. In the dzokchen tradition, laziness is defined as "being busy," being constantly preoccupied with various activities. This kind of laziness involves engaging in activity-based preconceptions. We have a concept of something that we want to get or achieve, and our desire, our hope and fear, provide the fuel to drive us forward. It is as if our lust for a "result" provides the driving force behind our relentless activity. This model of the person who is constantly "on the run," who never has a free minute, who goes from dawn until dusk, is held up as the ideal in modern culture, the model that everyone should emulate. Why, in dzokchen, is this regarded as the ultimate form of laziness? Because for dzogchen, the ultimate laziness is dwelling in ignorance, simply repeating one's habitual patterns over and over, and refusing to relate to the challenge of reality beyond ego. It is lazy in the sense that it reflects a desire to dwell in the morass and confusion of one's own self-absorption rather than step into the bright light and fresh air of reality, where what we are and how we spend our time may be called into question. "Being busy" in the modern sense, no matter how energetic it may appear on the surface, is ultimately lazy because it has no relationship to actual reality. It is based on mindless "cruising," attempting to impose our ego version of things on the world. In this, there is no respect for the other, no real communication, no opening, and no journey. This kind of energy has no staying power and leads to nothing but further suffering, sickness, and confusion.

On the other hand, every situation has its natural energy, intelligence, and inner imperative. The paramita of exertion involves trusting the energy presented in whatever occurs, opening oneself to it, and following its natural intelligence. Thus, because situations are always coming to us, we never miss an opportunity. Trungpa Rinpoche describes the fruition of exertion:

> In other words, it is joy, joyous energy. . . . This energy is joy, rather than the kind of energy with which we work hard because we feel we must. It is joyous energy because we are completely interested in the creative pattern of our lives. One's whole life is opened by generosity, activated by morality, strengthened by patience, and now one arrives at the next stage, that of joy. One never sees situations as uninteresting or stagnant at all, because the bodhisattva's view of life is extremely open-minded, intensely interested.[21]

MEDITATION (DHYANA-PARAMITA)

The meditation of shamatha and vipashyana developed in the Hinayana continues to be the foundation of dharma practice in the Mahayana. One continues to develop stillness through mindfulness of breathing or other similar techniques. And this practice nourishes the maturation of vipashyana, which, in the Mahayana, is the direct perception of shunyata, or emptiness.

However, as practiced in the Mahayana, meditation has a different context and a different motivation. Instead of meditating in order to benefit oneself, to create psychological comfort or protection, or to gain some other such end, now one's primary inspiration for practice is the benefit of others. The bodhisattva will notice that when he has a wandering mind, he is constantly being distracted from situations and from other beings, and is incapable of practicing the other four relative paramitas. He is instead agitated, confused, and led astray by his own discursive thinking.

Through the paramita of meditation, one trains again and again in bringing one's attention back to the breath, acknowledging and then letting go of thoughts when they arise, learning to be more and more fully present to one's object of mindfulness. This mindfulness practice, "on the meditation cushion," so to speak, is then easily and naturally transferred to one's ordinary life. When with others, particularly in difficult situations that one would rather avoid, one brings oneself back again and again. It is precisely when one is fully present to the situation that one can see its possibilities and can then engage the paramitas of generosity, discipline, patience, and exertion.

In its fruition stage, the paramita of meditation involves a continual awareness in which one sees situations with clarity and warmth. Here one rests naturally and spontaneously in the buddha-nature. Chagdud Tulku writes: "The mind falls naturally into its fundamental state, unobscured by thoughts of the three times—by memories, by thoughts of the present, or by anticipation of what may arise in the future."[22] At this stage, meditation provides the vast and unbroken field of awareness within which the other relative *paramitas* can appear spontaneously as called for by situations.

TRANSCENDENTAL KNOWLEDGE (PRAJNA-PARAMITA)

The first five paramitas are known as relative practices because they involve a subject who is the bodhisattva, an object who is a suffering sentient being, and an action, such as giving something that is needed. The sixth, prajna-paramita, is known as ultimate because it is the non-dual awareness of the true nature of reality. This is an absolutely direct and nonconceptual state in which all ideas of subject and object have disappeared and one is face-to-face with the profound emptiness that is the essential nature of all things.

On one level, without prajna-paramita, the other five paramitas would be blind; the sixth paramita brings the element of intelligence or insight, so that the other five can operate with precision and accuracy. Trungpa Rinpoche says, "Even if the bodhisattva has perfected the other five paramitas, lacking prajna the other actions are incomplete. . . . It says in the sutras that the *chakravartin* or universal emperor goes to war at the head of four different armies. Without the emperor to lead them, the armies have no direction."[23] With prajna-paramita as the awareness that sees situations exactly as they are, the bodhisattva's generosity, discipline, and so on, will be exactly appropriate, no more and no less than is needed.

Prajna-paramita also permeates the other actions so that at their fruition level they are nonconceptual and nondual. Without the sixth paramita, the other five would be strictly relative practices that would not be paramita, transcendent. What makes the first five paramitas transcendent is that while they begin in the kind of duality described above, they end in a direct awareness of reality.

This process is illustrated by what is know as the "threefold purity." For example, in the case of generosity, as long as a bodhisattva gives with the idea that he or she is a person who is giving, that there is a recipient who is receiving, and that there is an act of giving, the giving will just be ordinary, not the *paramita* of generosity. In that case, it will accrue the ordinary benefit and merit that giving on the Hinayana level would entail. By contrast, according to the threefold purity, the bodhisattva is asked to recognize no giver, no receiver, and no action of giving. He or she is called to engage in giving in a completely nonconceptual space, with no reference of the giver back to himself. Thus one gives—literally without giving it a thought. The insight into the need for the gift arises spontaneously as an expression of the bodhisattva's inner buddha-nature, and the act remains free from conceptualization and thus pure.

Some Specific Practices

The six paramitas provide a general context and set of guidelines for bodhisattva activity. In Tibetan tradition, a number of detailed and specific practices are also given that help the bodhisattva to develop the paramitas. All of the following practices are contemplative. They cannot be done simply by reading about them or even thinking about them. They must be applied on the meditation cushion through diligent and repeated application.

The practices described here are active and involve the imagination. They should always be preceded and followed, in any meditation session, by the formless meditation of shamatha and vipashyana. Formless practice at the beginning of one's session provides the mental processing, slowing, and opening necessary for the practice of the more active contemplations. Formless practice at the end of one's session enables one to let go of and "dissolve" whatever occurred during one's active contemplations, rather than turning it into grist for the mill of ego, either by providing food for endless thought and speculation or acting as grounds for an increasingly grandiose opinion of oneself.

"All Sentient Beings Have Been My Mother"

This practice is based on the idea that, over the course of our innumerable lifetimes, we have had every possible relationship with every sentient being. Thus each being has been our parent, child, friend, enemy, and so on. In the present instance, we are asked to remember that each sentient being has been, at one or another time, our mother. The practice begins with generating feelings of love, tenderness, and protectiveness toward our own mother for having given us life and for caring for us. We are then to think over the billions of past lives that we have lived, and realize that during those lifetimes there is not one sentient being who has not been our mother countless times over. Thus we may feel toward every sentient being, as our mother in many lives, both gratitude and love.

In modern Western culture, with its devaluation of the feminine and lack of respect for motherhood and homemaking, and with the stress that absent fathers or mothers put on the family, many have grown up ambivalent about their early years, their natal family situation, and their mothers. In a similar way, many women feel ambivalent about their mothering roles. The end result is that people have a hard time connecting with feelings of love and gratitude toward their own mothers. In this situation, one may pick another person for whom one has felt love in the course of his or her life. One may then generate tenderness and gratitude toward this person and gradually extend those feelings to all sentient beings.

Since we have been in every kind of relationship with every sentient being throughout our lifetimes, this means that we have loved not only those we are now close to, but also our current enemies and those we do not know. Moreover, the person who is now against me once loved me and cared for me in another time and place, perhaps at the risk of his or her life. This brings us face-to-face with the changeability of human relationships and the transience and fickleness of human emotions. Even in this very life, friends have become enemies and enemies have become friends. We need to feel the love and connection that we have with each sentient being, which underlies the continual changes that characterize samsara.

THE FOUR IMMEASURABLES

A practice done by many Tibetan Buddhists on some regular basis is that of the "four immeasurables." In this practice, one generates loving-kindness (*maitri*), compassion (*karuna*), sympathetic joy (*mudita*), and equanimity (*upeksha*) toward all beings. The four immeasurables are a meditation practice that one does in order to soften one's aggression, increase one's awareness of the suffering of others, and extend one's good feelings toward them. The change of heart brought about through the four immeasurables can then not help being reflected in one's interactions with suffering sentient beings. These practices are called immeasurable because, since sentient beings are limitless, so our love for them and desire to help them must likewise be without limit. They are also immeasurable because one does them for all sentient beings freely, without preconditions or qualifications. In Tibetan tradition, the four immeasurables may be developed one by one, as described below, or as a group by chanting and contemplating the meaning of the following verses:

> May all beings enjoy happiness and the root of happiness
>   [maitri];
> May they be free from suffering and the root of suffering
>   [karuna];
> May they not be separated from the great happiness devoid
>   of suffering [mudita];
> May they dwell in the great equanimity free from passion,
>   aggression, and delusion [upeksha].

Maitri, "loving-kindness," is the sincere wish that all sentient beings experience happiness, both the conditioned happiness of ordinary life and the ultimate happiness of liberation. To do this practice, we begin with someone close whom we love. We then consider how this person longs to be happy. Then we visualize that person obtaining all the happiness in the world, including the joy and freedom of enlightenment. Having done this with one person who is near and dear, we repeat the contemplation with someone we are not fond of. Finally, we extend the contemplation to larger and larger circles of sentient beings, those in our extended family, for example, then our neighborhood, our town, our state, and so on until all sentient beings are included.

Karuna, "compassion," is universal love that extends to all sentient beings throughout time and space. We begin, as before, selecting a person for whom we feel particular love. We visualize this person, and open our hearts to feel as deeply as possible the love that we have for him or her. Then we pick some other person that we know and try to extend this same love to him or her, realizing that in some former life we felt as much for that person. Next we extend this love to an enemy. And finally, we extend it to all beings.

Mudita, "sympathetic joy," involves rejoicing in the happiness of others. As Chagdud Tulku puts it, "We rejoice in others' worldly blessings—their health, wealth, wonderful relationships—and in their spiritual good fortune. We don't allow jealousy to overtake us, nor wonder, 'Why do they get this or that, and not me?' Instead, we make the wish that their happiness will be long-lived, and we do everything we can to make that happen."[24] As in the previous meditation, we pick a person whom we love and visualize whatever good things this person may have in his or her life. We consider each of these, and rejoice that these fine things have occurred to our beloved friend. Next we pick someone we do not like, to whom we would ordinarily wish ill. Then we think of whatever good things this person may have in his or her life, and we rejoice in those. Finally, we extend the contemplation to all sentient beings.

Equanimity is a state of mind in which, in Chagdud Tulku's words, we "live free of prejudice or bias, without making a division in our minds between friends and enemies."[25] This contrasts with our normal, habitual state in which we care for those with whom we identify, such as family and friends, but have little or no real concern about others. We may even feel satisfaction when something bad happens to someone we consider an enemy. "Through the practice of equanimity, we develop a noble attitude of compassion for all beings without distinction, from the depths of our heart."[26]

We practice equanimity by reflecting that over the course of our innumerable existences there is no sentient being with whom we have not been in every conceivable kind of relationship. Every sentient being without exception has been father, mother, sibling, wife, husband, child, teacher, student, supporter, detractor, friend, enemy, and so on. Then we pick a person and visualize him or her in every one of these relationships with us. In the course of this practice, we may alternately select a friend, an enemy, and a person about whom we have neutral feelings.

The ordinary logic of ego is that we become angry or jealous if anything good happens to others and conversely feel delight when they suffer misfortune. The four immeasurables reverse ego's habitual logic and cause disarray, as Trungpa Rinpoche says, in the central headquarters of ego. This disarray then provides cracks in ego through which the love of the buddha-nature, where the four immeaurables exist in their pure form, can stream. Khenpos Palden Sherab and Tsewang summarize:

> We already have the Four Immeasurables within the natural state of our mind, so practice is actually a matter of progressively clarifying and revealing them. To do this, we have to be purified of ego-clinging, grasping, and attachment to dualistic knowledge and experience. Such activities obscure our primordial nature and put severe limitations on these four precious powers.[27]

TONGLEN

Tonglen means "sending and taking," sending positive qualities to others and taking their pain upon oneself. Tonglen is one of the most challenging of all Mahayana practices, but also one of the most powerful. The Ven. Shamar Rinpoche was once asked which Vajrayana practice he found the most powerful and the most help. Although it is usually classified as Mahayana practice, he named tonglen. Like the four immeasurables, tonglen is best done in stages, beginning with a subject that is most easily accessible and only later moving into larger and more challenging arenas. The ultimate goal is to extend one's practice to all sentient beings.

Tonglen "rides upon the medium of the breath," meaning that the practice is synchronized with the natural inflow and outflow of breathing. As one breathes in, one visualizes that the pain of the other is coming toward oneself and dissolving into one's body. In this phase of the practice, one is taking on the pain of the other. As one breathes out, one imagines that relief and happiness are going out from one's body, giving to the other one's own well-being. In this sense, the practice should be felt as very personal.

Tonglen may be divided into several stages:

1. Initially, we meditate for a few minutes with shamatha and vipashyana practice. During this time, one tries to sense the peace, the openness, and the emptiness of the buddha-nature within.

2. Next, we visualize the cyclical alternation of the tonglen process, in-breath/pain, out-breath/relief. We begin with the abstract qualities of pain and relief. First, on the in-breath, one imagines pain in the form of black, dirty, defiling smoke coming toward us from all directions and dissolving into the pores of our body. On the out-breath, we visualize relief, peace, happiness, and sanity in the form of clear, soothing, white light going out from our pores and extending into space.

3. Now we select a person for whom this practice of tonglen will be the easiest and most natural. Perhaps there is a new baby in the family for whom we feel intense love. Or perhaps a close friend is in the midst of some kind of tribulation, a lost job, a failed relationship, a period of deep depression. Or perhaps a parent is dying in a great deal of physical and mental anguish and we would do anything to be able to alleviate his or her suffering. It could also be an animal whose suffering has touched us deeply.

   You begin by visualizing this person sitting in front of you. Next you imagine their pain, their anguish, their suffering. Now you visualize that their pain is coming toward you in the form of black smoke. On your in-breath, this black smoke dissolves into your body. On the out-breath, you radiate toward them the white light of relief in the form of peace, well-being, and joy. On the next round of in-breath and out-breath, you repeat the sequence of taking on the other's pain and sending them relief. One continues this practice until one's heart becomes tender, loving, and open, and one feels the inspiration to extend these feelings further.

4. Next you might pick a person for whom it will be more challenging to practice *tonglen*.

5. The final step in the *tonglen* practice is to generalize completely, extending the taking of suffering and the sending of relief to all sentient beings in the world and beyond. Thus on the in-breath, we visualize the suffering of all beings coming toward us and dissolving into ourselves; on the out-breath, we send relief in the form of white light to all sentient beings.

Tonglen is not an easy practice. Particularly when we move beyond those we love, it becomes difficult to visualize ourselves taking on another's suffering. After all, our entire ego orientation is about getting rid of our pain and maximizing our happiness. The reversal of this process in tonglen takes constant work. Being unable to do the practice very well should be no cause for alarm. Whether the practice comes easily or is monumentally difficult, the important point is making the effort. If we do so, we are working at the boundary of our ego's territory.

Sometimes beginning tonglen practitioners express the fear that in taking the suffering of others on themselves, they will feel worse than they already do or will get sick. They need to be reassured that this is not how the practice works. When we take the suffering of others into ourselves, it has nowhere to stick and flows right on through. This is possible, of course, because of the foundation of shamatha and vipashyana practice, in which we have become familiar with the process of letting go of thoughts and other mental contents, and returning to the breath. Taking the suffering of others on ourselves unleashes the power of our buddha-nature. This power purifies all negativity and transforms even the most self-absorbed hatred into selfless love.

One need only try tonglen to see how magical and miraculous it is. Let us imagine that you are in a screaming fight with someone you love. On some deep level, you love this person, but at this exact moment you are overcome with anger, defensiveness, and aggression. You can feel yourself down at the end of a long, dark hallway; way down at the other end of this hallway, you can barely see this person you are screaming at. As you shriek insults, blame, and hateful words, you feel yourself dropping into one of the cold hells, where—in rejecting love—you are isolated, deadened, and alone.

Realize that you have to make some kind of switch or leap. If you keep going along this course, there is no other destination but the deepest anguish. At this moment, an opportunity will appear. You will have the choice to begin doing tonglen. Take the risk. Throw your life over a cliff. Begin to breathe in the black air of your partner's pain, at that very moment. Then breathe out relief to him or her. Repeat this process a few times. See what happens. This is a practice that is exceptionally powerful and transformative in your most intimate relationships, whether you are getting along or not, whether there seem to be any apparent problems or not. If you are really interested in moving your relationship to a higher level and giving it the injection of immortality, this is the way to do it.

APPLICATION

Regarding all sentient beings as one's mother, the four immeasurables, and tonglen are essentially meditation practices. Hearing about them, reading about them, or thinking about them can be useful. But their raw power is unleashed only when they are put into practice in a sustained way through meditation.

It is best if one can make these practices part of one's daily or weekly meditation routine. The contemplation of all sentient beings as one's mother can be done in a few minutes at the beginning of the practice session. In the case of the four immeasurables, if done daily, one could devote a minute or two to each one or perhaps do them sequentially, giving five or ten minutes to one on one day, to the second on the next day, and so on. If done weekly, one might take half an hour for all of them. Tonglen can similarly be done daily for a short period of time or weekly for a longer period.

The Mahayana practices should be done, as mentioned, on a regular basis. If this is not feasible, then they should at least be undertaken when we are having difficulties carrying out our bodhisattva vow. Perhaps one of our children is in a rebellious phase and we find ourselves in a continual state of irritation, paranoid alert, and struggle. Perhaps we are not getting along with our spouse. Perhaps a person at work is attempting to undermine us and we find ourselves with ill will toward him. These are all ideal times to practice tonglen or the four immeasurables.

It is also recommended to devote all or part of a group meditation intensive or solitary retreat to the Mahayana practices. In such a case, one might divide one's day into three or four sessions, beginning each with a period of shamatha and vipashyana, then devoting the rest of the session to the practices described here. The impact of such an intensive practice of the active contemplations can be truly astounding. I personally have seen relationships in a state of total disarray turned around because one of the parties was willing to practice tonglen for his or her partner. It seems like such a simple thing. And yet, shockingly, through the practice a level of resource is unlocked that is more than a match for any difficulty.

RESULT

The goal of the Mahayana path is the complete and perfect enlightenment of a world-redeeming buddha. It is possible to aspire for something less. If one remains in the Hinayana and elects not to take the bodhisattva vow and enter the Mahayana—something almost unheard of in Tibet but still theoretically possible—one may still aim for enlightenment. According to the Hinayana, if one follows the Hinayana dharma of the Buddha, adhering to one's shila and practicing shamatha-vipashyana, one will eventually attain the realization of an arhant. This realization involves, as mentioned, the cessation of the three poisons and the attainment of the peace of nirvana. The Hinayana also advances another ideal, called the pratyekabuddha, the solitary awakened one. These are forest renunciants who lived prior to the time of the Buddha and thus have no direct connection with the lineage deriving from him. However, they are inspired by the idea of enlightenment and, through a life devoted to meditation, are able to attain the same general type of realization as the arhant. The realization of both arhant and pratyekabuddha are considered limited from the Mahayana point of view, because they involve awakening primarily for oneself and leaving out of consideration the vast sea of sentient beings that remain trapped within samsara. The enlightenment of these two is deficient because it stops short of seeing the condition of suffering beings throughout space and it is lacking in the compassionate motivation to help them all.

For the Mahayana, the only worthy goal is to become a buddha like Shakyamuni, whose wisdom has no boundaries and whose compassion is likewise limitless. Thus, through the bodhisattva vow, one aspires to follow the same path as Shakyamuni Buddha and eventually to be born, like him, into a world where the dharma is not known, attain complete and perfect enlightenment, and establish the tradition of dharma.

The path to this full awakening is said to be almost endless, stretching over three incalculable aeons. During this vast expanse of time and through billions of lifetimes, the bodhisattvas are reborn over and over within the afflicted world, practicing the six paramitas and sacrificing their own happiness for that of others. Although they have long since transcended the karma of rebirth in the six realms, through the force of their vow, they continue to take rebirth, experiencing all of the various conditions and situations that sentient beings face. Someday, as buddhas, they will be omniscient. This omniscience means that they know fully every kind and moment of suffering that sentient beings experience, and they know this because they themselves have been in precisely the place of each and every being, and have felt exactly what they feel. The omniscience of a buddha is thus really the knowing and the love of a heart that has suffered everything.

The path from the bodhisattva vow to complete buddhahood is described in terms of ten stages, or bhumis. In Tibetan tradition, a quite sizable literature exists on these various levels of development. Sometimes additional bhumis are added to make thirteen. As one is born in life after life, practicing meditation and assisting beings, one gradually makes one's way toward the awakening of a buddha. At the first bhumi, one has the first direct experience of emptiness. At the sixth, one has attained the realization of an arhant. As one traverses the final bhumis before buddhahood, one no longer takes birth as a being of flesh and blood but is born as an immaterial being who carries forward the bodhisattva vow in more ethereal and expansive ways. For example, one can multiply one's body, to assist many more sentient beings than before. As the master Asanga tells us in the "powers" chapter of the *Bodhisattvabhumi,* one can also take the shape of rain to alleviate drought, food in the time of famine, or a doctor in the midst of an epidemic.

The bhumi literature sometimes has the appearance of being abstract, scholarly, and unrelated to the spiritual life. However, if we read it closely, we find some challenging and helpful perspectives. For one thing, the outline of the bhumis shows us how vast the journey that we are undertaking really is. For ordinary people like us, with our day-to-day preoccupations and limitations, we might tend to think of our path as confined to this mundane human realm and to things that we are familiar with. The bhumi literature makes it clear that our journey goes far beyond the road that we see immediately ahead. In fact, it ascends a mountain on which the variety of meadows, cliffs, and waterfalls, the delicacy of the tundra, the vastness and starkness of the snowfields, and the wild beauty and desolation of the upper reaches we cannot possibly imagine. Moreover, this is a mountain whose ultimate height is completely beyond our ability to conceive.

Descriptions of the bhumis also make clear just how limitless are the time perspectives with which we are working. The road to full awakening is so vastly long that, in fact, from our point of view it has the appearance of being endless. Recognition of this has the effect of undercutting all speed, ambition, and spiritual arrogance. The practitioner really is left with no choice but to relax and give up his or her goal orientation. The mind may be able to live in tomorrow or next year, but it has a very hard time living in a future that is a billion lifetimes away. This recognition allows the practitioner to be fully present in this moment, to experience it fully, and to see what imperative toward the future it may hold.

The bhumi teachings also make us think twice about the way we regard the so-called ordinary reality of our everyday lives. They make the claim that our world is filled with presences and powers that we cannot see—the nonmaterial bodhisattvas—who are with us and watching over us. Moreover, these beings are engaged in endlessly providing sustenance, support, and help. In the bhumi texts we are told that when, on a blistering day, a cloud passes over the sun, it is not a purely physical event, but the incarnation of a bodhisattva. When we are nourished by the earth, warmed by fire, cleansed by water, cooled by a breeze, these are all the activities of high-level bodhisattvas. When we are in any kind of trouble and relief comes, that is the work of a bodhisattva. When we seek relief from suffering but continue to be led down dark hallways, our guide is a bodhisattva who is helping us exhaust our karma and develop understanding and love. The bhumi literature tells us that the habitual, desacralized reality that we think we live in is our projection, and that, in actual fact, in this world of ours far more is at work.

Eventually, in some time out of mind, we will achieve the realization of a fully enlightened buddha and establish the dharma in some universe we cannot now imagine. What then? Is the spiritual journey over? Has something definitive been achieved? Many years ago, someone asked Trungpa Rinpoche this very question. "What happens when you become a buddha?" Rinpoche responded: "That is just the beginning."

The Nirmanakaya

In Tibetan Buddhism, as mentioned above, buddhahood is described as having three "bodies" or dimensions. On one level, the most accessible and concrete, it manifests as a physical person. Thus Shakyamuni Buddha was himself a nirmanakaya, a human being of flesh and blood. *Nirmanakaya* means "created body" and does not refer to the body of an ordinary person, but rather to one who is, so to speak, "in the world but not of the world." By virtue of his realization, a buddha's body has a certain purity, beauty, and power not shared by those of ordinary people. For example, his form gives off a luster and radiance that is hard to look at. His speech is mellifluous and compelling, communicating to others just what they need. And his mind, resting in the enlightened state, brings others naturally into deep peacefulness and a feeling of the "isness" of the world.

The Sambhogakaya

There is also another dimension to buddhahood, namely the sambhoga-kaya, or "body of enjoyment." Once again in Tibetan tradition we are confronted with what we may call "the invisible world." There are physical buddhas like Shakyamuni, but these are few and far between. In our world age, Shakyamuni is in fact the only physical buddha there will be until the future buddha, Maitreya, appears on earth many thousands of years from now.

However, we are not left bereft. At this moment, there are many other buddhas who live in the timeless realm of the sambhogakaya. These buddhas have a glorious spiritual form that can be seen by realized people, but that is normally invisible to ordinary people like ourselves. Some of these sambhogakaya buddhas were once human beings, while others have been celestial buddhas since the beginning. While we cannot normally see them, we can certainly supplicate them and their responses can appear powerfully in our lives.

In Tibetan Buddhism, a number of celestial buddhas are particularly important. Although as fully enlightened sambhogakaya deities these buddhas are alike, on another level they each have their specific individuality in terms of what they provide to human beings. For example, there are five buddhas that are organized according to the principle of the mandala: Vairochana, the buddha of all encompassing space, in the center; Akshobhya, the immovable one, in the east; Ratnasambhava, the source of all generosity, in the south; Amitabha, the embodiment of love and compassion, in the west; and Amoghasiddhi, essence of accomplishment and transformation, in the north. There are also quite a number of important female buddhas. In the mandala, at each of the four directions, there stands a female buddha, the consort or feminine counterpart of each of the buddhas, such as Lochana, Pandara, and Tara.

The Dharmakaya

The third and ultimate "body" of a buddha is the dharmakaya, the "body of reality itself." Not only is the dharmakaya beyond all physical-ity, it is even beyond all form. It is the "mind-essence" of the buddhas of the three times, the state of unimpeded emptiness and clarity, the enlightenment that includes everything and that goes on and on without end. This attainment brings us back to the very beginning, of course, for the dharmakaya is nothing other than the essence of our own mind, which has been covered with obscurations since beginningless time and which has finally shed those obscurations.

It is frequently said in Tibetan tradition, as mentioned, that the three kayas are inseparable. Shakyamuni Buddha is who he is because in his enlightenment, he has attained all three bodies. His enlightenment itself is inseparability with the dharmakaya. His powers point to his attainment of the sambhogakaya. And his having attained enlightenment as a human being is the nirmanakaya. Taken from the other end of the scale, the dharmakaya, as pure and limitless wisdom and compassion, has within it the seeds of the sambhogakaya and the nirmanakaya. As itself, it naturally gives rise to the sambhogakaya and the nirmanakaya to help sentient beings.

On one level, the three kayas of a buddha are completely beyond us. They are inconceivably far from our present state and lie unimaginably far into the future. From our perspective as ordinary people, the nirmanakaya of Shakyamuni is gone forever, we are too insensitive to see the sambhogakaya, and the dharmakaya is completely hidden from us. Thus as ordinary people, we have and can expect to have little or no experience of the three kayas.

At the same time, however, in another way, the three kayas are as close to us as can be, for they reside within us as our buddha-nature. They are thus the very basis of our personality and our very being. In Vajrayana Buddhism, in fact, we can begin to see how the whole mechanism of ego is a defensive reaction to the three kayas within us. We are so ego-driven, in fact, because we are subliminally aware that within us, on fire and literally bursting to get out, are the three kayas.

We also know the three kayas in another way, in the persons of our teachers. Particularly in the Vajrayana context, one begins to glimpse dimensions of one's own guru that correspond to the three kayas.

PART FOUR

Buddhist Philosophy
THE THREE TURNINGS OF THE WHEEL OF DHARMA

ALTHOUGH BUDDHISM ORIGINATED AS A MEDITATIVE tradition, as we have seen, from the very beginning it has included an important philosophical dimension. This sets forth the "view" or conceptual standpoint without which the spiritual life itself would be impossible. As noted in chapter 3, Tibetans understand the essentials of Buddhist philosophy to have been articulated in three progressive "turnings of the wheel of dharma," given by Shakyamuni Buddha during his lifetime. It is these three turnings, with their sutra foundations and their commentarial elaborations, that are examined in the next three chapters.

Tibetans spend a great deal of time and energy memorizing the important texts of the three turnings, studying and hearing teachings on them, and clarifying them through debate. Although, as suggested above, the process of scholarly learning can be extensive and although considerable human and material resources are expended in its service, it has never been considered an end in itself. Rather, it is valued because it provides the understanding necessary to the successful practice of meditation, from the most simple and elementary shamatha at the beginning up to the challenging terrains of mahamudra and dzokchen at the end. In this way, scholarly study and meditation practice go hand-in-hand throughout the journey to enlightenment.

Within Tibetan Buddhism, the proper relation of study and practice is articulated in the concepts of *trangdön,* "straightforward or literal meaning," and *ngedön,* "true or actual meaning." Trangdön is the conceptual version of the dharma, the words as they exist in the texts and in discursive teaching. Ngedön is the inner meaning as realized in meditation. Trangdön is like the *idea* of an ice-cream cone, while ngedön is the *actual experience* of eating that ice-cream cone. It is through coming to study and understand the trangdön that the way is open for us to recognize ngedön when it arises in our practice. Trungpa Rinpoche compares trangdön to the photograph of a person, while ngedön is the actual person him- or herself. Imagine that we are supposed to meet someone at the airport whom we have never seen before. If we are not given a photograph, when the passengers debark, we will have no way to recognize the right person from among everyone else. However, if we have been given a photograph, then when the person that we want to find passes before us, we will know, "This is the one I am looking for." In the present context, the three turnings of the wheel of dharma are like the photograph, the true reality of which we discover, in progressive stages throughout our journeys, through meditation practice.

A traditional Zen analogy is helpful: trangdön is like the finger pointing to the moon, while ngedön is the moon itself. The finger pointing to the moon is necessary so that we know where to look. But until we see the moon itself in our unobstructed vision, we miss the intention of the pointing finger. Trangdön and ngedön are thus closely related. Ngedön is the actual experience of unthinkable reality, while trangdön is that verbal expression which, among all necessarily imperfect verbal expressions, comes the closest to pointing to the actual nature of things as they are.

The critical importance of trangdön is illustrated by a not uncommon experience in my introductory Buddhism classes. We will be reading about egolessness, and sometimes students will report some version of the following: At some point in their life, often during adolescence, they have had an experience in which they realized that they did not exist. They saw their own insubstantiality, their ephemeral nature, their emptiness. Such experiences, which are relatively common among young people, can be very distressing and leave one feeling shaky indeed. Often, they will attempt to talk about the experience with parents, teachers, or other authority figures. In modern cultures, one can look long and hard, without success, for someone to validate and interpret the wisdom in such insights. Not infrequently, my students have found their way to medical authorities. Typically their reports are met with prescriptions for antidepressants or anti-anxiety medications. And yet they have remained unconvinced by the various kinds of rejection and dismissal that they have met. Their impression that they have experienced something critically important remains intact. And when they encounter the Buddhist teachings and hear it said that absence of sub-

stance of ourselves is the final word about our existence, they are relieved, amazed, and sometimes exhilarated. Our culture, it seems, is
wanting in an effective trangdön, such as the three turnings, to prepare
its members for experiences that go beyond those of conventional reality.

The relation of trangdön, or the "words," and ngedön, or the "essential meaning," is a complex and subtle one. In fact, the entire path in
Tibetan Buddhism involves journeying back and forth from trangdön
to ngedön, back to trangdön, then to ngedön, and on and on. We read
about impermanence. When we experience it in meditation, it may be
difficult to handle, but we can say to ourselves, "Okay, what I'm experiencing is what the teachings of dharma are talking about." We integrate
a certain level of insight of impermanence into our lives, then study
further, then experience further impermanence. Not infrequently, we
experience things in our meditation that are fresh and unexpected, and
we are grateful that we can turn back to our books and our teachers for
clarification.

The integral role of trangdön on the path and its close indicative
relation to ngedön are important also on a cultural level. One sometimes
encounters Western Buddhists who feel that it doesn't matter what comprehensive view of reality they hold, that their own spiritual progress
and the integrity of their Buddhism will be maintained no matter how
they view the universe. They feel that a conventional Western view of
the world is entirely compatible with their Buddhism. This may be the
case. But consider the example mentioned in chapter 1. Many Western
Buddhists hold the view of scientific materialism, including the idea
that the natural cosmos is fully explained by the "laws" of conventional
physics, biology, and botany, that the universe visible to scientific observation is the only one that exists, and that nature is dead and lifeless, as
described since the Western "enlightenment."[1] In other words, they hold
the view that the modern, conventional Western trangdön (conceptual
version of reality) works just fine with the Buddhist ngedön—what one
actually experiences on the path of meditation. However, as we shall
presently see, according to Tibetan Buddhism, meditation eventually
leads inevitably to an experience of reality that shatters the Western

views of a dead and mechanistic universe. If one is too invested in maintaining that modern Western view, then one runs the risk of becoming stuck at the lower, initial levels of awareness or of walking unprepared through a door into the much vaster, unfamiliar cosmos revealed by meditation—and becoming unglued in the process.

14

The First Turning

ABHIDHARMA

IN THE VIEW OF TIBETAN BUDDHISM, AS MENTIONED, Buddha Shakyamuni gave three relatively distinct cycles of teaching in the course of his life. Each of these "turnings of the wheel of dharma" were unprecedented and groundbreaking. As we saw, the first turning corresponds to the Hinayana portion of the path, while the second and third turnings correspond to stages on the Mahayana path. Each turning is a presentation of the view appropriate to a particular level of training and understanding. Each provides a conceptual orientation on the basis of which one can progress more deeply in one's meditation practice.

To review, the first turning of the wheel of dharma was promulgated by the Buddha at Sarnath, at the Deer Park in Benares, following his enlightenment. The audience consisted of his first five shravaka disciples. The content of the first turning is the four noble truths. These teachings are found in the Hinayana "buddha word," the instructions given by the Buddha to his early disciples. In Tibetan Buddhism, these Hinayana teachings are articulated in the four reminders, discussed above. Thrangu Rinpoche explains:

> Buddha Shakyamuni presented the Middle Way view many times in different ways—all of which can be subsumed in the three turnings of the Wheel of *dharma*. Sakyamuni first taught in Sarnath, shortly after his enlightenment. . . . [He taught the] four truths. He taught that all ordinary existence is suffering, that this suffering results from our own karma, and that this karma is created through the defiled nature of our own minds.

Defiled mind, he said, comes from our clinging to a notion of individual self or ego. Thus the Buddha showed the suffering nature of existence in the world and its source. Then he showed that it was possible for us to free ourselves from this suffering by attaining nirvana. In order to attain nirvana, it is not enough to have a moral inclination or a feeling that one might attain it; one must practise the path in order to reach the complete cessation of suffering and defilements which is nirvana. In this context "the path" means counteracting the clinging to a notion of ego or self.[1]

The teachings of the first turning are given their most rigorous, systematic philosophical expression in the Abhidharma, or "higher dharma," which provides a detailed examination of egolessness, karma, and enlightenment. The Abhidharma developed largely within Buddhist monastic circles, as a response to the need of institutionalized Buddhism to give a coherent, consistent, and credible account of itself within the learned, religious culture of India. As Buddhism evolved, it found its doctrines critiqued by other schools and sects. In the climate of competition among traditions for patronage and protection, it found itself called upon to systematize and rationalize the core Buddhist teachings, always in relation to other schools, both Buddhist and non-Buddhist. Thus one finds in the Buddha's Abhidharma teachings, and even more in the commentaries, evidence of a tremendous background of learning spanning the great traditions of ancient India.

The Abhidharma constitutes a critical part of the curriculum followed by Tibetan monastics in the shedras, or monastic colleges. In some sense, the Abhidharma is considered the foundation of all Buddhist learning because it lays out the basic vocabulary, central concepts, and critical perspectives that underlie all later discussions of doctrine in Tibetan Buddhism. At the same time, owing to the sophistication of the Abhidharma, its full study is often postponed until one has progressed to a relatively advanced level in one's scholarly training. Its root texts are found in the Abhidharma section of the Kanjur, the words of the Buddha. The Tenjur, consisting of commentaries by various scholars, contains various elaborations and explanations. Among the multiple Abhidharma traditions developed within Indian Buddhism, Tibetans follow the traditions of the Sarvastivadins and, more particularly, of the Indian master Vasubandhu in his seminal text, the *Abhidharmakosha,* with revisions, elaborations, and refinements of the Yogacharin teacher Asanga in his *Abhidharma-samucchaya.*

THE NOTION OF A DHARMA, OR "ELEMENTAL REALITY"

The central concept of the Abhidharma is that of a *dharma* or "elemental reality." A dharma is the smallest unit of experience that human beings can have. Dharmas are momentary appearances in our experience and follow one another in rapid succession. Ordinary people crudely and ignorantly apply a conceptual label to the impermanent and ever-changing stream of dharmas, the label of "I," "me," and "mine." By contrast, meditation brings into view the fact that what we think of as "I" is in fact a continuous stream of constantly changing moments of experience. To see that the "I" is nothing more than a figment of our own imagination is to attain the Hinayana level of realization.

In the Abhidharma, the notion of a dharma receives technical definition. In the Sarvastivadin tradition, seventy-five distinct types of dharmas are known, elaborated to one hundred different kinds in the Yogachara. A dharma is said to be an instantaneous flashing or appearance. It appears and then disappears in an instant. It has no duration. It is an eruption of energy. Categories of time and space are again conceptual labels applied to momentary dharmas. According to the Abhidharma, the nature of our actual experience is timeless; it has no duration and is beyond any notions of past, present, and future. A dharma is defined entirely by its manifestation. What it appears to be—how it appears—is what it is, and there is nothing "behind" the appearance. The appearance of each dharma defines its essential "characteristic" or "mark." For example, the experience of insight is a dharma that is quite different in its character from the experience of hatred, another dharma.

Consciousness is enumerated as one dharma in the Sarvastivadin system. In order for us to have a moment of experience, consciousness must appear in conjunction with other dharmas that provide the content of which consciousness is aware. Thus each moment of experience involves consciousness arising in conjunction with other dharmas. This grouping of dharmas arises and then disappears in an instant. Thus the momentariness of the dharmas is of particular importance. What we normally and habitually think of as continuous experience is, in fact, the succession of momentary experiential events.

A dharma is thus a momentary event that comes into being in dependence on karmic causes and conditions. Examples of conditioned dharmas are passion, aggression, delusion, faith, energy, and so on. These and the other conditioned dharmas underlie what most of us consider our ordinary, day-to-day human experience. The conditionality of these dharmas is extensive and all-pervasive. Each moment of our experience arises based on previous causes, which are multiplicitous, and in dependent relation to the vast web of reality that exists in the present.

A full understanding of the concept of dharmas requires an explanation of conditioned coproduction, or *tendrel* (Skt., *pratitya-samutpada*). Conditioned coproduction says that whatever arises in our experience does so only as a result of causes rooted in the past and in conjunction with everything else that exists now. Kalu Rinpoche remarks, "The Tibetan word *tendrel* means interaction, interconnection, interrelation, interdependence, or interdependent factors. All things, all our experiences, are tendrel, which is to say that they are events that exist because of the relationship between interrelated factors. This idea is essential to the understanding of *dharma*."[2] He then provides an illustration:

> When you hear the sound of a bell, ask yourself, What makes the sound? Is it the body of the bell, the clapper, the hand that moves the bell to and fro, or the ears that hear the sound? None of these elements alone produces the sound; it results from the interaction of all these factors. All the elements are necessary for the sound of a bell to be perceived, and they are necessary not in succession but simultaneously. The sound is an event

whose existence depends on the interaction of these elements; that is *tendrel*.[3]

The analogy can be extended. The sound of the bell is also dependent upon having a bell to ring in the first place. The existence of the bell depends upon the materials out of which it is made, the process of production, and those who produced it. To take just one of these, the bell metal depends upon the mining of ore that was smelted to make the metal, and this in turn depends upon those who mined the ore, all of whom depended upon their families of origin and so on. Again, the sound of the bell depends upon a person to hear it, and the existence of this person depends upon a vast array of karmic conditioning as well. This process of exploring the causes and conditions of the sound of a bell, both those that extend back in time and those that support the sound in the present, can be carried on until virtually the entire universe in time and space is included. The sound of this bell can be heard in just this way because of the cooperating causality of all time and space.

Take, as another example, a single drop of rain. While appearing as a separate individual, it is in fact in relation with past, present, and future, the end product of a series of events that stretch back through infinite time. In this temporal perspective, it is the result of the immediate storm in which it occurs; the prior evaporation from river, lake, or perhaps ocean; the weather patterns that brought it to this place at this moment; and so on. More distantly, its falling relies upon the very existence of the earth, which formed at some time in the past and, beyond this, with the origin of the universe. Our drop of rain, in fact, has some causal connection with every event—however remote—that has taken place in the past within the realm of manifestation. It incarnates within its being—if we had subtle enough perception to see it—the karmic imprint of the rest of the universe.

In terms of the present, the drop of rain has some relationship with the air through which it falls, the other raindrops in the storm, the ground upon which it drops, and so forth. Since the gravitational force of physical bodies is an ever-diminishing force, the drop of rain feels the pull of all matter everywhere. In this moment, then, it is connected, in however subtle a manner, with all the other phenomena that exist throughout space. In terms of the future, the raindrop will impact the ground upon which it falls, be taken up by plant or animal life, and contribute its karmic force to whatever future there may be. The teaching of karma or conditionality is vast and mind-boggling. What I am in this moment is the result of causes and conditions that reach back to beginningless time and extend to limitless space. If anything had been different anywhere along the line, I would be different. The fact that I am this way and no other, with all of my problems and potentials, is an attestation to the entire realm of being. To understand myself, I need to understand this vast web of conditioning that I represent. When I do so, I see that the notion of an individual, isolated, existent "I" is merely a thought with no reality.

So far, we have been speaking about conditioned dharmas. Dharmas may also be unconditioned. An unconditioned dharma—such as space or nirvana—is not based on causes and conditions but exists beyond the realm of causality. Therefore, unconditioned dharmas are permanent and unchanging. In the Sarvastivadin system, there are seventy-two conditioned and three unconditioned dharmas, while in the Yogachara there are ninety-four conditioned and six unconditioned dharmas. The most fundamental distinction in the Abhidharma is between the realm of conditioned dharmas, or samsara, and the realm of unconditioned dharmas, or nirvana. The purpose of the path is to arrive at the point of cessation of samsara, which, in and of itself, involves attainment of the dharma (or permanent experience) of nirvana, or Hinayana enlightenment.

THE FIVE SKANDHAS

In the Abhidharma, several different ways of organizing the dharmas are given, each of which contributes something important to our understanding of egolessness. The most well-known and accessible arrangement is perhaps that of the five skandhas, or aggregates (mentioned above), the five types of experience that make up our supposedly solid self. Kalu Rinpoche remarks, "Our feeling of existing, of being a 'me,' 'my body,' 'my mind,' is the experience of individuality. This individuality is made up of five heaps or aggregates."[4] In other words, if we examine our experience, we discover five different kinds of experiential events (dharmas), but no solid, stable "I" or "self." The five skandhas show us that we can view and explain the totality of our experience without any need for the additional category of a "self." The five skandhas include the following:

1. *Form (rupa)* includes the physical elements (earth, water, fire, air) as well as the five sense organs (eye, ear, nose, tongue, and body) and their corresponding sense objects (visual, auditory, olfactory, gustatory, tactile). "Form" refers to those momentary events that we experience as "physical."

2. *Feeling (vedana)* refers to the primitive sensation of positivity (pleasure), negativity (pain), or neutrality (indifference) that attends any experience that we have, however momentary and fleeting.

3. *Perception (samjna)* refers to the experience of rudimentary perception in which we recognize and type what we see, hear, smell, taste, touch, and think. For example, as we walk along a wooded path, trees, plants, and stones may appear in our field of vision. The "perception" skandha slots these into our experience as familiar. If a rabbit suddenly jumps into our path startling us, it is the perception skandha that recognizes the rabbit as a rabbit, something we are familiar with. If we encounter a person we do not know, before consciously thinking so, we experience the "unfamiliarity" of that person.

4. *Karmic formations (samskara)* are all of the habitual concepts, identifications, labels, and judgments—all of the extra mental baggage—that we attach to the experiences of the first three *skandha*s. They cause us to react to things as we do and lead us to act in particular ways.

5. *Consciousness (vijnana)* is the circumscribed, self-referential field of awareness within which we become conscious of the first four

skandhas. Consciousness is like a field surrounded by an electric fence. Within the field is our consciousness governed by motives of self-protection and territoriality. When anything potentially helpful or harmful comes in contact with our consciousness, it mobilizes the other four skandhas to pull in the incoming object if it promises pleasure, to push it away if it appears threatening, or to ignore it if it does neither.

Sakyong Mipham Rinpoche points out that the consciousness skandha later provided a rich arena of exploration for the Abhidharma thinkers of the Mahayana. In the Yogachara school, for example, the fifth skandha of consciousness is seen as composed of eight aspects, differentiable according to function. These are the "eight consciousnesses," about which one hears so much in Tibetan Buddhism. They include the five sense consciousnesses: the eye consciousness (the aspect of consciousness that registers the visual impressions of the eye organ) and, likewise, the ear, nose, tongue, and body consciousnesses. The sixth is that aspect of the consciousness that registers the "mind organ's" perception of mental objects. The five sense consciousnesses are concept free—that is, they merely register the sense experience. The sixth consciousness is also concept free, insofar as it only registers the direct and unmediated experience of its object, without adding onto it.

Rinpoche remarks that in the Yogachara system, the "seventh consciousness" is known as the creator of duality. Here the bare experience given by the six senses is separated into "I" and "other." The seventh consciousness adds the idea of "I," "me," and "mine" onto our experience of the six consciousnesses. It taints every experience with the idea of a self and imposes the false idea of a self on everything that happens.

The eighth consciousness is known as the *alaya,* the "storehouse consciousness" where karmic seeds that have been created are "stored." The analogy requires explanation. Every experience that we have ever had has left an impression on our consciousness. This impression remains, from one moment to the next, from one year to the next, from one lifetime to the next, until it is resolved, which may happen either through the natural occurrence of one's suffering or through deliberate spiritual practice. This is what karma is, namely the collection of impressions that we have received since beginningless time. The sum total of these impressions exists at the most subtle level of our consciousness. Even when, at death, all of the more superficial levels of consciousness disappear, this most subtle alaya consciousness remains. It exits the body at the moment of death and passes on to a new birth, carrying all of our karma.

It is important not to think of the alaya as a "thing," and here is where the analogy of the storehouse breaks down. All of the five skandhas are momentary, including the eight consciousnesses. One moment of consciousness, with the alaya as its most subtle level, carrying our particular karma, dies. As it does so, it transmits this karmic "load" to the next moment of consciousness. Thus what we call the alaya is really the succession of moments of the most subtle dimension of our consciousness.

How do the eight consciousnesses work together? Let us take the example of seeing an orange. In the first moment of perception, our eye organ senses the orange, and this is registered by our visual consciousness.

MOMENT 1: visual object (orange) → eye organ → visual consciousness

In the next moment, the sixth consciousness, the mental consciousness, perceives the datum of the visual consciousness (the mental object).

MOMENT 2: mental object → mind organ → mental consciousness

In the next moment, various evaluations and concepts are added onto the bare perception of the visual object. Here we identify the perception as an orange, and this brings with it all of our accumulated, habitual judgments. In this process, the alaya supplies various recognitions, locations, and associations from its karmic reservoir, while the seventh consciousness supplies the notion of personal ownership of the now identified perception.

The unconditioned dharma of nirvana is outside of the five-skandha system. When one attains the dharma of nirvana, one has identified with a dimension of awareness that is beyond causes and conditions. When this occurs, the five skandhas as components of ego cease, and one attains what is known as cessation (nirodha), the third noble truth.

THE TWELVE NIDANAS

Other important ways of organizing the dharmas divide them into the twelve *ayatanas* (sense organs and sense fields), the eighteen dhatus (sense organs, sense fields, and consciousnesses), the twelve *nidanas,* or links in the chain of conditioned coproduction, and the scheme of the seventy-five (or one hundred) dharmas, mentioned above. Like the scheme of the five skandhas, these other arrangements all converge at the same point, so that when we look closely at our experience, we find a never-ending cascade of sensations, perceptions, feelings, thoughts, and so on, all arising in accordance with karma, wherein no "I" or self is ever found. To realize that this is all we are is, again, to attain nirvana, realization at the Hinayana level of the path.

One of the most important groupings of dharmas in the Abhidharma is that of the twelve nidanas, which illustrate the principle of conditioned coproduction in a particularly vivid way. The twelve nidanas are particularly helpful because they show in a clear and unmistakable manner how karma works, illustrating how our current situation is the result of past actions and how our present actions will determine our future circumstances. The stream of dharmas that makes up the experience of each individual is unique and reflects the particular karma of that person. Actions that we take in the present affect the arising or non-arising of dharmas in the future. In that way, we can influence the direction of our lives. The twelve nidanas also address the all-important question of "free will," indicating where, from the Buddhist point of view, our lives are determined and unfree, and just where human freedom can be found. Finally, they show how past, present, and future are karmically linked to one another.

The importance of the twelve nidanas appears in its central place in the Buddha's life. When Shakyamuni attained enlightenment beneath the bodhi tree at Bodhgaya, we are told that he did so by seeing the twelve nidanas. When the Buddha saw the twelve nidanas, he understood how everything that arises does so based on karma. He saw that there is no "self" to be found anywhere. At that moment, he attained enlightenment.

Whatever happiness or unhappiness arises, whatever pleasurable or painful circumstance occurs, it does so in accordance with the unfolding of karma, as the result of the ripening of the totality of the past. The operation of karma occurs even at the most subtle and seemingly insubstantial levels of our lives. Every thought that arises, every perception that happens, every feeling and emotion that we experience, all happen as the inevitable and unavoidable results of the totality of past karma. Within this framework, there is no independent, substantial "I" to be found.

From this point of view, the extensive domain of free will that we human beings think we have is an illusion. If I walk into an ice-cream store and see endless rows of flavors to choose from, it is only an illusion that, in selecting one of them, I am making a free choice. In fact, it is my own physical, emotional, and intellectual predispositions that lead me to pick the flavor that I do. If I am aware of the doctrine of karma and decide to flout it by choosing a flavor that I do not like, I am still within the grip of karma, being driven as I am by my anger, resentment, and opposition to the idea that I am not free in my choice.

The twelve nidanas describe the process of birth and rebirth, illustrating how our past life has given rise to our present existence, and how this life will lead to a future rebirth (see figure 14.1; see also commentary on imagery on pages 387–88).

Past Existence

The first two nidanas refer to the life immediately preceding this one and show what part of our past life is pertinent to the present one. They illustrate the fact that it is not possible to have a present without a closely supporting past existence. They answer the question, "What part of the

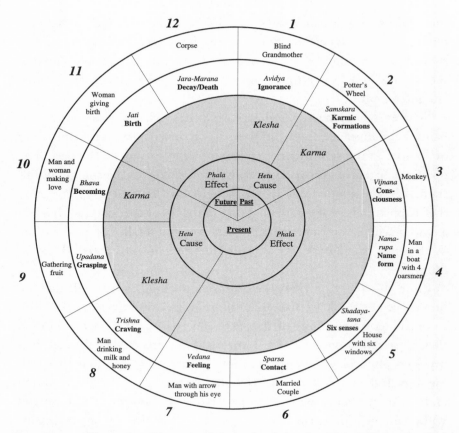

12 — Corpse — Jara-Marana **Decay/Death**
1 — Blind Grandmother — Avidya **Ignorance**
2 — Potter's Wheel — Samskara **Karmic Formations**
3 — Monkey — Vijnana **Cons-ciousness**
4 — Man in a boat with 4 oarsmen — Nama-rupa **Name form**
5 — House with six windows — Shadaya-tana **Six senses**
6 — Married Couple — Sparsa **Contact**
7 — Man with arrow through his eye — Vedana **Feeling**
8 — Man drinking milk and honey — Trishna **Craving**
9 — Gathering fruit — Upadana **Grasping**
10 — Man and woman making love — Bhava **Becoming**
11 — Woman giving birth — Jati **Birth**

Klesha — *Karma* — *Phala* **Effect** — *Hetu* **Cause** — **Future** **Past** — **Present** — *Hetu* **Cause** — *Phala* **Effect** — *Karma* — *Klesha*

FIGURE 14.1 *The twelve nidanas, or links in the chain of conditioned coproduction.*

past life participates actively in the present? They show the foundation laid by the past life, upon which the present existence can stand.

1. *Ignorance (avidya).* According to the classic *Gateway to Knowledge,* by the great Nyingma scholar Jamgön Mipham Rinpoche (1848–1912), ignorance refers to not knowing the four noble truths and to taking the impersonal rise and fall of the skandhas to be a solid and enduring self.[5] Our present life depends upon our having maintained this ignorance in our past life. The fact of our failing to realize our own nonexistence in our past lifetime has provided the necessary ground for this present life to arise.

378

2. *Karmic formations (samskara).* Each samsaric being shares the same ignorance, but we differ in terms of the particular bundle of karma that we carry around. Actions based on passion, aggression, and delusion that we committed in the past have left a karmic imprint on our consciousness that will express itself sooner or later. Put in traditional terms, those actions have sown karmic seeds in our alaya, or deepest consciousness, that will ripen and become manifest at some point in the future. These imprints or seeds are karmic formations. Mipham Rinpoche says, "[Karmic] formation therefore means that seeds of reincarnation are being planted in the consciousness."[6] Karmic formations in conjunction with ignorance from our past lifetime, then, give birth to our present existence.

Ignorance is classified as klesha, or "defilement," because it is the driving force that in the last life produced new karma. Karmic formations are considered "karma" because they are the results of the karma creation of the previous life. Both klesha and karma are considered *hetu,* or "cause," because they both function as causes in giving birth to the present lifetime. (See figure 14.1.)

Present Existence

The nidanas of the present, links three through ten, are divided into two groups. The first group, nidanas three through seven, are called karmic result; the second, links eight through ten, are known as karma-producing. The karmic-result nidanas are those aspects of our present situation that occur as the automatic fruition of past actions and occur with necessity.

KARMIC RESULT (PHALA, "EFFECT")

3. *Rebirth consciousness (vijnana).* Karmic formations, resting on ignorance, in Mipham's words "give rise to the consciousness which goes to the birthplace of the next existence."[7] Mipham Rinpoche divides consciousness into two aspects: "The seed placed in the [*alaya*] consciousness which propels one to the [next] rebirth is called impelling consciousness,

and that which leads to the birthplace of that life once the conditions have come together is called the consciousness of the impelled result. Both of these are in fact one, in terms of being the link consciousness that establishes a rebirth."[8]

4. *Name and form* (*nama-rupa*). In order for conception to occur, three causes must come together: the woman must be in her season; male and female must unite; and there must be a consciousness seeking rebirth in the kind of karmic situation provided by the potential mother and father. If these conditions are present, the male substance (sperm) and the female substance (ovum) join, and the consciousness enters to produce an embryo. This is explained as the arising of the five skandhas: *rupa* (form) and the four nonmaterial skandhas (*nama,* or name: feeling, perception, karmic formations, and consciousness). In the traditional terms, it is said that the consciousness conjoins with the male and female substances and is joined by the other three nonmaterial skandhas. Mipham Rinpoche says that these five "constitute the body of that existence by means of mutually supporting each other, as in the case of the roof-beams of a house."[9] Now the new being has the basic psychophysical structure necessary to a human existence.

5. *The six sense organs* (*shad-ayatana*). Mipham Rinpoche says, "Following that, when the period of name-and-form has been fully completed, the inner six sources of the eye and so forth arise."[10] The five skandhas, then, give birth to a further system of "wiring," that of the six sense organs, which receive impressions from sense objects. These include the material sense organs of eye, ear, nose, tongue, and body, and the mental sense organ, mind. Now the rebirth consciousness has the infrastructure needed to begin to experience things.

6. *Contact* (*sparsha*). With the complete psychophysical infrastructure in place, the next stage of karmic unfoldment is contact, the meeting of each sense organ with its corresponding sense object. In terms of the physical senses, the eye has contact with visible objects, the ear with sounds, the nose with scents, the tongue with tastes, and the body with touchable objects. The mental sense, the mind or receptive conscious-

ness, now has contact with mental contents such as thoughts, mental images, feelings, and complex emotions. Each meeting of sense organ with sense object is registered or cognized by a corresponding consciousness. For example, the eye perceives a visual object and this is registered by the eye consciousness. Again, the datum of the eye consciousness itself becomes an object for the mind organ that is registered by the mind consciousness. The six sense organs, six sense objects, and six sense consciousnesses are known in the Abhidharma as the eighteen *dhatus,* or aspects.* In Mipham Rinpoche's words: "Thereafter the objects, sense faculties and consciousnesses will meet together and the six contacts will arise, such as perception through the contact of the form of an object meeting with the eye. This is the link of contact."[11]

7. *Feeling (vedana).* Contact leads to basic or rudimentary experience, and this is felt as positive (pleasurable), negative (painful), or neutral. Mipham: "From this contact arises the experience of the three aspects of pleasant, painful, or indifferent sensations."[12] It is important to recognize that feeling, as one of the karmic result nidanas, represents the inevitable fruition of past karma. In other words, whether a particular experience is felt as positive, negative, or neutral is choiceless, being determined by the karma that has been accumulated in the past.

The preceding nidanas are all "karmic result" in the sense that they are the natural and unavoidable result of the multiplicity of past causes and conditions that are now coming to fruition. The karmic result nidanas provide the "givenness" of our lives over which we have no control. In this important sense, these nidanas are all morally neutral. This means that whatever arises in our experience, including our own feelings of pleasure or pain, has no particular moral direction essential to it and in and of itself produces no future karma, either good or bad.

---

*The term *dhatu* in Sanskrit has several meanings. As we saw in chapter 1, it may refer to the three realms of existence, as in "the three *dhatus.*" In the present context, dhatu indicates the arenas or fields (*dhatus*) of the object—organ—consciousness triad for each of the six modes of experience (eye, ear, nose, tongue, body, mind). In a third meaning, also found in Buddhism, *dhatu* can indicate one's physical makeup, constitution, or general state of being.

In some ways, this teaching runs counter to habitual ways of thinking common in the modern West. For example, many people feel that if a particular negatively charged thought or emotion appears in their minds, something morally bad is happening. They feel that, in experiencing pain, they must be guilty of some offense and generating negative karma. Buddhism replies that while present pain is the result of previous negative action, its appearance at this moment is neutral and in and of itself generates no future karma. The karmic implications of past karma ripening in the present depend entirely on how we respond to it.

KARMA-PRODUCING (HETU, "CAUSE")

Karma is produced only in nidanas eight through ten. It is true that we have no control over the ripening of past karma in the present moment. This does considerably limit the scope of human freedom. However, the next three nidanas make it clear that the Buddhism doctrine of causality is far from fatalism, and in fact insists on the reality and critical importance of the freedom that we do have.

8. *Thirst* (*trishna*). How do we respond to the positive and negative feelings that occur in our lives? Typically, we become immediately embroiled in "thirst." We thirst to pull the positive toward us and possess it, making it part of our personal territory; and we thirst to drive away the negative and keep it far from us, outside of our ego domain. This is ego's attempt to further fortify and aggrandize itself. Thirst is impulse that is acceded to. It involves the complicity of ego. In thirst, we experience an impulse and we say yes to it, we go along with it. We deliberately jump into a pool of wanting, hankering, desiring, hungering, craving, coveting, lusting. Thirst is not something that is given in our experience, in the givenness that we experience in *nidanas* three through seven. It is something that we intentionally manufacture based on self-serving motivations of ego aggrandizement. The movement into thirst involves the generation of new karma. Mipham Rinpoche explains:

> Based on sensation arises the eager craving of desiring not to be separated from a pleasant sensation, the fearful craving of desir-

ing to cast away an unpleasant sensation, and a self-sufficient abiding in regards to indifferent sensations. Thus arises a craving towards the six objects [of the six senses], from forms to mental objects. In short, the link of craving is to experience the taste of the objects caused by sensation, and to draw in these objects because of taking delight in clinging to them.[13]

9. *Grasping (upadana)*. Thirst is a state of mind and does not yet involve any activity. Once we have concocted our "thirst," we move very quickly to the next nidana, grasping. The attempt to grasp involves the effort of putting our thirst into action. Either we try to grab onto that which we feel is positive or we try to ward off that which we feel is negative. While thirst is mental, grasping usually involves either the body, in the case of physical actions, or speech, in the case of verbal actions. As the attempt to actualize our thirst, grasping involves further intentional, self-serving activity and generates further karma. Mipham Rinpoche provides the traditional explanation: "This craving greatly increases the eager craving of [thinking] "May I not be separated from what is beautiful and pleasant!" Hence the actual involvement in fervently grasping for objects is the link of grasping."[14] As Mipham Rinpoche remarks, four classes of objects are said to be the objects of grasping: the objects of sense desire (the objects of the five sense organs), views or beliefs about reality (the objects of the mind organ); clinging to rituals or disciplines (the grasping of the religious fanatic); and the idea of a self.[15]

10. *Being (bhava)*. The tenth nidana brings the process of the generation of new karma to its culmination. Based on our grasping, we arrive at the point of a seemingly solid self. It does not matter whether or not we have been able to possess the object of our grasping. If we have managed to possess it, we conceive of ourselves as one who has gained that particular object. If we have been unsuccessful, then we think of ourselves as one who has not gained that particular thing. In either case, the belief in a solid self has now reached its culmination and fruition. Once this point is reached, all the seeds have been planted for a future lifetime.

Within the framework of nidanas eight through ten, thirst and grasping are classified as kleshas because they involve explicitly intentional activity that produces karma. Being, although an integral part of the process of creating new karma, is considered karma—that is, karmic result—because it comes about as a result of the activity of thirst and grasping.

Nidanas eight, nine, and ten thus involve activity that produces further karma. For most of us, the activity of these nidanas involves manipulating, ignoring, and harming others. This produces negative karma and will lead to future suffering for us, either rebirth in a lower realm or at least increased suffering as a human being. The precise degree of negative karma we produce depends on the degree of passion, aggression, or delusion in our actions and on the negative impact on others.

At the same time, we can engage in nidanas eight through ten in a way that produces positive instead of negative karma. How does this occur? Perhaps we are disgusted by our own self-serving actions, feel some sympathy for others, and are afraid of the negative karma that we have been accumulating. Suppose that we identify some worthy person that we could help, perhaps someone who is poor or ill, and suppose we help them in some way. This will produce positive karma. It is important to realize that this process is not without ego and does involve nidanas eight through ten. We experience pain because of who we are, and we are afraid of our own future pain, so we give something. Here we are thirsting to attain better karmic circumstances (nidana number eight), we put this thirst into action by our help (nidana number nine, grasping), and we end up feeling some satisfaction in what we did, thinking of ourselves as a person who has helped someone else and who, in the process, has improved his or her karmic lot (nidana number ten, being).

The karma thus created is positive because, as the action was meritorious, it sowed the seeds for our own future happiness and well-being, material and psychological as well as spiritual. Trungpa Rinpoche comments that, although meritorious and demeritorious actions are similar in that both produce karma, they differ in the solidity of the egocentricity they involve. Demeritorious actions, which generate negative karma, proceed from a strong belief in the separateness of one's "self" and in the legitimacy of aggrandizing oneself at the expense of others. Demeritorious actions thus imply a solid and self-absorbed ego. In this case, the buddha-nature within is more or less completely occluded. By contrast, meritorious actions, which generate positive karma, have a much less solid and walled-off sense of "I." In fact, by acknowledging one's interconnectedness with others and one's moral obligation to respond to their needs, meritorious actions imply an ego that is relatively lighter and less occluded than that of a completely self-centered person. We might say that such actions reflect an ego that is more or less transparent to the unconditioned, selfless buddha-nature within. This is a transparency to qualities such as selfless love and compassion that are evident though not entirely without the taint of ego, as the individual has not attained realization.[16] Meritorious actions thus manifest a moment when we are closer to enlightenment and sowing seeds to generate conditions enabling us to advance further in that direction.

The preceding raises an important question: are we as human beings condemned to move from the karmic-result nidanas, three through seven, to the karma-producing nidanas, eight through ten? Must we always be engaged in creating karma, whether negative or positive? The answer is no. Between nidanas seven and eight, there is a gap in the process of ego. Between feeling, the final karmic-result nidana, and thirst, the first karma-producing nidana, there is an open space. There is no inevitability here and no predetermination. Here is the point at which we have freedom. Whether one takes the next step to thirst really is a matter of choice, though it is a step we habitually take without acknowledging that choice was present. Why do we do so? Because it is more comfortable and less painful, more robust and fortifying to our sense of ego, to ignore the gap. Like the Pied Piper's rats, it is easier to run with the pack, on to nidanas eight, nine, and ten.

It is, then, possible for us to rest in the open space after feeling and before thirst. In other words, we can stay with our pleasure and pain, without trying to do anything about it. However, the gap between feeling and thirst is a fleeting one and it is generally most difficult for us to see this place, much less to be able to rest in it. For this reason, we need a method to enable us to take advantage of this openness in our own state of mind, to find it and rest in it. This is the purpose of meditation. If we learn to be increasingly present to our own experience through mindfulness and through developing insight into the process of our own experience, our rampant discursiveness begins to slow down. As it does so, we begin to see our impermanent experience as it comes into being and disappears. And we begin to become aware of the nidanas and how one link leads to the next.

In particular, through this process, we begin to notice the gap between feeling and thirst. We begin to see that phenomena arise in our state of being (nidanas three through seven). They appear as the givenness of our experience at each moment. Moreover, we see that there is an additional movement on our part—and one that is neither inevitable nor necessary—when we go from this givenness to the activities of thirst, grasping, and being. This, in turn, shows us the possibility of resting with the bare givenness of our experience (the karmic-result nidanas up through feeling) and of resisting the temptation to manipulate our experience through thirst, grasping, and being. In fact, it may be said that the entire Tibetan Buddhist path, including the Hinayana, the Mahayana, and the Vajrayana, consists in nothing more nor less than learning to rest in the gap between feeling and thirst, ever more deeply and subtly, and in learning to see the implications of this resting for the way in which we live our lives.

One may ask: Is it possible to engage in thirst and not proceed to grasping and being, or to engage in grasping and not proceed to being? Buddhism holds that it is possible to stop the karmic process at feeling, the culmination of the process of karmic result. However, once we have taken the step to thirst, our process moves inevitably to grasping and being, and then on to a new rebirth.

Future Existence

If we ignore the opportunity provided by the gap between nidanas seven and eight and instead rush on to thirst, then—our investment in the option of manipulation having been made and confirmed—we will be impelled to grasping and being, with no further opportunities to step out of ego's game. In this case, we will then move from bhava, the last nidana of the present life, to a new lifetime epitomized by nidana eleven, birth, and twelve, old age and death.

11. *Rebirth (jati)*. If we do not rest in the gap between feeling and thirst but continue on to being, then all of the karma has been created for rebirth, and the inevitable result will be a new lifetime. Mipham: "By the power of this becoming [or being], once the conditions have assembled, the link of rebirth is to first actualize the rebirth in the birth-place of that reincarnation, to fully develop a body and to remain as one's similar class. It is the basis for experiencing all kinds of suffering through that [bodily] support."[17]

12. *Old age and death (jara-marana)*. Birth is inevitably followed by old age and death. Mipham again: "From rebirth comes aging, which is the change in the continuity of the aggregates [the five skandhas], and death, which is the ceasing of that continuity."[18] He continues:

> Illustrated thereby, from this arises the sorrow which is inner anguish, the lamentation uttered therefrom, the misery which accompanies the five sense consciousnesses, and the unhappiness which accompanies the mind consciousness. In addition arises distress caused by the unpleasant subsidiary disturbing emotions. In short, this great mass of total suffering results from rebirth within samsara.[19]

The future lifetime is summarized in birth followed by old age and death to show clearly that, if we do not succeed in arresting the nidana process between nidanas seven and eight, we will be condemned to a new cycle of samsaric existence, with all of its suffering.

As a further aspect of the teachings on the twelve nidanas, Tibetan tradition has assigned images to each. The purpose of these images is twofold: first, they clarify the meaning of each nidana; second, they give popularized form to the nidana teachings by being included as the outer rim of the well-known "wheel of life" depictions (figure 14.2). This is perhaps the single most frequently appearing image in Tibetan Buddhism, found on monastery gates, in thangkas, in frescoes, and so on. Thus [1] the blind grandmother represents ignorance, the stubborn blindness of the previous generation to anything new; [2] the potter's wheel, the blind momentum of karma; [3] the monkey, the active and atavistic intelligence of the rebirth consciousness; [4] the man, as consciousness, the four oarsmen as the other four skandhas; [5] the house with six windows as the six senses that provide access to the objective world; [6] the married couple, the coming together of the two poles of sense and sense objects; [7] the man with an arrow through his eye, the penetrating quality of feeling; [8] the man drinking milk and honey, the craving and "thirst" with which we respond to feeling; [9] the gathering of fruit, the action of attempting to possess the objects of our desire; [10] the man and woman making love, the result of thirst and grasping, namely the new creation of karma; [11] the woman giving birth; and [12] the corpse, aging and death.

Mipham Rinpoche comments that if one understands and accepts the process of the nidanas, ignorance will be eliminated and one "will be confirmed in unexcelled enlightenment by all the buddhas." He concludes that it is thus that

> these twelve aspects of interdependence will continuously evolve for as long as ignorance has not been relinquished. The past causes, ignorance and formation, make the present consciousness that is the impelled result appear, and the following links, down to the disturbing emotions craving and grasping, gather the karma that produces a rebirth. Thus, up to becoming [being], eight evolve. Continuing therefrom, there is the taking of birth in the realm corresponding to one's karma and through that [bodily] support one will undergo the samsaric suffering of aging, dying and so forth.[20]

CONCLUSION

Looking back over this teaching, one notices that the different nidanas are not all equivalent in status or function. The past existence, the pres-

FIGURE 14.2 *The "wheel of life" with its depiction of
the six realms of samsaric existence.*

ent lifetime, and the future birth are all essentially the same in being complete lifetimes. However, they are expressed differently in the nidana system in accordance with their status as past, present, and future. For example, the first two nidanas, ignorance and karmic formations, represent a complete lifetime, as that lifetime occurred in the past and as it is viewed from the vantage point of the present. When that lifetime was a present lifetime, it would have been described in terms of eight nidanas, namely three through ten. When that same past lifetime still stood in the future as a future birth, it would have been best described by nidanas eleven and twelve.

Within the karmic-result nidanas, there are also some important differences. Consciousness, name, and form, and the six senses develop in the embryo at the very beginning, setting in place the structure of possible human experience. This development obviously happens once in each lifetime. However, contact and feeling happen over and over throughout our lives, in every moment. The karmic-producing nidanas, numbers eight through ten, also happen in each moment. Each new moment of our lives, there is ripening of previous karma and, in ordinary samsaric existence, a new jump to craving, grasping, and being. Each time we proceed through nidanas eight, nine, and ten, we are sowing the seeds for a future rebirth.

I have presented the nidanas as if they were strictly sequential, and in the Sarvastivada Abhidharma, there is an emphasis on linear causality. However, in their Mahayana interpretation, they are read not only as sequential but also simultaneous. In one sense, as we have seen, they describe the way in which one element (or dharma) in our experience leads to another. Ignorance and karmic formations lead to consciousness and so on. But in another sense, they describe twelve elements that occur simultaneously, mutually conditioning one another. Ignorance and samskara remain, in some sense conditioning the other links in the chain. Again, when we focus on rebirth consciousness, we must see that it is supported not only by ignorance and karmic formations, but by the seeds of nidanas four through twelve that lie as potencies and possibilities within it. While the Abhidharma interpretation of the nidanas is primarily in terms of sequential, linear causality, the simultaneous interpretation is implicit within it, later to be exploited by the great Madhyamaka master Nagarjuna.

Thus the first turning of the wheel of dharma, addressed to the Buddha's first shravaka disciples, articulates the view of Hinayana, as found in the Abhidharma. Within the perspective of the first turning, the goal of spiritual practice is to realize the nonexistence of the "I" or self. Through study and meditation, one sees experience as a stream of momentary events, the dharmas, which follow one another in accordance with one's karma. Through realizing that what had been labeled a self is nothing more than the arising and ceasing of dharmas, one realizes one's own nonexistence. This realization removes the need to defend and aggrandize the nonexistent self. There is no longer a basis for thirst to feed this illusion. With the removal of thirst, suffering ceases and one attains personal liberation or nirvana. Within the Tibetan three-yana path, the teachings of the first turning of the wheel of dharma are only, as mentioned, the first stage on the path to ultimate liberation. Tibetans understand the Hinayana recognition of the absence of a personal "self," the "onefold egolessness" discussed above, as limited because it continues to see the individual dharmas that make up the self as existent. It is the contribution of the second turning of the wheel of dharma, presently to be examined, to point out that even the dharmas are without coherent self. This points toward the realization of "twofold egolessness," in which not only the individual self but all dharmas whatsoever are without substantial being. Nevertheless, although the Hinayana attainment is limited in this way, the goal articulated in the first turning is noble and profound.

15

The Second Turning
MADHYAMAKA

SOMETIME AFTER PRESENTING THE FIRST TURNING OF
the wheel of dharma, the Buddha promulgated the second turning. According to Dudjom Rinpoche, in the second turning,

> In places such as Vulture Peak near Rajagrha and chiefly to the
> communities of bodhisattvas, [the Buddha] revealed the *Bodhi-*
> *sattvapitaka* of the greater vehicle, which extensively teaches the
> ineffable, unthinkable, inexpressible reality of just what is,
> whereby all things from form to omniscience are totally di-
> vorced from substantial existence.[1]

The content of the second turning is the nature of ultimate reality, or
emptiness (shunyata). The Buddha's teaching on emptiness is found in
the *Prajnaparamita Sutras,* such as the *Eight-Thousand-Line Prajnapara-*
mita, the *Heart Sutra,* and the *Twenty-five-Thousand Line Prajnapara-*
mita. Thrangu Rinpoche summarizes:

> Later, in Rajgir, in Northern India, Sakyamuni taught the sec-
> ond turning of the wheel of dharma, the teachings on the lack
> of fundamental characteristics. He taught the sixteen modes of
> emptiness: outer appearances are empty; the inner world of
> thoughts is empty; both outer and inner things taken together
> are empty; and so on, in sixteen stages. In doing so he demon-
> strated that not only in the ordinary sense is there no ego, but
> no inherent reality can ever be found in anything, no matter
> where we look.[2]

The teachings on emptiness are given definitive form in the works of a number of important Indian commentators. The most important of these is the sage Nagarjuna (first to second century), who is known in Tibet as the human progenitor of the Mahayana and revered virtually as a second Buddha. Nagarjuna set forth the philosophical articulation of emptiness known as Madhyamaka in texts such as the *Mulamadhyamaka-karika,* or Root Verses on the Middle Way. Other important Madhyamaka masters include Aryadeva, who wrote the *Four Hundred Shlokas on Madhyamaka;* Chandrakirti, who composed the *Madhyamakavatara;* and Shantarakshita, who authored the *Madhyamakalankara.*

The second-turning teachings on emptiness speak about the two levels of selflessness. First is the absence of personal self or ego expounded in the first turning to the shravakas and detailed in the Abhidharma. The self of the individual, the "I" that we think exists, is revealed to be a label attached to a stream of impersonal dharmas; the recognition of this leads to the abatement of thirst and the cessation of suffering. Khenpo Tsultrim Gyamtso explains this in relation to the higher attainments of the Mahayana.

> The goal for the Sravaka is the removal of suffering. That goal is called nirvana. The Sravaka is not trying to remove the suffering of all beings, nor is he trying to attain Buddhahood. He does not have the vision, the understanding, or the confidence necessary to do that. His aim is relatively modest. It is simply to remove the cause of his own suffering. Nonetheless, one cannot say that his realization of emptiness is not very profound. It is said that it corresponds to that of Bodhisattvas on the first to the sixth levels. It removes the veils of ignorance and confusion that make deeper and more subtle levels of emptiness so inaccessible. Therefore, by realizing the not-self emptiness of the skandhas one is preparing for the higher vehicles, whose goal is not just the removing of one's own suffering, but the suffering of all beings.[3]

The Mahayana moves beyond the shravaka's understanding in two ways. First, the Hinayana aspiration is seen as limited, being aimed at the liberation of only oneself. A deeper aspiration for the awakening of all beings needs to be generated. Second, while the ego is fruitfully deconstructed into momentary dharmas, the understanding of dharmas as "real" is problematic. In particular, it sets up a dualism between the conditioned dharmas of samsara and the unconditioned dharma of nirvana. Each of these is reified, and liberation is conceived as the abandonment of samsara and the attainment of nirvana. The Prajnaparamita teaches that in addition to the egolessness of one's own self, one must meditate more deeply and uncover a second level of egolessness, that of the dharmas themselves. All of the dharmas of samsara and nirvana are themselves empty of essential nature. "Samsara" and "nirvana" are nothing more than conceptual labels that are put on a reality that is ineffable and beyond any conceptualization whatsoever. The Prajnaparamita also shows how the egolessness of dharmas and the aspiration to save all beings are connected. In projecting one's own liberation from samsara, one ignores the piteous cries of suffering beings throughout time and space. In realizing that samsara and nirvana are conceptualizations, one realizes that there is nothing to reject and nothing to attain. This realization leaves one aspiring to be nowhere other than where one is, among suffering beings, and this freedom opens a floodgate of compassion for all that live.

THE VIEW OF MADHYAMAKA

The Madhyamaka, the commentarial tradition on the second turning, was founded by Nagarjuna in his explanations and elaborations of the Prajnaparamita teachings. In his biography preserved in Tibetan, Nagarjuna is depicted as a brahman who, in the midst of the political chaos in his homeland, was inspired to give away all of his wealth and become a monk. After much study, he attained mastery of the five major branches of learning then current in India and available in monastic education. His works show him learned in the non-Buddhist philosophical schools of his day, in the various Hinayana philosophies, and in the Prajnaparamita. It was during this monastic phase of his life that he composed the great works that form the root texts of the Indian Madhyamaka tradition. Subsequently, Nagarjuna felt called to intensive meditation, received a vision of the deity Tara, and left the protection and comfort of his monastery to wander forth in search of full realization.

A keynote of Nagarjuna's Madhyamaka orientation is the identification of emptiness, shunyata, with the twelve nidanas and the principle of pratitya-samutpada, or conditioned coproduction. According to Nagarjuna, if we understand conditioned coproduction fully, we will be face-to-face with emptiness. It may be asked, how can Nagarjuna understand this central Hinayana teaching as equivalent to the Mahayana notion of emptiness? It may be recalled that the Sarvastivada Abhidharma interpret the twelve nidanas in terms of sequential, linear causality, which supports its "realistic" interpretation of the dharmas as being freestanding entities, each with its own "essential nature." At the same time, as noted, a more "simultaneous" interpretation is implicit within the nidana teachings.

Nagarjuna critiqued the Abhidharmic interpretation of the twelve nidanas as underplaying their important and, from his viewpoint, critical relational dimension. In fact, each nidana only has existence and meaning in relation to and in mutual dependence upon the others. Feeling makes no sense apart from a body-mind apparatus in which it appears. Rebirth consciousness has no meaning apart from ignorance. To give a mundane example, categories like hot and cold are relative. What is hot for a summer day is cold for a stovetop. What is hot in Iceland may be cold in equatorial South America. What is tall among Pygmy people is short among Watusi. Male and female only make sense in relation to one another. For Nagarjuna, the Abhidharmic idea that each nidana, as a dharma, is an entity with a definite and independent "essence" is incorrect. The deeper truth is relational: no single nidana has any nature that stands independent from the web of relationships in which it is appearing. Rather, that nidana is the effect of the entire realm of being with which it is causally connected. And this totality, which alone is what this nidana is, can never be put into thought or words. It is thoroughly and profoundly "empty" of individual self-nature, of conceptual attribution. Thus the naught and the plenitude of emptiness.

Later Madhyamaka luminaries were similarly monks who advanced these "middle way" teachings in ways appropriate to their day. Some, like their master, eventually retired from their scholarly, monastic careers to pursue meditation and realization in retreat. Thus the Madhyamaka, like the Abhidharma, developed primarily within the settled monastic culture of India. And, like the Abhidharma, it arose in response to the need to provide systematic and scholarly explanations of buddha-word, this time the Prajnaparamita. As in the Abhidharma, one finds in the Madhyamaka treatises evidence of a broad and multifaceted background of learning in contemporary Indian philosophical schools, both Buddhist and non-Buddhist.

After Nagarjuna, the Madhyamaka developed into a number of different schools. Buddhapalita (fifth to sixth century) is seen as father of the Prasangika Madhyamaka, while Bhavaviveka (sixth century) is credited with founding the Svatantrika Madhyamaka. Chandrakirti (seventh century), through his critique of Bhavaviveka, definitively established the supremacy of Prasangika in his *Prasannapada* and *Madhyamakavatara*. Shantideva (eighth century), also understood as a Madhyamikan, gave teachings on the six perfections in his famous *Bodhicharyavatara,* including a ninth chapter, on emptiness, that is widely famed in Tibet. Later masters, notably Shantarakshita and Kamalashila, developed the Yogachara-Madhyamaka, a synthesis of those two schools. The Madhyamaka teachings came to Tibet in two waves: Shantarakshita and Kamalashila brought the synthetic Yogachara-Madhyamaka from India in the eighth century, and Atisha, trained in the Madhyamaka in Suvarnadvipa (Sumatra) by the master Dharmakirti, brought a new infusion in the eleventh century. Although all four Tibetan schools follow the Madhyamaka teachings, the Gelukpas and the Sakyapas have particularly championed the unrivaled ascendancy of Madhyamaka among Mahayana views.

From the Tibetan point of view, the most important and profound Madhyamaka school is that of the Prasangika. Most of the great Madhyamaka masters and scholars of the Geluk, Sakya, Kagyü, and Nyingma considered themselves followers of the Prasangika school of Nagarjuna, Buddhapalita, Chandrakirti, and Shantideva. In this discussion, we take them as epitomizing the heart of Madhyamaka.

The Prasangikas argue that any philosophical tradition that attempts to conceptualize the ultimate is deficient. They criticize not only non-Buddhist schools for this fault but also the Hinayana Abhidharma and the Madhyamaka Svatantrika. They point out that if we look closely at the way in which the rational, conceptual mind works, we can see that it is completely inadequate to provide us with a demonstration, explanation, or proof of the ultimate. Unlike the Prajnaparamita, wherein meditation is the primary vehicle to realization of ultimacy, the Prasangika Madhyamaka, reflecting its urbane, settled monastic culture, advocates the use of reason. Nevertheless, reason is not to be used to prove anything. Rather, through a self-reflexive process of deeper and deeper questioning, reason comes face-to-face with its own limitations. Very much like the Zen koan, but in a different style, the Prasangika brings the conceptual mind to such an intensity of self-contradiction that it ceases. And when this mind ceases, reality hoves into view.

Khenpo Rinpoche comments about the Prasangika method:

> They are adamant in not positing anything either positive or negative. Some argue that this is a dishonest view in the sense that one is simply side-stepping issues and refusing to allow opponents to refute one's views. However, there is something very profound in this method. It is quite uncompromising in its systematic refutation of all conceptual attempts to grasp the nature of the absolute. The original Prasangikas in India and Tibet did not assert anything about the relative appearance of phenomena either. They considered the nature of this also to be beyond even the most subtle concepts of existence, non-existence, etc.[4]

The Prasangika, then, follows the teachings of Prajnaparamita that all the dharmas of samsara and nirvana are empty of essence, devoid of a self-nature. This means that the normal activity of conceptual mind, which attributes qualities and characteristics to all experience, whether worldly or supermundane, misses the truth. This feature of the Prasangika cuts through the tendency to separate ultimate truth from the actual nature of relativity. The fact is that from the beginning, the relative world presents itself as empty of essence. To see the truth of relativity is to see the ultimate. To see samsara as it truly is, is to see its emptiness, which is itself a realization of the ultimate. The same is true of nirvana. The truth is that all experience, whether labeled samsara or nirvana, conditioned or unconditioned, is ineffable, beyond the reach of language. Khenpo Rinpoche explains:

> This amounts to a complete destruction of all conceptual views, leaving one with no alternative [other] than a non-conceptual view of the nature of reality. The aim of the Prasangika is to silence completely the conceptual mind, allowing the mind to rest in absolute freedom from concepts. Absolute freedom from concepts is what Prasangikas call emptiness. . . . Finally, therefore, the Prasangikas are not saying anything about the ultimate nature of reality or of emptiness. That is not the aim of their system. Their aim is to free the awareness of its conceptualizing habit and to let the ultimate nature of reality reveal itself in a totally non-conceptual way. It is a very powerful system in that it gives the conceptual mind nothing to grasp onto at all.[5]

THE PRACTICE OF MADHYAMAKA

The actual method of the Madhyamaka uses philosophical exposition, critique, and debate to bring the mind to its own nemesis. In his useful book *Open Door to Emptiness,* Thrangu Rinpoche summarizes a section of Mipham Rinpoche's *Gateway to Knowledge* on the "four skills of Madhyamaka" to illustrate the way in which the Madhyamaka method is applied.[6] These four skills include arguments that span the Indian Madhyamaka tradition but converge in their intention to render the conceptualizing mind inoperative. Each of the skills takes up a different area of conceptual thinking and explores it in depth. Thus the first skill examines our attribution of an origin or a source to things; the second, our thinking about results; the third, our conceptualizing essential nature; and the fourth our using these three habitual ways of thinking together. But although each of the four skills begins from a different starting point, they all arrive at the same destination, namely a view of the relational and finally empty nature of any and every phenomenon. Let us look briefly at these "four skills" in order to get a taste of the Madhyamaka method in action.

The Tiny Vajra

The argument of the "tiny vajra," or "little diamond," was developed by Chandrakirti. It approaches the reifying mind by examining the way in which we habitually conceptualize the *sources* of phenomena, the origins from which they arise. It is true that when we think about things, the concept of their "source" or "origin" is generally central. It certainly seems as if particular phenomena come from particular sources. When we plant a seed, that seed will give birth to a plant. But when we take any existent thing, is it possible to find a single definitive source for it? When we look closely, does the concept of a source, birth, or origin of things really make sense? Chandrakirti suggests four possible angles we could take in looking for a source. Something could be the source if the result derives from something identical with itself; from something entirely different from itself; from both itself and something other than itself; and from neither.

1. Something does not arise from itself or from something identical with itself. A seed does not directly produce another seed. It is followed by a seedling, then a plant, then a plant in flower, and eventually a plant with seeds. A source and its result cannot be identical.

2. Do things arise from something entirely different and distinct from themselves? In ordinary experience, a particular thing does seem to be produced by a specific other thing. Yet, when we examine closely, this conventional way of thinking cannot stand up. Three arguments are put forward to refute this possibility.
   a) Certainly, the seed seems completely different from the plant. But for things to have a relationship of otherness or difference, it is

necessary for them to exist at the same time in order to be in relation with one another. Yet the source invariably disappears prior to the arising of the result. The seed is destroyed in the process through which the result comes to be. Since the source and the result do not occupy the same time, logically speaking they cannot really be compared with one another, and a relationship of total separateness cannot be established. The result occurs after the cause, placing it in some kind of karmic relation with the cause, and the result is also in proximity with it, again indicating some kind of close relationship.

b) It may be thought that there is some kind of purposiveness in the source that carries over into the result, making it happen. Thus, while the source may disappear prior to the result, its inner causal potency may inevitably express itself in the result and thus it may be designated as "the cause." However, in the example of the seed and the plant, the plant is very different from the seed and has come about, not just because of the seed, but because of a multitude of causes and conditions. One does need good seed, but in order for the plant to result, there must be someone to plant the seed, fertile soil in which to plant it, the right temperature, the appropriate balance of sunshine, fresh air, and rain, and so on. Thus there is nothing inevitable flowing from the seed to the plant, such that the seed would become "the source." The seed is thus not "the cause" of the plant, but one of many factors that collaborate to produce a situation in which the plant occurs.

c) Finally, someone might argue that our experience suggests that, as the source disappears, it immediately produces a result, that this then becomes another source producing another result and so on in linear fashion. But the fact is that this is not how our experience works. If we look closely, we see that things always arise out of a complex past situation, and we can never be certain what the outcome of any present situation will be. We often have the experience of thinking that we know the cause of something, perhaps some kind of interpersonal disagreement or problem. After talking with one person, we may have a pretty good idea of the problem and its origin. At this point, we may well have a fairly linear understanding of the causal pattern. But, the more we talk to those involved, the more our idea of *the* source of the problem begins to change and we begin to see a much greater range of causal factors involved in the picture. If we go far enough with this process, we encounter the universe in all of its infinite multiplicity, its mystery, and its karmic inevitability.

3 and 4. The remaining two options—that something arises from a source that is both the same and different from itself and that it arises from neither—are more easily disposed of. A thing does not arise from a source that is both the same and different from itself, because each of these individual options has been previously refuted. Putting them together thus achieves nothing. And we can easily see that things do not arise from no source whatever. There is clearly some regularity in the way in which things work in the world. There is some kind of relation of seed with plant, although it is not a simple, substantial, and linear connection. Seeds do not produce rocks or iron.

Thus we cannot point to anything as a source of anything else. This discovery has a profound impact on the way in which we think about and interact with the world. For example, suppose someone insults me. Initially I will think, "That person said a nasty thing to me; he did it out of his jealousy, competitiveness, and aggression. I do not like him." Having determined the source of my hurt feelings, I may then begin to strategize how to get back at this person or be ready for him the next time he tries anything. I may maintain this way of thinking for hours, days, or even longer. Sometimes an unkind remark can stay with us for years and form part of our regular mental inventory.

But suppose we really begin to look closely at what we think is the source of our pain, this other person. The more we look, the more discoveries we are likely to make. For example, we may begin to see the pain this person is in. We may acquire some understanding of what he is dealing with, how hard he tries to work his life out, and the many obstacles he feels. We may further remember past interactions where we have been unkind or unfair with this person, something that we had completely blocked. At this point, we begin to see his insult partially as a response to the way we have been behaving toward him, perhaps for a long time. We may begin to feel that actually his insult was a justified response to our own behavior and we may end up feeling that we are primarily responsible for the situation. As our understanding grows, the anger we feel begins to dissipate, and we start to feel sympathy for our "enemy." We may even come to a place of seeing his good intentions: we may begin to recognize in his insult an attempt—albeit unconsciously driven—to open up some kind of communication with us and resolve bad feelings. All this, from looking deeply at our habitual way of trying to pin down a source in any situation and from realizing that that kind of thinking is purely a function of ego's attempt to secure itself and its world, to make things simple, solid, linear, and controllable.

Thrangu Rinpoche summarizes: "We have now refuted the four possible modes of arising of phenomena: from self or from something of identical nature; from other; from both self and other; and from neither self nor other, that is, causeless arising."[7] Thus we cannot locate an origin or a source of anything. Any concept we may give to the notion of "source" is merely a selection, from the plenum, of one factor as the responsible party in the present situation. This may be our stubbornly held idea of the arising of a phenomenon, but it is an idea that does not accord with reality. Even if we select a few sources, we are still caught in our own game. Only when we realize that it does not make any sense to talk about a source of phenomena, that things arise without coming from any particular place or origin, that they are born from the totality about which nothing can be said, are we beginning to sense emptiness.

If we cannot locate any actual source for something, then we cannot talk about its having been born. Why? Because the concept of birth implies being born from something else. Something cannot arise out of nothing. Yet that is our situation, because we cannot locate any "thing" that anything has been born from. Since no source or origin can be identified, we cannot talk about birth. Thrangu Rinpoche concludes:

> We can thus see that there is no way for anything to arise; nonetheless, things continue to appear. That is, in the common mode of experience, things unceasingly arise in a functional and structured relationship with a basic source, conditions which are necessary for that source to come to fruition, and so on. If we

examine how they arise, it becomes obvious that this arising is itself an absurdity and that all arising of phenomena is empty, has no objectifiable reality of its own.

In the ultimate sense, if there is no way for anything to arise, it follows that there is no way for anything to stay; to abide. There is nothing actually there, nor is there anything that can pass away. In the Buddhist commentaries, this is called "the horns of a rabbit." If rabbits have no horns, the length of time that horns stay on a rabbit is meaningless, as is any talk about a rabbit losing his horns. According to this example we can see that since there is no way for things to arise in an ultimate sense, there can be no abiding or passing away. All appearance is mere appearance, which occurs but has no reality in itself.

Just as there is no abiding of phenomena, then neither can there be an arising and nonarising of phenomena, nor can there be neither an arising nor nonarising. In an ultimate sense, everything is totally beyond any conception whatever. This is what is meant by saying that everything is of the nature of emptiness—it is beyond any kind of conception.[8]

Looking at Results

The second skill, developed by Jnanagarbha, the teacher of Shantarakshita, looks for the supposed results or outcomes of any situation. Much of our habitual thinking is based on attributing results to things. When we act in the world, we do so with the idea that we are going to produce some kind of result. On the conventional level, situations do seem to produce definite results. However, when we look closely at the nature of things, can we say that anything ever actually produces a true, independently existing result?

Jnanagarbha suggests four perspectives to examine in looking for results: Do results exist at the point of their arising? Do they not exist, or both exist and do not exist, or neither exist nor do not exist at the point of their arising? [1] Results do not exist at the point of their arising because then they would exist along with their causes and would no longer be results. [2] Results are also not entirely nonexistent at the point of their arising because that would require them to pass from a state of nonexistence to a state of existence.

Thrangu Rinpoche:

> The argument that prior to the occurrence of a particular effect, there was a non-existence of that effect which then is transformed into existence at the point of arising can be refuted by reference to the mutual exclusiveness of being and nothingness. There is no way for something which does not exist to suddenly transmute into existence, for appearances do not occur causelessly out of nothing at all, rather they appear in dependence on previous conditions and causes. The notion that whatever obviously did not exist has come into existence is a mere intellectual construct, a projection about a particular situation having no genuine reality.[9]
>
> . . . Any notion of things arising out of nothingness, or passing into nothingness, is just a *post factum* judgement. That is, in observing a particular, previously unnoticed phenomenon, we imagine that it has newly come to be, or we fail to observe a previously noticed phenomenon and we suppose that it has ceased to be. This is merely a mental construct with no actual reality behind it.[10]

Recall the example of the person insulting me. From my point of view, the only "result" was my feeling of pain and anger. Any other possible result was for me, literally, not worth thinking about. Having identified the result as the sole, intended outcome of the cause, I felt confirmed in my own feelings and my ill-will toward my "enemy." However, suppose I begin to look at the result more closely. I may begin to see the impact of the insult on the person who made it. I may remember a look of remorse on his face right as he blurted forth his insult, a fact that I had conveniently blocked out before. I may recall the reactions and feelings of others who witnessed the insult, perhaps the hope of someone who had been wanting me and the other person to begin dealing more directly with one another, or the fear of another who wanted us to get along. Then there is the way this incident will impact the dynamics of the group of which we are both a part. The more I think, the more the outcomes of the insult proliferate. It is clearly not possible to identify a definitive result of the incident. I begin to realize that my attempt to identify a single result of the insult is inaccurate conceptualization, the attempt to contain a very large situation—which caused me distress—into a small, convenient, comfortable conceptual box of my own fabrication.

The fact is that the original insult arose out of a vast, unimaginably complex web of causes and conditions. There was no single origin and the situation of origin is ultimately beyond our concepts or language. Likewise, there is no single result of the insult, although I had a personal investment in thinking that there was. The results, like the causes, are multitudinous and beyond our ability to conceptualize.

[3] If we cannot say that resultant conditions exist at the point of arising or that they are entirely nonexistent, then, these two options having been refuted, we cannot say that they both exist and do not exist. [4] Finally, to say that resultant conditions neither exist nor do not exist doesn't make any sense.[11]

Thrangu Rinpoche concludes:

> In examining the outcome of any given cause, any specific source, we can see that there is no particular truly existent thing which can be designated as the result but neither is there a mere nothingness, for results are not totally non-existent. Conventionally speaking, resultant conditions appear, but from an ultimate point of view there has never been any result to anything, there being no truly existent causes.[12]

> There is no arising of phenomena or no passing away of phenomena and there is no abiding of or lack of abiding of appearances; there is no self-nature or lack of self-nature in phenomena. Everything that appears is mere appearance with no essence at all. In the final analysis there is nothing that can be said about phenomena. We cannot validly indicate any arising, any passing away, any coming, any going, any increase, any

recognition, or any obscuration of anything. Everything that appears is mere appearance, without further identifiable characteristics.[13]

Examining the Essence, Essential Quality, or Identity

The third skill of Madhyamaka, developed by Shantarakshita, looks to see whether we can locate the essence, the essential quality, or true identity of any phenomenon. For Madhyamaka, the essence or identity of anything is the idea or conceptual image that we have of it. This idea or concept represents our previous experience of that phenomenon, manipulated through our having selected some features, changed some around in our minds, and ignored still others, until we arrived at a version of the phenomenon in question that our egos can live with. The essence of a phenomenon can be gross, as when we meet a person from a culture that we do not like and we give rise to the thought, "This person comes from X, which I do not like; I do not like this person." The essence can also be subtle indeed, as when we recognize someone on the street, without any awareness of any thinking having occurred. Such an experience is concept operating at the level of the third skandha, perception, before we attached any labels to it, as in the fourth skandha. However, the unreliable nature of such a subtle, unconscious, perceptual attribution of "essence" is revealed by the following example. One day I was walking along a street in Chicago when I saw approaching me a lovely and gentle young woman whom I had known many years before and had cared for very much. As she approached and I recognized who she was, I suddenly found myself feeling the very same emotions I had experienced so long ago—here they were, so fresh and new. So familiar were her walk, the tilt of her head, the sweep of her hair. She came closer and my mind was racing, thinking, "What can she possibly be doing in Chicago?" and attempting to come up with something to say and wondering how it would be to talk with her again. Then, as she drew very near, I suddenly saw: *This was not her at all!* The saying was literally true: my mind had played a trick on me. Yet, for those few moments, I had the full and complete experience of seeing her. It *was* her! All this occurred through my attributing the same "essence" or "identity" to this other person.

In our daily life, it is true that we are constantly conferring an essence, a concept, an identity to everything we experience. We perceive and relate to things based on the particular identity that we attribute to them. When I walk through the mountains at nightfall, that large, dark shape looming ahead of me shocks me into alertness. It is a huge bear, standing stock-still by the side of the trail, watching and waiting as I approach, blocking my only way home. Bears attack people, do they not? I am frozen with fear. But moments pass and the shape still does not move. Looking more closely, I see a harmless oblong boulder along the trail. Now I can relax and move ahead, continuing whatever train of thought I had been engaged in. My attribution of an essence created a false reality for me. But what if part of that dark shape on the path ahead of me is a mountain lion crouching on top of the boulder? The alacrity with which I "recognized" a harmless boulder, my relieved attribution of an essence to that shape, may have blinded me again, and this time to a much more serious danger.

Shantarakshita wants to find out whether the habitual attribution of "essence" or "own being" has any basis in reality. He is asking whether the way in which we take things as certain known quantities, with certain definite qualities and characteristics, can stand close scrutiny. Since this process of attribution is something we are engaged in all the time and something we base our lives on, it is certainly an interesting question to ask. Shantarakshita explores this issue by asking himself: If an essential quality to anything were to be found, would it be unitary or multiple? When we look at multiplicity, we immediately see that multiples are made up of units. We can only have multiplicity because we first have single things that then collectively make up the multiplicity. So our question becomes: What kind of single, unitary essential quality can we find in anything?

Thrangu Rinpoche, commenting on Shantarakshita's argument, bids us consider the example of a hill. When we think of a certain hill that we have visited, a picture comes into our minds, and we experience the identity, the essential being, of that hill as the hill that is so familiar to us. Perhaps as a child we spent many happy hours lying in the warm summer grass at the top, watching clouds sail by. Perhaps, older, we spent time here with a sweetheart. Yet if we go to look at this hill, we see in a most dramatic way that the actual reality is not the same as our thought. We will see that the hill has a top, sides, a lower part, and various directions. It does not have one shape, size, or mood—it appears differently depending on where we stand. The hill may have rocks, meadows, trees, and bushes upon it, and perhaps a stream, but only some of these have contributed to our memory. Moreover, unlike our memory, there is no young child there watching the clouds go by or sweethearts sitting idly and contentedly in the warm, musty field grass. There is no one here, and the contrast of our memory of the hill and the stark, lonely reality can give rise to a feeling of sorrow and desolation. What, then, is "the hill," really? We must ask ourselves, can we find any one thing that is actually "the hill"? Where is this mental image that we see every time we think of the hill? It does not exist. Nothing in reality corresponds with the "essence" that I attribute to the hill in my own mind. There are many aspects to the hill, many features, but no unitary thing, "the hill."

By way of another example, let us consider our car. When we think of it, we form a definite picture and see clearly before us its identity, defined by certain features and characteristics. Yet, when we go to look at that car, we see that it is made up of many parts such as wheels, a windshield, an engine, a roof, seats, and so on. Where is the essential nature of the car located, exactly? If we begin removing parts of the car, at which point does it stop being a car? The answer is that there is no point at which it stops being a car other than when I stop thinking of it in that way. It is my attribution that locates this expensive mass of metal as a car. Moreover, in taking the car apart, ten people would probably have ten different points at which they felt that the essential nature of car had ceased to be. This indicates clearly that essential nature is not something residing in the object, but rather something that resides just in our own thinking. The car, in and of itself, possesses no essential nature.

What if we take one of the elements that, together, make up a car?

Let us consider a tire. When we think of this tire, we seem to see a specific, existent thing, with a particular essence or meaning. However, when we look at the tire, we see that it also is multiple, made up of a rim, rubber, a valve, various nuts and bolts, and so on. So it too is multiple, without essential nature. Let us consider one of the nuts that hold on the tire. It too is a compound, being made up of a metallic alloy, shaped in a certain way, threaded, with top, bottom, and sides. That nut may seem unitary in our thinking, having an essential nature, but when we look at it, we find all of these distinct elements and are in a quandary exactly where the essence of the nut is to be found.

The previous examples have been drawn from the external world of appearances. Would it be possible to find a single, essential essence to our inner mental world? Most of us think we have a "mind" and we have some idea what the essence of our mind is. However, what we call our "mind" is, like external phenomena, in fact multiple, being composed of various kinds of consciousness—visual, auditory, and so on—and various kinds of mental contents including feelings, perceptions, and karmic formations. Even what we may identify as the second skandha, feeling, does not have an essential nature, as it is made up of pain, pleasure, and neutral feelings. Let us consider "pain." We would certainly all admit to knowing what this word refers to, and each of us can probably readily call up an image of "pain," revealing that we have an idea of its essential nature. Yet, if we look closely at the actual and literal experience of that which we call pain, we may be in for a surprise. We may find that what we label as pain is, in fact, made up of an infinite variety of experiences—of appearances, for want of a better word—of energy of different temperatures, colors, intensities, and so on. In fact, there appears to be nothing in the experiences themselves that invariably and definitively marks them all as one thing, pain. The only common thing we may be able to find in what we call pain is that each of us chooses to think of certain experiences in that way and labels them as "painful."

In a similar fashion, we might look at elemental realities of our lives, such as time. It is obviously so central to my life that I definitely think that I know what time is. It certainly seems to have an essential nature, an identity that I can picture. But let us look more closely and ask, what is time and what is its essential nature? Time, again, is multiple, being dependent on the existence of past, present, and future. If only the present existed, if past and future did not exist, then where would be no time. Let us consider the past. Surely when I think of the past, I have a clear idea of what the essential nature of the past is. Yet in looking closely at "the past," we see that it is only an experience that occurs in the present that we choose to call "the past." When we are thinking about "yesterday," we are experiencing certain images in this present moment. Ultimately, "the past" is a label given to certain currently occurring thoughts and images that we designate "memory." Yet how is a memory different from a simple image and how is this different from an intimation of the future? There is no difference in essence, only the difference that we choose to impute.

Thus is it that no single phenomenon is unitary in nature with a single, essential nature. Everything that appears is a compound. Thrangu Rinpoche concludes, "In examining objective appearances in this way, it becomes obvious that there is no essential quality to any of it. There being no essential quality in any of the appearances which nonetheless occur, we may conclude that all is Emptiness, all is of the nature of Shunyata."

> Thus we can conclude from the foregoing analysis that there is no way for there to be any particular single real nature or essential quality to anything. And if there is no single real nature, there could also not be any multiple real nature, because multiplicity is based on single units and if there is no single unit there can be no multiple. These being the only possible alternative modes in which a real essential nature or quality might exist, we can see from this one method of examination that there is no self in any appearance, no self in any dharma, no essential nature to anything at all.[14]

Recognizing the Interdependent Nature of Everything

The fourth and final skill of Madhyamaka, attributed to Nagarjuna, is to recognize the interdependent, relational nature of everything. This skill puts together the three previous skills and examines causes, results, and essential nature together, without dividing them up. To illustrate how this works, let us again bring up the example of a hill to illustrate this point. Thrangu Rinpoche points out:

> If we are standing on a hill, the hill we are standing on is the hill over here, and the hill we see in the distance is the hill over there. But if we go over to the other hill, the hill we are then standing on is the hill over here, and the hill we were standing on before is the hill over there. Like that, things that are interdependent exist only in a relative sense—they do not exist in their own right but are always conditioned, dependent on circumstances.[15]

When we attempted to try to find an objectifiable source for things, we could not do so. Nevertheless, we also saw that things do not arise arbitrarily. There is some regularity in the world. When we attempt to contravene that regularity, we are hit with an unmistakable karmic effect, such as when we touch a hot stove, stub our toe against a rock, or say something mean to a friend.

> Phenomena have no discoverable essence or real nature, but appear without any objectifiable reality, like reflections in a mirror, due to causes and conditions. Phenomena, having no objectifiable real nature, are not eternal, but neither are they merely nothing. They do not come from anywhere, nor do they go anywhere. There is not real arising of them, nor is there any actual passing away of them. They do not exist independently, but occur interrelatedly due to the presence of sources and appropriate conditions. Thus all phenomenal occurrence[s] are beyond any possible conception.[16]

How are phenomena, then? They may be compared to the image of a person in a mirror. The image certainly appears, but we do not think that someone is actually there in the mirror. We do not attribute the essence or identity of "actual person" to the image. The image may be alive, breathing, even smiling and laughing, but we are aware that it is an image, not the real thing. There is no real arising of a person in the mirror and no passing away of such a person. It is similar with all of our experience.

> Phenomena are merely an unending succession of momentary arising, structured in a particular fashion, having no independent existence. They are not describable by any of the four propositions of being, non-being, both and neither, either in their sources or in their results. No particular real point of their arising can ever be discovered, and partial notions about them, such as that they are permanent, impermanent, and so on, are all inadequate to describe their actual nature. This unreal, apparitional existence of reflections in the mirror is of mere appearances occurring due to causes and conditions. And these conditioned appearances are in no way distinct from the fundamental emptiness.[17]

Upon close analysis, then, we do not find any objectifiable essence to anything. As we saw, this does not mean that things are completely nonexistent, a mere nothingness, but that they continue to appear. At the same time, their actual appearance is beyond any definitive objectifiable identity or essential nature. So it is that the ordinary things of this world, the people, places, and situations that we encounter every day, all these phenomena are fundamentally beyond thought, ineffable, and empty of essence. Thrangu Rinpoche:

> The lack of objectifiable reality nonetheless permits the continued expression of all kinds of experiences. When investigating the ultimate nature, we discover that there is no fundamental characteristic, no essential reality, no objectifiable reality to anything, so it is said that all things are empty, that there is no true reality at all. However, Emptiness is not distinguishable from the appearance of the phenomena we experience. These phenomena themselves are not separated from the fundamental nature, so our basic experience in the world is, in reality, never

anything but fundamental Emptiness, or lack of reality in everything. So the conventional truth concerning the way all appearances and experiences function, and the ultimate truth concerning the lack of objectifiable reality in everything, are inseparable; they are not two different things, but rather an integrated whole. This is the basic viewpoint of Madhyamaka as expounded by Nagarjuna, and it is a description of the actual viewpoint on reality of an enlightened Buddha.[18]

THE RESULT OF MADHYAMAKA

The method of Madhyamaka, as mentioned, is not an abstract intellectual exercise without practical meaning or results. In fact, realizing the absence of any inherent nature in phenomena has profound effects on the practitioner of Madhyamaka. Most fundamentally, that person is plunged into the essence of what is sometimes called in Zen "don't-know mind." One sees one's thoughts and preconceptions as transparent and without substance or reality. One does not fall into the trap of coming to definitive conclusions about things. One is always waiting and watching.

In such a state of suspended belief, one's senses and one's intuition become more and more highly attuned. If one cannot rely on what one thinks, one must then rely on what one sees. One must look closely at the nature of the present moment in order to know what is so.

The present moment reveals itself as empty of essence, empty of self-nature or any objectifiable reality. But, for all that, it is not utterly empty and void, either. It cannot be said to be nonexistent either, for then it would again have an essence, the essence of nonexistence. One is then left only with the indescribable, ineffable reality that composes the fabric of our experience.

It is this ineffable reality, the very nature of emptiness, that, according to the Mahayana, alone provides a sound basis for ethical conduct. The bodhisattva, rather than acting toward sentient beings based on his opinions of what is "good" for them, knows that he does not *know* and can never *know* what sentient beings need. All he can do is wait and watch until he sees, with direct and unmediated insight, what is called for.

The bodhisattva's patience, then, is based on his realization of emptiness. Knowing that he does not know, he does not act prematurely. He waits until this moment discloses its secret, which is its indefinable appearance, its "call," such as that may be.

What about the "future?" When the present is seen fully as it is, without conceptual overlay or preconceptions, the future literally takes care of itself. How is this so? Because part of the nature of the present is that it is pregnant with karma. Karma implies some kind of movement and direction. The realized Madhyamikan is free not only to boycott action that represents an impatient rejection of the present; in addition, he or she is free to act in a way that responds genuinely to the karmic direction or, we might say, *needs* expressed as an aspect of the present.

How is this so? For example, part of our most fundamental nature as human beings is, as mentioned, the deep desire to alleviate the suffering of other sentient beings in distress. It is only our own opinions and preconceptions that get in the way of the expression of this aspect of our nature. Through Madhyamaka, we are literally brought into a state in which we do not know what to think. Or if a thought does occur, we don't know what it is or what to do with it. This occurring thought, then, is like an image drawn on water. Finding no home, immediately it takes shape, it disappears. This represents real freedom from discursive thinking. Free from what we think, we are left only with what is. And what is, by its nature, calls for our response. With our habitual ideas disabled, there is room for the spontaneous compassion of the buddha-nature to manifest itself.

Let us take an example. Suppose I am counseling a student who is thinking of dropping out of school. Perhaps I begin the meeting with the idea that this student should not drop out of school. Yet suppose that the student is giving me every reason to see that dropping out of school is exactly what is needed in this situation. Still, because of my own blindness and preconceptions, I am unwilling to see what he is saying. Then, at a certain moment, I suddenly become aware that I am stubbornly hanging on to my own idea and that, behind this cloud, is the brilliant sun of what the student actually needs. At this moment, I have glimpsed, in an incipient way, the emptiness of my own thought, and, seeing this insubstantiality, I am free to do and say what the situation requires.

In traditional Tibet, it was said that a full realization of emptiness as expounded in the second turning could have far-reaching implications for one's relationship to the relative world. The biography of Milarepa provides a vivid example. One day, two jealous and contentious scholars from the monastery below appear at the entrance to Milarepa's cave. They taunt him with a challenge to debate Buddhist philosophical issues. Their motivation is a desire to defeat and humiliate the unlettered yogi. Seeing an opportunity to teach, Milarepa accedes and, invited to question the scholars, puts to them a series of queries. "Is space obstructing or unobstructing?" he asks. The head scholar replies, "Of course space is unobstructing." Milarepa responds, "But I think that space is obstructing." The scholar replies, "What is your reason for daring to make such a presumptuous assertion?" The story continues:

> In the meantime, Milarepa had entered the "Samadhi-of-Solidifying-Space and replied, "Let us see whether space is obstructing or non-obstructing! Now, will you please stand up and move around, or stretch your limbs?"
>
> The scholar then tried to move but found he could not do so. He had to remain in his original posture, unable even to open his mouth, and sat stiffly [like a dead image]. Whereupon the Jetsun [levitated] and walked, stood, lay down, and sat in the lotus posture, right out in space. Then he emerged from Samadhi and said to the scholar, "You have maintained that space is non-obstructing, but why cannot you move your body?"[19]

Unlike the scholars, Milarepa does not "believe" space to be a certain way or to possess a definitive essence. Moreover, he sees how "belief" conditions how reality appears and that reality can therefore appear any way. To demonstrate this fact, he enters a state in which space takes on the exact opposite of it usual appearance.

This wonder astounds and angers the scholars, who demand a rematch. This time, they challenge him to show that a solid rock is nonobstructive.

> Whereupon, the Jetsun entered the Samadhi-of-Space-Exhaustion, making the rock permeable, and then passed through it from the top to the bottom and from one side to the other; also, he kept half of his body in the rock and half outside of it. Then, he threw the rock up and let it fall. Finally he lifted up the rock with his hand, and cried to Rechungpa, "Bring a pillar!" Rechungpa brought a pillar-shaped stone and set it up. [Milarepa then placed the huge rock upon it,] leaving his handprints indented on the rock. These marks can be seen to this very day.[20]

Milarepa, in a similar manner, does not attribute to the rock any particular essence. In being free of the deep and ingrained belief of "solidity" as an essential reality, he is free to play with the boulder as he sees fit.

Chagdud Tulku tells a very similar story, only this time from the more recent past. The following is an account of one of his own previous incarnations, Chagdud Tanpai Gyaltsan. The moral is the same as in the story of Milarepa.

> Not attributing any inherent existence, permanence or solidity to appearances, [he was] able to manipulate them spontaneously. . . . One day Chagdud Tanpai Gyaltsan, who had been drinking a good quantity of *arak* [liquor], rode up to a friend's house. There was no place to tie his horse so he stabbed his riding crop into a rock to make a post. It was a completely unrehearsed gesture, an action beyond concept. In a way it was of no particular benefit—there are other ways to secure horses—yet the demonstration of the nonsolid nature of that rock certainly benefited those who witnessed it.[21]

Modern Westerners may choose to take stories such as these as no more than a metaphor. But even at this level, something profound is revealed. When we do not jump to conclusions about what an apparent situation is, we are left with much more room to work creatively with it. In the case of the person insulting me, by resisting the temptation to attribute an "essence" to the situation, to come to definitive conclusions regarding right and wrong, blameworthy and blameless, a great deal more of the situation can show itself and the response can be that much more accurate and helpful.

The Madhyamaka method, then, is a way of using the conceptual mind to bring about its own demise. Madhyamaka is considered the most clear and powerful presentation of emptiness that can be made in words. In this sense, it acts as the great purifier of the "wrong view" that remains trapped in some kind of substantialism. The ultimate value of Madhyamaka is that, in its critique, it enables the spiritual life to remain free and open.

Particularly in Western religious traditions, there is a tendency for people to think that a firm and unwavering belief in certain tenets or doctrines is the necessary prerequisite for a religious person. Belief is here equated with unquestioning faith and unchanging adherence to certain dogmas. It is often felt that without this an uplifted, ethical, spiritually informed life is not possible. In Tibetan Buddhism, unquestioning belief and rigid adherence to certain doctrines are considered the great enemy of the spiritual life. Anytime that we hear an attractive idea, gain some insight, or have a religious experience, there is always the tendency to want to attribute to it an essence, to turn it into some kind of solid reference point that we can hang on to and refer back to in the future. Following any strong insight or spiritual experience, for most of us, is the thought, "Aha. Now I have the answer!" We want to think that somehow we have been lifted permanently out of the human condition and can henceforth live on a spiritual plane where there is no more pain, frustration, or grief. Within the Tibetan Buddhist perspective, spiritual insights and experiences occur to us precisely to help us live as human beings in the human realm, being ever more humble and helpful to others. We get into trouble when we try to objectify and solidify something that has occurred so that we can protect ourselves from now on. This tendency is what Trungpa Rinpoche has called "spiritual materialism," using spiritual ideas and experiences to build up and fortify ego. The purpose of the second turning of the wheel of dharma is to show, in a final and definitive way, the view of emptiness that cuts the ground out from under our spiritual materialism. It is this view that is to be fully actualized in the Tibetan Vajrayana, particularly in the practices of formless meditation known as mahamudra and dzokchen.[22]

16

The Third Turning
Buddha-Nature

THE BUDDHA TURNED THE WHEEL OF DHARMA FOR A third and final time shortly before his death. According to Dudjom Rinpoche:

> In places such as Mount Malaya, the Point of Enlightenment, and Vaisali, at indeterminate times and to the host of great bodhisattvas who required the essential training, [the Buddha] excellently analyzed all things from form to omniscience in accord with the three essential natures of the imaginary (parikalpita), the dependent (paratantra), and the absolute (parinispanna); and having established the nature of the ground, path and result, he extensively revealed the abiding reality of the nucleus of the tathagata [tathagatagarbha, rendered here as "buddha-nature"].[1]

The essential content of the third turning, then, is twofold, including, on the one hand, the "three essential natures" (*tri-svabhava*) and, on the other, the buddha-nature. The Buddha's teachings on the three natures are first found in the *Sandhinirmochana Sutra* (Sutra That Elucidates the Mystery). They are given further expression in sutras such as the *Lankavatara* and the *Avatamsaka*. The Buddha's teachings on the buddha-nature are found in a number of sutras, including the *Tathagatagarbha Sutra,* the *Shrimaladevi Sutra,* and the *Dharanishvara Sutra.* The third-turning teachings are systematized, elaborated, and explained in a series of commentaries and subcommentaries by members of the Yogacharin school founded by Asanga.

According to the *Sandhinirmochana Sutra*—the Indian text where the third turning is explicitly mentioned for the first time—the first turning of the wheel of dharma, though true and profound, represents a provisional teaching. The second turning, while providing a more profound articulation of the dharma than the first, also represents a provisional rather than an ultimate teaching. The third turning of the wheel of dharma, however, represents the Buddha's final statement and is to be taken as his ultimate and unsurpassable teaching.

What Remains in Emptiness?

The first turning taught the four noble truths, while the second elucidated the doctrine that all phenomena are empty of self-nature. The third turning speaks about the world that appears once we realize that our conceptual/perceptual versions are all empty. It is certainly true that, strictly speaking, nothing can be said about this reality because it is ineffable and beyond thought. Nevertheless, one can point, one can draw analogies, one can evoke that reality. It is necessary to do this, as a step beyond the second turning, because the negative language of the second turning could give the impression that ultimate reality is nothingness, a blank void. It is certainly not that the second-turning teachings are saying this; in fact, they present the most refined and pure expression of emptiness that one could ever imagine. Yet the relentless negativity of the language of the second turning could, if unchecked, lead practitioners to a nihilistic viewpoint. It could allow them to think that everything is empty and meaningless, that nothing has any validity, that the spiritual path is bogus, and that they should turn to a life without values or just give up and die. The ultimacy and finality of the third turning in comparison with the second is not that it presents a different reality from the second, but rather that its manner of articulating emptiness is more complete and less potentially misleading.

The third turning calls our attention, then, to "what remains in emptiness." It does this first through the doctrine of the so-called three natures. Like the second turning, the third recognizes the ultimate emptiness of self-nature in all of reality and the false covering of concepts that conceals it. In the third turning, however, we find a third category added, that of what we may call the "dependent nature," or *paratantra*. Asanga argues that if we misconstrue our world through thinking about it, it is not the case that our concepts are labeling nothing at all, absolute nonbeing. Rather, they are labeling the ineffable world of "thusness" or "things as they are" experienced by the buddhas. This ineffable world is the one of causes and conditions that the Buddha saw on the night of his enlightenment and articulated in the doctrine of the twelve nidanas the conditioned coproduction.

The three natures pave the way for what is the essential teaching of the third turning, that of buddha-nature, or tathagatagarbha. The buddha-nature resides within the heart of every sentient being. Moreover, it is identical with the dharmakaya, the mind of the enlightened ones. As it exists within all sentient beings, this dharmakaya is fully developed and matured. The only difference between the buddha-nature as it exists in an ordinary sentient being and a fully enlightened buddha is that in the former, it is covered over by adventitious defilements and goes by the name of "buddha-nature" while in the latter, all the coverings have been removed and it is called "dharmakaya," "enlightenment," and so on. This buddha-nature is an expression within human beings, of emptiness. However, the buddha-nature is not nothing; rather, it is endowed with the power of cognizance and other qualities that are inseparable from emptiness. In practical terms, when emptiness is realized, then all the buddha qualities of wisdom and compassion with which the buddha-nature is endowed are free to express themselves.

Why Were the Teachings of Buddha-Nature Given?

Tradition points to five specific reasons why the Buddha gave the third-turning teachings on buddha-nature.[2]

1. If people are told, as they are in the second turning, "You are empty of any inherent reality," and if nothing more is said, they could feel faint-hearted, and depressed, and lose confidence. They could feel that they have no capacity to attain full enlightenment and might give

up. The third turning is given to assure such people that they have the realization of a fully enlightened buddha already within them.

2. Some people who consider themselves advanced Mahayana practitioners could look down disdainfully at others who have not yet entered the path, thinking, "They don't know very much," or "They don't have much compassion." The buddha-nature teachings are given to humble such arrogant folks, to show them that in worth and capacity, they are no better than anyone else.

3. Some people, overwhelmed by their own faults, tend to focus on these as if they were real. The buddha-nature teachings show that one's faults are not real; they are merely inessential stains that cover the buddha-nature but have no effect on it and do not compromise its truth and power.

4. Some people, when they experience the buddha-nature itself, dishonor it, thinking it is nothing. The third-turning teachings counteract this view, pointing to the wisdom, power, and other enlightened qualities that are inherent within the buddha-nature.

5. The third-turning teachings reveal the buddha-nature within all sentient beings. In so doing, they open the way for the arising of that great compassion which sees self and other as not fundamentally different.

The Commentarial Lineages of the Third Turning

The third-turning commentarial traditions, principally the Yogachara and lineages deriving from it, have their roots in the mountain hermitage rather than the monastery. Asanga, considered the founder of the Yogachara school, was born into a Buddhist family in the region of Gandhara in northwestern India.[3] As a child, he was drawn strongly to meditation but was also schooled in the major divisions of learning then current in India, including writing, debate, mathematics, medicine, and the fine arts. Asanga was a brilliant student and excelled at whatever he tried. At an early age, he took Buddhist ordination within a Hinayana sect, the Mahishasaka, known for the great importance it attached to the practice of meditation. Asanga trained under several teachers, mastering the Hinayana scriptures and studying Mahayana sutras. When he encountered the Prajnaparamita sutras, however, he found that while he could read their words, he did not really understand their inner meaning or the awakening they described. Asanga felt compelled by these teachings and recognized that the only way he could gain the transcendent wisdom that he longed for would be to enter into a meditation retreat. Having received instruction from his guru, he now went into strict retreat on Mount Kukkutapada. He spent his time meditating and supplicating his personal deity, the future buddha, Maitreya, for guidance, inspiration, and teaching.

We are told that Asanga's retreat, which lasted a full twelve years, was a most difficult one. For much of this long period, he felt that he was practicing in vain. No matter what effort he put into his meditation, no results whatever seemed to be forthcoming. He attempted to abandon his quest on three separate occasions. Each time, however, before he had gone very far from his cave, circumstances conspired to drive him back to the solitary work. Finally, after twelve years had passed and Asanga had more or less given up all hope, he received a vision of Maitreya. The future buddha revealed that he had been close by Asanga's side during the entire twelve years but that Asanga could not see him because of his obscurations. These were now dispelled, and Asanga beheld Maitreya in all his beatific glory.

When Asanga requested help in spreading the Mahayana dharma, Maitreya carried him to his celestial residence, the Tushita heaven, where he revealed to him five texts, today known by Tibetans as the "five dharmas of Maitreya." One of these is a commentary on the Prajnaparamita, the other four are works specifically on the third turning of the wheel of dharma.

On the Prajnaparamita
    1. *Abhsamayalamkara*

On the three natures and other classical Yogacharin themes
    2. *Mahayana-sutra-alamkara*

3. *Madhyanta-vibhanga*
4. *Dharma-dhamata-vibhanga*

On the buddha-nature

5. *Uttara-tantra Shastra*

Asanga himself subsequently wrote commentaries on these texts and also composed his own works including, we are told, the massive summaries of the path contained in works such as the *Shravakabhumi,* the *Pratyekabuddha-bhumi,* and—most notably—the *Bodhisattva-bhumi.* Asanga's younger brother, Vasubandhu, converted to the Yogachara and became one of its most astute and prolific commentators. Yogachara, having originated in "the forest," now became a strong and respected Mahayana school and was studied, debated, and developed within the Indian monastic culture. Masters such as Sthiramati and Dharmapala carried the Indian tradition forward. During the Indian period, the teachings on buddha-nature were integrated with the Yogacharin philosophy, reflected in texts such as the *Lankavatara Sutra,* producing a synthesis that was to have tremendous impact on Tibet.

The Yogachara teachings were initially made known in Tibet in the eighth century by Shantarakshita and Kamalashila. Subsequently, they became an important part of the curriculum of all four schools. The buddha-nature texts, and the Yogachara/buddha-nature synthesis, seem to have appeared in Tibet somewhat later. In the thirteenth century, we find the teachings of Yogachara and buddha-nature fully integrated into one system, in the Jonang school discussed in chapters 7 and 9. As we saw, the Jonangpas played an important and influential role in Tibetan Buddhism for about three hundred years until the seventeenth century when, at the time of Taranatha, the school was forcibly closed down. Today, elements of the Jonangpas' teaching survive among scholars and practitioners of all four schools, and particularly among the Nyingmapas.

Shentong and Rangtong

To review, the Jonangpas are known for their advocacy of the unrivaled supremacy of the third turning in a position known as shentong, "empty of other." They held that while all of the phenomena of samsara are empty of self-nature (as stated in the second turning), the buddha-nature cannot be said to be empty in the same way. While empty of self-nature in the ordinary sense of nothing being able to be said about it, it is in another sense *not empty*. It is not empty of its essential qualities of clarity or wisdom, compassion, and power. The only way we can fruitfully speak about the emptiness of the buddha-nature is to say that *it is empty of all those things that are not itself,* namely the adventitious defilements that cover it over. In this sense, it is said to be "empty of other," empty of everything that it is not.

Those who follow the shentong view distinguish themselves from the Rangtongpas, those who hold the teachings of the second turning in particularly high regard. *Rang* means "self" (i.e., self-nature), and *tong* means "emptiness"; the compound means those who advocate for the "emptiness of self(-nature)." This refers to those people, lineages, and traditions that place particular emphasis on the absence of self-nature in all phenomena, as set forth in the second turning. There has been a lively and—usually—constructive debate between Rangtongpas and Shentongpas over the centuries. In this chapter I discuss the third-turning teachings as they are understood within the shentong orientation.

The shentong masters identify their third-turning orientation as Greater Madhyamaka, *uma chenpo,* to distinguish it from the ordinary Madhyamaka of the Svatantrika, Yogachara-Madhyamaka, and Prasangika Madhyamaka. The distinctive feature of the "Greater Madhyamaka" is its teaching that "ultimate emptiness" is inseparable from qualities of wisdom, compassion, and power, and also its establishment of enlightened wisdom of the buddhas as truly existing. The shentong masters, then, see themselves as carrying out the ultimate intentions of the Buddha when he taught about emptiness and as uniquely taking the Madhyamaka tradition to its fulfillment. Khenpo Tsültrim Gyamtso:

When we say ultimate emptiness, we mean the final, genuine, correct emptiness. When we speak of the thoroughly established nature being empty in the context of shentong or empty-of-other, we are not speaking about the sort of emptiness that is indicated in the rangtong, or empty-of-itself, school. In the rangtong school, the emptiness of which one is speaking is some phenomenon's lack of its own nature. We are not positing that in regard to thoroughly established natures. In the way that they are presented in the shentong school, they are not empty of their own nature. Rather, the emptiness of the thoroughly established nature is an emptiness of complexity and defilements [i.e., "empty of other"].[4]

THE THREE NATURES

The central doctrine of the three natures is first found, as mentioned, in the *Sandhinirmochana Sutra,* the root text of the Yogachara. It is further explained in some of the five dharma of Maitreya, namely the *Mahayana-sutra-alamkara, Madhyanta-vibhanga,* and *Dharma-dhamata-vibhanga.* Asanga discusses it in texts such as the Tattvartha chapter of the *Bodhisattvabhumi,* and Vasubandhu discusses it in works such as the *Trisvabhava-nirdesha* (Treatise on the Three Natures). In the shentong orientation, the three-natures doctrine was integrated with that on buddhanature. The following account draws primarily on teachings on shentong given by Khenpo Tsültrim Gyamtso Rinpoche, at Rocky Mountain Shambhala Center in the summer of 1991, supplemented by his *Progressive Stages of Meditation on Emptiness.*

The Imaginary Nature (Parikalpita)

The imaginary nature is the essence or own being that we attribute to phenomena. It is the conceptual imputations that we give to our world. The imaginary nature is our version of reality, built up and refined in support of our egoic safety and security. The concepts that we attribute to phenomena are known as "complexities" and the path involves cutting off or severing these complexities so that we may rest in the nature of what is.

The imaginary nature is utterly nonexistent. In other words, the reality that it purports to point to has no existence whatever. Khenpo Tsültrim: "Imagined natures do not exist. We are speaking here about those phenomena that are just imputed or designated by conceptuality. Forget about them existing ultimately. They do not exist even relatively speaking."[5] The Prasangika Madhyamaka acknowledges the imaginary nature. In the Prasangika system, it is "relative truth" that is seen to be empty of own being. According to Khenpo Tsültrim, the relative truth of the Prasangika and the imaginary nature of shentong are the same thing.

Suppose I view a certain person as an enemy. When I bring to mind a conceptual image of this person, it is defined by his nature as "enemy." Yet that concept of enemy has no existence in fact. The person to whom I am attributing this particular identity or self-nature is not identical to my concept. The actual person is both much more and much less than my attribution. In this sense, there is no actual, concrete person whom fulfills my projection, who corresponds to my idea of "enemy."

Another example of the imaginary nature is the six realms. In a traditional analogy, the same reality is conceptualized as divine elixir by the gods, water by human beings, pus by hungry ghosts, and molten iron by hell-beings. What is it that leads sentient beings to view the same reality in these different ways? It is the imaginary nature that each puts forward as an imputation. In fact, there is no external, objective phenomenon that directly corresponds to elixir, water, pus, and so forth.

Khenpo Tsültrim summarizes:

> Imagined natures are just imputations by mind. Their nature does not exist, is not established. When one recognizes them as mere imputations, one is able to stop clinging, adhering to them, or regarding them as true. It is like an appearance of a snake in a dream. When one recognizes that the snake is just a dream appearance, then one stops hanging onto it as something true. What is important is to stop hanging onto things, clinging to things, discriminating things as true. When one does that, when one recognizes them as mere mistakes, one is able to stop cling-

ing to them as true. At that point, one separates from such superficial phenomena. Separating in that way, wisdom becomes manifest.[6]

The Dependent Nature (Paratantra)

The dependent nature is the world of causes and conditions that Shakyamuni Buddha saw on the night of his enlightenment. The dependent nature is what arises in experience before it is labeled, before an essence or self-nature is imputed to it.

The Prasangika does not explicitly acknowledge the dependent nature. They say simply that all phenomena are devoid of self-nature, that they are empty, and leave it at that. But Asanga makes the important point that if we engage in false imputation, there must be some basis upon which we are making that false attribution. It is not as if there is nothing, an empty blackness, and then we just manufacture an array of concepts and, suddenly, there is our world. According to Asanga, there must be a basis for false imputation, and this is the paratantra.

This difficult notion can perhaps be clarified by using the nidana framework as an analogy. In this scheme, paratantra would be nidanas three through seven, in other words, those nidanas that arise based on previous causes and conditions, that represent the "givenness" of our lives. Paratantra, as these nidanas, is thus morally neutral. In addition, because they precede thirst, grasping, and being, they may be said to be "preconceptual." They are that "karmic fruition" part of reality that is beyond concept and ineffable. Parikalpita, then, represents nidanas eight through ten in which we take the ineffable appearance of the world and subject it to the thirst, grasping, and being—in other words the conceptualizing process—of ego. While parikalpita is said to be utterly nonexistent, paratantra is thus understood as "relatively existent," as the twelve nidanas and conditioned coproduction define relative existence based on causes and conditions.

Although this analogy is imperfect, it does provide some insight into the interesting question of what enlightened experience might be like. Clearly, it is true that Shakyamuni Buddha after his enlightenment did not experience nothing. He lived and taught for forty-five years after his awakening, seeing what was before him, hearing the voices of others, smelling the scents of the Indian night, tasting his meals, feeling the touch of the wind, conversing with his disciples, and so on. Yet we are told that he lived without creating any new karma (as in the nidanas of thirst, grasping, being), simply exhausting whatever residual karma remained (nidanas three through seven). He "experienced" the world (nidanas three through seven) but did so without attributing "own being" to it (nidanas eight through ten). In the language of the three natures, the Buddha "experienced" paratantra, without overlaying it with the veil of parikalpita. He refrained from the pattern of conceptualizing his world, parikalpita, that is pursued by ordinary beings.

The concept of paratantra allows further insight into the operation of parikalpita. When we engage in this latter, we impute concepts to our experience. It is important to realize that the concepts being used to impute self-nature themselves do exist in a relative way. This is because they arise in our minds based on causes and conditions. Yet the objective referent that they postulate is utterly nonexistent. Our problem, then, comes not from having thoughts, but from taking these thoughts as if they referred to external, objectively existing phenomena.

Khenpo Tsültrim summarizes the importance of the concept of the paratantra in shentong:

> This emptiness of the nonexistent, the emptiness that is characteristic of imagined natures when we are speaking from the point of view of the shentong school, if we posited that as the only emptiness, if we spoke of nothing other than that, then we would not be able to indicate the basis [paratantra] for samsara or the basis for nirvana. We would not be able to talk about the basis for becoming confused in samsara and we would not be able to talk about the basis for release or liberation from samsara, the basis for achieving nirvana. It would be like talking about the various sorts of appearance in space like the appearances of a rainbow. They have no basis at all. We would not be able to indicate how it is that one becomes confused in samsara, how one becomes released into nirvana.[7]

If we speak about it in the way that the empty-of-other or shen-tong school discusses the various sorts of emptiness, we can distinguish the basis for becoming confused in samsara and becoming liberated into nirvana. This is something that becomes clear when one achieves enlightenment. Just how it is that one becomes confused within samsara, within cyclic existence and how, when the basis for confusion has been exhausted, worn out, or extinguished, then wisdom becomes manifest. That is the basis for release into the nirvana of complete enlightenment or buddhahood.[8]

The Fully Perfected Nature (Parinishpanna)

The fully perfected nature refers to the wisdom of the buddha-nature. It is free of all conceptual imputations (parikalpita) and also beyond causes and conditions (paratantra). It is also called the *dharmata,* the essential reality of all things.

What is the existent status of the fully perfected nature? Whereas the conceptualized nature is utterly nonexistent and the dependent nature is relatively existent, the fully perfected nature is truly existent. As Khenpo Tsültrim says, "the dharmata is not empty of its nature because of not changing. If something does not change, it is not empty of its nature."[9] This kind of "true existence" affirmed of the fully perfected nature in the third turning is, again, not the kind of existence that is refuted in the second turning. There, "existence" referred to the imputation of self-nature or own being to phenomenal appearances. The fully perfected nature does not exist in that way. Khenpo Tsültrim:

The thoroughly established nature is not imputed by conceptuality. It is not imputed by thought. For that reason, it does not exist relatively but it does exist ultimately. In this context, if something exists relatively, then it is necessarily an imputation by conceptuality. That is the meaning of relative here. It is a very profound way to understand things. One of the implications of this is that because the thoroughly established or perfectly existent nature is not imputed by conceptuality, it is something that ordinary people do not know anything about.[10]

The thoroughly established nature is said to be permanent, partless, and present in all, omnipresent, all pervasive. Khenpo Tsültrim asks, "To what do these qualities refer?"

> We are saying that the luminous, clear mind that is the wisdom that is free from complexity is without change. From the point of view that it is unchanging, it is permanent. When we say that it is partless, we mean that it cannot be discriminated into different portions that make it up. It cannot be chopped up into different parts. When we say that it is present in all, this is like the way we talk about things in the context of mahamudra or dzokchen. . . . Speaking of this final nature as being permanent and partless is the sort of language that one finds in many different places, both in sutras and in tantras. The discussion or characterization of it as pervading all, as present in all, is like the language that one finds in mahamudra or dzokchen.[11]

An Analogy of the Three Natures

A traditional analogy may be useful in clarifying the three natures. Consider a clear crystal with a yellow cloth held near it so that the color is reflected in the crystal. Suppose a person sees this crystal and believes that she is looking at gold. In this analogy, "the gold" that the person thinks she sees is the imaginary nature, the parikalpita. It is an identity imputed to the yellow-appearing crystal and that identity, the gold, exists nowhere except in the mind of the observer. She is utterly mistaken about what she is looking at. Like the essences attributed in parikalpita, the imaginary nature, the "gold" has no objective existence at all. The *yellow appearance* of the crystal is the paratantra, because it arises based on causes and conditions (the yellow cloth held in proximity to the clear crystal) and is what is actually there, yet is mistakenly taken by the observer to be real gold. The clear crystal itself is the perfected nature, the parinishpanna, because it is empty of appearance and beyond causes and conditions and is able to reflect whatever appears to it.

Emptiness and the Three Natures

The three natures teaching speaks about three kinds of emptiness. Parikalpita is empty as something that is nonexistent is empty. Paratantra manifests the emptiness of something that is only relatively existent, being based on causes and conditions and lacking any permanent self-nature. And parinishpanna manifests an ultimate emptiness, wisdom inseparable from compassion and power. Khenpo Tsültrim remarks:

> If one does not make the sort of distinction that is being presented in the shentong system, if one describes emptiness just in the way that it is described in the consequence or prasangika school, one ends up with liberation being a mere nothingness, just a cessation of body and mind. How is that? If one describes emptiness as just being a nonexistence of conceptual complexity, then when conceptual complexity has been extinguished, mind is extinguished. Mind just stops, ceases. There is nothing to become manifest. That is the problem that comes about if one does not distinguish well the basis for samsara and the basis for nirvana in terms of different sorts of emptiness.[12]

The Khenpo then provides the following analogy:

> If we connect these three types of emptiness to the example of the suffering that one experiences through being burned by a fire in a dream, we would speak about the way in which the different elements of that particular experience of emptiness, the fire that burns oneself, the dreaming consciousness or the dreaming conceptuality, and the true nature, dharmata, or reality of that conceptual dreaming consciousness are empty. We would say that the fire is an emptiness of the nonexistent because this fire does not exist as what it seems to be. It is not an external phenomenon in the way that it appears to be. It is not

fire. It does not exist even relatively. It is an emptiness of the nonexistent. As for the conceptual dreaming consciousness, its emptiness is an emptiness of the existent, even if it is confused about what is going on. Nevertheless, that consciousness does exist. Its emptiness is an emptiness of the existent. If we speak about the dharmata of that dreaming consciousness, in which case we are speaking about its clear, luminous, brilliant nature, its being wisdom free from complexity, the way in which it is empty is that it is an ultimate emptiness. It is a naturally pure nature. This is the way in which each of those three would be empty. These are good ways to be empty.[13]

The three natures, although philosophical in nature, have an intimate connection to the religious life. The teachings on relativity, in particular, are critical to an energetic, creative, and genuinely engaged spirituality. The doctrine of parikalpita provides a way to identify an experience of the phenomenal world that is conventional and conceptual. Parikalpita is a human projection and involves the ignoring and denial of otherness. At the level of parikalpita, we do not encounter a genuine other but only our own preconception, and no actual relationship, engagement, or interchange is possible. The doctrine of paratantra, on the other hand, points to another kind of experience of the relative world, in and of itself and on its own terms. For this reason, while parikalpita is always gained through concepts, paratantra is always beyond the range of that which we can conceive. It is ineffable as all genuine otherness is ineffable. In the experience of paratantra, then, we meet a genuine other, find ourselves in relation with that other, and are already entered into engagement, communication, and interchange.

THE BUDDHA-NATURE

The classical teachings on buddha-nature are given in a series of sutras on the tathagatagarbha among which ten are the most famous in Tibet. When studying buddha-nature, however, Tibetan scholars usually do not use these sutras directly, but rather the *Uttara-tantra Shastra,* the last of the five dharmas of Maitreya. This text is itself a commentary, providing a synthesis and analysis of the buddha-nature doctrine as found in the tathagatagarbha sutras, as well as quotations from these texts. The text itself is complex, containing root verses, further verses commenting on the root verses, and then an extensive prose commentary drawing on a wide range of scriptural sources. When one studies buddha-nature with a Tibetan lama, it is likely that one will encounter the *Uttara-tantra Shastra* as the basis of the presentation.

Buddha-Nature As Ultimate Emptiness

The buddha-nature, tathagatagarbha or *sugatagarbha,* exists within the heart of all sentient beings. It is the ground and source of their personality, their intelligence, and their very being. Khenpo Tsültrim: "It is clear light luminosity, which constitutes the fundamental ground of being."[14] Its nature is wisdom free from complexity and it is unstained by any mental contrivance. Unlike the imaginary nature, which is utterly non-existent, and the dependent nature, which is only relatively existent, the clear light luminosity of the buddha-nature is truly existent. To speak in this way, however, makes it sound as if the buddha-nature might be a thing, an existent among other existents. This is most emphatically not the case, for the buddha-nature is emptiness. Thus its "true existence" does not contradict its ultimate emptiness. Khenpo Tsültrim:

> It is important to understand that this true existence does not mean that it can be conceptualized. If it were even the most subtle object of the conceptual process, it would be refuted by Prasangika reasoning. The non-conceptual Wisdom Mind is not something that even supreme wisdom (prajna) can take as its object. Anything that can be an object of consciousness, however pure and refined, is dependently arising and has no true existence.[15]

Thus the truly existent wisdom mind of the third turning is the ultimate emptiness inseparable from qualities of wisdom, compassion, and power.

Some Names of the Buddha-Nature

The buddha-nature is the enlightened mind of the fully realized buddhas, known as the dharmakaya. In the tradition, it is known under many names and designations. Khenpo Tsültrim:

> [It] is called the Transcendence of Supreme Wisdom (Prajnaparamita). It is none other than the non-conceptual Wisdom Mind (Jnana) itself. It is also called the non-dual Wisdom Mind (Jnana), the Clear Light (prabhasvara) Nature of Mind and Dhatu (spacious expanse or element). Elsewhere it is called Dhatu and awareness inseparable, clarity and emptiness inseparable, bliss and emptiness inseparable. It is also called the Dharmata and the Tathagatagarbha.[16]

The Buddha-Nature Unrealized and Realized

The buddha-nature, the essence of the awakened state, is *the same,* as it exists in ordinary sentient beings and in the enlightened buddhas. At the same time, it is *not the same* in the way in which it appears or manifests itself. In ordinary sentient beings, the dharmakaya is covered over by inessential, adventitious defilements. Yet, though these superfluous stains cover and hide the Dharmakaya within, they do not harm or taint that wisdom in any way. No matter how confused, neurotic, and even crazy we may be, the Dharmakaya wisdom within us remains always itself, always full and complete, utterly untouched by those stains. Thus, those stains can be separated from it, leaving the unimpeded clear light wisdom. "To say that these are separable means that they do not belong to the essence of the sugatagarbha itself. These stains are incidental in the same sort of way as the clouds which appear to obscure the sky."[17] When the awakened state of the buddhas is covered over in this way, it is referred to as buddha-nature that exists within the heart of all sentient beings. When all the stains have been removed, it is referred to as enlightenment, the fully manifested Dharmakaya, and so on. Khenpo Tsültrim:

The Buddha qualities are the qualities of the non-conceptual Wisdom Mind, which, when it is purified, is called the Dharmakaya. When the Wisdom Mind is not purified the qualities are not manifest and it is called Tathagatagarbha.[18]

The Ground, Path, and Fruitional Phases of the Buddha-Nature

Khenpo Tsültrim speaks about the buddha-nature in its three roles as ground of being, that which is the object of realization on the path, and as the fruition of the buddhas of the three times:

> [Ground:] Basic buddha-nature refers to the clear light luminosity naturally present as the fundamental nature of mind in all beings. This basic state is obscured or covered over. So buddha-nature in this context constitutes a base in the sense of being that base from which the obscurations are to be removed.
>
> [Path:] What is referred to as path buddha-nature describes the situation in which direct realization of fundamental mind has been achieved and as a result delusion in its coarse form has been eliminated. This is path in the sense that one is in the process of removing delusion in its subtler or finer form.
>
> [Fruition:] When one has removed all trace of delusion together with the habitual tendencies producing it, this is called fruition buddha-nature. States of confusion do not belong to the essence of mind. When they have been removed, clear light luminosity, which is essential to mind, directly manifests. When this takes place, fruition sugatagarbha has been achieved.[19]

The Nonstainability and Unchangeability of the Buddha-Nature

The *Uttara-tantra Shastra,* the fifth dharma of Maitreya, presenting the classical teaching on buddha-nature, describes its central features. Two of these are its nonstainability and its unchangeability or unalterability. The Khenpo gives the example of space to illustrate both.

Even though space goes through temporary situations alternating between being obscured by clouds or not, the essence of space itself does not change. Just as clouds do not affect the essential nature of space itself, the cloudlike adventitious stains of delusion taking the form of thoughts in one's mind obscure the clear light nature of that mind without that essential nature changing or becoming stained. It is comparable to space.[20]

It may be asked, why is the unalterability of the buddha-nature so important? The Khenpo replies:

Suppose that sugatagarbha were a changeable phenomenon. What would be the problem there? What would be the fault of that? If sugatagarbha were something that changed, it would be impermanent. If it were impermanent, it would be a composite or conditioned phenomenon. If it were a composite or conditioned phenomenon, it would not be an effective antidote for samsara because it would be something that would just fall apart. It would be something that would disintegrate and collapse. If one's antidote, the factor that enabled one to achieve liberation were itself something that has a nature of falling to pieces, then one's liberation, even when achieved, would similarly disintegrate. One would fall back. It would not endure.[21]

The Buddha-Nature Is Not Empty of Inseparable Qualities

An essential teaching of the third turning of the wheel of dharma is that while the buddha-nature is empty of any conceptualized essence or own being, it is not empty of the buddha qualities that are essentially and inseparably part of itself.

These excellent qualities which have this characteristic of being inseparable from buddha-nature are spontaneously present. Wherever there is mind, there is mind's fundamental clear-light buddha-nature and within that the whole set of spontaneously present excellent qualities.

Because they are spontaneously present, at the very instant the adventitious stains of delusion are relinquished the clear light buddha-nature directly manifests, that is, buddhahood is attained, and these qualities become self-evident.[22]

The contention of the inseparability of the buddha qualities from the buddha-nature represents a point of difference with the rangtong view. Khenpo Tsültrim:

These qualities are the essence of the Wisdom Mind. They are not divisible from its essence as if the mind's essence were one thing and the qualities another. If they were like that they would have been shown to be empty of own nature by Madhyamaka reasoning. The essence would have arisen dependent on the qualities and the qualities dependent on the essence. Such qualities or such an essence could not have any self-nature or true existence.

However, the Buddha qualities are not like this. They cannot be grasped by the conceptual mind and are not separable from the essence of the Wisdom Mind (which also cannot be grasped by the conceptual mind). Thus the Buddha qualities are not compounded or conditioned phenomena, which arise, stay and perish. They exist primordially.

The Shentong criticizes the view of other Madhyamikas who say that the Buddha's qualities arise as a result of the good deeds, vows and connections made by Bodhisattvas on the path to enlightenment. If the qualities arose in this way then they would be compounded and impermanent phenomena, not beyond samsara and of no ultimate use to beings. The Shentong accepts the doctrine of the Tathagatagarbha sutras that the Buddha qualities are primordially existent; nevertheless, good deeds, vows and connections are necessary for removing veils.[23]

SHENTONG AND THE PATH

Formulation of the Process of the Path

How is the path described in shentong? Khenpo Tsültrim:

> One talks about stopping all of the ways in which the mind apprehends objects. The true nature comes forth, becomes manifest. Everything that is extra in the way in which the mind apprehends things crumbles, is destroyed. The mind settles into itself or falls into self. One speaks about it as separation from all such ways in which mind apprehends, as the absence of ordinary ways of apprehending, and as the crumbling, falling apart, or destruction of mental complexity of whatever sort.[24]

Samsara and Nirvana

The Buddhist path involves the process of abandoning samsara and attaining nirvana. How are these two conceptualized in the shentong system? Khenpo Tsültrim:

> As long as this basic wisdom, freedom from complexity, is obscured, covered over, blocked, obstructed by the imagined natures, by confusion and mistakes, then that is the state of being of a sentient being. When that has been extinguished, exhausted, worn out, used up, then that is nirvana. If one talks about it in that way, then it is easy to make the distinction between samsara and nirvana.[25]

Providing Confidence

The view of the third turning of the wheel of dharma, as understood in the shentong orientation, provides a unique support for the spiritual path. For one thing, the teachings on Buddha-nature give great confidence to all sentient beings. They show us that the awakened state of mind not only is not far away but exists as the very heart and root of our present being. Therefore, not only is buddhahood a possibility for us, but we will not have fully discovered and fulfilled who we most essentially are until we attain full enlightenment ourselves. The realization of the buddhas of the three times is an imperative written into our most basic genetic code, so to speak.

Showing the Buddha-Nature as an Inner Resource

As confused beings, we may feel that we have no way to realize the wisdom and compassion described in the teachings. The third-turning view encourages us, however, not to feel that we are lost and without resources on the dark and stormy ocean of samsara. Khenpo Tsültrim:

> At the point when the buddha-nature is obscured by the adventitious stains of delusion one might think, "If the basic nature of my own mind is obscured by the incidental stains coming from my own delusion, how am I supposed to know how to rectify the situation?" The point is that such knowledge is accessible, because buddha nature contains within it the seeds of knowledge (prajna) and compassion. Because the seed of knowledge is basically present, listening to, reflecting over and meditating on the dharma is able to catalyze a growth and development of this knowledge. This growth in knowledge in turn corrects the deluded state.
>
> Because the seed of compassion is already present, meditation on the instructions related to compassion is able to produce growth and development of compassion. Whatever is still lacking in one's compassion is able to develop from its present state and all the way up to buddhahood. When buddhahood has been attained, one has achieved the maximum degree of compassion, which means "great noble heart."[26]

Clarifying the Process of Meditation

The third-turning teachings also show us what is to be affirmed in our meditation and what is to be rejected. According to shentong, the two truths do not provide a sufficient basis for the path because they do not make this distinction. The three natures do provide that sufficient basis: in order for a path to be viable, within relative truth, it is necessary to distinguish what does not exist at all (parikalpita) from that which exists relatively (paratantra) and that which exists ultimately (parinishpanna). Khenpo Tsültrim remarks:

When one is involved in the work of severing the complexities and determining what the view is, it is necessary to distinguish what exists from what does not exist [as is done in the three natures doctrine]. If one does not assert existence and nonexistence, if one does not distinguish that which exists from that which does not exist even in a relative or conventional way, if one has no assertions whatsoever in the way the . . . madhyamaka prasangika school does not make any assertions about such things, then there is no basis for one's analysis and it is not possible to proceed. Therefore, [the shentong masters] feel that it is vitally necessary to make such distinctions.[27]

The Prasangikas do not admit that the experience of complete freedom from conceptual contrivance is the experience of the clear light nature of mind. The shentong holds that the failure to see this identity suggests a limited experience of freedom from conceptuality. Khenpo Tsültrim:

The Shentong contention is that the experience of complete freedom from conceptual contrivance (nisprapanca) must also be the experience of the Clear Light Nature of Mind. In their opinion a Prasangika who denies this must still have some subtle concept which is obscuring or negating this Reality; in other words he has not truly realized complete freedom from conceptual contrivance. This happens because for a long time the meditator has been cutting through illusion and seeing emptiness as a kind of negation. This becomes such a strong habit that even when the experience of Absolute Reality, the Clear Light Nature of Mind, starts to break through like the sun from behind the clouds, the meditator automatically turns his mind towards it to subtly negate it. The Shentong argues that if there really were no conceptual contrivance in the mind the Clear Light Nature would shine forth so clearly and unmistakably that it would not be possible to deny it.[28]

This suggests how very important the correct view is when one practices meditation. Suppose one is practicing with a Prasangika view. One might then be subtly expecting the realization of emptiness only as an absence. One might have developed very well the habit of cutting everything that appears in the mind and reducing it back to an emptiness as a pure absence, a negation. Everything that arises will be grist for the mill of emptiness. What happens, then, if one has a glimpse of the wisdom mind, if the clear light wisdom dawns within one's experience? This, too, is liable to be subjected to destruction, distancing, and cutting, and one will revert to thinking that one has experienced nothing at all.

Nature of Enlightenment

In the shentong, enlightenment is described as the attainment of the ultimate. What is this ultimate? Khenpo Tsültrim:

> In this empty-of-other or shentong school, one speaks of the ultimate as wisdom free from complexity. This wisdom that is free from complexity is the dharmata of the imaginary or imagined phenomena. When all of those imagined phenomena have been worn out or used up, then this wisdom that is free from complexity becomes manifest. That is buddhahood."[29]

Enlightenment may be conceived in terms of either wisdom or compassion:

> When the unsound state consisting in the deluded state of mind has been eliminated, in other words, when the knowledge which realizes nonself has been brought to final perfection, this is buddhahood. Or we could look at it from the other angle, when great compassion imbued with loving kindness has been brought

to final perfection, the name "buddha" is used to describe the person who has accomplished this.

The result is that through the power inherent in compassion one works for the benefit of beings and through the power inherent in finally perfected knowledge one comprehends fully and in their infinite variety the ways of benefitting beings in individual cases.[30]

Enlightenment in shentong is further conceived as the realization of real or true emptiness. What is this true, real, or ultimate emptiness? Khenpo Tsültrim:

It is the wisdom that illuminates itself and knows itself, that is devoid of or empty of apprehended and apprehender, that is primordially existent, existent from the start, that is empty of any stains whatsoever, the inseparability of awareness and the expanse of space, the undifferentiability of luminosity and emptiness, unpolluted in any way whatsoever. That wisdom is what needs to be realized. . . . What is presented as the ultimate? Just this wisdom that is empty of apprehended and apprehender, empty of duality, that is the true nature, that is the undifferentiability of luminosity and emptiness, the undifferentiability of awareness and space or expanse.[31]

CONCLUSION

The Three Turnings in Tibetan Buddhism

Within Tibetan tradition there is, as has been mentioned, a lively debate about the proper interpretation of the three turnings. The Shentongpas, belonging primarily but not exclusively to the Nyingma and Kagyü schools, tend to accept the linear progression of the three turnings as outlined in the *Sandhinirmochana Sutra,* but often with a modification. The second and third turnings are often both viewed as ngedön, ultimate, with the third turning as being, among these two, somewhat more definitive. The Rangtongpas, belonging primarily to the Geluk and Sakya traditions but also found among the other schools, hold that the second turning of the wheel is the highest, because it presents emptiness as the ultimate nature of reality. In this interpretation, the third turning is regarded as trangdön, that is, provisional.

The Shentongpas do not dispute the ultimacy of the second turning, in the sense that emptiness is the supreme teaching of the Buddha. However, they point out that the presentation of emptiness in the second turning could be mistaken for nihilism. The third turning, by contrast, also speaks of emptiness, but in a way that is more discriminating: it shows what does not exist at all, what exists relatively, and what exists truly, namely the buddha wisdom within.

The Rangtongpas hold that the Buddha gave his final teachings in the second turning. However, some beings, through fear of emptiness or lack of acuity, were unable to grasp the full import of the second turning teachings. To them, the Buddha gave a third turning, which presented a middle ground between the preliminary teaching of the first turning and the ultimate presentation of the second. This middle ground seemed to affirm the substantial existence of buddha-nature within. The Rangtongpas see this as not literally true but as something that—like the Hinayana teachings—was presented to help beings move along the path, only later to be refuted. For the Rangtongpas, then, the first and third turnings of the wheel of dharma are provisional, while the second turning is unsurpassable and final. This contrasts with the Shentongpas' view that the first turning is provisional, while the second and third are definitive, with the third still retaining some precedence in terms of ultimacy.

To some extent these differences reflect different environments. If a Tibetan happened to live in an area where the Gelukpas were strong, it would be natural to receive ordination within Geluk tradition and take up residence within a Geluk institution. Within the Geluk, the rangtong viewpoint predominates and the Mahayana philosophical training is based primarily on texts reflecting a Rangtongpa orientation, emphasizing study of the Prasangika Madhyamaka. At least traditionally, the shentong viewpoint was seen only through the eyes of its rangtong critics. On the other hand, those taking ordination within a Nyingma or

Kagyü monastery might well find themselves engaged in a curriculum in which the Shentong viewpoint is a major, if not controlling, "view" within which study occurs.

The rangtong-shentong debate also reflects different temperaments and priorities. Some people are most helped in their spiritual life by a via negativa or apophatic approach, in which "the way things are" is arrived at through a process of pure negation. Others find a more positive, kataphatic approach more useful and consider analogies and evocations of the ultimate more productive. Again, those who are drawn to the realm of analytical reasoning, study, and debate may find the rangtong approach the more fruitful one. Others, who may be more drawn to intensive meditation practice in retreat are perhaps more likely to find the shentong approach more appealing. In any case, these are only the most general of trends, and there are a multitude of exceptions that would need to be examined in a more nuanced discussion.

Khenpo Tsültrim emphasizes the importance of cogent reasoning and of "what makes sense" in the preference of rangtong or shentong as one's basic orientation.

> If through one's own analysis and reasoning, one comes to prefer one to the other, one does not necessarily have to favor the other just because it is supposed to be better. One is allowed to examine this with one's own intelligence and reasoning and come to one's own conclusions. If one happens to like and prefer the rangtong or empty-of-itself school, then that is fine. One does not have to take up the shentong view on the basis of faith or feeling that one is supposed to. On the other hand, if one has a great confidence in the shentong school, that is fine. One does not have to take up the rangtong position. This is to be settled on the basis of investigating it with reasoning. It is not settled by faith.[32]

The Three Turnings and Vajrayana Buddhism

The three turnings of the wheel of dharma have to do with "view," with the way in which one regards and conceptualizes reality. How, then, are the three turnings related to the Tibetan Buddhist path and to the phases and stages of spiritual development? In brief, it is said that the first turning of the wheel sets out a view that is appropriate at the beginning of one's practice, after taking refuge and prior to taking the bodhisattva vow, when one is concerned primarily with one's own welfare. The second turning is most appropriate for the bodhisattva practicing the conventional Mahayana including the four immeasurables, six paramitas, tonglen, and so on, and is particularly practical for those living in a monastic context, studying, analyzing, and debating.

The views articulated in second and third turnings of the wheel of dharma provide the basis of Vajrayana. The second turning, with its elucidation of emptiness, and the third, with its presentation of the non-conceptual wisdom mind, provide the foundation upon which alone one can engage in the Vajrayana practices. The role and importance of both the second and third turnings in the Vajrayana are examined in detail in my book *Secret of the Vajra World*.

As shall be seen there, the Vajrayana includes tantric practices of visualization and liturgy, as well as the traditions of more "formless" meditation known as mahamudra and dzokchen. These various types of meditation all presuppose that one has passed through the fire of the second turning and has, to some extent, understood the teaching on emptiness. The Vajrayana can only be practiced in an authentic way when the practitioner is able initially to emerge from emptiness, to engage in the practice without substantializing it, and to return to emptiness at the completion of the session. Moreover, when one is moving about in the world between meditation sessions, there can never be any question of one's actually existing in a substantial way—to fall into this extreme would be to break one's tantric vows and to incur all sorts of difficulties.

In terms of the role of the third turning in the tantric vehicle, it may be pointed out that all the various practices that make up the Vajrayana aim at the attainment of the wisdom mind of the buddhas. As the Khenpo says:

> So what is the non-conceptual Wisdom Mind? It is something
> that one realizes through means other than the conceptual proc-

ess. One experiences it directly just as it is and any conceptual fabrication obscures it. All the teachings of Mahamudra and Maha Ati and the whole of the Tantras are about this non-conceptual Wisdom Mind and the means of realizing it.[33]

In other words, the basis of the practice of Vajrayana is the buddha-nature that exists within all sentient beings, the clear light mind of wisdom. In the Vajrayana, the various tantric practices—including both the visualization of oneself and one's environment as a deity and the inner, tantric yogas—all aim at stripping the adventitious defilements from the buddha-nature within, leaving only the resplendent wisdom mind itself. And the various "formless" practices of mahamudra and dzokchen similarly seek to lay bare the naked state of awareness.

Conclusion

In this modern world with its unprecedented levels of technology, information, and materialism, it is tempting to regard Tibetan Buddhism as an anachronism. In this view, the Buddhism of Tibet represents a kind of dinosaur, a remnant of one of the last remaining "traditional" cultures, quaint and mildly interesting, but of no relevance to our contemporary situation.

This point of view misses the critical point that, most fundamentally, Tibetan Buddhism addresses human suffering and alienation—aspects of existence that are certainly prominent and even primary realities in the lives of all of us. The Tibetan dharma offers a way for human beings to address these familiar human afflictions by reconnecting with the wisdom, sanity, and warmth that, so we are told, characterize our most basic nature.

It is interesting that Tibetan Buddhism has appeared in our environment at just the moment when, perhaps for the first time, the majority of Westerners no longer believe in the modern myth of eternal progress, that every problem can be solved with more power, whether technological, economic, political, or military. Indeed, there is, as we know, a growing despair, that the blind and aggressive optimism of the past two centuries has led us to the brink of disaster—personal, societal, and global. Indeed the disasters are already upon us. Apart—perhaps—from certain small enclaves of the moneyed and privileged, people in the world today find themselves in states of woe that, in most previous generations, could not even have been imagined. It is self-evident that we human beings have brought this situation on ourselves. Science, technology, and medicine, in spite of their wonders and their gains, have by their very success worked together to give birth to calamitous overpopulation; to rampant disease, famine, and war; to the reduction of cultural values to the monovalue of consumerism; to the gradual suffocation of a natural world once abundant and unfettered; and to the barbarism of military dictatorships, political juggernauts, and economic organizations that oppress and dehumanize increasing numbers of people living today.

Within this abysmal context, the open and guileless optimism of Tibetan Buddhism—that human fulfillment and happiness are possible—appears almost laughable. It would seem the ultimate naiveté that the accelerating cataclysms of our world could be addressed in any significant way by sitting down to explore one's own mind and by expressing the warmth and feelings of kinship that arise from that process.

And yet the contents of this book may cause us to reconsider this view, particularly since the versions of reality to which we in the West have so firmly clung are so manifestly no longer adequate. Part one described the traditional Tibetan view of the cosmos—as multileveled, composed of both seen and unseen worlds—and of the need for an understanding and intimate relation with these spheres of being for a fruitful human life. Do we modern people deny the existence or relevance of normally unseen realms because these realms have no basis in reality? Or is it perhaps because we are so narcissistically mesmerized with our manmade habitats that we have lost the eyes to see or the ears to hear anything else? And if the cosmos is living and inhabited beyond our habitual way of seeing things, what might be the impact on us of failing to perceive or connect with it?

Part two presented a picture of the history of Buddhism in Tibet, beginning in India and continuing down to modern times, focusing on the practitioners whose lives and struggles have enabled the lineage of the dharma to be transmitted from one generation to the next. Perhaps these stories are about far-off times and places, and perhaps their subjects' lives have no bearing on ours. But may it not also be that these stories are about ourselves and about realities and possibilities that are alive in us? A person like Milarepa began in despair, discovered some inspiration, and pursued it through an extremely taxing path, to full possession of himself. Is it not possible that his life illuminates for us the geography of a journey that is encoded within ourselves as well?

Part three described the basic Buddhist path—its core teachings, its practices, and its fulfillments. As we saw, this is a path that begins with one's own condition of suffering and confusion, and ends with no less a goal than the salvation of the world. What is noteworthy here is that no human state or condition is regarded as too degraded a foundation for the spiritual path, and that a concrete and practical path of transformation is outlined, stage by stage. In the modern world, we are taught to seek fulfillment by looking outside and beyond ourselves, whether in traditional theisms or through an atavistic frenzy of consumerism. Are we so certain that who we already are and the resources we already possess should be so easily disparaged and discounted?

Part four detailed the basic Tibetan Buddhist perspectives of the three turnings of the wheel of dharma. Here we saw that, according to Buddhism, the world, reality, is not any one particular way but depends upon our degree of spiritual maturity and the keenness and subtlety of our perception. From one point of view, yes, life consists of suffering. But seen in another light, reality is transparent: walls, boundaries, and barriers are not as solid as they as first appear; and there is immense room and inspiration to engage others in a warm and selfless way. And from still another standpoint, this world and all of its beings are—in Thomas Merton's felicitous expression—charged with dharmakaya. In other words, they possess—to continue Merton's imagery—the freshness, beauty, and sacredness of the dawn of creation. Mightn't we do very well, then, to realize that this world is an open-ended realm and that what we think and what we experience, both our hells and our heavens, are our own creation? That even the impasses that we now feel are, to a very large and shocking extent, unbreachable and impenetrable because our minds have become frozen and petrified to think so? Such a realization, according to Buddhism, is profoundly and radically transformative and enables us to become agents of creation instead of its victims or its destroyers.

In this day and age, we are clearly, as a planet, in a cul-de-sac from which there appears no escape. The same old methods of technology and control, applied with greater frenzy and force, even if camouflaged with more and more information, are most likely going to make things worse. One thing only will help us, and that is magic. We need now, literally, to be able to see through walls and walk through mountains, and this is something that no extension of science or technology can make possible. We need to discover a new manner of perceiving our world and engaging it. We need to find new solutions that are not humanly created but, perhaps, may be given to us if we are willing to develop ourselves in the right way.

Or perhaps it is rather very old solutions that we seek. In the younger years of our species, as anthropology and the history of religions show us, people found intelligence, balance, and—in the preferred terms of our day—sustainability. Moreover, as we know, there was culture, spirituality, and a deeply felt significance to life. We in the West have been through a trying and confusing period of adolescence in which we have tried to force the world to conform to our own immature expectations and ideas. We have discovered our own independence and potency, although, like adolescents everywhere, we have done so by cutting ourselves off from our own roots. Now our suffering is bringing maturation and leading us to a point also reached by other adolescents, that of beginning to realize that where we came from, the world and the values that gave birth to us—our parentage, so to speak—have much more to do with who we are than we thought. Now we are faced with the need to find a way back.

Tibetan Buddhism is unique in this world because, as I have said, it does provide that way back to what we are most fundamentally as human beings, to—in Buddhist terminology—our "original nature." The Tibetans, like few others, have carried on their lineage of insight, kindness, and awakened perception of the world such that it has remained vital and effective—such that it can be received and understood by people as "heady," as alienated, and as distraught as ourselves. This tradition, in my view, deserves our interest, our support, and our protection. But, actually, it deserves much more. It deserves to be taken seriously by us and to be taken on as a life resource and discipline, for in fact it is in this way and in this way alone that it will survive for future generations.

Conclusion

* * *

This book has outlined the basic perspectives, teachings, and practices of Tibetan Buddhism, as they existed in traditional Tibet and as they are making their way into the modern world. The ways and traditions described above provide what is needed for a decent, creative, and benevolent life. And they provide all that is required for the journey to the utter fulfillment of enlightenment.

Yet there is another dimension of Tibetan Buddhism that remains to be explored, namely the Vajrayana or tantric traditions that have been frequently alluded to in the preceding pages. As we have seen, these largely esoteric teachings came to Tibet along with the basic Hinayana and Mahayana traditions examined above. The Vajrayana teachings did not, again as we have seen, present something fundamentally different from the journey outlined in the Tibetan synthesis of Hinayana/Mahayana. Rather, they provided particular methods of meditation and yoga that were held to accelerate greatly the process of spiritual maturation. As the Vajrayana evolved in Tibet, it also came to provide the overall frame of Tibetan Buddhism and to pervade the atmosphere of Tibetan culture itself. A full understanding of the Buddhism of Tibet, then, requires exploration of its tantric traditions and teachings. That exploration is carried out in the companion volume to this one, *Secret of the Vajra World: The Tantric Buddhism of Tibet* (Boston: Shambhala Publications, 2001), and I invite the reader to continue there the journey that we have begun here.

Chronology of Tibetan Buddhist History

563–483 BCE	Conventional dates for life of Buddha Shakyamuni[1]

563	Birth at Lumbini
534	Renunciation
528	Enlightenment
483	Death at Kushinagara

4th century BCE ff.	Pre-Mahayana ("eighteen") schools in formation
100 BCE–100 CE	Appearance of the Mahayana

ca. 150 CE	Nagarjuna, founder of Madhyamaka school
3rd–4th century	Asanga, founder of Yogachara
4th century	Aryadeva, Madhyamaka patriarch
4th–5th century	Vasubandhu
5th–6th century	Dignaga
7th century	Dharmakirti

pre–7th century	Vajrayana in formation
end of 7th century	Vajrayana appears as nonmonastic tradition.
9th century ff.	Vajrayana appears in conjunction with monastic life.
8th–12th century	Eighty-four siddhas of Vajrayana tradition
8th century	Padmasambhava
ca. 8th–10th century	Mahasiddha Virupa

988–1069	Mahasiddha Tilopa
1016–1100	Mahasiddha Naropa
11th century	Siddha Maitripa
1200	Institutionalized Buddhism largely disappears from India.

7TH–9TH CENTURY CE: EARLY SPREADING OF BUDDHISM IN TIBET

ca. 600	Namri Lontsan of Yarlung made king of region.
609–649	King Songtsen Gampo
	641 Marriage with Chinese princess, Wen-ch'eng
	Marriage with Nepalese princess
	Thönni Sambhota sent to India to procure alphabet.
650–700	Tibet's rise as a military power in Central Asia
754–797	King Trisong Detsen
	Shantarakshita in Tibet
	Padmasambhava in Tibet
775	Founding of Samye monastery
792–794	Samye debates
815–836	King Ralpachan
836	Murder of Ralpachan; Langdarma takes over; disenfranchisement of Buddhism along with persecution.
842	Murder of Langdarma by the monk Palgyi Dorje
842	Beginning of roughly two centuries of political decentralization. During this time, Buddhism in state of disenfranchisement. Buddhism continues to be passed on and develop in noninstitutional contexts.

10TH–12TH CENTURY CE: LATER SPREADING OF BUDDHISM IN TIBET

Early 10th century	Three monks, in refuge in East Tibet, return to Central Tibet.

958–1055	Rinchen Sangpo
982–1054	Atisha, Tibetan founder of Kadam
993–1077	Drogmi, Tibetan founder of Sakya
1042	Atisha arrives in Tibet.
1008–1064	Dromtön, primary disciple of Atisha
1056	Reting monastery founded by Dromtön; center of Kadam order.
1073	Founding of Sakya monastery, center of Sakya order, by Jonchog, disciple of Drogmi
1012–1096	Marpa, Tibetan founder of the Kagyü
1040–1123	Milarepa (disciple of Marpa)
1055	Machik Labdrönma is born.
1079	Gampopa is born.
1110	Gampopa becomes disciple of Milarepa.
1092–1158	Sakyapa Künga Nyingpo
1110–1193	Tüsum Khyenpa
1158–1189	Monasteries of some of the Kagyü subsects are founded.

1158 Phagmotrupa founds monastery of Thil.
1175 Monastery of Tshal is founded.
1179 Drikung monastery is founded.
1189 Tsurphu monastery is founded by Karmapa Tüsum Khyenpa (1110–1193).

13TH–14TH CENTURY CE: PERIOD OF MONGOL OVERLORDSHIP

1182–1251	Sakya Pandita
1207	Tibetan chiefs are forced to submit to Genghis Khan.
1235–1280	Phakpa

1249	Sakya Pandita is appointed Tibetan viceroy by the Mongols.
1260	Phakpa, successor to Sakya Pandita in 1253, is made viceroy of Tibet by Kublai Khan.
1284–1339	Rangjung Dorje, third Karmpa
1286–1343	Rigdzin Kumaradza
1290–1364	Putön, responsible for Kanjur and Tenjur compilations
1308–1363	Longchen Rabjam
1354	Conflicts between Sakyapas and Kagyüpas; former defeated; end of Sakya hegemony; beginning of Phagmotrupa rule
1358	Changchub Gyaltsen takes over power.

15TH–16TH CENTURY CE: RISE OF GELUKPAS TO POLITICAL DOMINANCE

1357–1419	Tsongkhapa
	1397 Tsongkhapa joins Reting monastery.
	1408 Establishes Monlam New Year festival
1391–1475	Gendün Druppa, disciple of Tsongkhapa, is retrospectively recognized as first Dalai Lama.
1408	Emperor Yung-lo invites Tsongkhapa to China; a disciple is sent.
1409–1447	Foundation of principal Geluk monasteries
	1409 Ganden
	1416 Drepung
	1419 Sera
	1437 Chamdo in Kham
	1447 Tashilhünpo in Tsang
late 15th century	Schools struggle with one another; political conflicts.

late 15th, 16th centuries	Second to fourth Dalai Lamas [2] Gendün Gyatso [3] Sönam Gyatso [4] Great-grandson of Altan Khan
1578	Sönam Gyatso (1543–1588), the third Dalai Lama, is given the title Dalai Lama by Mongol leader Altan Khan.
1617–1682	Fifth Dalai Lama, Ngawang Losang Gyatso
1641	King of Tsang defeated by Mongols; fifth Dalai Lama given political control of Tibet.
1642–1659	Consolidation of the Tibetan theocracy under Geluk rule
Second half of 17th century	Building of major monasteries by Nyingma[2] 1676 Mindröling 1659 Dorje Drak 1665 Palyül 1685 Dzokchen
1730–1798	Jigme Lingpa
1735	Shechen monastery is built on earlier foundations.[3]
1876–1920	Thirteenth Dalai Lama
19th century	Ri-me movement
1848–1912	Ju Mipham Rinpoche
1934	Fourteenth Dalai Lama born (enthroned in 1940)
1949	Chinese Communist invasion of Tibet; occupation and suppression of Tibetan culture begins.
1959	Chinese crackdown against Tibetan resistance to continued occupation. Dalai Lama flees to India.
1959–present	Chinese repression and destruction of Tibetan culture
1960–present	Tibetan teachers bring their traditions to the rest of the world.

---

[1]Robert Lester, *Buddhism,* 5.
[2]Date provided by Tulku Thondup, *Buddhist Civilization in Tibet,* 23.
[3]Ibid.

Notes

Tibet: People and Place

1. Following Snellgrove and Richardson, *A Cultural History of Tibet,* 29–31.
2. Quoted in Samuel, *Civilized Shamans,* 135–36.

Chapter 1. The Cosmos and Its Inhabitants

1. James George, "Searching for Shambhala," 12.
2. Chagdud Tulku, *Lord of the Dance,* 232.
3. Chögyam Trungpa, *Glimpses of Abhidharma,* 88–89.
4. Heinrich Harrer, *Seven Years in Tibet,* 207–208.
5. Delog Dawa Drolma, *Delog,* vii.
6. Chagdud Tulku, *Lord of the Dance,* vii.
7. Ibid.
8. George, "Searching for Shambhala," 14–15.
9. See Tambiah, *Buddhist Saints of the Forest and the Cult of Amulets,* 81–110.
10. Urgyen Rinpoche, *Rainbow Painting,* 90.
11. See Geoffrey Samuel, *Civilized Shamans,* 166–67.
12. Helmuth Hoffman, *Religions of Tibet,* 20.
13. Ibid., 20–21.
14. Samuel, *Civilized Shamans,* 166.

Chapter 3. The Indian Wellspring

1. Urgyen Rinpoche, *Rainbow Painting,* 28.
2. Ibid.
3. See Reginald A. Ray, *Secret of Vajra World,* chaps. 9 and 10.
4. See Ray, *Secret of Vajra World,* chaps. 12 and 13.
5. Dudjom Rinpoche, *The Nyingma School of Tibetan Buddhism,* vol. 1, 440–41.
6. Lama Taranatha, *History of Buddhism in India,* 102–103.
7. Tulku Thondup, *The Tantric Tradition of the Nyingmapa,* 12.
8. Nancy Hock, "Buddhist Ideology and the Sculpture of Ratnagiri."
9. Chökyi Nyima Rinpoche, *Repeating the Words of the Buddha,* 9–10.

Chapter 4. Foundations: The Early Spreading

1. See Ray, *Secret of the Vajra World*, chap. 7.
2. Dudjom Rinpoche, *The Nyingma School of Tibetan Buddhism*, vol. 1, 513.
3. Evans-Wentz, *The Tibetan Book of the Great Liberation*, 182–83.
4. Ibid., 105ff.
5. Evans-Wentz, 117.
6. Tulku Thondup, *The Tantric Tradition of the Nyingmapa*, 146.
7. John Powers, *Introduction to Tibetan Buddhism*, 320.
8. David Snellgrove and Hugh Richardson, *A Cultural History of Tibet*, 79.
9. Giuseppe Tucci, *The Religions of Tibet*, 13–14.
10. Samuel, *Civilized Shamans*, 453.
11. Tucci, *The Religions of Tibet*, 14.

Chapter 5. Nyingma: The Ancient School

1. Dudjom Rinpoche, *The Nyingma School of Tibetan Buddhism*, vol. 1, 490 ff.
2. Summarized in Ray, *Secret of the Vajra World*, chap. 13.
3. Dudjom Rinpoche, *The Nyingma School of Tibetan Buddhism*, vol. 1, 494.
4. Tulku Thondup, *Buddhist Civilization in Tibet*, 15.
5. Ibid., 14.
6. Trungpa, *Crazy Wisdom*, 100–101.
7. Tulku Thondup, *Masters of Meditation and Miracles*, 111.
8. Ibid., 114.
9. Ibid.
10. Ibid., 114–15.
11. Urgyen Rinpoche, *Rainbow Painting*, 29.
12. Chagdud Tulku, *Lord of the Dance*, 11.
13. Ibid., 12.
14. Tulku Thondup, *Buddhist Civilization in Tibet*, 15.
15. Urgyen Rinpoche, *Rainbow Painting*, 30.
16. Tulku Thondup, *The Tantric Tradition of the Nyingmapa*, 5.
17. Ibid., 6.
18. Tulku Thondup, *Buddhist Civilization in Tibet*, 14.
19. Urgyen Rinpoche, *Rainbow Painting*, 37.
20. Tulku Thondup, *Buddhist Civilization in Tibet*, 21.
21. Ibid.

Chapter 6. The Later Spreading: Kadam and Sakya

1. Urgyen Rinpoche, *Rainbow Painting*, 46.
2. Trungpa, *Transcending Madness*, 4.

3. Ibid., 47.
4. David Snellgrove, *Indo-Tibetan Buddhism,* 235.
5. See Ray, *Secret of the Vajra World,* chaps. 12 and 13.
6. See Ngorchen Konchog Lhundrub, *The Beautiful Ornament of the Three Visions,* xi.
7. Samuel, *Civilized Shamans,* 487.
8. Victoria R. M. Scott, "Introduction," in Deshung Rinpoche, *The Three Levels of Spiritual Perception,* xxxiii.
9. Lama Yuthok, *Lamdre,* 196.
10. Ibid.
11. These themes of the Vajrayana path are discussed in more detail in Ray, *Secret of the Vajra World.*
12. For more on mahamudra, see Ray, *Secret of the Vajra World,* chaps. 9–11.
13. Lama Yuthok, *Lamdre,* 197.
14. In Lhundrub, *The Beautiful Ornament of the Three Visions,* xii.

CHAPTER 7. THE LATER SPREADING: KAGYÜ

1. Pema Karpo, *The Life of Tilopa,* translated by the Nâlandâ Translation Committee, © 1982 by Chögyam Trungpa, © 1996 by Diana J. Mukpo and the Nâlandâ Translation Committee.
2. Herbert V. Guenther, *The Life and Teaching of Naropa,* 25.
3. Taranatha, *History of Buddhism in India,* 426–27.
4. Nâlandâ Translation Committee, *The Life of Marpa the Translator,* 10.
5. Ibid., 199.
6. Ibid., 200.
7. Ibid., 201.
8. Lhalungpa, *The Life of Milarepa,* 18.
9. Ibid., 27.
10. Ibid.
11. Ibid., 43.
12. Ibid., 59.
13. Ibid.
14. Ibid., 73.
15. Ibid., 74.
16. Ibid., 75.
17. Ibid., 11.
18. Ibid.
19. Ibid., 14.
20. Ibid., 42.
21. Ibid., 46.

22. Ibid., 46–47.
23. Ibid., 55.
24. Ibid., 58.
25. Ibid., 58–59.
26. For a discussion, see Ray, *Secret of the Vajra World,* chap. 13.
27. Roerich, *The Blue Annals,* 437–39.
28. Vicky Mackenzie, *Cave in the Snow,* 158.
29. Khenpo Könchog Gyaltsen, *The Great Kagyu Masters,* 188.
30. Ibid.
31. Kalu Rinpoche, *Luminous Mind,* 179–80.
32. Jampa Mackenzie Stewart, *The Life of Gampopa,* 92.
33. Thondup, *Buddhist Civilization in Tibet,* 26. See Ray, *Secret of the Vajra World,* Chapters 15 and 16 for a discussion of the *tulku* tradition.
34. See Ray, *Secret of the Vajra World,* chap. 18.
35. See ibid., chaps. 14 and 15.
36. Tulku Thondup, *Buddhist Civilization in Tibet,* 43.
37. Ibid., 44.
38. See the account in Susan Hookham, *The Buddha Within,* 135 ff.
39. Either Joklay Namgyal or Kunpang Tukje Tsontu. See Hookham, *The Buddha Within,* 135, and Thondup, *Buddhist Civilization in Tibet,* 44.
40. Thondup, *Buddhist Civilization in Tibet,* 44–45.

CHAPTER 8. MODERN TRADITIONS: GELUK

1. See the discussion of these two approaches in Samuel, *Civilized Shamans.*
2. Ibid., 511.
3. Ibid., 509.
4. Robert A. F. Thurman (trans.), *Tsong Khapa's Speech of Gold in the Essence of True Eloquence: Reason and Enlightenment in the Central Philosophy of Tibet* (Princeton, N.J.: Princeton University Press, 1984), 17. Quoted in Samuel, *Civilized Shamans,* 511.
5. This section owes a considerable debt to John Powers's helpful discussion, *Introduction to Tibetan Buddhism,* 412–16.
6. See the useful discussion in Lopez, *Prisoners of Shangri-la,* 166–68.
7. Ibid., 168.
8. Lobsang Gyatso, *Memoirs of a Tibetan Lama,* 87.
9. Ibid., 87.
10. Ibid., 87–88.

CHAPTER 9. MODERN TRADITIONS: THE RI-ME (NONSECTARIAN) MOVEMENT

1. Personal interview with Ringu Tulku, April 1999.
2. Namkhai Norbu, *Rigbai Kujyug,* 56–57.

3. See Ray, *Secret of the Vajra World,* chap. 13.

4. Namkhai Norbu, *Rigbai Kujyug,* 57.

5. Ibid., 56.

6. The following summarizes the account given in Nâlandâ Translation Committee, *The Life of Marpa the Translator,* xx–xi, and Samuel, *Civilized Shamans,* 519.

7. The following account summarizes the biography given in Tulku Thondup, *Masters of Meditation and Miracles,* 122.

8. Ibid., 120.

9. See Ray, *Secret of the Vajra World,* chap. 11.

10. Thondup, *Masters of Meditation and Miracles,* 123.

11. Ibid., 128.

12. Ibid.

13. Ibid., 129.

14. Ibid.

15. See Samuel's summary, *Civilized Shamans,* 534–35.

16. Dudjom Rinpoche, *The Nyingma School of Tibetan Buddhism,* vol. 1, 852–53, 861.

17. The following account is taken from a lecture given by Jules Levinson at the Vajradhatu Seminary, Rocky Mountain Shambhala Center in Red Feather Lakes, Colo., 1996.

PART THREE

1. Sakyong Mipham Rinpoche Vajradhatu Seminary, Red Feather Lakes, Colo., 1999.

2. Ibid.

3. Ibid.

4. Ibid.

5. Kalu Rinpoche, *Luminous Mind,* 97–98.

CHAPTER 10. HINAYANA: THE VIEW

1. Chagdud Tulku, *Gates to Buddhist Practice,* 54.

2. Ibid., 50–51.

3. Ibid., 51.

4. Urgyen Rinpoche, *Rainbow Painting,* 138.

5. Patrul Rinpoche, *The Words of My Perfect Teacher,* 55.

6. Urgyen Rinpoche, *Rainbow Painting,* 139–40.

7. Patrul Rinpoche, *The Words of My Perfect Teacher,* 57.

8. Ibid., 114–15.

9. Chagdud Tulku, *Lord of the Dance,* 218.

10. Ibid., 216.

11. Patrul Rinpoche, *The Words of My Perfect Teacher,* 130–31.

12. See the classic statement in Louis de La Vallee Poussin (trans.), *Abhidharma-koshabhashyam*, vol. 2, 456–59. See Sadakata's summary in *Buddhist Cosmology*.
13. Patrul Rinpoche, *The Words of My Perfect Teacher*, 63.
14. Ibid., 66.
15. Ibid., 68.
16. Chögyam Trungpa, *Cutting Through Spiritual Materialism*, 138.
17. Sadakata, *Buddhist Cosmology*, 58.
18. Ibid., 72.
19. Patrul Rinpoche, *The Words of My Perfect Teacher*, 75.
20. Trungpa, *Cutting Through Spiritual Materialism*, 140.
21. Patrul Rinpoche, *The Words of My Perfect Teacher*, 77.
22. Francesca Fremantle and Chögyam Trungpa, *The Tibetan Book of the Dead*, 8.
23. Patrul Rinpoche, *The Words of My Perfect Teacher*, 79.
24. In Tibetan, *khyab pa 'du byed kyi sdug bsngal*, often translated as "pervasive suffering." The above ("suffering in the making") follows the felicitous translation in *The Words of My Perfect Teacher*, 380, n. 50.
25. Chögyam Trungpa, *Transcending Madness*, 243.
26. Patrul Rinpoche, *The Words of My Perfect Teacher*, 92–93.
27. Sadakata, *Buddhist Cosmology*, 54–55.
28. Chögyam Trungpa, *Cutting Through Spiritual Materialism*, 143.
29. Fremantle and Trungpa, *The Tibetan Book of the Dead*, 9.
30. John Grimes, *A Concise Dictionary of Indian Philosophy*, 165–66.
31. Patrul Rinpoche, *The Words of My Perfect Teacher*, 93.
32. Chagdud Tulku, *Gates to Buddhist Practice*, 43.
33. *Dilgo Khyentse Rinpoche, Excellent Path to Enlightenment*, 18.
34. Ibid., 24.

CHAPTER 11. HINAYANA: THE PRACTICE AND RESULT

1. Chagdud Tulku, *Gates to Buddhist Practice*, 101.
2. Talk, Shambhala Center, Boulder, Colo., Feb. 10, 1995.
3. Ibid.
4. Kalu Rinpoche, *Luminous Mind*, 104–5.
5. Ibid., 109.
6. Chagdud Tulku, *Gates to Buddhist Practice*, 66–67.
7. Ibid., 47.
8. Ibid., 67.
9. Ibid., 68.
10. Kalu Rinpoche, *Luminous Mind*, 119.
11. Ibid., 115.
12. Chagdud Tulku, *Gates to Buddhist Practice*, 67–68.

13. Vajradhatu Seminary, Red Feather Lakes, Colo., 1999.
14. Chögyam Trungpa, *The Heart of the Buddha,* 30.
15. Chögyam Trungpa, *The Path Is the Goal,* 18.
16. Ibid.
17. Urgyen Rinpoche, *Rainbow Painting,* 152–53.
18. Chögyam Trungpa, *The Path Is the Goal,* 21.
19. Talk, Shambhala Center, Boulder, Colo., Feb. 10, 1995.

CHAPTER 12. MAHAYANA: THE VIEW

1. Kalu Rinpoche, *Luminous Mind,* 125.
2. Glenn Mullin, *Death and Dying,* 101–103.
3. Chagdud Tulku, *Gates to Buddhist Practice,* 109.
4. Kalu Rinpoche, *Luminous Mind,* 127.
5. Ibid., 137.
6. Talk, Boulder, Colo., Feb. 2, 1995.
7. Ibid.
8. Ibid., 131.
9. Ibid.
10. Ibid.
11. Ibid.,131–32.
12. Ibid., 141.
13. Chagdud Tulku, *Gates to Buddhist Practice,* 127.
14. Kalu Rinpoche, *Luminous Mind,* 141.
15. Ibid., 142.
16. Ibid.

CHAPTER 13. MAHAYANA: THE PRACTICE AND RESULT

1. Chögyam Trungpa, *The Heart of the Buddha,* 108.
2. Ibid.
3. Ibid.
4. Ibid., 109.
5. Ibid., 110.
6. Ibid., 112.
7. Ibid.
8. Ibid., 113.
9. Ibid., 114.
10. Ibid., 110.
11. Ibid., 115.
12. Ibid., 116.
13. sGam.po.pa, *The Jewel Ornament of Liberation,* 130–31.

14. Ibid.
15. Trungpa, *Cutting Through Spiritual Materialism,* 172.
16. Ibid., 173–74.
17. Chagdud Tulku, *Gates to Buddhist Practice,* 123.
18. Trungpa, *The Heart of the Buddha,* 123.
19. Trungpa, *Cutting Through Spiritual Materialism,* 174–75.
20. Kalu Rinpoche, *Luminous Mind,* 145.
21. Trungpa, *Cutting Through Spiritual Materialism,* 175–76.
22. Chagdud Tulku, *Gates to Buddhist Practice,* 124.
23. Trungpa, *Cutting Through Spiritual Materialism,* 178.
24. Chagdud Tulku, *Gates to Buddhist Practice,* 118.
25. Ibid., 111.
26. Ibid.
27. Khenpo Palden Sherab Rinpoche and Khenpo Tsewang Dongyal Rinpoche, *Door to Inconceivable Wisdom and Compassion,* 91.

PART FOUR

1. Jeremy Hayward, "Unlearning to See the Sacred."

CHAPTER 14. THE FIRST TURNING: ABHIDHARMA

1. Thrangu Rinpoche, *Open Door to Emptiness,* 1.
2. Kalu Rinpoche, *Luminous Mind,* 43.
3. Ibid.
4. Ibid., 50.
5. Mipham Rinpoche, *Gateway to Knowledge,* 52.
6. Ibid.
7. Ibid., 53.
8. Ibid.
9. Ibid.
10. Ibid.
11. Ibid.
12. Ibid.
13. Ibid., 53–54.
14. Ibid., 54.
15. Ibid.
16. Chögyam Trungpa, *Glimpses of Abhidharma,* 41–43.
17. Mipham Rinpoche, *Gateway to Knowledge,* 54.
18. Ibid.
19. Ibid.
20. Ibid., 57.

Chapter 15. The Second Turning: Madhyamaka

1. Dudjom Rinpoche, *The Nyingma School of Tibetan Buddhism,* vol. 1, 154.
2. Thrangu Rinpoche, *Open Door to Emptiness,* 2.
3. Khenpo Tsultrim Gyatso, *Progressive Stages of Meditation on Emptiness,* 33.
4. Ibid., 65–66.
5. Ibid., 66.
6. Thrangu Rinpoche, *Open Door to Emptiness,* 51–97.
7. Ibid., 69
8. Ibid., 69–70.
9. Ibid., 79–80.
10. Ibid., 80–81.
11. Ibid., 80.
12. Ibid., 45–46.
13. Ibid., 81.
14. Ibid., 91.
15. Ibid., 46.
16. Ibid., 93.
17. Ibid., 94.
18. Ibid., 48.
19. Garma C. C. Chang, *The Hundred Thousand Songs of Milarepa,* 385.
20. Ibid., 386.
21. Chagdud Tulku, *Lord of the Dance,* 71.
22. The fulfillment of the second-turning teachings on emptiness in these traditions is treated in detail in Ray, *Secret of the Vajra World,* chapters 12 and 13.

Chapter 16. The Third Turning: Buddha-Nature

1. Dudjom Rinpoche, *The Nyingma School of Tibetan Buddhism,* vol. 1, 154.
2. Maitreya, *The Changeless Nature,* 69–73.
3. See the summary of the traditional biography in Janice D. Willis, *On Knowing Reality,* 5–12.
4. Khenpo Tsültrim Gyamtso, *A Presentation of the Two Truths in the Three Yanas and the Mahayana Philosophical Traditions,* 171.
5. Ibid., 169.
6. Ibid., 166–67.
7. Ibid., 171–72.
8. Ibid., 172.
9. Ibid., 168.
10. Ibid., 169.
11. Ibid., 174.

12. Ibid., 172.
13. Ibid., 171.
14. Ibid., 187.
15. Ibid., 76.
16. Gyamtso, *Progressive Stages of Meditation on Emptiness*, 78.
17. *A Presentation of the Two Truths*, 188.
18. *Progressive Stages*, 81.
19. *A Presentation of the Two Truths*, 187.
20. Ibid., 188.
21. Ibid., 168.
22. Ibid., 189.
23. *Progressive Stages*, 81.
24. *A Presentation of the Two Truths*, 175.
25. Ibid., 167.
26. Ibid., 188.
27. Ibid., 166.
28. *Progressive Stages*, 78.
29. *A Presentation of the Two Truths*, 166.
30. Ibid., 188.
31. Ibid., 176.
32. Ibid., 167.
33. *Progressive Stages*, 76.

Bibliography

Asanga. *The Bodhisattvabhumi*. 2nd ed. Edited by Nalinaksha Dutt. Patna (India), 1978.

Chagdud Tulku. *Gates to Buddhist Practice*. Junction City, Calif.: Padma Publishing, 1993.

———. *Lord of the Dance*. Junction City, Calif.: Padma Publishing, 1992.

Chang, Garma C. C. *The Hundred Thousand Songs of Milarepa*. New Hyde Park, N.Y.: University Books, 1962.

Choedak, Panchen Ngawang. *The Triple Tantra*. Translated by Lama Choedak. T. Yuthok, Canberra, Australia: Gorum Publications, 1997.

Das, Surya. *The Snow Lion's Turquoise Mane*. San Francisco: HarperSanFrancisco, 1992.

Deshung Rinpoche. *The Three Levels of Spiritual Perception*. Translated by Jared Rhoton. Boston: Wisdom Publications, 1995.

Dowman, Keith. *The Divine Madman*. London: Rider, 1980.

———. *Masters of Mahamudra: Songs and Histories of the Eighty-four Buddhist Siddhas*. Albany: SUNY Press, 1985.

Drolma, Delog Dawa. *Delog: Journey to the Realms beyond Death*. Translated by Richard Barron. Junction City, Calif.: Padma Publishing,1995.

Dudjom Rinpoche, H.H. *The Nyingma School of Tibetan Buddhism*. 2 vols. Boston: Wisdom Publications, 1991.

Evans-Wentz, W. Y. *The Tibetan Book of the Great Liberation*. Oxford: Oxford University Press, 1954.

Fremantle, Francesca, and Chögyam Trungpa (trans.). *The Tibetan Book of the Dead: The Great Liberation through Hearing in the Bardo*. Boston: Shambhala Publications, 1987.

sGam.po.pa. *The Jewel Ornament of Liberation*. Translated and annotated by Herbert V. Guenther. Boston: Shambhala Publications, 1986.

George, James. "Searching for Shambhala." In *Search: Journey on the Inner Path,* edited by Jean Sulzberger. New York: Harper and Row, 1979.

Grimes, John. *A Concise Dictionary of Indian Philosophy* (Sanskrit-English). Madras, India: University of Madras, 1988.

Guenther, Herbert V. *The Life and Teaching of Naropa*. Oxford: Oxford University Press, 1963.

Gyaltsen, Khenpo Konchog. *The Great Kagyu Masters*. Ithaca, N.Y.: Snow Lion Publications, 1990.

Gyamtso, Khenpo Tsultrim. *A Presentation of the Two Truths in the Three Yanas and the Mahayana Philosophical Traditions*. Translated by the Nâlandâ Translation Committee. Red Feather Lakes, Colo.: Rocky Mountain Shambhala Center, Summer 1991.

————. *Progressive Stages of Meditation on Emptiness*. 2nd edition. Oxford: Longchen Foundation, 1988.

Gyatso, Lobsang. *Memoirs of a Tibetan Lama*. Translated and edited by Gareth Sparham. Ithaca, N.Y.: Snow Lion Publications, 1998.

Harrer, Heinrich. *Seven Years in Tibet*. London: Reprint Society, 1953.

Hayward, Jeremy. "Unlearning to See the Sacred." In *The Heart of Learning: Spirituality in Education*. Edited by Steven Glazer. New York: Jeremy P. Tarcher/Putnam, 1999.

Hock, Nancy. "Buddhist Ideology and the Sculpture of Ratnagiri, Seventh through Thirteenth Centuries." Ph.D. dissertation. University of California, Berkeley, 1987.

Hoffman, Helmuth. *Religions of Tibet*. New York: Macmillan Co., 1961.

Hookham, Susan K. *The Buddha Within*. Albany: State University of New York Press, 1991.

Kalu Rinpoche. *Luminous Mind*. Boston: Wisdom Publications, 1997.

————. *Secret Buddhism*. San Francisco: ClearPoint Press, 1995.

Karpo, Pema. *The Life of Tilopa*. Translated by the Nâlandâ Translation Committee. Halifax, Nova Scotia: Nâlandâ Translation Committee, 1984.

Keown, Damien. *Buddhism: A Very Short Introduction*. New York: Oxford University Press, 1996.

Khyentse Rinpoche, Dilgo. *Excellent Path to Enlightenment*. Ithaca, N.Y.: Snow Lion Publications, 1996.

Kloetzli, W. Randolph. "Buddhist Cosmology." In *Encyclopedia of Religion,* vol. 4, edited by Mircea Eliade. New York: Macmillan and Co., 1987, pp. 113–19.

Lester, Robert C. *Buddhism*. San Francisco: Harper and Row, 1987.

Lhalungpa, Lobsang P. *The Life of Milarepa*. New York: Penguin, Arkana, 1992.

Lhundrub, Ngorchen Konchog. *The Beautiful Ornament of the Three Visions*.

Translated by Lobsang Dagpa and Jay Goldberg. Ithaca, N.Y.: Snow Lion Publications, 1991.

Longchenpa. *Kindly Bent to Ease Us.* 3 vols. Translated by Herbert V. Guenther. Berkeley: Dharma Publishing, 1975–76.

Lopez, Donald S. Jr. *Prisoners of Shangri-la.* Chicago: University of Chicago Press, 1998.

Mackenzie, Vicky. *Cave in the Snow: Tenzim Palmo's Quest for Enlightenment.* London: Bloomsbury Publishing, 1998.

Maitreya, Arya, and Acarya Asanga. *The Changeless Nature.* Translated by Kenneth Holmes and Katia Holmes. Eskdalemuir (Scotland): Karma Drubgyud Darjay Ling, 1985.

Mipham Rinpoche, Jamgon. *Gateway to Knowledge,* vol. 1. Translated by Erik Pema Kunsang. Hong Kong: Rangjung Yeshe Publications, 1997.

Mullin, Glenn. *Death and Dying: The Tibetan Tradition.* Boston: Penguin, Arkana, 1986.

Nâlandâ Translation Committee. *The Life of Marpa the Translator.* Boston: Shambhala Publications, 1995.

———. *The Rain of Wisdom: Songs of the Kagyu Gurus.* Boston: Shambhala Publications,1980, 1999.

Norbu, Namkhai. *Rigbai Kujyug: The Six Vajra Verses.* Singapore: Rinchen Editions, Pte Ltd, 1990.

Patrul Rinpoche. *The Words of My Perfect Teacher.* Translated by the Padmakara Translation Group. Boston: Shambhala Publications, 1999.

Poussin, Louis de La Vallee (trans.). *Abhidharmakoshabhashyam,* English translation by Leo M. Pruden, 4 vols., Asian Humanities Press, Berkeley, 1988–90.

Powers, John. *Introduction to Tibetan Buddhism.* Ithaca, N.Y.: Snow Lion Publications, 1995.

Ray, Reginald A. *Buddhist Saints in India.* New York: Oxford University Press, 1994.

———. *Secret of the Vajra World: The Tantric Buddhism of Tibet.* Boston: Shambhala Publications, 2001 (forthcoming).

Robinson, James B. *Buddha's Lions: The Lives of the Eighty-four Siddhas.* Berkeley: Dharma Publishing, 1979.

Roerich, George N. *The Blue Annals.* Delhi: Motilal Banarsidass, 1976.

Sadakata, Akira. *Buddhist Cosmology: Philosophy and Origins.* Tokyo: Kosei Publishing Co., 1997.

Samuel, Geoffrey. *Civilized Shamans.* Washington, D.C.: Smithsonian Institution, 1993.

Samuel, Geoffrey, Hamish Gregor, and Elisabeth Stutchbury. *Tantra and Popular Religion in Tibet*. New Delhi: International Academy of Indian Culture and Aditya Prakashan, 1994.

Sherab Rinpoche, Khenpo Palden, and Khenpo Tsewang Dongyal Rinpoche. *Door to Inconceivable Wisdom and Compassion*. Boca Raton, Fla.: Sky Dancer Press, 1996.

Snellgrove, David. *Indo-Tibetan Buddhism*. 2 vols. Boston: Shambhala Publications, 1987.

Snellgrove, David, and Hugh Richardson. *A Cultural History of Tibet*. New York: Frederick A. Praeger, 1968.

Stein, R. A. *Tibetan Civilization*. Translated by J. E. Stapleton Driver. London: Faber and Faber, 1972.

Stewart, Jampa Mackenzie. *The Life of Gampopa: The Incomparable Dharma Lord of Tibet*. Ithaca, N.Y.: Snow Lion Publications, 1995.

Tambiah, Stanley. *The Buddhist Saints of the Forest and the Cult of Amulets*. Cambridge: University of Cambridge Press, 1984.

Taranatha, Lama. *History of Buddhism in India*. Translated by Alaka Chattopadhyaya. Simla: Indian Institute of Advanced Study, 1970.

Thinley, Karma. *The History of the Sixteen Karmapas of Tibet*. Boulder: Prajna Press, 1980.

Thondup, Tulku. *Buddhist Civilization in Tibet*. Mahasiddha Nyingma Center, 1982.

————. *Masters of Meditation and Miracles*. Boston: Shambhala Publications, 1996.

————. *The Tantric Tradition of the Nyingmapa*. Marion, Mass.: Buddhayana, 1984.

Thrangu Rinpoche. *Open Door to Emptiness*. Translated by Shakya Dorje, edited by Michael L. Lewis and Clark Johnson, Ph.D. Vancouver: Karme Thekchen Choling,1997.

————. *Songs of Naropa*. Translated by Erik Pema Kunsang. Hong Kong: Rangjung Yeshe Publishing, 1997.

————. *A Spiritual Biography of Rechungpa*. Boulder: Namo Buddha Seminar, 1991.

Trungpa, Chögyam. *Born in Tibet*. 3d ed. Boston: Shambhala Publications, 1977.

————. *Crazy Wisdom*. Boston: Shambhala Publications, 1991.

————. *Cutting Through Spiritual Materialism*. Boston: Shambhala Publications, 1973.

————. *Glimpses of Abhidharma*. Boston: Shambhala Publications, 1975.

Bibliography

————. *The Heart of the Buddha*. Boston: Shambhala Publications, 1991.

————. *The Path Is the Goal*. Boston: Shambhala Publications, 1995.

————. *Transcending Madness*. Boston: Shambhala Publications, 1992.

Tsogyal, Yeshe. *The Lotus-Born: The Life Story of Padmasambhava*. Translated by Erik Pema Kunsang. Boston: Shambhala Publications, 1993.

Tucci, Giuseppe. *The Religions of Tibet*. Translated by Geoffrey Samuel. Berkeley: University of California Press, 1980.

Urgyen Rinpoche, Tulku. *Rainbow Painting*. Kathmandu and Hong Kong: Rangjung Yeshe Publishing, 1995.

————. *Repeating the Words of the Buddha*. Kathmandu: Rangjung Yeshe Publishing, 1992.

Willis, Janice D. *On Knowing Reality: The Tattvartha Chapter of Asanga's Bodhisattvabhumi*. New York: Columbia University Press, 1979.

Yuthok, Lama Choedak. *Lamdre: Dawn of Enlightenment*. Canberra, Australia: Gorum Publications, 1997.

Credits

TEXT

The author thanks the following publishers and individuals for permission to quote material to which they control the rights:

ALTA MIRA PRESS for excerpts from Patrul Rinpoche, *The Words of My Perfect Teacher*, trans. Padmakara Translation Group (San Francisco: Harper-Collins, 1994); reissued by Shambhala Publications, Boston, in 1998.

JAMES GEORGE for excerpts from his "Searching for Shambhala," in *Search: Journey on the Inner Path*, edited by Jean Sulzberger (New York: Harper and Row, 1979).

KHENPO TSULTRIM GYAMTSO RINPOCHE and SHENPEN HOOKHAM for excerpts from *Progressive Stages of Meditation on Emptiness*, 2nd edition, by Khenpo Tsultrim Gyamtso Rinpoche (Oxford: Longchen Foundation, 1988).

THE NÂLANDÂ TRANSLATION COMMITTEE for excerpts from *A Course on View: The Two Truths in the Three Yanas & The Mahayana Philosophical Traditions* by Khenpo Tsultrim Gyamtso Rinpoche, translated by Jules Levinson, Michele Martin, and Jim Scott © 1992 & 1997 by Khenpo Tsultrim Gyamtso and the Nâlandâ Translation Committee. Used by special permission of the Nâlandâ Translation Committee, 1619 Edward St., Halifax, Nova Scotia B3H 3H9.

NAMO BUDDHA SEMINAR for excerpts from Thrangu Rinpoche, *A Spiritual Biography of Rechungpa* (Boulder: Namo Buddha Seminar, 1991), and *Open Door to Emptiness*, translated by Shakya Dorje, edited by Michael L. Lewis and Clark Johnson, Ph.D. (Vancouver: Karme Thekchen Choling, 1997), reprinted by courtesy of Thrangu Rinpoche.

PADMA PUBLISHING for excerpts from Chagdud Tulku, *Lord of the Dance: The Autobiography of a Tibetan Lama* (Junction City, Calif.: Padma Publishing), © 1992, and from Chagdud Tulku, *Gates to Buddhist Practice* (Junction

City, Calif.: Padma Publishing), © 1993, reproduced by permission of the publisher.

RANGJUNG YESHE PUBLICATIONS (www.rangjung.com) for excerpts from Chokyi Nyima Rinpoche in Tulku Urgyen Rinpoche, *Repeating the Words of the Buddha*; Jamgon Mipham Rinpoche, *Gateway to Knowledge*, vol. 1, translated by Erik Pema Kunsang; and Tulku Urgyen Rinpoche, *Rainbow Painting*.

SHAMBHALA PUBLICATIONS for excerpts from *Masters of Meditation and Miracles* by Tulku Thondup, © 1996; *Cutting Through Spiritual Materialism* by Chögyam Trungpa, © 1987; *The Heart of the Buddha* by Chögyam Trungpa, © 1991; and *The Tibetan Book of the Dead* by Francesca Fremantle and Chögyam Trungpa, © 1992. Reprinted by arrangement with Shambhala Publications, Inc., Boston, *www.shambhala.com*.

WISDOM PUBLICATIONS for excerpts from the words of Kalu Rinpoche, ©Wisdom Publications 1997. Reprinted from *Luminous Mind: The Way of the Buddha* with permission of Wisdom Publications, 199 Elm St., Somerville, MA 02144, U.S.A., www.wisdompubs.org.

ILLUSTRATIONS

All photographs of artworks are from the Argüelles collection, The Allen Ginsberg Library, Naropa University. Reproduced courtesy of Naropa University.

Index

479

Index

Index

namic between, 4, 98, 99–100, 130, 171, 173, 174, 175, 176, 188, 189, 192

monasticism in, 12, 92–93, 97, 103, 128–129, 131–133, 134–135, 187–188, 446

nonharming, attitude of, 53

nontheism of, 44, 55, 77, 254, 281

oral and textual traditions in, 232

outside of Tibet, 7, 11

path, understanding of, 77, 121

persecution of in Tibet, 101–102

politics, role of in, 129, 146–147, 153, 188, 192

practice, importance of in, 229

regional differences in, 11, 12–13, 192

rangtong-shentong debate in, 425, 438, 443–445

religious diversity of, 13, 88, 188, 207

religious kings, significance of, 89–91, 92

ritual in, 37, 39, 40, 44, 52, 56, 62–63

schools of, 3, 184, 187, 189–190 (see also specific schools)

scholarship and study in, 87

sectarianism (sho-ri) in, 218–219, 220–221, 224–225

shamanic aspects of, 12, 102

spirits in, 26, 40, 44–46, 359 (see also nonhuman beings)

three turnings in, 71–72, 80, 363, 391, 443, 446, 451

three yanas in, 238–239, 298, 309

types of beings found in, 34–41

view, practice and result in, 241

vows, 283, 284, 288, 310 (see also bodhisattva vow, refuge)

in the West, 110, 236 (see also Western Buddhism)

worldview of, 26, 46

yogic tradition in, 159, 176–177, 178, 185–186, 188

See also Vajrayana Buddhism, Tantric Buddhism

Tibetan cosmology, 3

geography of, 17–18

Mount Meru, 17–18, 19 fig. 1-1, 262, 271, 273, 276

nature of, 26, 27

nonhuman beings, presence of, 26

modern experience of, 17, 25–26, 28

time in, 27

Tibetan pantheon, 35

Tibetan people, 12

exile of, 7, 192

Tibetan translators, 106

Tilopa, 34,120, 152–154, 157–159

Tiphupa, 163

togdenma, 178

tonglen (sending and taking), 331, 337, 351–354, 446

for beings in six realms, 54

trangdön (literal meaning), 363–365, 444

transmigration, 47

tripitaka (three baskets), 75, 98

triratna. See three jewels

Trisvabhava-nirdesha, 426

trishna (thirst), 261, 382–383, 386, 388, 393

Trisong Detsen, 90, 91, 92, 93, 94, 96–97, 98, 105

Trungpa Rinpoche, Chögyam, 315–316

on animal realm, 268

on becoming a buddha, 358

on bodhisattva vow, 331–332, 333, 340

on divination, 29–30, 33

on hell realm, 263–264

on Hinayana/Mahayana transition, 312

on human realm, 270

on "idiot compassion," 334

on jealous god realm, 272

on Kadam school, 135

on karma, 384–385

on paramita practice (various), 337, 339, 341, 342–343, 344, 346

on purification, 61–63

on samsara and the six realms, 261–262

on shamatha, 300–301, 303–304